Workers, Collectivism and the Law

ELGAR STUDIES IN LAW AND SOCIETY

Elgar Studies in Law and Society brings together critical and thought-provoking works by scholars from around the globe, on the most pressing topics and issues within the field of Law and Society. The books in this series reflect original, cutting-edge scholarship on aspects of the Law's role in modern society and its intersection with social structures and institutions, such as politics, gender, race, religion and ethics.

Titles in this series include:

The U.S. Supreme Court and Racial Minorities
Two Centuries of Judicial Review on Trial
Leslie F. Goldstein

Just Interests
Victims, Citizens and the Potential for Justice
Robyn Holder

Workers, Collectivism and the Law
Grappling with Democracy
Laura Carlson

Workers, Collectivism and the Law

Grappling with Democracy

Laura Carlson

School of Law, Stockholm University, Sweden

ELGAR STUDIES IN LAW AND SOCIETY

Edward Elgar
PUBLISHING

Cheltenham, UK • Northampton, MA, USA

Published by
Edward Elgar Publishing Limited
The Lypiatts
15 Lansdown Road
Cheltenham
Glos GL50 2JA
UK

Edward Elgar Publishing, Inc.
William Pratt House
9 Dewey Court
Northampton
Massachusetts 01060
USA

A catalogue record for this book
is available from the British Library

Library of Congress Control Number: 2018944042

This book is available electronically in the **Elgar**online
Law subject collection
DOI 10.4337/9781788112451

MIX
Paper from
responsible sources
FSC® C013056

ISBN 978 1 78811 244 4 (cased)
ISBN 978 1 78811 245 1 (eBook)

Typeset by Columns Design XML Ltd, Reading
Printed and bound in Great Britain by TJ International Ltd, Padstow, Cornwall

To my beloved daughter Lovisa,

for finally lifting her book ban.

Contents

Acknowledgments

My first and greatest thanks go to Professor Jan Kleineman for encouraging me both to write this book and to apply for the Stockholm Centre Oxford Fellowship. I also have the Stockholm Centre for Commercial Law, the Institute of European and Comparative Law, Oxford Law Faculty, and Christ Church College, University of Oxford to thank for generously sponsoring my fellowship. This work would not have been possible without the amazing cooperation between these institutions. On a more personal note, I would like to thank Jenny Dix, Dr. Benjamin Spagnolo, Dr. Andreas von Goldbeck, and Professor John Cartwright for making me a part of the home team.

I am also grateful to my family: my husband, Fredrik Gustafsson; my daughter, Lovisa Gustavsson; and my mother-in-law, Ragnhild Bok, for their loving support, as well as for Fredrik's eternal proofreading.

Abbreviations

Acas	Advisory, Conciliation and Arbitration Service
AFL	American Federation of Labor
CIO	Congress of Industrial Organizations
COE	Council of Europe
CUE	Coalition of University Employees
DAF	*Deutsche Arbeitsfront*
DGB	*Deutscher Gewerschaftsbund*
DO	*Diskrimineringsombudsman*
DOL	United States Department of Labor
EAT	Employment Appeal Tribunal
EC	European Community
ECHR	European Convention on Human Rights
ECSC	European Coal and Steel Community
EEOC	Equal Employment Opportunity Commission
ERA	Employee Relations Act
EU	European Union
FEPA	Fair Employment Practices Agencies
FLSA	Fair Labor Standards Act
GFTU	General Federation of Trade Unions
GG	*Grundgesetz*
GO	*Gewerbeordnung*
ICCPR	UN International Covenant on Civil and Political Rights
ICESCR	UN International Covenant on Economic, Social and Cultural Rights
IFPTE	The International Federation of Professional and Technical Engineers
ILO	International Labour Organization
ITUC	International Trade Union Confederation

LMRDA	Labor-Management Reporting and Disclosure Act of 1959
LO	*Landsorganisationen i Sverige*
NCF	National Civic Federation
NIRA	National Industrial Recovery Act
NLRA	National Labor Relations Act
NLRB	National Labor Relations Board
OECD	Organisation for Economic Co-operation and Development
PTK	*Privattjänstemannakartellen*
SACO	*Sveriges akademikers centralorganisation*
SAF	*Svenska arbetsgivareföreningen*
SAGE	Swedish Agency for Government Employers
SALAR	Swedish Association of Local Authorities and Regions
SEK	Swedish crowns
STUC	Scottish Trade Union Congress
TCO	*Tjänstemännens centralorganisation*
TEU	Treaty of the European Union
TFEU	Treaty on the Functioning of the European Union
TUC	Trade Union Congress
TULR(C)A	Trade Union and Labour Relations (Consolidation) Act 1992
UCU	University and College Union
UK	United Kingdom
UN	United Nations
UNDHR	United Nations Universal Declaration of Human Rights
US	United States
USSR	Union of Soviet Socialist Republics
WHD	Wage and Hour Division

Introduction to *Workers, Collectivism and the Law*

Nationalistic parties blazing across too many horizons, declining union density, Europeanization, and globalization have all contributed to a cauldron of change that strains the constellations of industrial relations forged in the nineteenth-century social movements. Further challenges have been posed in Europe by the delicate, if tenuous, balance in European Union law between freedom of movement, EU social objectives, and continued member state autonomy in the area of labor law. The EU Charter and the European Convention after the 2007 Lisbon Treaty have received greater attention, and it is arguable that a new era is beginning with this stronger focus on human rights and access to justice. Parallel to and fueled by these developments of greater emphasis on human rights at all levels—international, regional, and national—are expanded concepts of democracy. Given these forces, the time is ripe for a reappraisal of the institutional frameworks of employee collectivism against the background of these modern trends. The focus of this book is on different elements that can be identified as facilitating employee voice within the collective, particularly concerning employee grievances, as well as rights of procedural due process and access to justice as components of democracy.

To this end, first, developments in concepts of democracy as well as histories of collective labor organization are presented. The Western history of worker organizations has been inextricably intertwined with social unrest, mercantilism, nationalism, the voting franchise, industrialism, wars, and even plague. Four national systems—those of the United Kingdom, Germany, Sweden, and the United States—are laid out. The comparison first focuses on worker organizations in their incipient form—the guilds—and the transition from the medieval corporative structures to the modern labor union movements. The role of the law with respect to workers and the collective is generally traced throughout this history. The presentations of the modern labor law systems focus on how democracy has been inserted in the paradigms created by law, collective agreements, and custom in these industrial relations with respect to union members. Habermas' procedural democracy is a starting point for the analysis of the modern labor law models. It provides a framework by which to assess the issue of labor union members' rights/abilities to concretely influence the actions of both employers and labor unions internally and externally as defined by law and/or collective agreements, as well as the legal mechanisms existing regarding labor unions' responsiveness to members.

After the presentation of the general history and legal structures of the national labor law systems, the focus of the comparison narrows down to the specific topic of employee grievances, and the role of employers, employees, unions, works councils, tribunals and courts in facilitating the pursuit of employee grievances. The procedural focus on grievances was chosen to highlight the relationship between these different actors in a way that underscores questions of workplace democracy and access to justice. Many aspects of employee grievance procedures are set out in the legislation and/or in collective agreements. The issue was also chosen as it is indicative of union responsiveness to employee needs. Employees' rights regarding grievances, such as access to dispute resolution systems, are viewed in light of the alternatives provided in order to raise such complaints—either through the unions or, as is the case in Germany, works councils; to the employer directly or through a tribunal—and with regard to the decision makers handling such grievances.

This is a comparative work seeking to highlight how, as an aspect of industrial democracy, employee voice—both collective and individual—assumes different guises in the different models of legal and industrial relations. The objective is to identify issues of voice, access, and equality. At a time when certain labor rights are gaining status as human rights, a comparison of different systems, delineating the boundaries of such rights, is warranted by the protections sought and granted. The historical trajectories of these four systems have greatly affected their outcomes, in the form of today's national labor law models, as well as those key issues still contested in the different forums between the social partners, employees, and the state.

The book is divided into three sections, the first of which is this Introduction, which sets out the theoretical framework for the comparative analysis and includes a short history of the conception of democracy. Part I then addresses the historical origins of collective worker organizations in Northern Europe, originally in the form of the guild system; it moves on to take in the United Kingdom, and more specifically England; then Germany; and then Sweden. The transition from the guild systems, later expanded to journeymen's associations, to the modern worker organizations—first trade and labor associations, societies, and clubs, then ultimately trade or labor unions—is examined in Chapters 1 through 6. The United States is also included here, as a historical newcomer. Chapter 7 provides a short history of labor initiatives on the international and regional levels concerning labor conditions, originally with a focus on outlawing the slave trade, and then turning to improvement of worker safety. Modern international and regional efforts focus on strengthening employee rights by providing access to justice as well as damage awards that can deter unwanted conduct. This international and regional focus runs parallel to, and has greatly affected the evolution of, the national legal models. The chapters in Part II present the current individual national systems by country. The final chapter compares these different systems from the perspective of procedural democracy.

LABOR LAW AND MODELS

As an academic legal subject, labor law is a relative newcomer when compared to other topics, for example, such as the law of obligations, which finds its roots in Roman law. Traveling merchants and later tramping journeymen contributed early to the creation of a lay system—arguably already in place by the thirteenth century—in which a high degree and exchange of knowledge existed as to the law of the guilds, journeymen's associations, and later even labor unions. Academic investigations of labor law systems began at a comparatively much later stage, pioneered by German scholar Lujo Brentano and his books on the history and developments of the (English) guilds and origins of trade unions[1] in the early 1870s.[2] The English Fabian scholars Beatrice Potter Webb and Sidney Webb also contributed to this early research with their books *The History of Trade Unionism* (1894) and *Industrial Democracy* (1897),[3] with Beatrice Potter Webb coining the term "collective bargaining."

The emergence of labor law as an academic legal field was carried on by three generations of German scholarship, beginning with Philipp

---

[1] *See* Lujo Brentano, *Introduction* in TOULMIN SMITH, ENGLISH GILDS—THE ORIGINAL ORDINANCES OF MORE THAN ONE HUNDRED EARLY ENGLISH GILDS (Oxford University Press 1870) and LUJO BRENTANO, ON THE HISTORY AND DEVELOPMENT OF THE GILDS AND THE ORIGIN OF TRADE-UNIONS (London 1870).

[2] *See* LUJO BRENTANO, DIE ARBEITERGILDEN DER GEGENWART (Duncker & Humblot 1871).

[3] *See* SIDNEY WEBB & BEATRICE WEBB, A HISTORY OF TRADE UNIONISM (Longman, Green & Co. 1894) and INDUSTRIAL DEMOCRACY (1897).

Lotmar's *The Labor Contract* at the turn of the twentieth century.[4] His student Hugo Sinzheimer, seen as the father of German labor law in part for his contribution to the drafting of the labor law section of the Weimar Constitution,[5] carried Lotmar's work further, focusing on the normative function of the collective labor agreement.[6] Later, Sinzheimer's student Otto Kahn-Freund criticized the case law of the German Labour Court as fascist.[7] Both Sinzheimer and Kahn-Freund were forced to flee Germany during World War II. Sinzheimer died in 1945 from poor health caused by his imprisonment in a concentration camp; Kahn-Freund eventually became a professor of comparative law at the University of Oxford. There he had considerable influence in the academic establishment of labor law in the United Kingdom, as well as comparative labor law internationally, and articulated a conceptual framework of collective laissez-faire.

Swedish scholars were also addressing issues of workers and the social question, as seen in Carl Livijn's 1893 dissertation on social security for workers who had suffered industrial accidents,[8] and Östen Undén's focus in his 1912 doctoral dissertation on collective agreements under Swedish law.[9] American professor John Commons was lead editor of the ten-volume collection *A Documentary History of American Industrial Society*, published in 1910,[10] which formed the basis for his four-volume

---

4 *See* PHILIPP LOTMAR, DER ARBEITSVERTRAG NACH DEM PRIVATRECHT DES DEUTSCHEN REICHES (Duncker & Humblot 1902).

5 Certain scholars see Sinzheimer as the father of labor law universally; see, for example, Ruth Dukes, *Hugo Sinzheimer and the Constitutional Function of Labour Law* in THE IDEA OF LABOUR LAW 57 (Guy Davidov & Brian Langille eds. Oxford 2011).

6 *See* HUGO SINZHEIMER, DER KORPORATIVE ARBEITSNORMENVERTRAG: EINE PRIVATRECHTLICHE UNDERSUCHUNG (Duncker & Humblot 1907).

7 *See* OTTO KAHN-FREUND, DAS SOZIALE IDEAL DES REICHSARBEITSGERICHTS: EINE KRITISCHE UNTERSUCHUNG ZUR RECHTSPRECHUNG DES REICHSARBEITSGERICHTS IN ABHANDLUNGEN ZUM ARBEITSRECHT VOL. 7 (Bensheimer 1931).

8 *See* CARL LIVIJN, OM MODERNA SOCIALPOLITISKA LAGAR OCH LAGFÖRSLAG ANGÅENDE ARBETSKLASSENS BETRYGGANDE MOT DE EKONOMISKA FÖLJDERNA AF S.K. OLYCKSFALL I ARBETET (Beckman 1893).

9 *See* ÖSTEN UNDÉN, KOLLEKTIVAVTALET ENLIGT GÄLLANDE SVENSK RÄTT (Berlingska boktryckeriet 1921).

10 *See* A DOCUMENTARY HISTORY OF AMERICAN INDUSTRIAL SOCIETY, Vols. 1–10 (John Commons, Ulrich Phillips, Eugene Gilmore, Helen Sumner & John Andrews eds. Cleveland 1910) and John Commons, David J. Saposs, Helen

History of Labor in the United States. Commons also drafted the first workers' compensation program in the United States, adopted by the state of Wisconsin in 1911. Commons' doctoral student Edwin Witte later became the architect of the federal Social Security Act of 1935. The high degree of international awareness as to developments in labor law can be seen in the fact that an early 1900s judgment by the UK House of Lords that was negative to English labor unions led almost immediately to legislative discussions in Sweden.

The need for a specific field of labor law was deemed self-evident by these scholars given the lack of parity between employers and employees, who were no longer tied by status, as with masters and journeymen, but simply by contract. Social security also plays an important role in this field, strengthening the position of employees and lessening the power of employers in those systems providing strong social protection such as pensions, sickness insurance, occupational hazard insurance, vacation time, and parental leave. Where labor unions provide such social security, union membership is central to securing these benefits, and unions become quasi-state actors. Where the state provides social security tied to employment, the state becomes a necessary partner to employees and employers. Because of the insertion of social security benefits as well as worker protections, labor law in all of these models extends across both private and public law. Regardless of whether the system terms itself common law or civil law, legislation, case law, and common law principles all come into play in the field of labor law. Collective agreements are normative, but are given different degrees of status in the national labor law systems. Employer practices and agency codes also differ in the extent to which they are concretized in the different models.

An additional complication in the field of labor law is the role of collective organizations, on both the employee and employer sides, in determining norms for different sectors. The European countries chosen for study in this book represent several of the main European labor law models. The United Kingdom forms one end of the spectrum, with modern trade unions originally based on a "collective laissez-faire" economic model as coined by Kahn-Freund, having a strong preference that the state remain neutral and only the social partners should determine the

---

Sumner, E.B. Mittelman, H.E. Hoaglund, John B. Andrews & Selig Perman, HISTORY OF LABOR IN THE UNITED STATES, Vols. 1–4 (New York: Macmillan 1918).

conditions in the labor market through collective bargaining: "What the State has not given, the State cannot take away."[11] Germany provides a dual-channel Works Council model and Sweden offers an example of the Nordic model based on extensive self-regulation, perhaps the truest example of a one-channel voice system. The United States was chosen for its stark contrast to the European approaches, particularly from the perspectives of judicial and state intervention.

Industrial democracy is also a component in the delegation of social partners' roles. The treatment of industrial democracy is ideologically based on different premises, such as that greater control by individual workers increases their overall quality of life. Those employers supporting industrial democracy also do so for different reasons, most often to improve worker morale and productivity.[12] Industrial democracy can be categorized as either direct or indirect. Direct forms can be seen at the local level, where the employees most affected by a workplace decision have a voice in that decision. Representative or indirect industrial democracy involves the use of representatives, chosen or elected to represent either employers or employees, negotiating and/or deciding workplace issues. Labor unions often act as such representatives for their employee members, but other, nonunion forms also exist, such as works councils. There are five different levels of modern worker consultation that can be roughly identified: the provision of information; two-way communications; consultation in decision making; joint decision making/ codetermination; and the delegation of certain types of decision making.[13] The degree of worker autonomy increases incrementally with each of these types, and the national labor law models taken up here are located at different points on the scale. Issues of a "representation gap" can arise, for example, where groups of workers are excluded from these indirect forms of representation, such as unorganized workers where the labor union has strong rights, or temporary workers where permanent employment is required for representatives to be chosen.

These four national systems also run the gamut of legislative perspectives, from the Swedish minimalist approach to the more heavyhanded US and UK ones. Social democracy as a political movement is also a

---

[11] *See* Otto Kahn-Freund, *Labour Law*, in LAW AND PUBLIC OPINION IN BRITAIN IN THE TWENTIETH CENTURY 244 (Morris Ginsberg ed., London 1959).

[12] *See* GREG PATMORE, WORKER VOICE—EMPLOYEE REPRESENTATION IN THE WORKPLACE IN AUSTRALIA, CANADA, GERMANY, THE UK AND THE US 1914–1939 1 (Liverpool University Press 2016).

[13] *See* MICK MARCHINGTON, JOINT CONSULTATION REVISITED 7 (Centre for Research in Industrial Democracy and Participation 1985).

thread in this tapestry, playing a major role in the European transition from the guilds to trade unions and in the modern history of labor, with the United Kingdom, Germany, and Sweden having had social democratic governmental constellations over significant periods of time. The social democratic movement was seen as a third way between capitalism and radicalism and the period between 1945 and the early 1970s has been hailed as its "golden age," during which it "fought to entrench universal social citizenship encapsulated in the welfare state and a model of regulated capitalism that protected national populations from misfortune."[14] Despite this universal goal, social democracy began to take on different forms in the different European countries after its purported golden age, in efforts to reconcile social democratic models to the economic and ideological challenges presented in the post-Cold War period. Three models of social democracy can be identified: traditional, modernized, and liberalized. In traditional social democracy, the parties have largely retained their original objectives and policy instruments, and their heavy emphasis on state economic intervention is unchanged. Germany is an example here. In modernized social democracy, the objectives have remained the same, but new policy approaches have been adopted. Sweden is an example, with policies such as welfare to work (*arbetslinje*). In a liberalized social democracy, both the objectives and methods have changed, as can be seen in such policies as the replacement of the traditional emphasis on equality and redistribution with social inclusion. The United Kingdom is an example here.[15]

METHODOLOGY AND COMPARATIVE LABOR LAW

The idea of comparative labor law and industrial relations is neither new nor untouched. The pioneer in this field—again, Kahn-Freund—raised issues as early as the 1970s, when the United Kingdom was about to join what later became the EU, as to the limits of comparisons to—and, more importantly, borrowing from—foreign legal systems outside their context.

---

[14] *See* Patrick Diamond, *From Fatalism to Fraternity: Governing Purpose and the Good Society* in AFTER THE THIRD WAY—THE FUTURE OF SOCIAL DEMOCRACY IN EUROPE 3 (Olaf Camme & Patrick Diamond eds. London 2012).

[15] *See* Wolfgang Merkel, *Social Democracy in Power: Explaining The Capacity to Reform*, 1(1) ZEITSCHRIFT FÜR VERGLEICHENDE POLITIKWISSENSCHAFT 125–45, 134–5 (2007).

In his famous words:

> The use of the comparative method requires a knowledge not only of the foreign law, but also of its social, and above all its political context. The use of comparative law for practical purposes becomes an abuse only if it is informed by a legalistic spirit which ignores this context of the law.[16]

In the current work, in order to allow for a more contextual assessment, the system dynamics approach to comparative law is chosen as the framework of comparison. This approach,[17] whose object is to capture and represent influences as to the law as such, takes into consideration four principal sources: legal texts; institutions; decision-making communities; and patterns of thought or discourses. The texts here are legislation, case law, and collective agreements as well as the documented custom and usage of administrative agencies and employers. The objective is to "reveal patterns in the ways that texts operate in legal systems—how they influence decisions and are influenced by those decisions."[18] The institutions included here are those with decision-making functions: guilds; employers; employee and employer organizations; the state; and tribunals. The decision-makers and institutions are placed within their broader communities. Finally, the patterns of thought, or discourses, are compared as deciphered from the interaction of these three components and the historical development of the different labor law models. Given the number of systems examined, the ambition here is not to provide exhaustive accounts or comparisons of the national systems but rather to set out their main features—the bones, so to speak.

Aspects of a procedural democracy model will be assessed against this comparison of legal models, particularly regarding the alternatives employees have with regard to bringing grievances and issues of access to justices. In order to facilitate this assessment, an overview of democratic conceptual models is now provided.

---

[16] *See* Otto Kahn-Freund, *On Uses and Misuses of Comparative Law*, 37 MOD. L. REV. 1, 27 (1974).

[17] *See* David J. Gerber, *System Dynamics: Toward a Language of Comparative Law?*, 46 AM. J. COMP. L. 719, 722 (1998) and note 5 *citing* Eric Stein, *Uses, Misuses—And Nonuses of Comparative Law*, 72 NW. U. L. REV. 198 (1977) and Alan Watson, *Legal Transplants and Law Reform*, 92 L. QUART. REV. 79 (1976).

[18] *See* Gerber, *supra* intro. note 13 at 730.

CONCEPTUAL FRAMEWORKS FOR DEMOCRACY

Winston Churchill once said:

> Many forms of Government have been tried, and will be tried in this world of sin and woe. No one pretends that democracy is perfect or all-wise. Indeed, it has been said that democracy is the worst form of Government except for all those other forms that have been tried from time to time.[19]

This statement reveals much of the historical development, and skepticism, concerning democracy since its Western inception in Athens around 500 BC. This brief historical account begins there and continues up to modern times, exploring five conceptual models of democracy: direct democracy; indirect democracy, in the form of either liberal or republican democracy; deliberative democracy; and procedural democracy. The historical development of these different models can be seen as being mirrored in the evolution of workers' collectivism, beginning with the early guilds and their initial governance structures of direct democracy. Two aspects of Habermas' procedural democracy are taken up in the comparison of the different modern models of labor law at the conclusion of this work. Despite the complexity of the procedural model of democracy, these two aspects—the system's responsiveness to the needs of its constituency, as well as the interests actually represented—easily lend themselves to this analysis. These two aspects are key to the analysis of the different labor law systems examined below, and to the determination of democratic processes. These are used as support for the argument that a broader understanding of democracy needs to be incorporated in the structure of labor unions and the law in order to more successfully respond to employee interests and better anchor both in today's changing society.

THE ORIGINS OF WESTERN DEMOCRACY: ATHENIAN DIRECT DEMOCRACY

Dēmokratia, the term invoked by Athenians to describe their governance system, comprises *kratos* (rule by) and *dēmos* (the people).[20] Its roots are

---

[19] *See* RICHARD M. LANGWORTH & WINSTON CHURCHILL, CHURCHILL BY HIMSELF: THE LIFE, TIMES AND OPINIONS OF WINSTON CHURCHILL IN HIS OWN WORDS 57 (Ebury Press 2008), referring to a House of Commons speech given on Nov. 11, 1947.

[20] *See* M.H. Hansen, *Democracy/Athenian* in Oxford Classical Dictionary (2015) available online at classics.oxfordre.com.

found in Solon's law reforms during the sixth century BC, particularly with regard to increasing access by the poor to the law courts.[21] Cleisthenēs is seen as the architect of democracy through his reorganization of the citizen body a century later, extending political power beyond simply the wealthy to the entire *demos* of Athens. This extension, however, was still limited to only Athenian citizens, a minority group of males constituting about 30 percent of the free population.[22]

Insights into the internal perception of Athenian democracy can be gleaned from Thucydidēs' account of a speech made by Pericles, who began: "I shall speak first of our ancestors ... they by their valor transmitted to us a free state."[23]

> It is true that our government is called a democracy, because its administration is in the hands, not of the few, but of the many ... For we [Athenians] alone regard the man who takes no part in public affairs, not as one who minds his own business, but as good for nothing; and we Athenians decide public questions for ourselves or at least endeavour to arrive at a sound understanding of them, in the belief that it is not debate which is a hindrance to action, but rather not to be instructed by debate before the time comes for action.[24]

This idea of civic duty came to be seen as a cornerstone of the later French republic model of democracy. Athenian democracy lasted almost two centuries, until Macedonia conquered Athens in 338 BC.

That democracy was contested as a system as early as the time of the Greeks is evidenced by the writings of Thucydides, Socrates, Plato, and Aristotle. Plato's Socrates argued in *The Republic* that "such is democracy—a pleasing, lawless, various sort of government, distributing equality to equals and unequals alike."[25] Plato's critique of democracy was that the rule of the *demos* was the rule of the foolish, vicious, and always potentially brutal, and that any stability in such a rule was a sheer fluke.[26] The ideas articulated above—civic duty, democracy requiring instruction and debate, as well as democracy vulnerable to being reduced

---

[21] *See* JOHN DUNN, DEMOCRACY—A HISTORY 34 (Penguin 2005).

[22] *Id.* at 35.

[23] *See* THUCYDIDES, THUCYDIDES IN FOUR VOLUMES: VOL. 1, THE HISTORY OF THE PELOPONNESIAN WAR BOOKS I AND II 320–21 (Charles Forster Smith trans. Harvard University Press 1956). Thucydides lived from approximately 472 to 396 BC.

[24] *Id.* at 322–9.

[25] *See* PLATO, THE REPUBLIC 94 (Benjamin Jowett trans. Project Gutenberg 2008).

[26] *Id.* at 22.

to mob rule—still resonate today as central issues when grappling with concepts of democracy.

Almost two millennia then passed during most of which democracy was seen as neither positive nor reliable, but rather was marginalized and viewed with suspicion. Thomas Hobbes considered democracy an unstable form of government that would either revert to anarchy or become a de facto "aristocracy of orators, interrupted sometimes with the temporary monarchy of one."[27]

THE LIBERAL MODEL OF DEMOCRACY

Democracy did not surface again in a positive light until the ratification of the US federal constitution in the 1780s, in which a model of representative democracy was adopted. There were several reasons for this choice, but central to the discussion here was that representative democracy was seen to best balance fears of mob rule by placing the ultimate responsibility for decisions in the hands of elected, informed representatives. Another safeguard was the rule of law, the lawmaker being bound by the constitution, as the United States was (and still is), to be a "government of laws, not of men."[28] Certain fundamental rights and liberties of minority groups would then be guaranteed as against a rule by the majority, a caveat here being that women and slaves at this time had no participatory rights. An additional safeguard against the temporary monarchy of one orator was the separation of powers, as well as the system of checks and balances between the three different branches of government: the President, Congress, and the Court.

The American model places a great emphasis on voted leaders as opposed to civic duties, developing into what is now considered the liberal model of democracy. The classical liberal view, postulated for example by John Locke, was "wherever law ends, tyranny begins."[29] Locke emphasizes the impersonal rule of law and the protection of

---

[27] *See* Alan Apperley, *Hobbes on Democracy*, 19(3) POLITICS 65–171 (1999), *citing* THOMAS HOBBES, *DE CIVE PHILOSOPHICAL RUDIMENTS CONCERNING GOVERNING AND SOCIETY* (1651) in THE ENGLISH WORKS OF THOMAS HOBBES, Vol. IV 141 (William Molesworth ed. London 1840). Hobbes had translated Thucydides into English: THUCYDIDES, EIGHT BOOKES OF THE PELOPONNESIAN WARRE WRITTEN BY THUCYDIDES THE SONNE OF OLORUS DATE: 1648 (Thomas Hobbes trans. 1648).

[28] *See* John Adams, *7th "Novanglus" letter*, BOSTON GAZETTE, 1774.

[29] *See* JOHN LOCKE, TWO TREATISES OF GOVERNMENT Chapter XVIII Section 202 (Thomas Hollis ed. 1689).

individual freedom; democratic process is constrained by, and in the service of, personal rights that guarantee individuals the freedom to pursue their own goals and happiness. Legitimate government is defined in relation to the protection of individual liberty and human rights, and questions of private autonomy. The focus is instead on the individual's ability to govern herself, a departure from the medieval corporate conception of democracy—the right of a people to organize into a body free of external interference. The individual under this modern model is capable of self-restraint and no longer needs elaborate institutions to control human vice.[30]

THE REPUBLIC MODEL OF DEMOCRACY

Representative democracy as a model was quickly established thereafter in Holland and France; in turn, its reach was fairly quickly felt throughout much of Europe. In contrast to the liberal, elective-representative model developed in the United States, the French revolution led to a representative democracy with a greater focus on civic participation. This model of a republic emphasized the democratic process as a collective deliberation that ideally leads citizens to reach agreement on the common good. Human freedom is to be found not in the liberal pursuit of private preferences (happiness) but rather in self-governance through political participation: "liberty, equality and fraternity." Legitimate government is defined in terms of popular sovereignty and public autonomy.

Criticism—in particular of liberal democracy as a tool for capitalism—was raised by Karl Marx prior to World War I.[31] World War II brought further denunciation, as exemplified by Joseph Schumpeter's argument that the "reduced sense of responsibility and absence of effective volition" found in representative democracies results in the typical citizen dropping "down to a lower level of mental performance as soon as he enters the political field ... He becomes primitive again."[32] Schumpeter posited that the principle of democracy "merely means that the reins of government should be handed to those who command more support than

---

[30] *See* Joyce Appleby, *The Radical Double-Entendre in the Right to Self-Government*, in THE ORIGINS OF ANGLO-AMERICAN RADICALISM 275 (Margaret Jacob & James Jacob eds. London 1984).

[31] *See* JOSEPH V. FEMIA, MARXISM AND DEMOCRACY 18 (Oxford University Press 1993).

[32] *See* JOSEPH A. SCHUMPETER, CAPITALISM, SOCIALISM AND DEMOCRACY 261 (Martino Publishing, reprint 2011) (2nd ed. 1947).

do any of the competing individuals or teams,"[33] in a modern echo of Hobbes' fear of rule by orators.

DELIBERATIVE DEMOCRACY

Deliberative democracy—also referred to as discursive democracy—attempts to bridge, in part, Schumpeter's criticism of democracy as becoming mindless—that voters who have achieved political equality no longer deliberate when making voting choices. This imbalance is to be redressed through political equality and authentic deliberation. James Fishkin and Robert Luskin define political equality as comprising the equal consideration of everyone's preferences. Here, "everyone" refers to a relevant population or *demos*. "Equal consideration" entails three things: a process of counting so that everyone has the same voting power, that is, an equal chance to cast a decisive vote; anonymous voting; and the absence of voting track records or preferences.

Deliberation, for Fishkin and Luskin, is a weighing of competing considerations through discussion. Such a weighing is to be characterized by being informed, balanced, conscientious, substantive, and comprehensive.[34] The weighing is informed, and consequently informative, when the arguments presented are supported by appropriate and reasonably accurate factual claims. "Balanced" entails that counterarguments be presented in order to be able to more thoroughly assess claims. "Conscientious" requires that participants be willing to talk and listen with civility and respect. "Substantive" means that the arguments are to be considered sincerely on their merits, not by how they are made or who is making them. Finally, "comprehensive" means all points of view held by significant portions of the population are to be given attention.

In a somewhat ironic turn, the best known historical example of deliberative democracy in action is the drafting and ratification process of the US federal constitution in the late 1780s. It is ironic because this

---

33 *Id.* at 73.

34 *See* James S. Fishkin & Robert C. Luskin, *Experimenting with a Democratic Ideal: Deliberative Polling and Public Opinion*, 40 ACTA POLITICA 284, 285 (2005). *See also* generally, JAMES S. FISHKIN, WHEN THE PEOPLE SPEAK—DELIBERATIVE DEMOCRACY AND PUBLIC CONSULTATION (Oxford University Press 2009). Several others have delineated notions of deliberative democracy, including Joshua Cohen, Amy Gutmann, and Dennis F. Thompson. As the ambition here is to give a short history, the more nuanced aspects of each of these models have been omitted.

deliberative democratic process approved the instrument which ultimately created the imbalance that the deliberative model of democracy is attempting to redress. The drafting of the constitution began in a convention representing 12 states,[35] then went to committee for report; this report was then discussed by the convention again, compromise was reached, and a draft constitution was decided upon. Benjamin Franklin, when signing the draft, stated, in a manner much in line with the Churchill quote earlier in the chapter: "I consent, Sir, to this Constitution because I expect no better, and because I am not sure, that it is not the best."[36] The draft was then sent to the individual states for debate and ratification by general election. The debates held in the different states concerned the draft as well as issues raised by *The Federalist Papers*, a collection of 85 essays authored by Alexander Hamilton, James Madison, and John Jay in 1787–88.[37] This process is seen as one of the best examples of deliberative deliberation because of the level of detail the discussions engendered, the extent of the debates across the 13 states, and the number of individuals freely participating in the debate process.

PROCEDURAL DEMOCRACY

Jürgen Habermas puts forth a procedural concept of democracy that combines a procedural account of democratic legitimacy with deliberative politics.[38] Habermas attempts to resolve several issues with this concept, such as the tension between the liberal human rights model and the republic popular sovereignty model, as well as the imbalance between financial resources and power, on one side; and popular sovereignty, on the other. According to this procedural principle of democracy, "[o]nly those statutes may claim legitimacy that can meet with the assent of all citizens

---

[35] The State of Rhode Island and Providence Plantations did not attend for fear of a strong central power, and was the last state to ratify the constitution in 1790.

[36] *See* JAMES MADISON, NOTES ON THE DEBATES IN THE FEDERAL CONVENTION, TUESDAY SEPTEMBER 17, 1787, available at the website of The Avalon Project, Documents in Law, History and Diplomacy, Yale Law School: avalon.law.yale.edu.

[37] *See* ALEXANDER HAMILTON, JAMES MADISON, & JOHN JAY, THE FEDERALIST PAPERS (1787); *see* the e-text archives of Project Gutenberg, gutenberg.org.

[38] *See* Jeffrey Flynn, *Communicative Power in Habermas's Theory of Democracy*, 3(4) EUROPEAN JOURNAL OF POLITICAL THEORY 433 (2004).

in a discursive process of legislation that in turn has been legally constituted."[39] Law is to act as a transformer of communicative power. The exercise of state authority through administrative power is only legitimate if bound to this discursively generated communicative power. Two components can consequently be identified: communicative power; and a responsiveness by the political/administrative system to this communicative power.

The communicative power is of the citizenry. According to Habermas, the principle of democracy mandates that "[j]ust those norms are valid to which all possibly affected persons could agree as participants in rational discourses."[40] The communicative power of the citizenry is to be bound by a set of abstract rights that citizens recognize in order to regulate their lives together by means of legitimate, positive law. Habermas identifies five broad categories of such rights.[41] The first category comprises the basic rights that result from the politically autonomous elaboration of the right to the greatest possible measure of equal individual liberties. This category of a general right to equal liberties necessitates the following two corollaries:

- Basic rights resulting from the politically autonomous elaboration of the status of a member in a voluntary association of consociates under law; and
- Basic rights resulting immediately from the actionability of rights and from the politically autonomous elaboration of individual legal protection [due process guarantees].

These categories of rights regulate relationships among citizens. Citizens can each claim rights and bring them to bear as against one another. The general right to equal liberties, along with the correlative membership rights and guaranteed legal remedies, establish the legal code as such: in other words, "there is no legitimate law without these rights."[42]

The fourth category addresses rights to political participation. This is the basic right to equal opportunities, to participate in processes of opinion and will formation, in which citizens exercise their political autonomy and through which they generate legitimate law. The fifth category concerns the right to social welfare rights. If citizens cannot

---

[39] *See* JÜRGEN HABERMAS, BETWEEN FACTS AND NORMS 110 (Polity Press 1997).

[40] *Id.* at 107 and 111.

[41] *Id.* at 122–23.

[42] *Id.* at 125.

meet their basic material needs, neither private nor public autonomy will be effectively exercised. Basic rights relate to the provision of living conditions that are socially, technologically, and ecologically safeguarded, insofar as the current circumstances make this necessary if citizens are to have equal opportunities to utilize the civil rights listed in the first four categories above. Through this communicative power of the citizenry bound by the above categories of rights, Habermas resolves the tension between popular sovereignty and human rights.

Habermas links the communicative power of the citizenry with the lawmaker's result: "law represents … the medium for transforming communicative power into administrative power."[43] The procedural aspect of this model comes into place here. Only the state can act. State action, however, is legitimate only if the formal decision-making procedures within the constitutional state have a discursive character that preserves, under conditions of complexity, the democratic sources of legitimacy in the public at large. For there to be democratic lawmaking, formally institutionalized deliberation and decision must be open to input from informal public spheres. The political/administrative system cannot become an independent system, operating solely according to its own criteria of efficiency and unresponsive to citizens' concerns. Neither is it to be too subservient to particular interests that have access to administrative power through unofficial paths of influence that bypass the democratic process.

This requirement of responsiveness on the part of the political/administrative systems to the communicative power of the citizenry also provides a resolution to the tension between formal justice (a liberal paradigm) and substantive justice (a social welfare paradigm). According to the procedural democracy approach, any conflict between these two paradigms has the potential to be resolved by requiring, for the legitimate regulation of the issue, participation in the public discussions of the parties affected. The example given by Habermas concerns women's struggles for equality. Equal voting rights and access to education are based on formal equality and the liberal paradigm. Special aid to women with children to allow women to become better educated, as well as subsidized childcare, fall within the category of a social welfare paradigm (to achieve substantive justice eventually). This latter paradigm is in direct conflict with the first one of formal equality. Under a procedural democracy approach, in order for the regulation of these issues to be

---

[43] *Id.* at 169.

legitimate, women themselves have to participate in the public discussions determining which gender differences are relevant to issues of equality.[44]

The systems' responsiveness is explored in this work through the historical and legal parameters of workers and collectivism, beginning with the guild systems and ending with the modern national labor law models. Historically the guilds might seem far removed, but, as seen in the following chapters, the guild systems, and particularly the journeymen's associations, set out the basic structures for workers' rights: the early labor unions, and the twentieth-century systems of social welfare. The early guilds also demonstrate a model of direct democracy. When that democratic balance within the guilds was disrupted, the model no longer functioned, with journeymen engaging in industrial action against their masters. Today's labor law models are based on representative democracy, and the issue is whether they have made or should make the transition to a procedural democratic model.

Habermas discusses state action, and the question can be, and has been, raised whether labor unions are state actors. Each of the labor law models explored here involve degrees of self-regulation, in that the social partners determine the terms and conditions of employment through collective agreements, some of which, through *ergo omnes*, are declared nationally applicable in certain sectors. Given this degree of normative rulemaking by the social partners, the same components of procedural democracy should be addressed within labor law models in order to claim legitimacy. After tracing the historical and legal developments of worker collectivism, this work will conclude with a comparative analysis of the different current national labor law models from a procedural democracy perspective.

Part I examines workers, collectivism, and the law historically. "Trade unions are the successors of the old gilds"[45] was the conclusion reached by one of the very first scholars of labor law, the German Lujo Brentano, when tracing the history of the English trade unions. Though describing the English system, this statement is equally applicable to the German and Swedish labor law systems. However, each of these systems had a vital mid-stage, with journeymen's associations playing a central role in fighting for rights, first against the masters and then against employers.

---

44 *Id.* at 421–27.

45 *See Brentano*, supra intro. note 1 at clxv. *See also* CAROLA M. FREGE, EMPLOYMENT RESEARCH AND STATE TRADITIONS: A COMPARATIVE HISTORY OF BRITAIN, GERMANY AND THE UNITED STATES 17 (Oxford 2007).

The historical and legal development of the guilds, journeymen's associations, and labor unions is set out in this part. The transition from guilds to trade unionism in each of the four countries compared here—the United Kingdom, Germany, Sweden, and the United States—is then briefly traced, followed by a chapter looking at the internationalization of these collective worker efforts.

The history of trade unionism begins in England. There it dovetails into the decline of the guilds, the Reformation's social acceptance of profits, and the rise of journeymen's associations. England was the first country to have trade unions, a result in part of the early forging of a nation state, the early transitions from agricultural to mercantile and then industrial economies, and the parallel early commodification of labor and the tensions that arose between masters and journeymen. The rise of trade unionism in Germany and Sweden followed almost a century later, and almost immediately on the heels of the legislative abolishment of their guild systems. The guild system never quite permeated the American colonies or nation, with the history of the labor movement in the United States having as a starting point the concerns of colonialists focusing on survival in the face of labor shortages.

The modern labor law models of those four countries are set out in Part II. The general organizational structures of the social partners in each of the current national systems addressed here are blends of old unionism, with certain unions still organized in line with the trades or crafts, and new unionism, with union organization based on employer or industry. Each of these national labor organizational systems are also similar in their "bones," starting at the grassroots level with local clubs or unions, then with national unions comprising the locals, then with trade union federations or confederations comprising the nationals. Regional and international organizations, comprising national federations or confederations, add further layers to this structure. An example of the convergence of the organizational structures can be seen in the International Trade Union Confederation, with members from all four countries: the British Trades Union Congress; the German Deutscher Gewerkschaftsbund; the Swedish Landsorganisationen i Sverige, Sveriges Akademikers Centralorganisation, and Tjänstemännens Centralorganisation; and the American Federation of Labor and Congress of Industrial Organizations.

Organizational density is also a vital component in understanding these different labor law models. Historical peaks with respect to union density were reached for the United Kingdom in 1980 with 50 percent, Sweden in 1993 with 84 percent, Germany in 1991 with 36 percent, and the

United States in 1954 with 35 percent.[46] Union density in 2014, according to the OECD, was 25.1 percent for the United Kingdom (6.9 million members), 67.3 percent for Sweden (3.5 million members), and 10.7 percent for the United States (15 million members); 18.1 percent for Germany (7.4 million members). The general average for OECD countries in 2014 was 16.7 percent.[47] Employer organization is not as pervasive in most of these national systems; Sweden is the outlier, with an employer organizational density of more than 87 percent in 2014, surpassing that of labor union density.[48] Despite differences in numbers, the structures for employer organization in the different national systems are also quite similar in the different national systems, and often mirror the structures on the employee side.

The focus of each chapter in Part II is on the current basic labor law frameworks of the national systems, the legal status of employee organizations, recognition and collective bargaining, the legal status of collective agreements, employee consultation, industrial action, and the peace obligation. Relationships between the unions and employers, then between unions and members are then explored. Workers' ability to affect decisions at the local levels varies in the different national systems, which are all mostly systems of indirect democracy with organizations as members, and not individuals. Individual employee voice is then explored in situations of indirect industrial democracy, namely whether individual workers have sufficient means to hold unions accountable with regard to representing the employee's interests, particularly in grievance procedures. If such means are not available, the question then becomes whether other viable alternatives exist by which individual employees can seek

---

46 *See* MARTIN UPCHURCH, GRAHAM TAYLOR, & ANDREW MATHERS, THE CRISIS OF SOCIAL DEMOCRATIC TRADE UNIONISM IN WESTERN EUROPE: THE SEARCH FOR ALTERNATIVES (Ashgate 2009) and Jelle Visser, *Union Membership Statistics in 24 Countries*, 38 MONTHLY LABOUR REVIEW 39–49, 45 (January 2006).

47 These OECD statistics as to trade union density are available at the website of the OECD, at stats.oecd.org.

48 *See* Ewa Persson, *Högsta organisationsgraden på sju år för tjänstemannen*, ARBETSVÄRLDEN, 18 February 2015, available at arbetsvärlden.se. The degree of organization in Sweden in 2010 was 80 percent by private employers and 100 percent among public employers: *see* Anders Kjellberg, *Kollektivavtalens täckningsgrad samt organisationsgraden hos arbetsgivarförbund och fackförbund*, 2013(1) STUDIES IN SOCIAL POLICY, INDUSTRIAL RELATIONS, WORKING LIFE AND MOBILITY, RESEARCH REPORTS (Lund University 2013).

remedies within the national labor law models. An examination of worker voice—collectively or individually as to employers, and individually as to employee organizations, as well as access to justice in pursuing employee grievances—concludes each chapter.

PART I

Workers, Collectivism and the Law Historically

1. Guilds: brother[sister]hood, friendship, and mutual aid

The historical prototype for worker collectivism in the Western world is the guild model, which greatly influenced today's labor union structures.[1] The guilds also exemplify early struggles with democracy, as well as attempts by the law to harness worker collectivism, both of which are still pertinent issues for labor unions today. The origins of the guild system are found in prehistory, spanning several millennia. Craft guilds were known to have existed in Mesopotamia almost one thousand years prior to the Code of Hammurabi (1754 BC), which itself had several sections devoted to craftsmen.[2] The Gild of Stratford-upon-Avon,[3] in response to the 1388 royal demand to prove its origins, stated that its beginnings were "in a time before memory."[4] The account given here begins with the Roman *collegia* and then considers the early European guilds, revolving around the ethos of these organizations, their member

---

[1] *See generally* GEORGE HOWELL, TRADE UNIONISM NEW AND OLD 1 (London 1900).

[2] *See* DAVID B. WEISBERG, GUILD STRUCTURE AND POLITICAL ALLEGIANCE IN EARLY ACHAEMENID MESOPOTAMIA 52 (Yale 1967).

[3] Terminology is complicated due to the time period covered as well as the different languages involved. For example, the modern term (and spelling) of "guild" has many antecedents. The historical accounts referring to guilds can use the following terms, in Latin: *gildonia*, *confratriae*, *convivial*, *fraternitas*, *confranternitas*, *consortium*, *societas*, *solidatum*, *convivium*, *unio*, *conjuration*, or *collegia*; in English: guild, gild, fraternity, confraternity, mystery, mistery, corporation, brotherhood, company, commonalty, livery company, trading corporation, municipal corporation; in Swedish: *gilda*, *gille*, *skrå*, and *ambete*; and in German: *gilde*, *zeche*, *gaffel*, *genossenschaft*, *association*, *verien*, *einung*, and *zunft*, to list a few of the variations.

[4] *See* TOULMIN SMITH, *supra* chap. 1 note 1 at 211: "[P]redicta gild est, et incept fuit, a tempore cuius contrarium memoria non existit." The 1389 response goes on to speak of the duties of the "bretheren and sisteren" consistently throughout the document. *See also* J. MALET LAMBERT, TWO THOUSAND YEARS OF GILD LIFE—OR AN OUTLINE OF THE HISTORY AND DEVELOPMENT OF THE GILD SYSTEM FROM EARLY TIMES, WITH SPECIAL REFERENCE TO ITS APPLICATION TO TRADE AND INDUSTRY 1 (London 1891).

and societal functions, and the laws which eventually governed them. The argument has been made that, in contrast to their more modern negative reputation as monopolists, guilds were actually the "first and original basis for the theory and practice of popular democratic government in Europe" and the first to give worker organizations a role in the polity.[5]

THE GREEK AND ROMAN *COLLEGIA*

The origins of *collegia opficum* as a form of craft guild are found in both ancient Greece and Rome, but the specifics have been lost.[6] According to a legend preserved by Plutarch, Numa Pompilius, the second King of Rome, who reigned in the period 715–673 BC, divided the people of Rome by their trades and crafts into flautists, goldsmiths, carpenters, dyers, leatherworkers, curriers, blacksmiths, and potters, with all other occupations placed in one single organization.[7] Artisans, as social groups freed from households, began to make their presence felt in about the sixth century BC.[8] Associations of trades are mentioned in the laws of Solon (594 BC), which required fathers to teach their sons their trades. The Roman *collegia* were mentioned in the Twelve Tables (450 BC) as an imitation of a Greek model, perhaps the *phratria* (φατρία) that existed until about the second century BC.[9] As a rule, the earlier Greek collegia were less formally organized, while the Roman *collegia* could have extremely complicated organizational structures.[10] Greece later adopted the more formal Roman *collegia*.

---

[5] *See* ANTONY BLACK, GUILD & STATE—EUROPEAN POLITICAL THOUGHT FROM THE TWELFTH CENTURY TO THE PRESENT xvii (Transaction Publishers 2003).

[6] *See* GUNNAR HAZELIUS, OM HANDTVERKSAMBETENA UNDER MEDELTIDEN 8 (Nordiska museet 1906).

[7] *See* Plutarch (45–120 AD): THE RISE OF ROME: TWELVE LIVES BY PLUTARCH: ROMULUS, NUMA, PUBLICOLA, CORIOLANUS, CAMILLUS, FABIUS MAXIMUS, MARCELLUS, ARATUS, PHILOPOEMEN, TITUS FLAMININUS, ELDER CATO, AEMILIUS PAULLUS, NUMA chapter XVII (Christopher Pelling, Ian Scott-Kilvert, & Jeffrey Tatum trans. Penguin 2013).

[8] *See* HERBERT APPLEBAUM, THE CONCEPT OF WORK: ANCIENT, MEDIEVAL AND MODERN 44 (SUNY 1992).

[9] The phratries owned property that could then provide an income to be used to support feasting and other cultic activities, as well as financial loans to members. See *Phratries* in OXFORD DICTIONARY OF THE CLASSICAL WORLD (John Roberts ed. Oxford University Press 2007).

[10] Much of this historical account has been taken from Esmée Myfanwy Thomas, Guilds of Craftsmen and Small Traders in the Ancient World (exclusive

Collegia were controversial: at some times seen as seditious and rebellious, at others bundled with brigands. In 64 BC they were limited by law in response to a perceived Senate threat. Julius Caesar later adopted further restrictive measures. Emperor Augustus tightened controls in 7 BC through his *lex Iulia de collegiis*, requiring that any group of persons throughout Italy desirous of forming a craft guild had to seek authorization from the Roman government. Such privilege was only to be granted in consideration of the service rendered to the public by the grouping together of such individuals.[11] At this point the *collegia* were corporate bodies, legal persons in their own right.

The *collegia opficum* as a type of craft guild was a society of individuals formed for their mutual advantage, with activities revolving around religion, burial rights, and their craft or trade. They built temples; held religious rites, feasts, and memorials; guarded tombs; set trade standards; and secured monopolies as well as the good will of politicians. They supported sick or unemployed members as well as widows. The members of these voluntary *collegia* were expected to pay dues and participate. Full members were on an equal basis with respect to submitting proposals and voting. The general assembly and officials constituted the *collegia*, and officials were appointed by the assembly of members. The *collegia* had their own charters that were enforced against their members through self-policing. The business holdings of a *collegia* could be extensive; for example, the bakers of Rome owned land in Europe and Africa, buildings in Rome, and warehouses in Portus.[12]

The freedom of membership that marked much of the Greek and Roman history of the *collegia* began to be severely restricted during the third century AD, and was totally abolished by the fourth century under the Theodosian Code.[13] By granting state recognition, the *collegia* became part of the government machinery and were seen as indispensable for the production of the goods necessary for the Roman population. The occupations became synonymous with public responsibility, and no

of Egypt) from the Earliest Greek Times to the End of the 5th Century AD 75 (unpublished thesis, Oxford University, St. Anne's Society 1934).

[11] *See* SUETONIUS: THE LIVES OF THE TWELVE CAESARS; AN ENGLISH TRANSLATION, AUGMENTED WITH THE BIOGRAPHIES OF CONTEMPORARY STATESMEN, ORATORS, POETS, AND OTHER ASSOCIATES, ch. XLII (J. Eugene Reed & Alexander Thomson eds. 1889) Perseus Digital Library version available at perseus.tufts.edu.

[12] *See* APPLEBAUM, *supra* note 8 at 143.

[13] *See* Cod. Theod. VI, 20 1.17 (399), VII 20, 1.12 § 3 (400).

one could escape these obligations without committing an offense.[14] Vocation was now a public duty regulated by the state. Membership in the *collegia* became mandatory for the period of one's own life and for the lives of any of one's children, with sons having no choice but to remain in the same *collegia* as fathers, and sons-in-law becoming "wedded to the calling of [the wife's] family."[15] Freedom of movement was also limited, with craftsmen dragged back to the *collegium* and to their municipalities if they attempted to flee. Freedom of organization within the *collegia* was retained, however. Collective action such as strikes were few, but evidence does exist of such activity, in which craftsmen sought better terms and stricter enforcement of contracts with regards to payments, time limits, defaults, penalties, and prices.[16]

There is much debate about whether the Germanic and later European guilds stem from the Roman *collegia*. Roman *collegia* existed in Constantinople and Ravenna as late as 900 AD, and in Rome as late as 1030 AD.[17] At a minimum, the Catholic Church maintained the structure of the *collegia* in certain European areas. Regardless of whether there is a direct connection as to origins, legal issues concerning the European trade guilds were analyzed during the Middle Ages by Canon lawyers in accordance with the *collegia* structures found in Roman law. Consequently, traceable Roman influence in the interpretation of the law regarding guilds, at least, can be discerned.[18]

---

[14] *See* APPLEBAUM, *supra* note 8 at 142.

[15] *See* LAMBERT, *supra* note 4 at 13.

[16] *See* APPLEBAUM, *supra* note 8 at 142.

[17] The longevity of the Roman institution of *collegia* is outside the scope of this work. The Digest of Justinian, issued in 533 AD, includes *collegia*: see JUSTINIAN, DIGEST OF JUSTINIAN Vol. 4 Chapter 22 of Book 47 (Alan Watson trans. PennPress 2009). The lifespan of the *collegia* is inextricably intertwined with the survival of the reach of the Roman Empire, or at least the reach of its institutional structures. For the argument that these existed well past 476 AD, *see generally* CHRIS WICKHAM, THE INHERITANCE OF ROME: ILLUMINATING THE DARK AGES 400–1000 (Penguin 2010). *See also* LAMBERT, *supra* note 4 at 52 for the argument of continuity past the fifth century AD with respect to collegia, as well as W.J. ASHLEY, SURVEYS HISTORIC AND ECONOMIC 186 (London 1900) and HAZELIUS, *supra* note 6 at 13–15. But see STEVEN A. EPSTEIN, AN ECONOMIC AND SOCIAL HISTORY OF LATER MEDIEVAL EUROPE 112 (Cambridge University Press 2009) for an emphatic denial of any connection.

[18] *See* LAMBERT, *supra* note 4 at 52 and ASHLEY, *supra* note 17 at 186.

THE EVOLUTION OF THE NORTHERN EUROPEAN GUILD SYSTEM

The Northern European guild is often considered to have Germanic roots. The origins of the modern English term "guild," and its precursor "gild," are found in the Germanic/old Norse *gilda* and German *gilde*. In its first known use some time before 450 AD, *gilda* referred to a sacred banquet celebrating warrior feats, simultaneously confirming social solidarity through feasting and drinking.[19] The oldest Swedish use of the word *gilda* is found on the Viking Bjälbo runestone dating from around 1000 AD: "Valiant men raised this stone in memory of Greipr, their gild-brother—Lófi carved these runes—Júti's son."[20]

At this point of time, a guild was any group bound together by ties of rites and friendship, offering mutual support to its members upon payment of entry fees (German *geld*, Swedish *gäld*). The Germanic guilds created this social organization not based on blood ties or even social status, but rather to provide a type of social security as constructed families. The ties were expressed as being those of brotherhood, sisterhood, and friendship.[21] The members promised each other mutual aid and protection, providing burial services, for example, as seen with the Bjälbo runestone. Support for impoverished members or dependents of deceased members was eventually included, as was compensation at times for cases of fire or shipwreck, functioning as an early form of insurance. These early Germanic guilds were informal in that there were no legal requirements as to their formation, with the creation of a guild based on the intention of the members, not any official state consent.[22]

---

19 *See* BLACK, *supra* note 5 at 3. There is even a specific term for this type of feasting: in Old English, *gebeorscipe*; in Swedish, *gillesdrickningar*.

20 The Old Swedish reads: "DrængiaR ræisþu stæin þennsi æft Græip, gilda sinn, Lofi ræist runaR þessaR, Iuta sun"—see Project Samnordisk Runtextdatabas Svensk—Rundata entry for Ög 64, available at nordiska.uu.se/forskn/samnord.htm. There is a second runestone at Törnevalla, Sweden, also from around 1000 AD, that reads: "lveR/ØlveR ræistu stæin þenns[a] æftiR Dræng, ØygæiRs(?) sun, gilda sinn [Alver/Ölver raised this stone in memory of Dräng, Ögers (?) son, his gild brother]", which speaks to there being a merchant guild (*handelsgille*) in that area at that time—see runinskrift Ög MÖLM1960:230.

21 In the Wallonian region of the Netherlands, southern Germany, and France, "brotherhood" (*caritates*) was used as a designation instead of the term "guild": see HAZELIUS, *supra* note 6 at 35.

22 *See* OTTO VON GIERKE, COMMUNITY IN HISTORICAL PERSPECTIVE 19 (Antony Black ed. reprint Cambridge 2002) (originally published in German in 1868 as DAS DEUTSCHE GENOSSENCHAFTSRECHT, vol. 1).

These informal guilds became Christianized and ultimately Europeanized, institutionalized, and legalized during the Middle Ages. The earliest legal traces of guilds are found in the laws of King Ine of Wessex (688 to 726) banning turbulent proceedings at guild meetings.[23] In 779 Charlemagne prohibited those guilds based on mutual membership oaths upon the penalty of scourging, nose-slitting, and banishment, as oaths of loyalty were to be made only to the sovereign.[24] One of the earliest known English guilds was established during the reign of King Cnut (1016–35) by the Scandinavian thegn Orc, who founded Orcy's Gild among the frith-gildsmen of Abbotsbury.

An example of an early foreign guild in England is the Steelyard Merchants (*Gilda Theutonicorum*) of London, known as the Easterlings and later as part of the Hansa, settled prior to 967 and chartered in 1232.[25] The Easterling guild had a council of 12 headed by an alderman, lived together in a collegiate fashion with a guild hall, and owned warehouses.[26] The members had a common table and separate cells, and all men were required to remain unmarried. Marriage to an Englishwoman would result in the loss of privilege, later referred to as *Hanse*. This was a typical organization for the German guilds—both merchant and trade—abroad under the umbrella of the Hanseatic League.[27]

---

[23] A man who slew a thief had to prove that the victim was a thief and not an associate (*gegylda*): see Lambert, *supra* note 4 at 43.

[24] *See* BRENTANO, *supra* chap. 1 note 1 at 12.

[25] *See* WILLIAM HERBERT (LIBRARIAN TO THE CORPORATION OF LONDON), THE HISTORY OF THE TWELVE GREAT LIVERY COMPANIES OF LONDON; PRINCIPALLY COMPILED FROM THEIR GRANTS AND RECORDS WITH AN HISTORICAL ESSAY AND ACCOUNTS OF EACH COMPANY, ITS ORIGIN, CONSTITUTION, GOVERNMENT, DRESS, CUSTOMS, HALLS, AND TRUST ESTATES AND CHARITIES, INCLUDING NOTICES AND ILLUSTRATION OF METROPOLITAN TRADE AND COMMERCE AS ORIGINALLY CONCENTRATED IN THOSE SOCIETIES, WITH ATTESTED COPIES AND TRANSLATIONS OF THE COMPANIES' CHARTERS, VOL. 1 10 (London 1837). *See also* HELEN ZIMMERN, THE HANSA TOWNS AND THE HANSEATIC LEAGUE cxvi–cxxxu (Florence 1889).

[26] The German *Gild-Hall* or *Gildhalda Teutonicorum*, the Gildhall of the Dutch, the Easterling's House, or des Hansee städtischen stallhoffes: *see* EDWARD P. CHEYNEY, AN INTRODUCTION TO THE INDUSTRIAL AND SOCIAL HISTORY OF ENGLAND 25 (New York 1916).

[27] *See* GIERKE, *supra* note 22 at 66.

EARLY ENGLISH GUILDS

An early Anglo-Saxon secular guild, Knighten Guilde,[28] that existed at the time of King Edgar (959–75) was granted land in London "with the liberty of a Guilde for ever."[29] Edward the Confessor (1042–66) granted this guild's first written charter. Several other early English guild statutes,[30] including the tenth-century London Peace Gild ordinance, articulate the solidarity of these early guilds: "for friendship as well as for vengeance we shall remain united, come what may."[31] Under the eleventh-century Gild at Cambridge statute, the members agreed to take on the patron saint of the guild, swear faithful brotherhood towards each other not only in religious but also in secular matters, support each other in sickness and death, and protect each other from criminals and from each other's own wrongdoings: "If all misdo, let all bear it; let all share the same lot."[32]

The ethos of the guild was brotherhood (and in several cases sisterhood[33]), friendship, and mutual aid among guild members. Members had equal voting rights, entailing that these guilds were very much based on a direct democracy model. The guilds could own property, had bylaws which they self-policed, and provided complaint and resolution procedures including their own courts, practicing equality among members. Different types of guilds existed during the Middle Ages, including social, religious, priests, merchant (*gilda mercatoria*), burgher, town, crafts, and peace (frith) guilds.[34] Universities also began as guilds, with

---

28 Even here language and spelling are tricky, as this same guild is referred to during its history as the Enichten, Knigten, Cnughts, Cneughts, Anglische Cnuighten Gild, Cnithtegilda, Cnigtas Knytte gilda, Englisc Cnihtente gild, and Knighten gild.

29 *See* HERBERT, *supra* note 25 at 6.

30 The terms "customs," "privileges," and "statutes" are loosely used at this time, mostly because they are so intertwined in medieval society. Custom refers to the unwritten law "time out of mind." Privileges were usually a sovereign's acknowledgement of a custom, while a statute was a written compilation of custom or privileges or both: see MACK WALKER, GERMAN HOME TOWNS, COMMUNITY, STATE, AND GENERAL ESTATE 1648–1871, 35–37 (Cornell 1971).

31 *See* MARC BLOCH, FEUDAL SOCIETY 420 (Routledge & Kegan Paul Ltd. 1961).

32 *See* BRENTANO, *supra* chap. 1 note 1 at 5.

33 *See* Carole M. Nottingham, *The London Middle English Guild Certificates of 1388–9 in Historical Introduction*, 39 MEDIEVAL STUDIES 108, 111 (1995).

34 *See* HERBERT, *supra* note 25 at 3. Guilds performed many functions, with respect to both trade and society. Herbert explains the guilds as one of the "first

the colleges at Oxford and Cambridge comprising guilds of masters.[35] The early merchant guilds included handicraftsmen among their members, but this membership ceased when the craft guilds began to be formed in their own right.[36] The entire fabric of social, municipal, and trade life in the Middle Ages, with the exception of agriculture tied to the manor, was arguably kept within the circle of the guilds.[37]

The Rolls of the Exchequer during the reign of Henry I (1100–35) provide evidence of payments made for the right to form craft guilds, with guilds "amerced as adulterine" if founded without royal consent.[38] The first known grant of a charter to a craft guild was by Henry II (1154–89) to the London weavers. King John (1199–1216) required all guilds to receive a royal charter of confirmation of their status (in exchange for a fee), and later royals repeated this requirement as a way to insure control over the guilds by granting and revoking privileges—and also as a source of revenue for the Crown, through the payments for such grants.

---

political, and one of the grand elementary parts of our constitution." One of the societal functions of the guilds originated from the Saxon custom of frankpledge. Saxon law ordained that "every freeman of fourteen years old should find sureties to keep the pease, or be committed, certain neighbours, consisting of ten families, entered into an association, and become bound to each other to produce him who committed an offence or to make satisfaction to the inured party." To effect this, members raised a sum of money among themselves that they put into a common stock. When one of the pledges committed an offence and fled, the other nine would pay satisfaction out of this stock. To better identify each other, as well as to ascertain whether any man was absent on unlawful business, the members would assemble at stated periods at a common table, where they ate and drank together. *See* Horne's Mirror of Justices, fourteenth century, book one, lib.i.c.de la veue des franc pleges, 7 Selden Society 1, vol. VII 42 (W.J. Whittaker and F.W. Maitland trans. 1893).

35 *See* RICHARD HOFSTADTER & WALTER METZGER, ACADEMIC FREEDOM IN THE AGE OF THE COLLEGE 4 (Columbia University Press 1961). Two models were created by the end of the twelfth century: the Bologna model based on guilds of students, and the Paris model based on guilds of the masters. Oxford and Cambridge followed the Paris model. One of the arguments made against the Swedish 1852 repeal of the universities' legal rights to self-policing (*domsrätt*) was that equals should be judged by equals, see Ernst Kallenberg, *Akademisk jurisdiktion. Studenternas rättsliga undantagsställning*, 2 STATSVETENSKAPLIG TIDSKRIFT 97–121, 105 (1906).

36 *See* HAZELIUS, *supra* note 6 at 37.

37 *See* LAMBERT, *supra* note 4 at 2.

38 *See* STELLA KRAMER, THE ENGLISH CRAFT GILDS AND THE GOVERNMENT—AN EXAMINATION OF THE ACCEPTED THEORY REGARDING THE DECAY OF THE ENGLISH CRAFT GUILDS 17 (Columbia University Press 1905).

The growth in the guilds' sophistication and power at this time parallels the evolution of towns.[39] In the twelfth century towns became new centers of power, commerce, opportunity, and culture, moving the focus of the economy away from manors, monasteries, and great fairs.[40] Towns were often founded on charters and incorporated, either by the Crown, as was the case with London, or by a local noble having command of the land. Privileges were granted to towns under these charters in exchange, for example, for the payment of taxes or the supply of goods or military services. Citizens of the towns were free to pursue trades, giving rise to the German saying "the city makes you free."

Towns became centers of production and trade by the thirteenth century, with at least one merchant guild in every English town. These guilds included nearly all the principal town residents as members exercising the most important functions in trade, and also those closely bound to the municipal government. In some cases, the guilds founded the town. By this time, guilds were regularly also corporate legal bodies. Privileges were confirmed by royal or municipal charters which often now granted a monopoly and the regulation of all commercial interests within their domain, trade as well as geographic, as well as exemptions, for example, from paying trade tolls. Municipal positions were often held by guild members, and guilds were often mobilized for guard duty, militia and police functions, and public works.[41]

How thoroughly guild membership permeated the identity of their members as to their place in society can be seen from the following description taken from one guild's history:

> Adam's eldest son was educated as a plowman, and his brother a Grassier [grazier]. The Fall of Man introduced the liberal sciences, divinity, law and physick; But tho' we had continued pure, as when we dropt from the creating Fingers of our Maker, Mechanick Arts had been necessary. In the Infancy of the World, before the Wranglings of Lawyers, the Sophistry of Philosophers, and turbulent factions of divines had debauched mankind, artists were in the highest repute.[42]

---

[39] The peace guilds often became the foundation of towns, with guild duties becoming intertwined with civic duties. Eventually admission to a guild would be a requisite for admission to a city as a free citizen: see JACOB LUNDELL, OM HANDTVERKSSKRÅN, NÄRINGSFRIHET OCH ARBETS ORGANISATION 28 (Lund 1846).

[40] *See* APPLEBAUM, *supra* note 8 at 230.

[41] *See* APPLEBAUM, *supra* note 8 at 269.

[42] *See* ALEXANDER PENNECUIK, BURGESS AND GUILD-BROTHER OF EDINBURGH, AN HISTORICAL ACCOUNT OF THE BLUE BLANKET, OR CRAFTS-MEN'S

According to this guild version of history, artists practicing the crafts would have existed even if Adam and Eve had not fallen from grace.

At the height of their power, guilds could be seen as ruling most aspects of an individual member's life, both in terms of religion and of the mysteries of the craft. A principle of unanimity dominated craft guild decision-making, with members voting on their own statutes; electing their own officials, including the enforcers of the guild's statutes; and in some cases even electing their own courts.[43] The rights of free association, addressing grievances, and providing remedies, as well as mutual assistance, were central. Masters were the official members of the craft guilds, but journeymen and apprentices were also governed by guild rules and had a voice in decision-making processes at this point in time.[44] Advancing each other's interests and promoting the welfare of the members were the core aims of the early medieval guilds.[45] The guild also regulated the external affairs of its members, competition within the trade, price and wage setting, and mutual restraint for the mutual good, as well as obtaining necessary legislation and political good will.

To modern eyes, the rules governing apprentices and journeymen at this point of time were very invasive on a personal level. A youth of 14 years of age would often leave his birth family entirely and move in with the master, receiving everything—clothing, substance, and housing—from the master. An apprentice served for three years, as did a journeyman.[46] The goal was to become master and a member in the craft, for without such membership the individual was barred from practicing the trade. The balance in numbers between masters, journeymen, and apprentices was vital to the economic and social health of the trade. If a master took too many journeymen and/or apprentices—too many being more potential masters than the craft could bear—the entire system would topple. Trained apprentices would not be able to become journeymen, and trained journeymen not able to become masters. This early regulation of the number of journeymen and apprentices prevented gluts in the crafts. When the interests of the masters, journeymen, and apprentices were no longer kept in balance, as seen in Chapter 2—with masters

---

BANNER, CONTAINING THE FUNDAMENTAL PRINCIPLES OF THE GOOD-TOWN, WITH THE POWERS AND PREROGATIVES OF THE CRAFTS OF EDINBURGH & C. lii (Edinburgh 1722).

43 *See* BLACK, *supra* note 5 at 24.

44 *See* EPSTEIN, *supra* note 17 at 111.

45 *See* HOWELL, *supra* note 1 at 11.

46 *See* GEORGE URWIN, INDUSTRIAL ORGANIZATION IN THE SIXTEENTH AND SEVENTEENTH CENTURIES 13 (London 1957).

taking on more journeymen and apprentices than the craft could handle—this system began to disintegrate.

GERMAN *GILDE* AND *ZÜNFTE*

As with England, the Germanic notion of guilds, based on bonds of brotherhood, loyalty, and mutual aid, existed in fluid forms up to Charlemagne's ninth-century legislation.[47] The early German guilds often had overlapping aims and religious, social, moral, political, and private law objectives, such as providing funerals, taking care of the poor and sick, providing funds for travel, and offering insurance against shipwreck, flood, fire, theft, or robbery.[48] Evidence of German traders in England can be seen in the laws of London under the reign of Ethelred II in 978: "the people of the Emperor [Otto II of the Holy Roman Empire] have been judged worthy of the good laws, like to ourselves."[49]

Charlemagne's legislation effected state intervention in these early, fluid corporative forms, with greater requirements regarding loyalty to the sovereign—confining guilds to single purposes within private law, in contrast to the freedom of guilds in England at this time.[50] Early guilds include the Weavers' Guild in Mainz, evidenced by a letter dated 1099 from the Archbishop of Mainz to the guild,[51] and the Charter of the Watermen of Worms, dating from 1106. The first record of a German miners' guild fund (*Büchsen*) is from the reign of Emperor Wenzell II of Bohemia in 1300. Miners' funds set up their own hospitals, and when a fatal accident occurred, a decent funeral was arranged and the widow provided with financial support.[52]

Guilds, towns, and other corporative bodies had become so common and powerful that the German princes at the 1231 Diet of Worms expressed their marked disapproval of such organizations, perceived of as a clear threat to their own power.[53] The establishment of town councils at the beginning of the thirteenth century gave landholders and merchants

---

[47] *See* GIERKE, *supra* note 22 at 13.

[48] *Id.* at 23.

[49] *See* ZIMMERN, *supra* note 25 at x.

[50] *See* GIERKE, *supra* note 22 at xxiv and 28.

[51] *See* HAZELIUS, *supra* note 6 at 38.

[52] *See* K.P. COMPANJE, R.H.M. HENDRIKS, K.F.E. VERAGHTERT, & B.E.M. WIDDERSHOVEN, TWO CENTURIES OF SOLIDARITY—GERMAN, BELGIAN AND DUTCH SOCIAL HEALTH CARE INSURANCE 1770–2008 35 (Amsterdam 2009).

[53] *See* ZIMMERN, *supra* note 25 at xxx.

oligopolistic rights, often excluding the craftsmen.[54] Vocational guilds began to form (*Berufsgilden*) in addition to the trade guilds (*Gewerbsgilden*) such as the Hansa. The London Steelyard became a major Hansa trade center, with privileges granted by English kings that such traders be treated as subjects and friends.[55] Other ports, such as York, Bergen, Venice, Novgorod, and Stockholm, became Hansa cities. The Hansa associations of merchants became associations of cities, with Visby the German center of trade in the Baltic Sea, as blessed by Pope Honorius II.[56]

Craft guilds (*Zünfte*) began to emerge in the shadows of the merchant guilds during the thirteenth century, but were still relatively powerless. The different German guilds began to have explicit membership requirements in their charters, and persons who were not members of a trade guild in a city could not exercise their trade there (*Bannmeile*).[57] Many guilds received privileges as official suppliers of certain services or products to a certain city. The guilds were also given jurisdiction to enforce these regulations within the trade.

The fluid form of the Hansa cities and merchants became affixed in a constitution adopted at the Cologne Confederation in 1367 in response to the actions of the Danish King Waldemar III Attardag, who had plundered Visby and threatened the Hansa herring trade in the Baltic Sea. The deputies of 77 Hansa towns declared war, and stated that the towns would be the enemies of the King of Denmark and "help one another faithfully."[58] Towns that were too weak to aid in battle could contribute monies. Those not joining the war were declared outside the Hanseatic League, entailing that no Hansa town, burgher, or merchant would buy or sell goods, allow entrance to their ports, or unload goods in their domains to those towns (and their citizens) outside the Hansa. When contacted by Waldemar, the towns individually responded: "The Hanseatic League having resolved on war, they must submit themselves to the general resolution which bound them all."[59] After prevailing in the war, the Hanseatic League received as concessions from Denmark two thirds of the revenues from Scania (southern Sweden), possession of Scania's strongholds, free passage at sea, and the right to veto any choice of Danish King for a period of 15 years.

---

54 *See* ASHLEY, *supra* note 17 at 192.
55 *See* ZIMMERN, *supra* note 25 at xii.
56 *Id.* at xv and xviii.
57 *See* HAZELIUS, *supra* note 6 at 93.
58 *See* ZIMMERN, *supra* note 25 at xliii.
59 *Id.* at xliv.

Journeymen associations (*Gesellenvereinigungen* or *Gesellenschaften*), also referred to as brotherhoods (*Brüderschaften*), became more prevalent in the fourteenth century, based on similar structures and ideals as the guilds, but with a focus on better defending the journeymen's interests against masters as well as providing networks of self-help groups for young artisans on the tramp. These journeymen's associations began to take part in concerted collective action early on, for example with work stoppages in 1329 in Breslau and 1349 in Paris, and a ten-year work stoppage by the baker journeymen in Kolmar, supported by secondary actions throughout the Rhine Valley. The Kolmar dispute did not concern working conditions but rather the status and position of the journeymen in the church processional.[60] By the fifteenth century, the journeymen's associations had an established autonomy within the guild, with the right to hold periodic meetings and have their own treasury and systems of mutual aid. Membership was obligatory, and all journeymen had to abide by the decisions of the association. Refusal to do so resulted in the journeyman being declared dishonorable, which entailed losing their job, being excluded from the association, and losing all rights to aid as well as tramping (discussed below). Letters would also be sent to the associations in other towns to prevent the individual from gaining work elsewhere.[61]

Religious guilds/fraternities were repressed in certain German areas during the Reformation in the 1520s. Many German cities were in favor of the Reformation, and much of the Protestant movement originated in the lower and middle strata of town citizens, including craftsmen and artisans, invoking a strong sense of community, brotherhood, and friendship, as well as equality of all believers.[62] Certain parts of Germany abolished religious guilds/fraternities in 1524. The Peasant's Revolt in 1525 led to a tightening of state controls, similar to the Tudor legislation, hemming in the power of trade guilds. Just a few decades later, the Hansa began to lose many of their strongholds in the Baltic.

By the sixteenth century, the tramping system (*Wanderjahre*) was highly organized throughout the entire Holy Roman Empire. The *Wanderjahr* was an obligatory period of 4–5 years following a 3–4 year apprenticeship. Fairly detailed rituals were put into place regarding the tramping system, with a developed system of passports, lodgings, rules

---

[60] *See* HAZELIUS, *supra* note 6 at 141.

[61] *See* George S. Werner, *Traveling Journeymen in Metternichian South Germany*, 125 PROCEEDINGS IN THE AMERICAN PHILOSOPHICAL SOCIETY NO. 3 190–219, 211 (1981).

[62] *See* BLACK, *supra* note 5 at 111.

regarding welcome and work, and support in case of lack of work.[63] *Geschenkte Handwerke* were the artisan circles in which aid was given to travelers and *schenke* was the cup of wine offered to travelers.[64] The same tension seen in England between masters and journeymen began to manifest itself in the sixteenth century, with Imperial legislation passed to restrain the activities of journeymen—the Reformation of Good Order [*Polizey*]—in 1530, 1548, and 1577.[65] Certain German states maintained a strong guild presence up to the nineteenth century. Guilds dominated not only production and trade, but also politics, social life, and ethical conduct, with home-town regimes based on a definition of honor that meant "domestic, civic and economic orderliness."[66] The guilds maintained this equality by penalizing or excluding those who were seen as pushy, and by mutual agreement among the membership restraining expansion and promising security.[67] This localization of power within German home towns gave rise to a self-sufficiency and collective individualism unique to northern Europe. One good example of this independence within collectivism is that community law (home-town custom) was considered by many in the home towns to break book law (imperial or church law).[68] These home-town guild systems also provided extensive social welfare support to their members.

SWEDISH *GILLE* AND *SKRÅ*

Viking trade was extensively developed during the late eighth to mid-eleventh centuries, with routes starting in the Nordic countries and traveling out to the Middle East, Russia, Iceland, Greenland, and even North America.[69] During this period, Swedish towns were neither large, nor populated, nor powerful and held no monopolies, a legacy that would go down the centuries. Every individual was basically free to do what was necessary to survive.[70] Birka was the first significant Swedish

---

63 ROBERT A. LEESON, TRAVELLING BROTHERS 158 (Granada 1979).

64 *See* WERNER, *supra* note 61 at 194.

65 Reformation of Good Order [*Polizey*] in 1530, Tit. 39, 1548, Tit. 36 & 37 and 1577, Tit. 37 & 38, see WALKER, *supra* note 30 at 435.

66 *See* BLACK, *supra* note 5 at 124 and WALKER, *supra* note 30 at 102.

67 *See* BLACK, *supra* note 5 at 125 and WALKER, *supra* note 30 at 134.

68 *Id.* at 75.

69 *See generally*, KIRSTEN A. SEAVER, THE LAST VIKINGS: THE EPIC STORY OF THE GREAT NORSE VOYAGERS (Tauris 2014).

70 *See* LUNDELL, *supra* note 39 at 51.

trading center in the late eighth century, followed by Sigtuna in the eleventh century. There is evidence of craft production in the latter.[71]

The Christianization of Sweden occurred between the eleventh and twelfth centuries, after which the Church became a powerful ally for the King as well as a significant patron of the crafts.[72] As evidenced by the Bjälbo rune stone, Germanic guilds (*gillena*) existed in some form in Sweden by the eleventh century, the main four types being general guilds (*allmänna gillen*), priest guilds (*prästgillen*), merchant guilds (*köpmannagillen*), and craft guilds (*hantverksgillen*). The craft guilds never became as powerful as the merchant guilds. One reason given for this is that the Swedish guild system was strongly influenced by the Hansa trading system, with several Swedish cities part of the Hansa and given the accompanying influx of German traders and craftsmen, who often also held political power, particularly in Visby, Kalmar, and Stockholm.[73] Visby was the most powerful Hansa city in the Baltic Sea by the twelfth century.[74] Trade under the Hansa and Lübeck was in full swing by the mid-1350s, with textiles and linen the largest areas of import to Sweden.[75]

Craft guilds, or *skrå*,[76] began to emerge in Sweden during the thirteenth century. Each craft often had two guild organizations in place:

---

[71] *See* FOLKE LINDBERG, HANTVERK OCH SKRÅVÄSEN UNDER MEDELTID OCH ÄLDRE VASATID 38 (Prisma 1989).

[72] *See* MICHAEL NORDBERG, I KUNG MAGNUS TID, NORDEN UNDER MAGNUS ERIKSSON 1317–1374 191 (Norstedts 1995). Several facts complicate tracing the history of guilds in Sweden. Sweden as a huge land mass was sparsely populated and poor, the latter arguably up to the twentieth century. Pre-history in Sweden is seen as the period up to around 800 AD. A further complication is that many of the medieval documents were lost in the 1697 fire of the Stockholm royal castle, Three Crowns. The fire started in the archives, with up to 90 percent of the royal collection of medieval documents destroyed: see NORDBERG, *supra* at 11.

[73] *See* SIGFRID HANSSON, BLAND MÄSTARE, GESÄLLER OCH LÄRPOJKAR 8 (Norstedt & söners förlag 1931); *see also* ZIMMERN, *supra* note 25 at xxxvii and LUNDELL, *supra* note 39 at 56.

[74] *See* NORDBERG, *supra* note 72 at 262.

[75] *See* LINDBERG, *supra* note 71 at 17. Letters of privilege were issued to Lübeck by Birger Jarl in the thirteenth century and by Magnus Eriksson in 1336. By law, half of the mayors and councilmen in the Swedish cities in the fourteenth century were to be German, see Statdslagens konungsbalk, flock II. *See also* NORDBERG, *supra* note 72 at 122.

[76] The word *skrå* originally referred to a piece of leather, then to a parchment; later to the statute or charter written on parchment; then to the guild organization itself, becoming a type of shorthand designation for the business side of the organization, see HANSSON, *supra* note 73 at 7.

the social guild, *gille*, and the craft guild, *skrå.* Many times the social guild was founded first and the professional master craft guild (*ämbete*) organized later, with individuals usually belonging to both.[77] Journeymen and apprentices were part of this order, as seen from the charters. The journeymen association of saddlers (*Bältare Svennernes skrå*) has one of the oldest Swedish journeymen charters, dating from some time prior to 1437.[78] The interactions between the different types of guilds, masters, journeymen, towns and guilds, Swedes, and Germans can be seen at the Falun mine, Stora Kopparberget (literally, in English, "the big copper mountain"). In 1344, King Magnus Eriksson confirmed Lübeck's ancient privileges in the mine.[79] In 1347 masters and journeymen formed a guild there, which had the right to appoint 14 councilmen, of whom one would be the head of the mine and another a judge for all guild disputes.[80] A peace guild, St. Georgs gillet vid Stora Kopparberget, was also formed there by the Germans.[81]

A marked distinction between the town (as often controlled by merchants, a mayor, and a council) and craftsmen existed historically in Sweden. Cities with their own laws and charters began to be founded in the thirteenth and fourteenth centuries, and often under the influence of either the German Hansa or the Danes.[82] A rigid divide existed between those who lived in the country (*landtmännen*) and those who lived in towns or cities (*stadsmännen*), with different sets of laws in place for these two groups. The first national legislation was passed under the regency of Birger Jarl (1248–66)[83] and the first legislative code encompassing both city and country dwellers was passed in 1350 under King Magnus Eriksson, the great-grandson of Birger Jarl. The 1350 Code was

---

[77] *See* LINDBERG, *supra* note 71 at 73 and 74.

[78] *See* G.E. KLEMMING, Samlingar utgifna av Svenska Fornskrift-sällskapet—Skrå ordningar 3 (Stockholm 1856).

[79] Operations at the Falun mine are believed to have begun in the Viking period, spanning a period of almost a millennium. The oldest written document as to the mine (then referred to as Tiskasjöberg) is a letter of privilege dated 1288 and signed by King Magnus Ladulås. The mine produced two thirds of the copper in the European market by the 1600s and was Sweden's largest employer, with more than one thousand workers. It was also its largest sole income source and a significant basis for its power: *see generally* David Dunér, *Helvetet i Falun*, 3 POPULÄR HISTORIA 48–53 (2009).

[80] *See* LUNDELL, *supra* note 39 at 53–54.

[81] *Id. citing* J.H. SCHRÖDER, STATUTA CONVIVII A S. GEORGIO DICTI AD MAGNUM CUPRIMONTEM DALEKARLIAE (Uppsala 1833).

[82] *See* LUNDELL, *supra* note 39 at 52.

[83] *See* LINDBERG, *supra* note 71 at 12.

in effect until 1734.[84] Under it, every able-bodied adult had to either prove they had the means to be able to live for a year or be forced to work—a rule that remained in place until 1846.[85] The crowns of Denmark, Norway, and Sweden were combined in 1389 under the personal rule of the Danish Queen Margareta Valdemarsdotter, daughter-in-law to King Magnus Eriksson, and the Kalmar union was formed in 1397. The Kalmar union remained in place until Gustav Vasa broke free and was elected King of Sweden in 1523. The Hansa consequently dominated trade in the Baltic Sea and in much of Sweden, particularly Stockholm, until the sixteenth century.

The oldest known Swedish craft guild charter was for the Stockholm Tailors, issued by King Magnus Eriksson in 1356 and granting them a monopoly.[86] Under that charter, no individual was to be admitted as a tailor unless first approved by a master after an apprenticeship, and then by the mayor and the organization's leaders. Several similar craft guild charters were issued in the fifteenth century, granting rights of self-policing, monopoly, meetings, elections, member fees, member limits, price setting, and sanctions, as well as rights of masters, journeymen, and apprentices. The charters also regulated processions, often concerning the guild's patron saint. Four main themes can be identified in the charters: economic regulation of the craft; illness and funeral insurance; self-policing of internal membership disputes through arbitration; and the social aspects of drinking and feasting together, or *gillesdrycke*.[87]

The importance of the guilds' social aspects in any of the countries discussed here cannot be overexaggerated. Brothers and sisters eating and drinking together in the common hall, with detailed ceremonies both for religious and professional reasons, often as markers of achievement such as becoming a journeyman, then a master, were deeply ingrained in the organizations. The best example of this can be seen from the Swedish 1501 Charter of the Goldsmiths' Guild.[88] Upon the death of a goldsmith

---

[84] *See* NORDBERG, *supra* note 72 at 119.

[85] "Nu kan löskær man skeno göra, ok orkar ei til flriggia marka, fla skal han fangas sum för ær sakt ok haldas en manafla dag": *see Magnus Erikssons landslag* (1350). "Kan lösker man skeeno göra, oc orkar ey til III mark, tha scal han fangas oc haldas een maanadh": *see King Kristoffer's landslag* (1442) para. 37.

[86] *See* LUNDELL, *supra* note 39 at 58.

[87] *See* SUNE AMBROSIANI, FRÅN DE SVENSKA SKRÅÄMBETENAS DAGAR 2 (Stockholm 1920).

[88] One guild had no difficulty in creating a monopoly: the goldsmith's guild. This was most likely because the King wanted the goldsmith's guild to police the

or his wife, every guild brother was required to "follow them to the grave" and any member who failed to do so, regardless of whether or not they had received notice of the funeral, was to be fined, without exception.[89] Many charters also included the duty for members to contest any unfair funeral costs attributed to the deceased, and to hold masses.[90] Even in death the cohesion of the guild was to be maintained.

On occasion, it was possible for the original social guild to be converted to a craft guild by the King or a high noble. The charters issued afterwards became more and more craft- as well as rule-based—a professionalization and legalization of the crafts, in fact.[91] Granting monopolies to town guilds at this time and restricting those who lived outside the cities to only one trade was neither plausible, given the scarce population and extensive land mass, nor feasible, given the difficulties in enforcement. Neither were taxes assessed against the trade of handicrafts in the countryside at this stage, as seen from King Kristofer's country/provincial law of 1442.[92] Towns still did not constitute more than 5 percent of the Swedish population by the fifteenth century and did not dominate to the same degree seen in England because of the country's sparse population and the extensive geographic distance to be covered.[93]

The pattern of a career in the trades in Sweden basically followed that seen in England and Germany. An apprentice would serve their time in this role, become trained, receive a journeyman's certificate (*gesäll-brev*),[94] and enter the journeymen's association. The former apprentice

---

origins of precious metals and to ensure certain standards with respect to coinage: see JOHN KROON, GULDSMEDERNAS SKRÅ AV ÅR 1501 FAKSIMILTRYCK (Malmö 1959).

89 *Id.* at 124.

90 *See* LUNDELL, *supra* note 39 at 26.

91 *See* KLEMMING, *supra* note 78 at 5.

92 Kristofers landslag 1442 (Köpm B VII), part of the Växjöregulation of 1414.

93 The general population of Sweden at this time was about 500,000, with the nobility comprising fewer than two hundred families, only about ten of which were considered wealthier than farmers. About 2,500 individuals fell into the category of ecclesiastics including monasteries and cloisters, controlling 20 percent of the land and receiving a 10 percent tithe. Consequently, the demand for crafts was not very high during this period, as there was neither the population nor the wealth to engender any greater demand. This began to change after Gustav Vasa's reign: see LINDBERG, *supra* note 71 at 11 and 16.

94 *Gesäll* is the modern Swedish designation of "journeyman." Prior words included *sven*, *knekt*, and *lönedräng*: see KLEMMING, *supra* note 78 at 10.

would most likely stay with the same master after becoming a journeyman, with the same room and board, but now with wages. In order for the journeyman to experience and hone different skills with different masters, based very much on the German model, a period of two to four years of tramping was expected. A very complex Swedish tramping system was created, with regulations as to board (two pillows), the persons to be contacted, and the amount and time of work to be performed. The journeymen's association also eventually provided illness and funeral insurance.

The three European systems examined in this chapter show similarities in the development of their guild systems as well as the internal self-regulation of the guilds. Though proffered as a description of the English guilds, the following is equally true of the systems created in Germany and Sweden, in that they all were

> autonomous republics with their own employment, population and emigration policies and apparatus: their welfare system from orphan allowance to funeral benefit, their inner democracy, far more intricate and alive than the official democracy of the Parliament which excluded them; their own financial system, laws and customs, check points and passports.[95]

The guilds in this early period were pockets of democracy offering stability and support for their members in times of great social change.

---

[95] *See* R.A. Leeson, United We Stand—An illustrated account of Trade Union Emblems 7 (Adams & Dart 1971).

2. The golden age of the English guilds

Three different strands can be traced in the early English legislation concerning workers: the desire to prevent agrarian workers from leaving agriculture and taking up trades; the prohibition of any collective action by workers to negotiate better work conditions; and the need for the Crown instead of the guilds to regulate the conditions of work, specifically the relationships between guild masters, journeymen, and apprentices. This restrictive legislation, beginning in the early fourteenth century, governed during a time span of well over five hundred years.

Twin forces can be seen as causing changes in the English guild system. The first was the development of the nation state centered on the Crown, and the efforts of the Crown to harness the freedoms of corporate bodies as well as profit through charters and grants of privileges. The second was the Reformation and the growth of commerce, resulting ultimately in profits and capitalism, changing the rules of the game.[1] Profit was no longer seen as immoral—a basic tenant during the Middle Ages—but became desirable in the spirit of the Reformation as doing God's bidding,[2] ultimately further eroding the guild relationships of masters, journeymen, and apprentices. Masters began ignoring the delicate balance between the needs of the trade and the number of journeymen and apprentices, acting instead to exploit short-term individual profits, no longer taking care as to the future of the craft.[3] Journeymen's associations became more common and more active as a result of the growing tension between masters limiting access to the trades for greater individual profit.[4] The barriers created to prevent journeymen becoming masters eventually led to "journeyman" becoming a permanent rather

---

[1] *See* CHRISTOPHER L. TOMLINS, LAW, LABOR, AND IDEOLOGY IN THE EARLY AMERICAN REPUBLIC 114 (Cambridge University Press 1993).

[2] *See* APPLEBAUM, *supra* chap. 1 note 8 at 244.

[3] *See* LUNDELL, *supra* chap. 1 note 39 at 2 for a discussion of how guildsmen, academics, and artists fell outside the category of business during the Middle Ages as profits were not perceived as a part of their operations.

[4] *See* WEBB & WEBB (1894), *supra* Introduction note 3 at 26.

than transitory identity, unifying and strengthening the resolve of the journeymen's associations as well as expanding the scope of their demands.

LEGISLATIVE RESTRICTIONS IN THE FOURTEENTH AND FIFTEENTH CENTURIES

Despite the pastoral views of medieval life depicted in the many beautifully illustrated books of hours of the era, English medieval society was very much in a state of constant conflict, not only on the battlefield, but also in the courts. All classes of society except the very poorest guarded or contested their privileges through litigation. The courts existed at several levels—manorial, royal, and ecclesiastical—and there were also special market and guilds courts. In an effort to stem frivolous and unfounded legal activity arising as a response to this litigiousness, a 1304 act was passed setting out nascent conspiracy. The 1304 act, Who be Conspirators and Who be Champertors, defined conspirators as:[5]

> [T]hey that do confeder or bind themselves by oath, covenant or other alliance, that every one of them shall aid and bear the other falsely and maliciously to indite, or cause to indite, to falsely to move or maintain pleas … and such as retain men in the country with liveries or fees to maintain their malicious enterprises, and to drown the truth.[6]

Conspiracy was taken up again in a 1330 act (4 Edw. 3.) st. 1 concerning conspirators, confederators, and maintainers of false quarrels.[7] Though it was focused on spurious legal claims, this definition of conspiracy was expanded by the courts to encompass groups who agreed by oath to injure individuals.[8] Though originally only addressing litigants and false

---

[5] 1304 (33 Edw. 1) st. 2. The punishment of Champerty set out in 1305 (33 Edw. 1) st. 3 was three years' imprisonment and fines at the King's pleasure.

[6] The act was issued in Law French. This translation is from RICHARD BURN & SIR GEORGE CHETWYND, JUSTICE OF THE PEACE AND PARISH OFFICER VOL. 4 567 (1820). The fact that the 1304 Act was still included in an 1820 law book for justices of the peace demonstrates how enduring it was, being finally repealed in 1824.

[7] 1330 (4 Edw. 3.) st. 1.

[8] These fourteenth-century acts would come to greatly affect workers and collectivism up to the twentieth century as the legal bases for the long history of conspiracy in both England and the United States, under criminal and civil,

claims, the judicial interpretation of conspiracy in subsequent centuries would extend to combinations of workers being deemed unlawful.

Almost all the crafts had their own guild organizations by the fourteenth century, separate from the merchant guilds. The craft guilds were already self-policing their sectors. In 1306, London picketers assaulted strangers who had come to the city on royal contracts,[9] demanding that the strangers work for no less than the daily London rate of sixpence and an after-dinner drink.[10] A Royal Proclamation was issued against "congregations and chapters" of craftsmen in response to this picket.[11]

Collective labor action and the legal regulation of wages during the fourteenth century were mainly the result of the depopulation caused by the 1348 plague. The 1349 Statute of Labourers was enacted "[b]ecause a great Part of the People, and especially of Workmen and Servants, late died of the Pestilence, many seeing the Necessity of Masters, and great Scarcity of Servants, will not serve unless they may receive excessive Wages."[12] The 1349 Statute mandated that "Every Person able in Body under the Age of Sixty Years, not having to live on, being required, shall be bound to serve him that doth require him, or else committed to the Gaol, until he find Surety to serve." The statute went on to criminally sanction with prison any premature departure from service before the expiry of the contract term, and prescribed that the "old Wages, and no more, shall be given to Servants." Any artificer or workman receiving higher wages than those of old was to be committed to the gaol. This 1349 wage ceiling would remain in effect for more than two centuries, until 1562. The criminalization of any breach of an employment contract by leaving service early, or leaving work undone, would remain in effect for five centuries, until 1867, when the penal sanctions were finally removed. The 1349 Statute also put into place a system of private

---

statutory and common law, with respect to both journeymen associations and trade unions as discussed in the following chapters.

[9] A "stranger" or "foreigner"—from *forren*, taken from the Medieval Latin *forinseci*, referring to those from outside—was a person not born or apprenticed within a specific town or village. Someone from beyond the sea was an "alien": see LEESON, *supra* chap. 1 note 63 at 23. Foreigners had to buy their freedom to trade within a town: see MARGARET GAY DAVIES, THE ENFORCEMENT OF ENGLISH APPRENTICESHIP, A STUDY IN APPLIED MERCANTILISM 1563–1642 11 (Harvard University Press 1956).

[10] *See* LEESON, *supra* chap. 1 note 63 at 24.

[11] *Id.* at 25 *citing* R.W. POSTGATE, THE BUILDERS' HISTORY 4 (London 1923).

[12] 1349 (23 Edw. 3) stat. 1, c. 1–8.

enforcement by offering a share of any penalty exacted to the informer providing the information *qui tam* as to the violation.[13]

The wages for artificers and laborers were regulated by the Statute of Labourers of 1351.[14] The statute prescribed that "no workman shall take more, and no employer give more, than had been customary before the plague." The statute also outlawed beggary and idleness, mandating that every able-bodied worker under the age of 60 with no means of subsistence was to work for whoever required him or her to do so—in effect, it was a vagrancy law.

Collective worker action close to a boycott was also seen at this time, as evidenced by the 1353 Royal mandate concerning the workmen who had withdrawn from the works at the Palace of Westminster:

> [I]n contempt of us ... in our behalf strictly to be forbidden, that any one shall, on pain of imprisonment of his body at our will, and of grievous forfeiture unto ourselves, receive any such workmen upon his works, of whatsoever calling they may be, who shall have been before retained upon our works aforesaid, (unless they shall have had leave to depart therefrom) or in any way retain the same ... the receivers of them to be sent to our Tower of London without delay, there in prison at our will to remain.[15]

Additional laws concerning laborers departing service and fleeing to other counties, cities, or boroughs were enacted in 1360.[16] Craftsmen were limited to only one trade in 1362:[17] "[a]ll artificers and people of mysteries shall each choose his own mystery before the next Candlemas: and that having so chosen it, he shall henceforth use no other."

Not only were wages, vocation, location, and master regulated by law, but that same year the apparel of different groups was to be governed by law. Servants, handicraftsmen, yeomen, gentlemen, esquires, merchants, citizens, burgesses, knights, clerks, ploughmen, and at times also their wives and children were to be clothed in a manner reflecting their status. The dress of different social groups might seem a strange focus for royal attention, but a significant social problem was arising, again due to workers having a better bargaining position due to the shortage of laborers. The lower classes were clothing themselves in fashions similar to those of their superiors, and the entire social order was "risking"

---

13 *See* DAVIES, *supra* note 9 at 25.
14 1350 (25 Edw. 3) stat. 2, c. 1–7, Statute of Labourers 1351.
15 1353 (27 Edw. 3) Letter-Book G. fol. x. (Latin).
16 1360 (34 Edw. 3) c. 9–11, Labourers.
17 1362 (36 Edw. 3) stat. 1, c. 5–6, apparel in c. 8–14.

collapse due to the better economic position of workers and their aspirations to better clothing.[18]

Collective worker action again became a focus after the great Peasant Revolt in 1381. The Mayor of London, on behalf of the King, proclaimed in 1383 that:

> [N]o person should make congregations, alliances or covins of people, privily or open, and that those belonging to the trades more than other men, should not, without leave of the mayor, make congregations, conventicles nor assemblies, alliances, confederacies or conspiracies, or obligations to bind men together.[19]

The illegality at issue here is not the actual collective action, but rather the fact that the group did not first seek permission to form. This distinction would even haunt labor unions, as courts in both England and the United States would find that the mere forming of a trade or labor union,[20] without any further action, was in itself illegal.

The same depopulation led to legislation limiting entrance to apprenticeships and restricting movement, with a 1388 statute mandating that children who had reached the age of 12 working in husbandry and agricultural work "thenceforth shall abide by the same labour without being put to any mystery or handicraft."[21] Mobility from the manors to the towns was another natural effect of workers' better negotiating positions due to the scarcity of labor, so such mobility was outlawed. Servants were forbidden from moving, and penalties were exacted from both the payor and the payee if more than the statutory wage was paid. This is reminiscent of the limitation placed on Roman *collegia* a millennium earlier by the Theodosian Code, and for a similar reason, but now to guarantee a pool of agricultural workers rather than trade workers.

The Commons petitioned King Richard II at the 1388 Cambridge Parliament that "all gilds, fraternities and their common chests should be

---

18 *See* APPLEBAUM, *supra* chap. 1 note 8 at 270.

19 *See* LEESON, *supra* chap. 1 note 63 at 41.

20 As stated above, terminology is complicated when looking at different systems. "Trade union" is the term used in the UK with respect to unions, and thus in most of Europe when translating to English, while "labor union" is the term used in the United States. The attempt here is to be consistent in this usage, but for the purposes of this work the terms are interchangeable.

21 1388 (12 Ric. 2) c. 3–9. A similar statute was passed again in 1405 (7 Hen. 4) c.1 7.

abolished."[22] The King did not grant the request, but did instruct his sheriffs throughout England to make two proclamations: that the masters and wardens of guilds and fraternities were to certify any information to the Chancery about the foundation of their guilds, their organization and government, details of their meetings and oaths, and the value of their lands and chattels; and that the masters, wardens, and surveyors of misteries and crafts were to submit any royal charters or letters patent in their possession to the Chancery for inspection.

Many craft and trade associations were presumed to have already acquired the licenses to be produced for inspection under the 1388 proclamation, due to King John's twelfth-century orders regarding the reissuance of guild charters. The 1388 proclamation had as its main target informal, and consequently unregulated, guilds.[23] The Crown wished to govern the guilds by requiring a royal letter patent or charter in order to incorporate, with it exercising control through grants of rights and obligations as well as legal personhood. The enrollment of all company charters (including guild charters) consequently became mandatory once again under the 1388 act, upon penalty of charter revocation.[24]

The set of rights a guild could be granted under charter by Richard II included the right to hold property for conducting business, to relieve the poor, and to maintain a chapel and chantry. The guild was typically granted a geographically defined monopoly, as in a town. The guild could even found a town and/or become its governing body, the town then being referred to as "gildated." This reconstitution of the guilds made clear their fundamental principles: all members possessed an equal share in all rights not delegated; all were full brothers equally participating in both advantages and disadvantages; in cases of insolvency at death, funerals of poor members were to be equally respected; and elections of officers were to come by and from the assembled commonalty.[25] The charters also confirmed the ancient rights of the guilds to search their respective trades in order to detect dishonest practices and punish offenders and to self-police, and required that a craftsman's door always

---

22 *See* L.C. HECTOR & BARBARY HARVEY, THE WESTMINSTER CHRONICLE 1381–1394 356–68 (Oxford University Press 1982). The common chests, also referred to as boxes, contained the funds collected from the members for their mutual aid.

23 *See* NOTTINGHAM, *supra* chap. 1 note 33 at 109. More than 500 of the guild certificates produced in the 1388–89 inquiry are still extant.

24 1388 (12 Ric. 2) c. 1.

25 *See* HERBERT, *supra* chap. 1 note 25 at 41–42.

be open for inspection. Guilds self-policed working times and the quality of goods, and also banned individual advertisement. Wages were to be equal among those within the different categories of master, journeyman,[26] and apprentice.[27]

Another restrictive statute as to social mobility was passed in 1405:[28] that "[n]o Man shall put his son or daughter to be an apprentice unless he have twenty shillings in land or rent, but every person may put his son or daughter to school." This law again demonstrates the high degree of statutory control placed on wages, worker movement, and trade organization—legislative restrictions that would be in force for centuries. By this time, the trade that children could enter (that of their father), their place of work (that of their residence), and their wages, hours, dress, arms, mealtimes, leisure activities, were regulated by parliamentary statute as enforced by local justices of the peace. Movement, even if lawful, was difficult. Employment of strangers was often for a limited period, conditioned on the stranger leaving town when the period had expired. If work was available, the stranger would be told to either join the local guild after proving their skill by a test of competence and paying the relevant fee, or to leave town. If there was no work, the stranger would be entirely barred from the town.

The charters were again replaced by letters patent under the reign of Henry IV (1399–1413), rendering the companies and guilds bodies corporate and politic with perpetual succession and a common seal, becoming more and more institutionalized and legalized. Guilds could now hold and transfer land in fee simple, and plead or be impleaded, along with retaining the more traditional rights of self-regulation through bylaws and ordinances, the right of self-policing by searching through their several trades and punishing any such offenders, and the right to receive bequests. The royal fear as to collective action remained in place, with a 1425 prohibition of the stonemasons from meeting annually, in a royal attempt to prevent them from combining.[29] Henry VI (1422–61) again called for renewed reconstitution (and the accompanying payments) of all guilds.[30]

26 "Journeymen" is derived from the French *journée*, a worker paid by the day. The word "journey" later came to define the distance one could walk in a day: see LEESON, *supra* chap. 1 note 63 at 30.

27 *See* APPLEBAUM, *supra* chap. 1 note 8 at 312.

28 1405 (7 Hen. 4) c. 17.

29 1425 (3 Hen. 6) c. 1, *see also* 1360 (34 Edw. 3) c. 9, Labourers.

30 1436 (15 Hen. 6) c. 6–7.

INTERNAL GUILD STRIFE, PLAGUES, AND WAR IN THE SIXTEENTH CENTURY

Deep crevices in the guild system were starting to surface by the sixteenth century, long before industrialism came to England. The internal balance existing in the early medieval guilds between masters, journeymen, and apprentices was eroding. The larger guilds started to stratify power and profits, with the distances between masters also widening.[31] Brentano's central thesis, that guilds have been instruments of class struggle, is clearly supported by the events in sixteenth-century England.[32]

Most of the new larger guilds were divided into livery and yeoman sections at this time. Liveries were the merchant traders and larger craft masters, as distinct from the yeomanries of smaller masters and journeymen. The new charters conveyed perpetual succession of the craft leadership not on the masters as a body, but on the wealthier livery section. This was a radical departure from the historical model of direct democracy seen in the early guilds.[33] The livery went on to concentrate power through barriers limiting entry to master status, such as seven-year apprenticeships instead of three, three-year waiting periods after apprenticeships where previously there were none, and significant entrance fees to the trade where before, passing the master's examination of skills had been enough. The prohibitive entrance fees charged by masters in effect barred all but those very few who could pay.[34]

The yeomanry and journeymen attempted to safeguard their interests by assuming the more traditional tasks of craft government in their associations, exercising charter rights of self-policing by searching out illegal products and illegally employed strangers and apprentices. The journeyman identity began to solidify as an identity separate from their guild status, and journeymen's associations became more common during this period as a backlash against the perceived abuses by the wealthier masters.

Complaints were brought to the Crown about masters taking on too many apprentices and the lengthy service often required, as well as the fact that apprentice wage levels were not consistent and were often

---

31 *See* LEESON, *supra* chap. 1 note 63 at 50.

32 *See* TOULMIN SMITH, *supra* chap. 1 note 1 at cxcv.

33 *See* TOMLINS, *supra* note 1 at 116 and LEESON, *supra* chap. 1 note 63 at 46.

34 *See* KRAMER, *supra* chap. 1 note 38 at 79.

circumvented.[35] Criticism was also raised regarding greater monopolies and an absence of free competition, with price-setting cartel-like behavior as both buyers and sellers of goods, the guilds acting as gatekeepers for those who could enter the trade and impeding technological advances—as well as indulging in general licentiousness in terms of drinking and feasting.

One of the first legislative responses to these criticisms was the act of 1530, For Exactions not to be levied on Apprentices, which set a fixed fee for fully trained apprentices' entrance to the guild.[36] A second act in 1536 banned the practice of masters requiring apprentices and journeymen to swear not to set up separate establishments without a license from the master and wardens of their craft for or concerning their "Freedom of Occupation." As the divide between masters, journeymen, and apprentices widened, the larger guilds were becoming more and more powerful and monopolistic.

Many guilds were dissolved during the Reformation,[37] with only trade guilds and those having some form of public utility or corporate protection surviving this legislative purge. The surviving guilds forfeited those properties and trusts devoted to religious purposes to the King in 1547, and "all payments by corporations, misteryes or craftes, for priests' obits and lamps" would henceforth be made to him.[38]

The 1548 Bill of Conspiracies of Victuallers and Craftsmen was passed in the first year of Edward VI's reign, the year after the death of Henry VIII.[39] Various wars, including one against Scotland, had led to domestic economic turmoil, shortages of men and workers, and the need for war financing. Laborers throughout England were prohibited under section 1(2) of the 1548 act from combining to improve their pay and conditions concerning work hours, rates, and wages:

> And likewise Artificers, Handicraftsmen, and Labourers have made Confederacies and Promises, and have sworn mutual Oaths not only that they should not meddle one with another's Work, and perform and finish that another hath begun, but also to constitute and appoint how much Work they shall do in a Day, and what Hours and Times they shall work, contrary to the Laws and

---

35 *See* LEESON, *supra* chap. 1 note 63 at 50.

36 1530 (22 Hen. 8) c. 4.

37 1545 (37 Hen. 8) c. 4. The act specifically names the King's need for monies in order to conduct the wars against Scotland and France "for the preservation and defence of us your said Subjects."

38 The Act for Chantries Collegiate, 1547 (1 Edw. 6) c. 14.

39 1548 (2 & 3 Edw. 6) c. 15.

> Statutes of this Realm, and to the great Hurt and Impoverishment of the King's Majesty's Subjects.

The sanctions for such combinations were harsh:

> [T]hat then every Person so conspiring, covenanting, swearing or offending, being lawfully convicted thereof by Witness, Confession or otherwise, shall forfeith for the first Offence ten Pounds[40] to the King's Highness, and if he have sufficient to pay the same and also pay the same within six days next after his conviction or else shall suffer for the same Offence twenty Days Imprisonment, and shall only have Bread and Water for his Sustenance.

The second offense of such an unlawful act was penalized by £20 or punishment of the pillory. The third offense was sanctioned by £40 or the pillory and the loss of an ear, and also that the offender "at all Times after that be taken as a Man infamous, and his Saying, Deposition or Oath not to be credited at any Time in any Matters of Judgment."[41] The ultimate sanction for such collective demands concerning hours and wages was losing an ear and becoming a man infamous. Any organization supporting such claims was to be dissolved. Certain scholars argue that the early guild system ended during the reign of Edward VI.[42]

Guild behavior was harshly criticized as monopolistic, exploitative, and excessive. At the same time, there was a growing precariousness of employment as trades were glutted by journeymen—the actualization of the concerns raised by journeymen in the prior decades. The apprentice–master relationship developed into a more short-term and strictly contractual bargain to train skilled workers. Instead of the familial bounds of the early guilds, with the apprentice becoming a part of the master's family, apprentices now remained with their birth families in a "clubbing out" apprenticeship, only working or training with the master during the day.[43] This more distant situation foreshadowed the more modern concept of

---

[40] The harshness of the monetary fines can be seen from the time value of money. Based on the historic standard of living, £10 in 1548 would today be £5,256; based on labor earnings it would be £53,240, based on economic status £182,800, or based on the economic power value of that sum £2,221,000. These calculations are taken from MeasuringWorth.com. The sanctions of £20 and £40 are naturally correlatively greater.

[41] A man "infamous" was effectively stripped of any legal rights or legal personhood, entailing that anyone could basically rob or murder such a man without any fear of legal sanction.

[42] *See* HOWELL, *supra* chap. 1 note 1 at 14.

[43] *See* K.D.M. SNELL, ANNALS OF THE LABOURING POOR—SOCIAL CHANGE AND AGRARIAN ENGLAND, 1660–1900 255–59 (Cambridge 1985).

the employee–employer relationship, mirroring Sir Henry Maine's movement from status to contract.[44]

The Statute of Artificers of 1562 brought together two centuries of labor legislation into one law "concerning the retaining, departing, wages, and orders of apprentices, servants, and labourers, as well in husbandry as in divers other arts, mysteries, and occupations."[45] Certain workers were to remain in the agricultural sector. Others would need testimonials in order to move to different towns, and future employers could be penalized for failing to demand to see such testimonials. The 1349 legislative wage ceiling was finally lifted "as too small and not answerable to this time, respecting the advancement of prices of all things belonging to said servants and labourers." Wages were to be determined by meetings of the local justices of the peace, and eventually, later, parliament. The payment of excessively high wages was sanctionable for both employees and employers. Working hours were also set out and labor contracts were stated to be for a full one-year term in any of the sciences, crafts, mysteries, and arts, to counteract short-term exploitative contracts.

The ratio of apprentices and journeymen was also set out in Chapter 33:

> That all and every Person and Person that shall have three Aperrentices in any of the said Crafts, Mysteries or Occupations … shall retain and keep one Journeyman, and for every other apprentice above the number of the said three Apprentices, on other Journeyman, upon Paid for every Default therein ten Pounds.

This ratio requirement was in direct response to the journeymen's complaints that the masters were using cheaper apprentices, glutting the market and eventually eradicating the future prospects of both apprentices and journeymen.[46] The 1562 act is seen as creating and regulating a

---

[44] *See* SIR HENRY SUMNER MAINE, ANCIENT LAW 170 (London 1861, reprint Legal Classics Library 1982). *See also* JOHN V. ORTH, COMBINATION AND CONSPIRACY—A LEGAL HISTORY OF TRADE UNIONISM 1721–1906 2 (Clarendon Press 1991).

[45] 1562 (5 Eliz. 1) c. 4. The law is estimated to have covered approximately 5 percent of the English population at the time of its enactment: see LEESON, *supra* chap. 1 note 63 at 59.

[46] Private parties brought more than 95 percent of the cases for enforcement of the statute with respect to apprenticeships, in contrast to public prosecution. These private parties fell into two main groups: approximately one quarter of the complaints were brought by competitors of the wrongdoers, such as other trade

national (as opposed to regional or even town) labor market, establishing wage settings and controls, addressing employment conditions, and restricting labor mobility. In essence, it transferred some of the former guild gatekeeping and policing functions to the English Crown.[47] "Queen Betty's Law" would remain in effect until 1813.

THE LONDON LIVERY COMPANIES

Most craft guilds only exerted local influence, mainly in one town or city. The ties between guilds and incorporated towns and cities were perhaps most marked between the City of London Corporation and the Great Twelve, both of which exercised national and even international influence.[48] There is no surviving charter evidencing the original establishment of the City of London Corporation. William the Conqueror granted a charter to the citizens of London in 1067 confirming the rights and privileges that they had enjoyed under his predecessor, Edward the Confessor, "in all the law whereof they had been worthy in King Edward's day."[49] The 1215 Magna Carta ordains that "the city of London shall have/enjoy its ancient liberties." The 1225 Magna Carta under Henry III, chap. IX grants that "[t]he city of London shall have all the old liberties and customs, which it hath been used to have."

In the early fourteenth century the City of London Corporation formally drafted articles of regulation, ordained by its citizens for their internal government, approved by Edward II (1307–27) and incorporated

groups, and three quarters by professional informers based on information qui tam seeking a share of the penalty: see DAVIES, *supra* note 9 at 18. The Tudor reliance on private parties for law enforcement was a way to compensate for the absence of any extensive governmental agency enforcement power.

[47] *See* Donald Woodward, *The Background to the Statute of Artificers: The Genesis of Labour Policy, 1558–63*, 33(1) THE ECONOMIC HISTORY REVIEW, NEW SERIES 32–44 (Feb., 1980).

[48] Ian Anders Gadd & Patrick Wallis, *Reaching beyond the City Wall: London Guilds and National Regulation 1500–1700* in GUILDS, INNOVATION AND THE EUROPEAN ECONOMY, 1400–1800 288 (S.R. Epstein & Maarten Prak eds. Cambridge 2008). S.R. Epstein maintains that guilds were overall beneficial in premodern European economies in that they contributed to skill preservation and training, and that the economic environments created by guilds were conducive to technological innovation. *See also* Maarten Prak, *Preface in S.R. Epstein (1960–2007) and the Guilds* in THE RETURN OF THE GUILDS 1 (Jan Lucassen, Tine De Moor, & Jan Luiten van Zanden eds., Intl. Review of Social History supp. 16 2008).

[49] *See* KRAMER, *supra* chap. 1 note 38 at 14.

into a charter. The City naturally had the greatest number of merchant and craft guilds, as England's capital, largest city, and manufacturing center. The charter granted a monopoly to members of the Trades or Mysteries as to civic freedom through citizenship, demonstrating how closely entwined the guilds and City had already become, to the extent of the guilds being active in approving civic citizenship. Eventually, some of these guilds became the "Livery Companies" during the reign of Edward III (1327–77), due to their distinctive dress or livery.[50] At about the same time, an enactment transferred the right of election of all city dignitaries and officers, including members of parliament from the ward representatives, to the livery companies.[51] During the fourteenth and fifteenth centuries, the civic government of London was conducted by the Court of Aldermen, the Common Council, and the Great Congregation, in essence being completely within the hands of the livery companies.[52] Almost all of the "Great Twelve" livery companies were recognized by the time of Henry VI (1422–61), with even kings at times being members of particular livery companies.[53]

The relationship between the Crown and the Great Twelve was not always easy, with significant royal loans demanded, beginning with Henry VIII's desire to fund his war with Scotland. Membership in the Great Twelve was expanded from a basis in servitude (apprenticeship and journeyman service) and patrimony (inheritance) to redemption, where an individual not trained in the trade could redeem (buy) a membership. The divide between masters on one side and apprentices and journeymen on the other widened even more when the leadership of the Great Twelve came to comprise members who had not even practiced the crafts and mysteries.[54] The livery companies in London are perhaps one of the best examples of the pinnacle of guild power—a power existing in that city even today.[55]

---

50 *See* HERBERT, *supra* chap. 1 note 25 at 28. The fluid use of terms can also be seen here: the trade guilds became Livery Companies, also referred to as ancient trade corporations as well as Municipal Corporations.

51 1376 (50 Edw. 3) cc. 1–8.

52 *See* IAN DOOLITTLE, THE CITY OF LONDON AND ITS LIVERY COMPANIES—A HISTORY OF SURVIVAL 5 (Guildhall Library Publications 2010).

53 *See* HERBERT, *supra* chap. 1 note 25 at 106.

54 *See* LEESON, *supra* chap. 1 note 63 at 41.

55 More than one hundred London livery companies still exist, playing a major role in the election of the City of London's Lord Mayor, who still presides over the Court of Aldermen and the Court of Common Council. For more information, see the Livery Companies website at liverycompanies.info.

JOURNEYMEN IN THE SEVENTEENTH CENTURY

England was still predominantly rural and preindustrial in the seventeenth century, with the main market being the City of London.[56] The Civil War (1642–51) and Cromwell decades are seen as contributing to a general breakdown of the traditional medieval forms of corporate regulation, including the guilds.[57] The guilds were hit twice financially. First, both kings and parliaments requested large loans from London financed by the Great Twelve livery companies. Second, the Great Fire of London in 1666 resulted in extensive property devastation, including the destruction of 44 guildhalls.[58]

Thomas Hobbes's *Leviathan* was written during this turbulent period, arguing the benefits of a supreme ruler as well as defining "a man's Labour … [as] a commodity exchangeable for benefit, as well as any other thing."[59] Hobbes helped pave the way for the 1688 Glorious Revolution, after which a constitutional monarchy and parliamentary powers were confirmed by the 1689 Bill of Rights. Hobbes had articulated, for the first time, labor as a commodity exchangeable for benefit, bringing labor out of the guild system of solidarity and into a system of economic exchange.

This commodification of labor was also reflected by the collective actions of journeymen, who started to form trade union-like associations in the 1600s, one example being the Journeymen Hatters' Trade Union of Great Britain.[60] Journeymen artisans and craftsmen met at public houses designated as houses of call for certain trades, there receiving information about work and making donations to the mutual assistance fund, or the box, kept by the box club.[61] With the breakdown of the master and apprentice/journeyman relationship, these associations often looked after the interests of journeymen, despite the legal prohibitions against such "conspiracies." The friendly society began to appear at about the same

---

[56] *See* APPLEBAUM, *supra* chap. 1 note 8 at 339.

[57] Michael Berlin, *Guilds in Decline? London Livery Companies and the Rise of a Liberal Economy, 1600–1800* in GUILDS, INNOVATION AND THE EUROPEAN ECONOMY, 1400–1800 325 (S.R. Epstein & Maarten Prak eds. Cambridge 2008).

[58] *Id.* at 327.

[59] *See* THOMAS HOBBES, LEVIATHAN Chapter XXIV (1651) available at gutenberg.org.

[60] *See* BRENTANO, *supra* Introduction note 1 at 97.

[61] *See* C.R. DOBSON, MASTERS AND JOURNEYMEN, A PREHISTORY OF INDUSTRIAL RELATIONS 1717–1800 38 (London 1980).

time, an offshoot of some of the guild functions concerning mutual aid. Many of these societies began informally, perhaps with no more than an alms box for charitable purposes, and became more and more sophisticated over time, covering burial costs and providing pensions and provisions for loss of earnings through sickness, infirmity, or old age. The Oddfellows—comprising members from different trades, thus a group of "odd fellows"—is an example of this type of friendly society still in existence today.[62]

The journeymen's associations addressed four main issues: control of entry to the craft and its organization by apprentices, ensuring a strict ratio of employment of boys/apprentices to men/journeymen; the administration of friendly benefits for sickness, old age, and death; the regulation of behavior in workshops or clubhouses; and the traveling or tramping system.[63] The history of the tramping system in England is often traced back to the Masons, stonecutters who, as part of their work, were forced to travel from building site to building site. "Felaus" were taken in by the Masons during their travels under an elaborate set of rules as to conduct, work, and pay that were well documented by the fifteenth century. Traveling fellows needed passes stating that they had left their former employer on good terms. This Mason system is viewed as a precursor to the English tramping system of journeymen that later developed in the other trades. That this was an evolving system can be seen from its terminology, with the sixteenth-century "strange felau," the seventeenth-century strangers, the eighteenth-century travelers, and the nineteenth-century tramps.[64]

Journeymen's associations would fund the travels of stranger journeymen through the tramping system until they found employment, keeping employment within a trained pool of candidates while at the same time preventing noncertified, nonskilled competition from outside. The tramping system created a highly trained group of workers who were well traveled and had a network of contacts and information that covered much of Europe, functioning both as an employment and an unemployment service. As a secondary effect, the tramping system allowed for an

---

62 *See* JAMES BURN, AN HISTORICAL SKETCH OF THE INDEPENDENT ORDER OF ODDFELLOWS 17 (Manchester 1845) for the argument that the Oddfellows began in Ancient Rome. According to their website, the Oddfellows were an organization in London as early as the seventeenth century, with the earliest surviving rules of an Oddfellows Lodge referring to the Loyal Aristarcus Lodge in London dating from 1730: see oddfellows.co.uk.

63 *See* LEESON, *supra* chap. 1 note 63 at 14.

64 *Id.* at 57–58, 123.

early form of more regionwide industrial action: strikes. Where a master circumvented the system of hiring only local skilled journeymen by either hiring too many apprentices, strangers, or workers at too low wages, or refusing wages or other benefits, the journeymen could simply tramp en masse. The communication networks created also allowed for journeymen in certain sectors to coordinate this action by all leaving their work at the same time. Leaving work undone was still a breach of contract that was criminally punishable; achieving this through tramping had the beauty of both depriving the masters of all skilled employees at the same time and placing the tramping workers out of the reach of any reasonable efforts at law enforcement.[65] The masters' focus on profits can be seen as causing their eventual demise. By alienating the journeymen, the journeymen created an identity for themselves.

The fourteenth to sixteenth centuries saw the rise of the English guilds, and the beginning of their demise. The Reformation, with its acceptance of profit and the Crown's need to control corporate bodies, paved the way for a dissonance between masters and journeymen that eventually resulted in Queen Betty's law, with legislative control of wages and the conditions of work that had formerly been matters under guild control. The delicate balance that had been democratically achieved, with equal rights between guild members and consideration of apprentices and journeymen as future guild members, was abandoned in favor of a structure in which guild leaders, at least in the London Great Twelve, no longer even needed to have had practiced the trade in order to attain leadership. Freedom of trade and production developed earliest in England,[66] coinciding with or caused by those liberal theories articulated as an antithesis to medieval economic and legal models. On the theoretical plane, a conceptual apparatus as to the commodification of labor began to emerge under a liberal market theory approach. The seeds for the modern understanding of an employment relationship began with this commodification of labor, underscored by the breakdown in the relationships between masters and apprentices. The journeymen's associations created a sophisticated system of training and employment services through tramping, and also began to take over the guild function of providing mutual aid in times of unemployment, sickness, old age, and burials. By coming together, exchanging knowledge as to skills and employment opportunities, and enforcing the rules against the masters regarding hiring and pay, the journeymen not only created independence for themselves,

---

65 *Id.* at 250.

66 *See* BLACK, *supra* chap. 1 note 5 at 159.

but also laid the groundwork for collective worker actions. As the following chapters will show, the journeymen's organizations and friendly societies that were formed to support those who can now be seen more as employees became the precursors to the modern labor unions.

3. The rise of labor in England

The path to the modern British economy can be seen as comprising three stages. The first was the transition from a medieval agrarian-based to a mercantile-based economy in the sixteenth century, with the subsequent development of significant mercantile capital during the seventeenth century derived from the more technically advanced agrarian production and parallel greater trade. These gave rise to the third stage: the eighteenth-century transition to an industrial economy based on the mercantile capital investments in technology, particularly in the cotton industry. The English timeline with respect to industrialization is at least a century ahead of most of continental Europe. For example, German and Swedish industrialism, as will be seen below, took hold almost instantly, but was delayed until the latter part of the nineteenth century. English collective worker action in the form of journeymen combinations preceded industrialism by at least a century, as seen in Chapter 2. The different British timeline meant the chain of events and interests concerning workers, collectivism, and the law unraveled in a novel way that had repercussions in both Europe and the United States.

The final demise of the English guilds cannot be pegged to a specific date or year. The Reformation and the 1562 Statute of Artificers are argued to have brought about the end of the guild system. The widening divide between masters, journeymen, and apprentices in the sixteenth century also contributed to the erosion of the medieval corporative guild structure. Technological advances wrought significant changes in most trades, with certain jobs becoming obsolete while new ones arose outside the established structures. A piecemeal decline of the guilds by trade and geographic area can instead be traced. The guilds of mercers and drapers disappeared in the 1690s, manufacturing guilds abruptly in the 1740s and 1750s, and service guilds in the 1770s. Determining a date for the rise of trade unions is equally slippery, particularly given the varying terminology used in attempts to circumvent the reach of the different conspiracy and combination laws.

LIBERALISM V. RADICALISM IN THE EIGHTEENTH CENTURY

Journeymen in certain trades were already very active in labor disputes by the eighteenth century, particularly weavers, seamen, riverside workers, and the London tailors. These early trade disputes often ended in violence, leading to the conclusion that "collective bargaining by riot" was the distinguishing characteristic of the time.[1] Journeymen's associations systematically came to be seen as unlawful combinations not sanctioned by the Crown, first within certain specific trades and then by a general ban. The 1718 Proclamation Against Combinations of Woollen Weavers complained that these:

> [L]aw-less clubs and societies which had illegally presumed to use a common seal, and to act as Bodies Corporate, by making and unlawfully conspiring to execute certain By-laws or Orders, whereby they pretend to determine who had a right to the Trade, what and how many Apprentices and Journey-men each man should keep at once, together with the prices of all their manufactures, and the manner and materials of which they should be wrought.[2]

Such organizations were deemed to be criminal conspiracies based on the group's formation without state sanction, without any legal requirement for action to have been taken by the group.

Journeymen tailors, one of the most highly organized groups, were constantly involved in labor disputes in the eighteenth and early nineteenth centuries, including a 1720 strike of over 30,000 London tailors.[3] In 1721, 40 tailors leaving work undone because of striking were criminally prosecuted under the 1562 Statute of Artificers as well as the common law doctrine of conspiracy.[4] This led to the first combinations act that same year, the 1721 Combinations Act, prohibiting associations of journeymen and apprentices from collective action for better employment conditions.[5] A summary procedure before two justices of the peace was sufficient to prosecute instead of a court hearing, with the penalty two months in the common gaol. The tailors' case is one of the first in

---

1 *See* DOBSON, *supra* chap. 2 note 61 at 30.

2 4 Hughson's London 337. The proclamation was reprinted in Notes and Queries, September 21, 1867, from a copy preserved by the Sun Fire Office.

3 *See* DOBSON, *supra* chap. 2 note 61 at 60.

4 King v. The Journeymen Tailors of Cambridge, 8 Mod. 11 (Nov. 7, 1721). *See also* ORTH, *supra* chap. 2 note 44 at 181.

5 1721 (7 Geo. 1) st. 1, c. 13.

which criminal conspiracy was used against a combination of workers, here a combination to raise wages.

The 1721 Combinations Act not only prohibited combinations/associations of journeymen and apprentices, but also voided any agreements made by employers and employees regarding higher wages or fewer hours, with a sanction of two months' imprisonment for entering into such agreements. Leaving work unfinished or quitting before the end of a contract period continued to be criminally penalized. A similar act was passed in 1725 prohibiting combinations of weavers as well as combinations of brickmakers and tilemakers.[6] Despite these laws, journeymen's associations grew in numbers and in strength: "they further support one another, insomuch that they are become one Society throughout the Kingdom."[7] A more general anti-combination act was passed in 1749, again directed at journeymen's associations founded to improve employment conditions.[8] All these acts availed themselves of summary processes not brought before courts.

The masters began distancing themselves even further from the historical and more democratic corporative guild structure. By admitting an unlimited number of apprentices, the masters undermined their hold over the journeymen.[9] Journeymen began to argue under the 1562 Statute of Artificers for the protections there given as to employment and jobs, becoming more vociferous with demands concerning wages, working hours, and payment made in monies as opposed to in kind.[10] The journeymen wool combers of Norwich asked of their masters in 1752: "[W]e are social Creatures, and cannot live without each other; why would you destroy Community?"[11] Adam Smith noted in 1776 that "[w]hen masters combine together in order to reduce the wages of their workmen, they commonly enter into a private bond or agreement, not to give more than a certain wage under a certain penalty. Were the workmen to enter into a contrary combination of the same kind, not to accept of a

---

[6] 1725 (12 Geo. 1) c. 34 and 35.

[7] ANONYMOUS, A LOVER OF HIS COUNTRY, A SHORT ESSAY UPON TRADE IN GENERAL 40 (London 1741).

[8] 1748 (22 Geo. 2) c. 27.

[9] *See* ANONYMOUS *supra* note 7 at 91.

[10] Also referred to as the truck system: see LEESON, *supra* chap. 1 note 63 at 79.

[11] *See* Robert W. Malcolmson, *Workers' Combinations in Eighteenth-Century England* in THE ORIGINS OF ANGLO-AMERICAN RADICALISM 149 (Margaret Jacob and James Jacob eds. George Allen & Unwin 1984) cites omitted.

certain wage under a certain penalty, the law would punish them very severely."[12]

Because of the anti-combination and conspiracy legislation, journeymen's associations in the eighteenth century began to assume other guises, such as those of corresponding or friendly societies. Edmund Burke opined that "[w]hen bad men combine, the good must associate."[13] As with the journeymen's associations, these organizations were heavily influenced by the ethos of the guilds, with rituals, banners, processions, and initiation ceremonies used to create a shared sense of occupational identity.

Many journeymen's associations began working openly for broader social reform and political democracy. The tramping system provided extensive information networks for journeymen, who became very skilled at organizing in several workplaces within a sector so that all the masters would be forced to accede to comparable terms. The French revolution inspired several British authors to also agitate for social change, including Thomas Paine in *The Rights of Man* (1791) and Mary Wollstonecraft in *A Vindication of the Rights of Woman* (1792). At the same time, the prevalent belief among the British upper class was that they were the freest people in Europe, due to the 1688 Glorious Revolution and England's constitutional monarchy and parliament confirmed by the 1689 Bill of Rights. Many of those believing so belonged to the just over 5 percent of the population that had the right to vote: propertied male members of the Anglican church.

Friendly societies became regulated by a 1793 act "for the encouragement and Relief of Friendly Societies."[14] Their existence was to be registered and their rules to be evidenced by a writing confirmed by local justices. The act was amended in 1795 to include benevolent and charitable institutions.[15] Though seemingly peripheral, the state registration and approval of these societies' rules was vigorously contested as such state control had historically deprived organizations of rights as

---

[12] *See* ADAM SMITH, AN INQUIRY INTO THE NATURE AND CAUSES OF THE WEALTH OF NATIONS Book I, Chapter X, Part II (London 1776).

[13] *See* EDMUND BURKE, THOUGHTS ON THE CAUSE OF THE PRESENT DISCONTENT (1770), reprinted in THE WRITINGS AND SPEECHES OF EDMUND BURKE, VOL. 2: PARTY, PARLIAMENT, AND THE AMERICAN WAR: 1766–1774 315 (Paul Langford and William B. Todd eds. Oxford University Press 1981).

[14] 1793 (33 Geo. 3) c. 54. More than 7,000 friendly societies, many of them based in the crafts, existed by the late 1700s: see LEESON, *supra* chap. 1 note 63 at 98.

[15] 1795 (35 Geo. 3) c. 111.

opposed to protecting them—still a very pertinent issue today with respect to the issue of trade union registration.

Fears of French revolutionary ideas, radicalism, the need for a steady supply of goods for the war against France, and masters' complaints about unfair journeymen demands led to several parliamentary acts targeting collective worker action. Two 1795 acts—the Treasonable and Seditious Practices Act,[16] and the Seditious Meetings Act[17]—led to the collapse of the corresponding societies by 1797 as a result of fears of prosecution. A general combinations act, An Act to prevent Unlawful Combinations of Workmen, was passed in 1799, outlawing both journeymen's associations and collective agreements; it was adopted in response to a petition by master millwrights.[18] The master millwrights described the journeymen's acts—enforcing wage increases in London and the surrounding areas, refusing to work and preventing the employment of nonaligned individuals, creating a common fund to support such actions and any journeymen rendered unemployed because of such demands—as a "dangerous combination."[19] The 1799 Combination Act was novel in that it was generally applicable, as opposed to targeting only a certain sector. All collective agreements as to working conditions were void as of the date of the act, and criminal if entered into after that date. Combining to achieve such purposes was also rendered criminal, as was influencing another to leave work, preventing a master from freely hiring, refusing to work, attending meetings held, and paying monies for such unlawful purposes. Another novelty in the act was that masters were free to hire nonlicensed workers, that is, not journeymen, in the face of journeymen's refusal to work, striking a severe blow against the entire system of qualifications within the trades.[20]

The 1799 Combination Act was highly controversial, and replaced already by the next year with the 1800 Combination Act.[21] Parliament had received petitions from workers all over the country arguing that "the law is materially changed to the great injury of all journeymen and workmen,"[22] evidence again of the extensive journeymen's networks that could easily be deployed. Despite its being a repeal, many of the changes

---

16 1795 (36 Geo. 3) c. 7.

17 1795 (36 Geo. 3) c. 8.

18 1799 (39 Geo. 3) c. 81.

19 *See* ORTH, *supra* chap. 2 note 44 at 43–44.

20 *Id.* at 49.

21 1800 (39 & 40 Geo. 3) c. 106.

22 *See* ORTH, *supra* chap. 2 note 44 at 49 *citing* Commons Journal, 55 (1799–1800), 645–46, 665, 672, 706 and 712.

in the 1800 act were procedural as opposed to substantive. A new crime was added: combinations of masters to keep wages low. Collective action and collective agreements were still outlawed. The only lawful employment contract was the individual one between the master and worker, falling back on a very liberal paradigm.

Wages were now to be determined between masters and workers, no longer by the state, as in Elizabethan times, or by collective worker organizations. The latter were illegal at common law as conspiracies, as any agreement made by their members would prejudice either masters or other workers. Such combinations were also illegal by statute as they constituted agreements to affect working conditions.[23] The 1799 and 1800 Combination Acts have been characterized by certain scholars as the "highest point ever reached by repressive labor legislation in England."[24] The net result of the 1800 act was to render illegal and criminal any and every combination of masters or workmen fixing wages or work conditions. Despite this hostile legislative environment, the eighteenth century saw the continued rise of organizations of journeymen and workers as agitators for better working conditions and de facto social change, a legacy that was carried on by the trade unions in the next century.

WORKER COMBINATIONS IN THE NINETEENTH CENTURY

The nineteenth century was another turbulent period of social unrest, including dissatisfaction with worker and voting rights. The 1562 Statute of Artificers was repealed in 1813, against the protests mostly from the smaller guilds and journeymen who still invoked its protections, arguing that apprenticeships were necessary to maintain the quality of the craft.[25] Sympathy for the plight of the workers brought about an 1824 repeal of the 1799–1800 Combination Acts as well as other related suppressive legislation, including the 1304 Conspiracy Act. More difficult was the treatment of common law conspiracy, as parliament does not have the competence to repeal the common law. The legal technical solution

---

[23] *Id.* at 67.

[24] *See* PRAK, *supra* chap. 2 note 48 at 119.

[25] *See* SIMON DEAKIN & GILLIAN S. MORRIS, LABOUR LAW 7 (6th ed. Oxford University Press 2012).

adopted by parliament was to instead grant statutory immunity to the common law action of conspiracy through the 1824 Combination Act:[26]

> [T]hat journeymen, workmen, or other persons who shall enter into any combination:
>
> - to obtain an advance, or
> - to fix the rate of wages, or
> - to lessen or alter the hours or duration of the time of working, or
> - to decrease the quantity of work, or
> - to induce another to depart from his service before the end of the time or term for which he is hired, or
> - to quit or return his work before the same shall be finished, or
> - not being hired, to refuse to enter into work or employment, or
> - to regulate the mode of carrying on any manufacture, trade or business, or the management thereof,
>
> shall not therefore be subject or liable to any indictment or prosecution for conspiracy, or to any other criminal information or punishment whatever, under the common or statute law.

Immunity was not granted for violent acts or intimidation; criminal prosecution remained the sanction here. This technical legislative solution set the framework for the UK labor law model still prevalent today, with immunities from prosecution granted to trade unions rather than positive rights.

In response to a series of strikes taken under these newfound freedoms,[27] the 1825 Combinations of Workmen Act repealed the 1824 act.[28] The 1825 act in essence prohibited any combinations of workmen with the sole purpose of pressing for wage increases or changing working hours, and suppressed the right to strike by not granting prosecutorial immunity for such actions. Liability for violence and threats could be imposed on both individuals and combinations. Combinations of workers or masters were, however, immune from criminal prosecution if meeting solely for the purpose of discussing wages, prices, or work hours.

---

26 1824 (5 Geo. 4) c. 95.

27 The term "strike" began to be used for concerted work stoppages in the late eighteenth century, borrowed from the practice of sailors striking or lowering sails as protest. The 1824 legislative committee introduced the word into its resolutions, explaining it as a "suspension of work": see ORTH, *supra* chap. 2 note 44 at 118, *citing* OXFORD ENGLISH DICTIONARY (1st ed. 1884–1928) and the entry for "strike."

28 1825 (6 Geo. 4) c. 129.

Inequalities in political representation, particularly due to eligibility restrictions and voting district boundaries, led to protests that at times resulted in casualties. The Representation of the People Act 1832 finally expanded the voting franchise for elections to the House of Commons from approximately 400,000 to 800,000 men, out of the 14 million individuals then in England and Wales.[29] The final blows to the guild structures came from the Great Reform Act 1832 and the Municipal Corporations Act 1835.[30] Manors and guilds could now no longer nominate borough corporations, sweeping away "the last vestiges of guild and other chartered incorporations from the provincial towns."[31]

Despite renewed attempts to restrict worker combinations, they continued to exist, at times under different guises in order to avoid direct conflicts with the law. A change in name, however, was no guarantee of lawfulness. Six men, later referred to as the Tolpuddle Martyrs, were found guilty in 1834 of administering illegal oaths in connection with the "Friendly Society of Agricultural Labourers," and sentenced to seven years' transportation.[32] The members were found by the court to have taken an oath to combine and raise wages in their profession as agricultural workers. A demonstration against the verdict and sentencing was held by 30,000 people in London, and more than 800,000 signatures were collected in support of these men.

Another example of redesignation is the London Journeymen's Trades Hall, constituted in 1839 "in order to promote the moral and social improvement of the *Working Class*, erection of trade halls instead of public houses, library committee, lectures (free to wives and children)."[33] The slogan adopted in 1840 by the United Society of Brushmakers, "[u]nited to protect, not combined to injure," clearly emphasized that the focus of the organization was lawful.[34]

Factory conditions, extensive use of child labor, and the lack of poor relief became hotly contested issues in the mid-nineteenth century.

---

[29] 1832 (2 & 3 Wm. 4) c. 45.

[30] 1835 (5 & 6 Wm. 4) c. 76.

[31] *See* BERLIN, *supra* chap. 2 note 57 at 316.

[32] R v. Lovelass and Others (1834) 172 ER 1380. Given the small number of men present at the meeting, the question of how the authorities found out about the secret oath can be raised. Much of the Combination legislation, as was the case with the 1562 Statute of Artificers, made provisions for informers to receive part of the monetary sanctions—in some cases one half of a penalty, which could be up to £500 at that time: see ORTH, *supra* chap. 2 note 44 at 11.

[33] Laws for the Constitution and Government of the London Journeymen's Trades Hall Enrolled According to Act of Parliament (London 1839).

[34] *See* ORTH, *supra* chap. 2 note 44 at 175–211.

Attempts were made to build national unions, such as that by Robert Owen with the 1834 Grand National Consolidated Trades Union, which gained 500,000 workers as members within a few weeks but almost immediately lost most of its membership after the Tolpuddle Martyrs case.[35] Chartism became a movement five years later, initiated by a Charter drafted in 1838 by the London Working Men's Association addressing social conditions including voting rights.[36] The Charter was presented to parliament several times—in 1839, 1842, and 1848—and had millions of signatures. Chartism led to the founding of the first working-class political party, the National Charter Association. The year 1842 also saw the first General Strike, involving nearly one and a half million workers throughout Britain protesting a 25 percent wage cut in the cotton industry and demanding the Charter be made law. An English translation of the Communist Party manifesto was published in 1848, while Karl Marx and Friedrich Engels were in exile in London.

Britain was the strongest trading economic power in the world by the 1850s, reaping the benefit of her early lead through mercantile capital, industrialization, and colonialism. This prosperity expanded the gap between the working population and the wealthy middle class. The latter group included those referred to as the labor aristocracy, who often worked in profitable industrial sectors at highly skilled jobs, usually

---

[35] *See* G.D.H. Cole, *A Study in British Trade Union History. Attempts at a 'General Union' 1829–1834*, 4 INTERNATIONAL REVIEW OF SOCIAL HISTORY 359–462, 359 (January 1938). Robert Owen also argued for model worker societies and successfully championed the enactment of the Cotton Mills and Factories Act 1819: see APPLEBAUM, *supra* chap. 1 note 8 at 433 and LEESON, *supra* chap. 2 note 63 at 118.

[36] The 1838 Chartists' demands with respect to voting rights included: (1) a vote for every man 21 years of age, of sound mind, and not undergoing punishment for crime; (2) secret ballots; (3) no property qualifications for Members of Parliament; (4) payment of MPs; (5) equal-sized constituencies; and (6) annual parliaments. Most of these demands were met through the ten voting reform acts passed between 1832 and 1928. The 1832 act was followed by the 1867 Reform Act (30 & 31 Vict.) c. 102 which expanded the voting franchise to approximately 2.5 million men who met the property qualifications. The Representation of the People Act 1884 (48 & 49 Vict.) c. 3 widened the franchise among men to almost 60 percent of the male population, while retaining the property ownership qualification. Secret ballots were introduced in 1872 and campaign spending limits in 1883. A redistribution of the seats in the House of Commons with equally populated constituencies was passed in 1885, with the abolishment of property qualifications for men and introduction of limited female suffrage for women over the age of 30 in 1918. The last reform, in 1928, granted women voting rights equal to those of men.

requiring apprenticeships or involving artisan skills, receiving higher wages and better benefits. Many of the worker associations were based on groupings within this labor aristocracy, with efforts focusing on the benefits of these highly skilled groups. Cooperatives and friendly societies also flourished during this period,[37] with the Friendly Societies Act 1855 strengthening the standing of such organizations by creating stronger protections for member funds.[38]

New unionism, a new model of trade unionism nationally covering a broader range of unskilled workers, also emerged at this time.[39] Higher membership subscriptions led to the financing of permanent union officials, which in its turn facilitated collective bargaining negotiations as well as arbitration procedures, both consequently becoming more accepted practices. The first conciliation and arbitration board, with the social partners nominating the members, was established in 1860 for the Nottingham hosiery trade. The umbrella employer and employee organizations, the Trades Councils and the Trade Union Congress ("TUC"), were also founded at this time.[40]

In its 1860 report on trades societies and strikes, a legislative investigative committee expressed its surprise at the cooperation of the trades societies, stating that this "demonstrates the great advance that has been made since the olds of secret societies."[41] The report defined a trades society as a combination of workmen to enable each to secure the conditions most favorable for labor.[42] Other institutions associated with

---

37 *See* Observations on the Rise and Progress of Friendly Societies 55 (1824). *See also* Rev. J.T. Becher, Observations upon the Report from the Select Committee of the House of Commons on the Laws Respecting Friendly Societies (1826).

38 1855 (18 & 19 Vict.) c. 63.

39 *See* Sidney Webb & Beatrice Webb, The History of Trade Unionism 1666–1920, Vols. 1 and 2 380 (1920, Palgrave reprint 2003).

40 *See* Orth, *supra* chap. 2 note 44 at 55.

41 *See* Committee on Trades' Societies, Trades' Societies and Strikes, Report of the Committee on Trades' Societies appointed by the National Association for the Promotion of Social Science, Presented at the Fourth Annual Meeting of the Association at Glasgow, September 1860 vii–viii (London 1860).

42 This was much in line with the Act 1859 (22 Vict.) c. 34 explanatory to the 1825 Combinations Act, further defining immunity with respect to trade union membership: "[N]o workman or other person, whether actually in employment or not, shall by reason merely of his entering into an agreement with any workman or workmen or other person or persons, for the purpose of fixing or endeavoring

the trades societies in the report included benefits and insurance societies. The report listed a number of activities of the trades societies, including:

- periodically publishing the state of the trade in different regions of the country;
- keeping a book of names of unemployed men and of employers wanting men;
- assisting men from town to town in search of employment and occasionally to emigrate;
- regulating the number of apprentices in the trade;
- maintaining men in resistance to their employers;
- regulating the number of working hours and the rules of the trade; and
- organizing strikes.

These, in essence, are the activities of the journeymen's associations that were arguably already in place by the eighteenth century. The committee found that trades societies were increasing in number while moderating their demands and setting better rules, and that the "slightest return to the old policy of prohibiting combinations would be most mischievous, and that no legislative measures for preventing strikes and lock-outs would be effectual."[43] Despite the conciliatory tone of the Committee, the courts' hostility to such associations continued. In the 1867 case of *Hornby v. Close*,[44] the court found that the Bradford branch of the United Order of Boilermakers and Iron Ship Builders had no standing to bring a case to recover unlawfully withheld union funds. The court noted that though the union had the function of a friendly society, it also had an illegal purpose as a union of workers in the restraint of trade, and thus was an unlawful organization.

Parliament heeded the recommendations of the 1860 Committee and a decade later the Trade Union Act 1871 was passed,[45] repealing the 1825 Combinations Act, for the first time both using the term "trade union" in statutory language and legalizing their existence. Trade unions were given immunity and not deemed unlawful in criminal or civil law simply

---

to fix the rate of wages or remuneration at which they or any of them shall work … be subject to any prosecution or indictment for conspiracy."

43 *See* COMMITTEE ON TRADES' SOCIETIES, TRADES' SOCIETIES AND STRIKES xix.

44 Hornby v. Close, 10 Cox CC 393 (QB 1867).

45 1871 (34 & 35 Vict.) c. 31 s. 2. The 1871 act has today been superseded by the Trade Union and Labour Relations (Consolidation) Act 1992.

for the reason that they were in restraint of trade. The criminalization of the organization of labor was removed, with the act stating that "[t]he purposes of any trade union shall not, by reason merely that they are in restraint of trade, be deemed to be unlawful so as to render any member of such trade union liable to criminal prosecution for conspiracy or otherwise."[46] Unions and associations were not legal persons and consequently had no statutory requirements as to registration, with the act instead providing a system of voluntary registration. Trade unions and organizations were autonomous bodies that were free to determine their own constitutions.[47] None of the internal rules of trade unions were to be enforceable as contracts, so that unions could not sue but neither could they be sued for breach of such rules. Collective agreements between trade unions and employers' associations consequently could not be given legal force by the courts. The act also gave union members the right to access union financial records.[48]

Contemporaneously, the 1871 Criminal Law Amendment Act effectively reinforced existing law rendering strikers criminally liable for intimidation, molestation, and obstruction. An 1872 prosecution of gas workers made it clear that common law conspiracy could still be used against workers. The 1875 Conspiracy and Protection of Property Act legalized peaceful picketing and granted prosecutorial immunity for those actions taken in trade disputes between employers and workers if such an act would have been legal had it been committed by only one person.[49] The 1875 Employers and Workmen Act removed the remaining inequalities of masters-and-servants law and made breach of contract a matter purely of civil law, as opposed to criminal law. The legal status of the TUC was clarified and made more secure by legislation in 1871–5 and again in 1906. The years 1873–96 witnessed an economic depression in Britain due to the loss of colonial markets and competition. New unionism gained even more ground among unskilled workers following the successful London Dock strike of 1889.[50] A Scottish umbrella trade

---

[46] Restraint of trade was an additional judicial doctrine rendering labor combinations unlawful under the common law because of potential harm to the public due to the restraint of trade. The first case explicitly announcing this doctrine was Rex v. Marks et al., 3 East 157 (1802). This UK common-law line of reasoning also had significant impact in the United States.

[47] *See* DEAKIN & MORRIS, *supra* note 25 at 985.

[48] Now sections 28–30, Trade Union and Labour Relations (Consolidation) Act 1992.

[49] 1875 (38 & 39 Vict.) c. 86.

[50] *See* BLACK, *supra* chap. 1 note 5 at 172.

union organization was founded in 1897, the Scottish Trades Union Congress ("STUC"), partly as the result of a dispute with the TUC. A second English national umbrella trade organization, the General Federation of Trade Unions ("GFTU"), was founded in 1899 at a special Congress of TUC along the lines of new unionism.[51]

The close of the nineteenth century saw the end of much of the legislative and judicial hostility to worker combinations, now referred to explicitly as trade unions. Immunities granted by the different statutes carved out a safe zone not only for trade unions, but also for the use of negotiations and eventually collective bargaining to resolve worker disputes. Sidney Webb and Beatrice Potter Webb gave expression in 1897 to the preference for collective rather than individual bargaining:

> Individual bargaining between the owner of the means of subsistence and the seller of so perishable a commodity as a day's labour must be, once for all, abandoned. In its place, if there is to be any genuine "freedom of contract", we shall see the conditions of employment adjusted between equally expert negotiators acting for corporations reasonably comparable in strength.[52]

The beginning of the nineteenth century was characterized by state control over wages and many aspects of working life. By the century's end, the groundwork for the model of "collective laissez-faire"—as it was termed by Kahn-Freund—as the accepted state policy was laid, highly characterized by labor's resistance to legal regulation, corporate form, and binding collective agreements.

LABOR IN THE EARLY TWENTIETH CENTURY

The twentieth century saw labor increasing as a political force. Social welfare legislation was promulgated parallel to the extension of the voting franchise. First came the Workmen's Compensation Act 1897,[53] followed by the more extensive 1906 Workers' Compensation Act,[54] old

---

[51] Despite its foundation in new unionism, GFTU today supports specialist unions, with 35 affiliates covering about 214,000 union members. For more information on GFTU, including access to a digital archive of all of its records since 1899, see its website at gftu.org.uk.

[52] Sidney Webb & Beatrice Potter Webb, Industrial Democracy 842 (1897).

[53] 1897 (60 & 61 Vict.) c. 37.

[54] 1906 (6 Edw. 7) c. 58.

age pensions,[55] regulation of the working hours of adult males in the mining sector,[56] the first state labor exchanges,[57] minimum wage legislation in sweatshops,[58] and national sickness and unemployment insurance.[59] A dual system was effected, with a separation of the statutory and voluntary sectors. The statutory regulations set a floor of rights, with the voluntary sectors, the social partners, regulating the terms of work through collective agreements. This dualism arose due to fears that statutory attempts to introduce compulsion into arbitration and conciliation procedures and enforce the terms of collective agreements against unions would provoke "the most embittered resistance from the whole body of Trade Unionists."[60] The Labour Party was formed in 1906 after Labour won 29 seats in the House of Commons. Membership of the TUC grew steadily, from 700,000 in 1889 to two million in 1900, and reaching 8.5 million workers in 1920. This was partly due to the extension of membership to less skilled workers, white-collar workers, and female workers in the already organized trades, as well as the unionization of hitherto unorganized industries and firms.

The Trade Disputes Act 1906 was passed with the support of the new Labour Party.[61] This act strengthened the role of trade unions by extending the immunity of trade unions with respect to criminal conspiracy to also include the tort of civil conspiracy, rejecting the holding in the *Taff Vale* case.[62] Immunity was also granted in trade disputes for breach of contract (when the sole basis), also defanging any judicial developments in the tort of interference with economic relationships. The 1906 act remained fairly undisturbed until the 1970s. The Trade Union Act 1913 gave unions the right to distribute membership fees/subscriptions between political and social funds, with members having the right to opt out of the political funding.[63]

---

55 1908 (8 Edw. 7) c. 40.

56 The Coal Mines Regulation Act, 1908 (8 Edw. 7) c. 57.

57 1909 (9 Edw. 7) c. 7.

58 1909 (9 Edw. 7) c. 22.

59 1911 (1 & 2 Geo. 5) c. 55.

60 *See* DEAKIN & MORRIS, *supra* note 25 at 20 *citing* Parliamentary Papers (1894) XXXV.9 at 154.

61 1906 (6 Edw. 7) c. 47.

62 Taff Vale Rly. Co. v. Amalgamated Society of Rly. Servants [1901] UKHL 1 held that a union could be held liable for damages arising from the acts of trade unionists, giving rise to significant vulnerability caused by the exposure of union funds to tortious liabilities.

63 1913 (3 & 4 Geo. 5) c. 30. This act was repealed by the Trade Union and Labour Relations (Consolidation) Act 1992 ("TULR(C)A 1992").

The focus during World War I was on prevailing in the conflict, which necessitated unprecedented cooperation between the state and social partners. Statutory regulation was in place concerning profits, wages, worker mobility, and compulsory arbitration. In 1920 the UK, like much of Europe, was hit by a severe depression, with unemployment reaching 14 percent by 1922. This economic situation led to discussions of the use of joint industrial councils, a proposal that was never enacted. A movement referred to as Guild Socialism began in the 1920s, seeking worker freedom in a societal model based on the guilds. All industries and services would be run by national guilds working not for profit but for service, much as cooperative societies: "Not only must capitalism be destroyed: the workers must also reorganize Society on the basis of a democracy of free associations working together, each in its appointed sphere, for the fullest social achievement under conditions of the fullest personal liberty for all its members."[64]

The General Strike of 1926, involving more than 1.5 million workers, led to the Conservative government passing the Trade Disputes and Trade Unions Act 1927.[65] The act rendered sympathy actions outside the scope of trade unions' immunities from civil and criminal sanctions. Mass picketing giving rise to intimidation of workers was proscribed as unlawful. Trade union members now had to contract in to any political funds (levy) paid by unions, as opposed to the contracting out that was the system under the Trade Union Act 1913. Civil service unions were prohibited from affiliating with TUC and from having political objectives. The 1927 act was eventually repealed by the Trade Disputes and Trade Unions Act 1946, which returned the legal situation to that which had existed under the Trade Union Act 1913.[66] A Trade Union Disputes Act 1965 was passed by the Labour government of that period as a response to a court ruling that trade union action constituted civil intimidation.[67]

---

[64] *See* for example THE NATIONAL GUILDS LEAGUE, THE POLICY OF GUILD SOCIALISM 23 (London 1921). *See also* G.D.H. COLE, GUILD SOCIALISM 9 (The Fabian Society 1920), arguing guild socialism to be the better choice as compared to trade unionism, as guilds take into account all workers and would look after the interest of both workers and the industry.

[65] 1927 (17 & 18 Geo. 5) c. 22.

[66] 1913 (3 & 4 Geo. 5) c. 30. This act was repealed by the Trade Union and Labour Relations (Consolidation) Act 1992 (TULR(C)A 1992).

[67] Rookes v. Barnard [1964] UKHL 1. The case concerned the negative freedom of association in a closed shop context. The fired employee sued the union, successfully claiming that the union officials had used unlawful means to

LABOR AS A POLITICAL BATTLEFIELD

The Industrial Relations Act 1971 was passed by a Conservative government, repealing the Trade Union Act 1871.[68] The 1971 act imposed a system of legal regulation of internal trade union affairs, the complete antithesis to the collective laissez-faire system created during the nineteenth century.[69] The 1971 act introduced an entirely new system of collective labor law, replacing the common law liability and statutory immunities as to industrial action with a system of unfair labor practices somewhat modeled on the American Taft-Hartley Act of 1947, as discussed in Chapter 6. Procedures for prestrike ballots and cooling off periods were adopted. A Registrar of Friendly Societies was created. Trade union protections from civil liabilities were included, but made conditional upon the trade unions being registered under the act. Such registration would entail that the trade union would become a body corporate and would have to subject their rule books to potential legal review. Most of the trade unions refused to register as part of the TUC boycott of the entire act, and those unions registering under the act were expelled from the TUC.[70]

The 1971 act also created a bill of rights for union members. Its provisions included making it unlawful to unreasonably exclude or expel a person from membership; making it unlawful to unreasonably refuse a member their vote, their participation in union meetings, or their standing for office, or to discipline a member for refusing to strike; setting out procedures to be followed in cases of member discipline; establishing a right to resign from union membership; and voiding any agreement limiting a member's right to recourse to litigation. A National Industrial

---

intimidate his employer and that he was the victim of tortious intimidation. The House of Lords found for the employee, *citing* Lumley v. Gye (1853) 2 E. & B. 216.

[68] 1968 *Report of the Royal Commission on Trade Unions and Employers' Associations* (the "Donovan Report"), 23(4) RELATIONS INDUSTRIELLES 686–98, 687 (1968). The Report was the fifth Royal Commission report, those prior being issued in 1871, 1874, 1891, and 1903. The Donovan Report recommended employee protections from unfair dismissals, as well as improving the conditions for collective bargaining.

[69] PATRICK ELIAS & KEITH EWING, TRADE UNION DEMOCRACY—MEMBERS' RIGHTS AND THE LAW 12 (Cengage Learning 1987). For an argument as to the resilience of collective laissez-faire to the present day, *see generally* ALAN BOGG, THE DEMOCRATIC ASPECTS OF TRADE UNION RECOGNITION (Oxford University Press 2009).

[70] ELIAS & EWING, *supra* note 69 at 13.

Relations Court was established, only to be proven a failure as the unions refused to honor its orders.

The United Kingdom became a EU member in 1973. The 1971 Industrial Relations Act was repealed by the 1974 Trade Union and Labour Relations Act when Labour came to power. The 1974 act regulated trade union functions and legal status, including the presumption that a collective agreement is not binding. The immunity of trade unions under the 1906 pattern of statutory immunities was restored. The legislation included protections against unreasonable exclusion or expulsion of members where the workplace was a closed shop, as well as anti-discrimination provisions as to race and sex. The Certification Officer replaced the Registrar of Friendly Societies as a result of the 1975 Employment Protection Act enacted by Labour. Both collective bargaining and union membership reached their peaks at the end of the 1970s, with two thirds of workplaces with 25 or more employees recognizing unions for collective bargaining purposes, covering 70 percent of their employees. Trade union membership density in 1979 was 55.4 percent, with 13.2 million members. In 1977–78, more than 40 percent of companies in the manufacturing industry with 50 or more employees had consultative committees.[71] This restoration of trade union rights was shortlived, however. Prime Minister Margaret Thatcher came to power in 1979 determined to weaken the trade unions, viewing them as a source of Britain's then weak economy.

The period from 1979 to 1997 was dominated by the Conservative government's neoliberal focus and its concomitant liberalization and economic deregulation. The Employment Act 1980 limited the right to strike, with trade unions placed under a high degree of external regulation and supervision. The Conservative Party reintroduced restrictions on secondary industrial action in 1980, finally banning it altogether through the Employment Act 1990.[72] The Employment Act 1982 restricted closed shops by imposing high ballot requirements (85 percent), allowed employers to terminate the employment of strikers, and reduced compensation in cases of employment dismissals. Union protections from being sued were lifted so that claims could be made against union funds for up to £250,000 per offense.

The Trade Union Act 1984 introduced strike ballots on the penalty of forfeited union immunities; mandatory elections of certain officials every

---

71 *See* MARK HALL & JOHN PURCELL, CONSULTATION AT WORK: REGULATION AND PRACTICE 15 (Oxford University Press 2012).

72 This is now codified in the Trade Union and Labour Relations (Consolidation) Act 1992.

five years; and the validation of political objectives and funds every decade, under the guise of strengthening union member democracy. The Employment Act 1988 created the Commissioner for the Rights of Trade Union Members, to which body trade union members could lodge complaints against their trade unions. The Conservative government's argument was that democracy in trade unions was hampered when individual union members could not exercise their statutory rights against the trade unions.[73] Few complaints were lodged with the Commissioner initially, as many workers saw this as invoking "Tory legislation to beat the trade unions."[74]

The Trade Union and Labour Relations (Consolidation) Act 1992 and the Trade Union Reform and Employment Rights Act 1993 removed certain of the floor rights with respect to wages. The Commissioner for Protection against Unlawful Industrial Acts was created to support third party claims regarding harms arising out of unlawful industrial action. The mandate of the Certification Officer was extended to include administrative, judicial, and investigative responsibilities. The categories of persons not entitled to statutory employment protection were broadened, and unfair dismissal protection was lowered, extending the six-month trial employment period before any protections became effective to two years. Thatcher's anti-union strategy was successful, as evidenced by the rapid decline in union density during the 1980s and 1990s. In workplaces with more than 25 workers, union density fell from 65 percent (12.6 million members) in 1980 to 47 percent (9.8 million) in 1990 and 36 percent (7.8 million) in 1998.[75] In 2016, the number of trade union members was 6.2 million and the proportion of employees was 23.5 percent.[76]

Given the Conservative Party's political hostility to trade unions, as well as the unions' weakened position as a result of the accompanying bevy of legislation, employers began to refuse to recognize bargaining arrangements, offering employees incentives against union membership and conducting anti-union campaigns in a trend of union derecognition.

---

73 *See* Graeme Lockwood, *An Epitaph to CROTUM and CPAUIA,* 31(5) Industrial Relations Journal 471–81, 472 (2000).

74 *Id.* at 477.

75 *See* Deakin & Morris, *supra* note 25 at 35.

76 Department for Business, *Energy & Industrial Strategy, Trade Union Membership 2016,* Statistical Bulletin May 2017; *see also* Department of Employment Statistics Division (1892–1974), Certification Officer for Trade Unions and Employers' Associations (1974–2013), available at the UK data.gov website at data.gov.uk.

Sectoral-level bargaining gave way to more local, plant-level bargaining. There were fewer strikers, but greater potential tort liabilities for unions. Changes in the strike balloting laws resulted in more complex and cumbersome procedures for union industrial action.

Labour came back to power in 1997 under the banner of "New Labour." The New Labour approach was postulated as a third way between Conservative and traditional Labour approaches, promoting labor and employers working together. Many of the restrictive trade union provisions passed under Thatcher's reign consequently were not repealed under this version of the Labour Party, including the complicated notice and strike balloting systems. The broader immunities which trade unions had formerly enjoyed with regard to industrial action were not restored. However, collective bargaining rights were strengthened for the majority union, which could now require employers to enter into negotiations over pay and certain employment terms under the Employment Relations Act 1999.[77]

A coalition Conservative–Liberal Democrat government came to power in 2010, with labor regulation once again a focal point of the political agenda, this time in order to reduce red tape. The Conservatives came back to power in 2015 and, according to newspaper headlines, the "biggest crackdown on trade union rights for 30 years" was launched.[78] The 2016 Trade Union Act addresses industrial action, trade unions, employers' associations, and the functions of the Certification Officer. With respect to industrial action, the 2016 act introduced a heightened voting requirement of 50 percent of those asked to strike, otherwise the action is to be deemed unlawful. If a strike in key services is at issue, 40 percent of those asked to strike must vote in favor of the strike. This double threshold in the public sector entails, for example in the case of teachers, that of 100 eligible voters, 50 votes are required for a quorum and 40 votes must be in favor of the strike. Two weeks' notice of industrial action is to be given. Strike ballots are to be renewed every four months.

The 2016 Trade Union Act places caps on the time public sector union representatives may spend on union activities. A government Certification Officer is to be appointed the power to impose a fine of up to £20,000 for a trade union's failure to comply with reporting rules. This tightening of strike rules under the 2016 act is interesting in light of the

---

77 *See* DEAKIN & MORRIS, *supra* note 25 at 43.

78 *See* Patrick Wintour, *Trade Unions—Biggest Crackdown on Trade Union for 30 Years Launched by Conservatives*, THE GUARDIAN, July 15, 2015.

fact that the number of lost work days in 2014 was 788,000, compared to a high of 29.5 million in 1979 and the all-time high of 162 million days in 1926.[79]

The eighteenth to twentieth centuries in the UK saw the death of the guilds and the rise of journeymen's associations to provide former guild support and mutual aid, which functions were eventually assumed by trade unions. A system of collective laissez-faire was established at the turn of the twentieth century, with the state setting floors through legislation governing work conditions, and the social partners using collective bargaining to flesh out these rights. Kahn-Freund declared in 1954 that there perhaps is "no major country in the world in which the law has played a less significant role in the shaping of labour management relations than in Great Britain."[80] This conclusion rested partially on the technique of immunities created in the Trade Union Act 1871, facilitating collective bargaining for wages, working time, and other terms and conditions of employment for most workers.

The state nonintervention noted here was however eradicated by Conservative legislation in the period 1979–97, with ever tighter regulation of trade unions in a conscious attempt to reduce their power. The past 30 years have continued this political–legislative battle, with often radical legislative changes, depending on the government. UK trade unions today appear to be hostages to political will, the latest round of which has been seen in the case of the 2016 Trade Union Act. This susceptibility within the UK labor law model to changes in the political and legislative winds is highly unusual in comparison to the legislative stability of the other three national systems examined here—Germany, Sweden, and even the United States.

---

[79] Office for National Statistics, Labour Disputes; UK;Sic 07; total working days lost; all inds. & services (000s), Source dataset: Labour Market Statistics time series dataset (February 15, 2017) available at the website of the Office for National Statistics at ons.gov.uk/employmentandlabourmarket.

[80] *See* Otto Kahn-Freund, *The Legal Framework*, in THE SYSTEM OF INDUSTRIAL RELATIONS IN GREAT BRITAIN: ITS HISTORY, LAW, AND INSTITUTIONS 42–127, 44 (Alan Flanders and Hugh Clegg eds. Oxford 1954).

4. Labor in Germany: rapid transformations

It is difficult to fully grasp the lateness of Germany's industrialization and capitalization, when set against the period of several centuries over which those processes took place in England. At the beginning of the nineteenth century, the lands associated with the German peoples, from the Tyrol to the Baltic, were divided into several hundred sovereign territories, "ranging from the Austrian and Prussian monarchies to tiny principalities of imperial knights within the Holy Roman Empire."[1] Each of these territories had its own political and legal infrastructure, and Germany was not unified as one nation until 1871. Industrialism began in certain German regions as early as the 1830s, for example in Saxony and Prussia.[2] However, in the early nineteenth century only 10 percent of the German population lived in communities of 5,000 people or more, and only 2 percent in cities of more than 100,000 inhabitants. By 1848, only 5.5 percent of the German population worked in factories or the mining industry.

Germany had five joint stock companies in 1800, increasing to a little over one hundred by 1850.[3] By 1745, bank notes were used fairly extensively as currency in Britain, in line with the rise of mercantile capital; the use of paper money was still only being discussed in Germany in the 1830s. By 1873, there were more than 140 kinds of

---

[1] *See* BOB HEPPLE (ED.), THE MAKING OF LABOUR LAW IN EUROPE—A COMPARATIVE STUDY OF NINE COUNTRIES UP TO 1945 Appendix 1 p. 315 (Bloomsbury 1986).

[2] *See generally* BO STRÅTH, THE ORGANISATION OF LABOUR MARKETS—MODERNITY, CULTURE AND GOVERNANCE IN GERMANY, SWEDEN, BRITAIN AND JAPAN 27 (Routledge 1996).

[3] *See* THEODORE S. HAMEROW, RESTORATION, REVOLUTION, REACTION—ECONOMICS AND POLITICS IN GERMANY, 1815–1871 6 (Princeton University Press 1970) 6; *see also* CAROLA M. FREGE, EMPLOYMENT RESEARCH AND STATE TRADITIONS: A COMPARATIVE HISTORY OF BRITAIN, GERMANY AND THE UNITED STATES 97 (Oxford University Press 2007).

paper bank notes and monies in circulation in the German Empire.[4] Despite these disparities and its lack of unity, Germany had become Europe's leading industrial nation by 1914, outstripping Britain and second only to the United States as the leading manufacturing country globally.[5]

Given the number of German states and their changing borders, and the consequent lack of an overarching state structure, the history of worker collectivism starting with the guilds is more complicated to trace in the German context. The fate of the guilds in Germany came to be intimately intertwined with questions of conquest, nationhood and democracy in a unique manner, with Germany achieving national status in 1871, long after Britain, Sweden, and even the United States.

THE GERMAN GUILD STRUCTURE BY THE EIGHTEENTH CENTURY

Variances in the structures of the German guilds roughly reflect the geographical boundaries of the different German states. The Hansa league established merchant guilds in certain German cities as early as the thirteenth century, and the dominance of the merchant guilds in those cities continued well into the eighteenth century. Craft guilds were most prevalent in home towns, independent self-contained microcosms of a size somewhere between that of a city and that of a village. These craft guilds often had a charter (articles or statutes) that was voted on by the guild members and then confirmed by a local authority, giving public force to the private agreement. The guild charter outlined the guild's training program, the regulations governing the trade, membership and election rules, the specific economic activity (*Zunftzwang*) involved, and

---

4 *See* RICHARD KOCH (ED.), NATIONAL MONETARY COMMISSION, GERMAN IMPERIAL BANKING LAWS, 61ST CONGRESS 2D SESSION DOCUMENT NO. 574 (Washington DC 1910) 3.

5 *See* Dick Geary, *Socialism and the German Labour Movement before 1914* in LABOUR AND SOCIALIST MOVEMENTS IN EUROPE BEFORE 1914 102 (Dick Geary ed. Berg 1992). One comparative study gives the following statistics with respect to commerce: England 1840, $853 million and 1900, $3.965 billion; Germany 1840, $263 million and 1900, $2.4 billion; and the United States 1840, $223 million and 1900, $2.24 billion: see FRANK MCVEY, MODERN INDUSTRIALISM 10 (New York 1904).

the geographical area (*Bannmeile*) over which the guild had a monopoly. The guilds were self-policing with respect to the rules adopted in the charter.[6]

The ties between apprentices, journeymen, and masters were economic and familial. Both apprentices and journeymen served and lived with a master, not marrying and setting up their own households until they themselves achieved master status. Journeymen had higher status than apprentices, often owned their own work tools, and had a higher degree of independence from the master, with their own associations (albeit that these were under the supervision of the masters). Journeymen tramped during their *Wanderjahr* and upon their return were required to submit themselves to the town guild, which was to decide the master for whom they would work. The journeyman then would be taken around the shops in the town so that all the masters could have an equal chance to hire (*Umschau*). To become a master, a journeyman had to produce a masterpiece, which master exam was approved by the guild, after which the town magistrate accepted the applicant as burgher with civic rights and duties. Despite this dependence on the goodwill of masters, journeymen could and did assert their rights within the guild structure. One scholar points to more than 300 cases of strikes led by journeymen's associations within the guild structures in the 1700s.[7]

The different German state powers began attempts to rein in the journeymen's associations in the early eighteenth century. Laws were passed restricting these associations in their different forms, including correspondence and cooperative societies, and taking away their treasury rights.[8] A 1731 Imperial law to Remedy Abuses among the Guilds had the purpose of governing the relationship between masters, apprentices, and journeymen, as well as any associations of such, but was adopted only in Brandenburg-Prussia.[9] Within five years, Brandenburg-Prussia had issued more than 61 additional laws governing in detail the guilds in

---

6 *See* WALKER, *supra* chap. 1 note 30 at 78–83.

7 *See generally* ANDREAS GRIESSINGER, DAS SYMBOLISCHE KAPITAL DER EHRE: STREIKBEWEGUNGEN UND KOLLEKTIVES BEWUSSTSEIN DEUTSCHER HANDWERKSGESELLEN IM 18. JAHRHUNDERT (Ullsteing 1981).

8 *See* WERNER, *supra* chap. 1 note 61 at 211.

9 A 1731 Imperial law to Remedy Abuses among the Guilds, signed in Vienna, August 16, 1731. This 1731 Act renewed and was based on a 1654 Imperial act. An English translation of the 1731 Act can be found in WALKER, *supra* chap. 1 note 30 at 435–51. *See also* J. BREUILLY, LIBERALISM AND LABOUR IN NINETEENTH-CENTURY EUROPE 295 (Manchester University Press 1992), and see WERNER, *supra* chap. 1 note 61 at 193.

the major trades, converting the 1731 law's prohibition as to guild abuses into state control as exercised by the police or military.[10] The 1731 law declared unlawful all associations whose charter had not been confirmed, on penalty of being excluded from the craft within the entire Holy Roman Empire. It also addressed the "senseless rebellion and refusal to work" of the journeymen. Journeymen's associations were totally forbidden, while masters could continue to uphold the guilds and their traditions in the manner prescribed.[11]

THE INFLUENCE OF FRANCE AND LIBERALISM 1791–1870

Further evolution of the guilds and journeymen's associations was derailed in several of the German states by the arrival of Napoleon. The French 1791 National Assembly had removed all restrictions on craft membership, outlawing all trade associations seeking to regulate wages and working hours.[12] Napoleon brought this new freedom of labor to parts of Germany through conquest, seizing the Rhineland in 1793 and placing it under French rule. He imposed a number of reforms, including prohibiting all employer and employee organizations. The Prussian *Allgemeines Landrecht* of 1794 made worker combinations generally illegal. Serfdom was abolished in Prussia in 1807, with the right to possess land now free. That same year citizens were given the right to engage in the trades, with compulsory membership in certain guilds abolished by 1811.

As Napoleon took over northern Germany, from 1814 guilds were outlawed in the Electorate of Hanover, the Grand Duchy of Oldenburg, and the Hanseatic cities, with the Kingdom of Westphalia and the Grand Duchy of Berg following in 1808 and 1810, respectively. The craft guilds and journeymen's associations were more or less abolished in certain German states, depending upon the zealousness of the statute's enforcement. The debate as to the freedom to choose one's occupation (*Gewerbefreiheit*) did not have the same liberal basis as that in England but was rather more often a question of replacing guild control with state control of the individual. The guilds continued to do business as usual in those states free of French rule, for example, in the Kingdoms of Saxony, Württemberg, and Bavaria and in the Grand Duchy of Baden.[13]

---

10 *See* WALKER, *supra* chap. 1 note 30 at 95–96.

11 *Id.* at 436.

12 *See* HAMEROW, *supra* note 3 at 22.

13 *See* WERNER, *supra* chap. 1 note 61 at 192.

After the fall of Napoleon, the 1815 German Confederation (*Deutscher Bund*) was formed under Austrian leadership, comprising 39 states, excluding Prussia. The social consequences of the economic and political upheavals, wars, increasing technology, movement from the countryside to the cities, and commodification of labor led to social welfare demands.[14] In response, guilds were reintroduced in some of the German states by the 1830s, mostly in unindustrialized areas and where the guild structures had historically provided positive community support. In other states, the lack of enforcement of the statutory prohibitions against guilds entailed that the guild structures were still strong despite the prohibitive legislation.[15] The rights of the cities' monopolies were terminated in certain parts of Germany and new masters moved in, with systems of state concessions in the licensing of masters introduced. A Bavarian 1825 Trade Law abolished guilds' rights to limit entry to the crafts, instead placing the rights with the state, and master exams were to be carried out by the police.

The debate concerning the role of guilds in German society at this time differed greatly from that in Britain. German traditionalists wished to keep the guild structure because of its societal support and provision of social security. More liberal forces saw guilds as impediments to modernization efforts in line with the French arguments.[16] The reforms that occurred in the different German states generally addressed specific narrow issues instead of the entirety of the structure, reflecting a system of compromise. Some German states broke up the craft monopoly by legislating that payment of a fee and being of sound character were the only requirements allowed for entry of a trade. Others decided that the state would determine the numbers of those admitted to certain crafts, with the abolition of geographic monopolies. Legislation allowing individuals to engage in more than one craft was also passed. Guild membership became entirely voluntary and guilds could be dissolved by

---

[14] *See* MICHAEL STOLLEIS, ORIGINS OF THE GERMAN WELFARE STATE: SOCIAL POLICY IN GERMANY TO 1945 (GERMAN SOCIAL POLICY) 32 (Springer 2014).

[15] *See* HAMEROW, *supra* note 3 at 26. *See also* MICHAEL J. NEUFELD, THE SKILLED METALWORKERS OF NUREMBERG—CRAFT AND CLASS IN THE INDUSTRIAL REVOLUTION 35 (Rutgers 1989).

[16] General social welfare reforms also began in Prussia at this time, first with an 1839 Act prohibiting the employment of children under the age of nine in mines and factories. The act also limited the working day of children under the age of 16 to ten hours (later raised to 12 hours in 1853), while the working day of children under the age of 14 was limited to six hours: see STOLLEIS, *supra* note 14 at 63.

member vote, with individuals allowed to withdraw through resignation. The self-policing function was transferred to the state and the guilds' specialized courts were dissolved. Other guild functions were also transferred to the state to be administered by the police, particularly social insurance, the issuing of passports, and the registration of worker movement.[17]

Pressure was on the German states to create a national German trade system that could function effectively from the perspectives of customs, currency, transportation, and legal regulation. One of the apparent mismatches among the different German states was the liberal industrial regulation in the west and the traditional guild control of the east. Prussia passed the *Gewerbeordnung* ("GO") of 1845 extending liberal economic principles to all of Prussia; abolishing the monopolistic rights of the guilds, including the power to grant industrial concessions; and ending the towns' exclusive trading privileges. Corporate organizations of tradesmen could exist as benevolent voluntary associations supervising the education of apprentices, administering benefit funds and savings accounts, and providing benefits for widows and orphans. In certain sectors, the right to be employed as an apprentice could still be contingent on guild membership. Discussing, threatening, or engaging in strike action, however, was completely banned.[18]

During this period of changes wrought by greater interstate cooperation, the dismantling of medieval structures including the guilds, and the path toward liberalism and industrialism, Germany suffered economic depressions almost every decade. The 1840s depression led to hunger riots and eventually the 1848 uprising.[19] One outcome of the 1848 uprising was the extension of the voting franchise. Before 1848, the working class had no vote with regard to any state political institution. The German and Prussian parliaments were elected on the same day in 1848, with expanded voting rights based on universal male suffrage, but still with certain restrictions. Karl Marx's Communist Manifesto was published that same year, while workers in Berlin demanded that the Prussian King establish a ministry for workers.[20] The typographers' unions were pioneers, drafting a program at their 1848 Mainz meeting which included the collective regulation of employment conditions by the unions.

---

17 *See* LEESON, *supra* chap. 2 note 63 at 160 and WERNER, *supra* chap. 1 note 61 at 193.

18 *See* HAMEROW, *supra* note 3 at 29.

19 *Id.* at 75.

20 *See* STOLLEIS, *supra* note 14 at 33.

A backlash against the liberalism espoused after the 1848 uprising occurred almost immediately. A national artisan congress was formed later that year, the General Fraternization of German Workers (*Allgemeine Deutsche Arbeiterverbrüderung*), appealing "to our brothers in trade." In its address, the congress stated that it was most firmly opposed to industrial freedom and that "[w]e declare ourselves to be competent and qualified to conduct our own affairs and hence also to undertake the solution of the social problem."[21] Industrial freedom in France was argued to have resulted in a "propertyless and uprooted proletariat always ready to embark upon revolution," a fate Germany could avoid if it abandoned its policy of encouraging factories and obstructing guilds. The proposed solution was a return to the corporate organization of production in the form of guilds, which had historically kept the market, employment, and other social concerns in balance.[22]

The conservative measures adopted in 1849 were in line with those proposed by the national artisan congress and were the ultimate result of the 1848 uprising. These measures included guild approval of trade membership by trade examinations and apprenticeship requirements. The simultaneous practice of several trades was restricted. The benevolent labor associations created under the 1845 act were strengthened, including cooperatives, friendly societies, and educational associations.[23] Industrial councils comprising both employer and employee representatives were put in place, and municipal trade courts to address disputes between masters and journeymen, industrialists and trade hands, and merchants and helpers were reestablished.[24] The conservatives' tactics involved outliberalizing the liberals with welfare programs that would assure the loyalty of the lower classes and consequently defang liberal arguments, resulting in a renaissance of sorts of the guild system as a means for providing social security.

This guild renaissance was however shortlived, lasting only a decade until political power was transferred from the ailing King Frederick William IV of Prussia to Prince William as regent in 1858. Prince William immediately began reforms favorable to the liberal bourgeoisie. One world-class reform concerned education, and saw 97.5 percent of all school-aged children in Prussia attending school by 1860. This reform was founded on the idea that the state had the obligation to instruct its citizenry, as an educated society was the foundation of a moral society.

---

21 *See* HAMEROW, *supra* note 3 at 144.
22 *Id.* at 145.
23 *See* GEARY, *supra* note 4 at 106.
24 *See* HAMEROW, *supra* note 3 at 190.

The link between formal vocational, technical, and scientific education and industrial progress was strongly argued.[25] The creation of trade and technical schools is considered to have contributed to the eventual demise of the journeymen's tramping system, as travel abroad was no longer necessary to learn skills.[26] The state was taking over the guild functions of training and education.

The 1860s saw the rise of trade unions in the midst of this liberal–conservative debate. Many of these trade unions began in those trades in which journeymen's associations had been active—basically highly skilled, relatively well-paid fields, such as construction and engineering. Consequently, the early trade unions were much influenced by journeymen's associations, particularly as the requirement of tramping meant coming into contact with new ideas.[27] The General German Workers Association (*Allgemeiner Deutscher Arbeiterverein*)[28] was founded in 1863 with the aim of representing the interests of the working class, including the right to universal, equal, and direct suffrage,[29] with national unification placed high on their agenda.[30] This approach of social democratic reformism was in direct contrast to the aims of classlessness and statelessness to be achieved through revolution as espoused by Karl Marx and Friedrich Engels.

A 1868 procedural decree made a shambles of guild rights: employers were free to hire as many workers as desired, a trade could be practiced

---

[25] *See* APPLEBAUM, *supra* chap. 1 note 8 at 427.

[26] *See* WERNER, *supra* chap. 1 note 61 at 202.

[27] For example, one of the most well-known German Socialists prior to 1848 was Wilhelm Weitling, a traveling tailor-journeyman highly regarded in the German journeymen's associations and in both Paris and Switzerland. Weitling was active in the League of the Just, which Karl Marx and Friedrich Engels joined in 1847 and which shortly thereafter merged with the Communist League: see HELGA GREBING, HISTORY OF THE GERMAN LABOUR MOVEMENT—A SURVEY 20–21 (Berg Publishing 1969).

[28] The Social Democratic Workers' Party (*Sozialdemokratische Arbeiterpartei Deutschlands*), founded in 1869, differed from the 1863 General German Workers' Association on issues of statehood. However, the two merged in 1875 under the name of the Socialist Workers' Party of Germany (*Sozialistische Arbeiterpartie Deutschlands*), adopting the party's current name, Social Democratic Party of Germany, in 1890 after the bans were lifted. Consequently, the year 1875 is taken as the date the Social Democratic Party was founded: see MANFRED WEISS & MARLENE SCHMIDT, LABOUR LAW AND INDUSTRIAL RELATIONS IN GERMANY 28 (4th ed. Kluwer 2008).

[29] Of the nine original workers in that association, seven were tailors, joiners, cobblers, or cigar-makers: see GEARY, *supra* note 4 at 107.

[30] *See* GREBING, *supra* note 27 at 34.

outside guild regulations, and buyers could purchase wares in any market and from any dealer. Under then Prussian Prime Minister Otto von Bismarck, a national code of manufacture was drafted for the North German Confederation and adopted in 1869, repealing the 1845 GO. Under a liberal economic philosophy, workers were now allowed to combine to present wage demands but severe restrictions were placed on the means that could be used legally in the furtherance of trade disputes. Workers could also set up collective benevolent self-help associations with, for example, savings or educational purposes. However, those associations active in the area of social policy needed state permission, which would be granted only after the submission of a membership list.[31]

A liberal trade union was founded in 1869,[32] in principle accepting capitalism as the structure of the economy and trying to strengthen the hand of workers by combining their forces in the negotiation of working conditions. Thus even prior to the founding of the German Reich in 1871, three competing union movements were in place: the reformist social democrats, the liberals, and the radical communists inspired by Marx and Engels.[33] Some argue that the focus on nationalism and trying to create a German national identity contributed in part to the widespread general lack of class consciousness at this time.[34]

THE GERMAN EMPIRE 1871–1918

Germany achieved statehood when Prussian King Wilhelm I was proclaimed its Emperor in 1871, with the North German Federation converted into the German Empire under the auspices of now Chancellor Bismarck. The German Empire comprised 25 states, excluding Austria. Though now a nation state, Germany was still far from a system of universal democracy, with much power still in the hands of the royal family and the aristocracy. At the top of Bismarck's agenda was stemming the rise of socialism. A severe depression in the 1870s exacerbated social unrest, with great strike waves in 1869, 1872/3, and 1889/90. In 1873 the Typographers' Union succeeded, after extensive industrial action, in establishing wage tariffs in a collective agreement

---

[31] *See* WEISS & SCHMIDT, *supra* note 28 at 164. According to Weiss, the membership list requirement in the 1869 law is a reason why many labor unions are still not registered as legal entities to this day.

[32] *Id.* at 28.

[33] *See* BLACK, *supra* chap. 1 note 5 at 172.

[34] *See* STRÅTH, *supra* note 2 at 9.

valid for three years, considered the first significant collective agreement in Germany.[35]

Industrialism was taking root at an extraordinary pace and workers were moving to the cities, causing housing shortages with subsequent rises in rents and food prices. Triggered in part by two assassination attempts against William I in 1878, Bismarck successfully introduced the "Law Against the Publicly Dangerous Endeavors of Social Democracy" (*Gesetz gegen die gemeingefährlichen Bestrebungen der Sozialdemokratie*) that same year, which was extended by parliament four times up to 1890. A prohibition as to the employment of women within three weeks after the birth of a child was enacted in 1878, as well as certain protections regarding health risks in certain industries and with night work.[36]

Germany was breaking ground in terms of employment protection at the same time as it was balancing ways of preserving the privileges of the political old guard. Bismarck's government passed social welfare laws as part of a strategy to counteract the socialists. Bismarck posited that "the healing of the social harms will have to be sought not exclusively through the repression of social democratic excesses, but equally so through the positive promotion of the welfare of the workers."[37] He also noted that "[t]he socialist element is nothing new, and the state cannot exist without a certain Socialism."[38] The laws passed from 1883 to 1889 created a social package based on an insurance solution, including health, accident, disability, and retirement insurance, very similar to the Prussia package adopted already in the 1830s as a way to counter the arguments of the guilds. Despite this social welfare approach embraced by the government, many industrial employers maintained a "Herr-im-Hause" (master in my own house) attitude: "Neither king nor emperor has any say in our workshops. We alone decide."[39]

---

[35] *See* AXEL ADLERCREUTZ, Kollektiv avtalet—Studier över dess tillkomsthistoria 85 (Lund 1954) and STOLLEIS, *supra* note 14 at 68.

[36] ALICE SALOMON, LABOUR LAWS FOR WOMEN IN GERMANY 4 (Women's Industrial Council London 1907, Leopold reprint 2010). All three of these issues would eventually become the focus of international labor conventions, the first being the 1890 Berlin conference convened by Wilhelm II which passed resolutions on child labor, women and children in mining, and night work: see Chapter 7.

[37] *See* MICHAEL STOLLEIS, A HISTORY OF SOCIAL LAW 63 (Springer 2013).

[38] *Id.* at 62 *citing* Bismarck in the Reichstag on March 15, 1884, Verhandlungen Reichstag, vol. 75, 72.

[39] *See* GREBING, *supra* note 27 at 53 and *see also* STRÅTH, *supra* note 2 at 34.

The General Commission of Trade Unions (*Generalkommission der Gerwerkschaften Deutschlands*) was established in 1890. Industrial employers were to ensure that the workplace was free of all threats of injury to life and health, as prescribed by the Decree of 1891. All industrial laborers were to be free on Sundays and holidays, and the length of the working day was to be regulated. Wages were to be paid in cash, with a prohibition as to the sale of goods on credit or payment of wages in public houses. Every employer with more than 20 employees was to draw up a schedule of Rules and Regulations to be posted in a suitable place inside the factory, and every new hire was to be presented with a copy. The schedule was to contain rules relating to hours of work, intervals for rest and meals, payment of wages, notice terms, and sanctions. Though Germany was a latecomer to both statehood and industrialism, the groundwork for social protections had been laid—in part by the guilds and their extensive reach into home town life, but also already beginning in Prussia in the 1830s. Acceptance of the social program crossed party lines due to this existing strong basis, allowing Bismarck to deflate many of the social democrats' arguments.[40]

The repeal of the anti-socialist law coincided with a dramatic increase in votes for the Social Democratic Party, almost doubling from 1887 to 1890.[41] The number of industrial wage earners increased from 4 million in 1882 to 8.6 million in 1907, with the number of white-collar workers increasing from 100,000 to 700,000.[42] Union organization in Germany also increased dramatically, from 19,000 members in the free trade unions in 1872, to about a quarter of a million workers in 1890, to 2.5 million workers in 1914.[43] By that year, Germany had the largest socialist party in the world, with one million fee-paying members and four million votes, or one third of the votes in the 1912 Reichstag election.[44] The employer side also organized into powerful corporate groups, cartels, and syndicates as a response to this increase in trade unions.[45]

Special industrial courts (*Gewerbegerichte*) were created in the 1890s with the objective of quicker and cheaper dispute resolution proceedings

---

40 *See* STOLLEIS, *supra* note 37 at 63.

41 *See* GREBING, *supra* note 27 at 60. In 1887 there were 763,000 votes (7.1 percent of the votes); in 1890 there were 1,427,000 (19.7 percent of the votes).

42 *See* STRÅTH, *supra* note 2 at 28.

43 *See* GEARY, *supra* note 4 at 82.

44 *Id.* at 101.

45 *See* STRÅTH, *supra* note 2 at 28 *citing* ROLF TORSTENDAHL, BUREAUCRATIZATION IN NORTHWESTERN EUROPE 1880–1895 97 (Routledge 1991).

in labor issues, with the social partners (masters and men) appointing the members of the court. Municipalities with populations of more than 20,000 were required by law to establish such courts. The first collective agreement, in 1873, was followed by the 1899 Construction Workers' collective agreement. The reasons for this long gap were both employer resistance and the fact that the unions themselves were not willing to be bound by such agreements. An 1899 union congress resolved that collective agreements were desirable, as strong organizations on both sides could then guarantee the execution and fulfillment of the agreement.[46] Collective agreements were judicially accepted as a specific type of contract in 1900, commencing the gradual process of uncoupling labor law from the traditional civil law. This was reinforced academically by two seminal works, Philipp Lotmar's *The Labor Contract* in 1902 and Hugo Sinzheimer's 1907 *The Normative Function of the Collective Labor Agreement*; however, industry resistance was still significant, with many employers seeing collective agreements as impinging on their employer prerogative.

Reformers were calling for bodies of worker representatives, such as factory or workers' committees, as early as the end of the nineteenth century. Plant-level workforce representation was included as part of the Prussian state modernization program, together with an industrial code, vocational training, and social insurance. Amendments to the Industrial Code in 1891 provided specifically for optional workers' committees, and in the mining sector these became mandatory in 1905. The unions of this period opposed such committees, with the leader of the Social Democratic Party, August Bebel, deeming them mere "fig-leaves of capitalism."[47] A 1916 special act passed because of World War I, the Act on Patriotic Services (*Gesetz über den vaterländischen Hilfsdienst*), provided certain rights for labor unions and imposed workers' committees in all factories of vital importance to the war effort and having more than 50 employees.[48]

---

[46] *See* ADLERCREUTZ, *supra* note 35 at 86.

[47] *See* Walther Müller-Jentsch, *Germany: From Collective Voice to Co-management* in WORKS COUNCILS: CONSULTATION, REPRESENTATION AND COOPERATION IN INDUSTRIAL RELATIONS 53–78, 53 (Joel Rogers and Wolfgang Streeck eds. Chicago 1995).

[48] *See* STOLLEIS, *supra* note 14 at 84.

THE WEIMAR REPUBLIC 1918–1933

The Weimar Republic was established after the November 1918 revolution that caused the abdication of the Kaiser, close on the heels of Germany's 1918 defeat in World War I. The country was ravaged by war, suffering greatly both economically and socially. The central agreement for the social partners, the *Stinnes-Legien* Agreement, was signed in November 1918. Employers agreed to recognize trade unions and the right of association, company unions would be banned, collective agreements would regulate labor conditions, Works Committees would be put in place in workplaces of more than 50 employees, the working day would be eight hours long, and arbitration would be the dispute resolution mechanism used.[49] Self-regulation by the social partners was the chosen alternative to state regulation. That same year, the Collective Bargaining Decree (*Tarifvertragsverordnung*) was adopted, guaranteeing the principle of collective bargaining autonomy (*Tarifautonomie*) by the social partners without state interference, as later confirmed by the 1919 Weimar Constitution. The early trade-based unions of the nineteenth century gave way to unions encompassing both skilled and unskilled workers, new unionism, leading to greater class consciousness.[50] The newly founded Communist Party of Germany attempted an unsuccessful coup that same year. The 1918 revolution ultimately led to fundamental changes in labor law, essentially the transition from individual to collective labor law.[51]

The 1919 Weimar Constitution, whose labor law section was partially drafted by the previously mentioned Hugo Sinzheimer, specifically addressed labor issues for the purpose of achieving uniform labor legislation.[52] Article 159 guaranteed freedom of association without limitations for the first time in Germany history. In Article 163 the constitution guaranteed that all "shall be given the opportunity to earn his living by economic labor," to enable access to and support of the extensive insurance system in place covering sickness, accidents, disability, and eventually unemployment.

The 1918 Stinnes-Legien Agreement mandated that the labor conditions for all private sector workers were to be determined through

---

[49] *See* STRÅTH, *supra* note 2 at 3. This was 20 years prior to the equivalent Swedish agreement, the Saltsjöbad Agreement of 1938.

[50] *See* NEUFELD, *supra* note 15 at 304.

[51] *See* STOLLEIS, *supra* note 37 at 125, cites omitted.

[52] Formally, the Constitution of the German Reich (*Die Verfassung des Deutschen Reichs*, referred to as the Weimar Constitution, *Weimarer Verfassung*).

collective agreements with employer organizations. By 1922, there were almost 11,000 collective agreements covering 890,000 businesses and 14.3 million employees. The National Labor Office was given the authority to declare, *ergo omnes*, collective agreements generally binding at the request of the social partners.[53]

Works councils were legally established in 1920 to preempt more revolutionary activity. The former workers' councils then became industrial works councils (*Betriebsräte*). Demonstrations were held by workers and trade unions to protest the act, and 42 demonstrators were killed by machine gun fire. Despite the Act's passage, works councils never fully developed at this time due to the perceived competition with unions. Labor arbitration and later a labor court system as created by the Labour Court Act of 1926 were put in place, granting original jurisdiction for all employment and labor law claims to the labor courts.[54]

The number of working days lost through industrial disputes between 1927 and 1930 was 3.7 million annually, and this figure doubled between 1930 and 1932 as the Great Depression hit.[55] Unemployment rose to four million by 1930 and to six million by 1932—almost 44 percent of the workforce. Adolf Hitler joined the German Workers Party in 1919 and gradually transformed it into the New Nationalist Socialist German Workers Party (*Nationalsozialistische Deutsche Arbeiterpartei*, the Nazi Party) in order to attract socialist votes. Public support for both the Nazi and the Communist parties grew during the Great Depression, based greatly on anti-Jewish and anti-Communist sentiment: "In Russia the eight-hour day has been abolished. There are no more workers' councils."[56] Hitler's rise to power depended to a significant extent on major funding from industry, in return for promises to win the working class away from Marxism.[57]

---

53 *See* STOLLEIS, *supra* note 14 at 123.

54 *See* Taylor Cole, *The Role of the Labor Courts in West Germany*, 18(3) JOURNAL OF POLITICS 479–98 (Aug. 1956).

55 *See* RICHARD GRUNBERGER, A SOCIAL HISTORY OF THE THIRD REICH 20 (Phoenix 1971).

56 *See* JOHN SIMKIN, TRADE UNIONS IN NAZI GERMANY 1 (Spartacus-educational.com 1997) *citing* ANTON DREXLER, A POLITICAL AWAKENING (1920). Despite this rhetoric, the works councils were abolished under Nazism.

57 *See generally* JAMES POOL, WHO FINANCED HITLER: THE SECRET FUNDING OF HITLER'S RISE TO POWER, 1919–1933 (Gallery 1979) and HENRY ASHBY TURNER, GERMAN BIG BUSINESS AND THE RISE OF HITLER (Oxford University Press 1987).

THE NAZI REGIME AND WORLD WAR II 1933–1945

The Nazi Party overthrew the Weimar Republic in 1933, remaining in power until 1945. Within a month of Hitler becoming Chancellor in 1933, many of the protections in the Weimar Constitution were immediately suspended under its emergency clause, including the freedoms of expression and association. Hitler achieved the destruction of any worker voice that same year, beginning with a law relating to industrial representation by which works councils members could be removed for working against the government or economy.[58] By May the unions were dissolved, their funds had been confiscated, their leaders had been arrested, and their headquarters had been occupied. Many union leaders were sent to concentration camps.[59] The 1934 Law for the Protection of National Labor created a new labor law structure, abolishing collective agreements and independent arbitration. Under the 1934 Law Regulating National Labour (the Charter of Labour), the employer was declared the master and workers were assigned the role of followers, without any voice or influence with management or its policies. Employers answered only to the state. Robert Ley, assigned to take over the unions, stated that the act was designed "to restore absolute leadership to the natural leader of a factory—that is the employer … Only the employer can decide. Many employers have for years had to call for the 'master in the house.' Now they are once again to be the 'master in the house'."[60]

Initially standing on a worker platform, the Nazi regime annihilated any worker voice. The German Labour Front (*Deutsche Arbeitsfront*, "DAF") was the only union organization allowed under the Third Reich, and had 20 million members. Ley appointed 12 state officials—labor trustees who were Nazi officials—to regulate wages, conditions of work, and labor contracts in each of their respective districts, and to maintain peace between workers and employers.[61] DAF was to put an end to the class conflict in manufacturing and industrial enterprises; workers were

---

[58] *See* Alf Lütdtke, *The "Honor of Labor": Industrial Workers and the Power of Symbols under National Socialism* in REWRITING HISTORIES: NAZISM AND GERMAN SOCIETY, 1933–1945 69 (David Crew ed. Routledge 2013).

[59] *See* GREBING, *supra* note 27 at 140 and MICHAEL THOMSETT, THE GERMAN OPPOSITION TO HITLER, THE RESISTANCE, THE UNDERGROUND AND ASSASSINATION PLOTS 1938–1945 80 (Crux 2016).

[60] *See* WILLIAM SCHIRER, THE RISE AND FALL OF THE THIRD REICH 203 (Mandarin 1999).

[61] *See* THOMSETT, *supra* note 59 at 80.

"rendered totally docile and … no longer had any voice in management."[62] The poor turnout experienced in works councils' elections suggests that the Labour Front representatives were not popular with the German workforce. As a result, no further elections were held after 1935. Some workers resisted, with illegal networks created in certain sectors, such as metal and wood workers, railwaymen, and seafarers.[63] In 1930, four million days of work were lost due to strikes; in 1933 the number was just over 96,000 days, and from 1934 to 1939 no days were lost. Strikes were classified as un-German.[64] The choice for workers was either to accept the Nazi regime and retain their employment, or be unemployed, or worse.

POST-WORLD WAR II

After World War II, Germans slowly, under the auspices of the Allied Control Council, began to rebuild a country left in ashes by the devastation wreaked by the war and the Nazi regime's actions. The issues of social protection and social law were taken up again, but in diverging ways in the different occupied zones, much reflecting the domestic politics of the United States, France, the United Kingdom, and Russia.[65] Trade union activities were initially restricted by the allied forces, but by 1949 the Confederation of German Trade Unions (*Deutscher Gewerkschaftsbund*, "DGB") had been established, founded on four basic principles. Of these, two were directly based on strengthening unions to be able to better prevent a repetition of Hitler's labor attacks in the 1930s and 1940s: the DGB was to be a general trade union with no religious, political, or other ties; and there would be a one company–one union principle so that all of an employer's workers belonged to the same union irrespective of their individual occupations. Third, a decentralized system of interest representation was created, with individual unions typically emulating the federal structure, having local, district, regional, and national offices, and inputs at each level as to shaping union policy. Fourth, the unions chose to rely on legislation for the protection of workers' rights, rather than on direct negotiations with employers. A

---

[62] *See* LÜTDTKE, *supra* note 58 at 69.

[63] *See* MICHAEL BURLEIGH, THE THIRD REICH: A NEW HISTORY 675 (Pan 2001).

[64] *See* Chris Trueman, *Trade Unions and Nazi Germany* (2013), available at the website of the History Learning Site, historylearningsite.co.uk.

[65] *See* STOLLEIS, *supra* note 14 at 158.

social partnership was built between employers and trade unions, setting wages and other working conditions through collective agreements.[66]

The Act on Collective Agreements (*Tarifvertragsgesetz*) was passed that same year in April, and has been in effect since. The act gives only the social partners the right to enter into collective agreements; specifically, only trade unions (and not works councils) are to represent employees in such bargaining. Collective bargaining originally occurred mainly at the central organization level, with such agreements (*Flächentarifvertrag*) still the dominant type today. East Germany (the German Democratic Republic)[67] and West Germany were also founded that same year as two separate states. The West German constitution, the Basic Law (*Grundgesetz* "GG"), was also adopted in 1949, stating that the new nation was "[c]onscious of their responsibility before God and man, Inspired by the determination to promote world peace as an equal partner in a united Europe."[68] The constitution specifically protects freedom of association (*Koalitionsfreiheit*) and the right to associate to safeguard working and economic conditions (Art. 8 GG) and occupational freedom (Art. 12 GG). Shortly after its adoption, the Social Democratic Party aligned with the Christian Democrats and won the election, remaining in power until 1967. The Confederation of German Employers' Associations (*Bundesvereinigung der Deutschen Arbeitgeberverbände*) was established by the Allies in 1950. An anti-capitalist spirit pervaded, however, fueled by German industrial support of Hitler.[69] German industry, particularly the steel industry, was dismantled by the allied powers, returning it to prewar levels.[70]

The 1949 Collective Agreements Act and the 1952 Works Constitution Act reinstated the prewar dual structure of employee representation through unions and works councils. The unions once again opposed the works councils, which they perceived as a dilution of union power, as works councils under the law were formally independent from, as

---

[66] *See* Deutscher Gewerkschaftsbund, *DGB—Functions and Principles* (2016), available at the DGB website, dgb.de. The DGB member unions today represent more than six million employees and are members of ETUC and ITUC.

[67] The Communist Party came to power in East Germany in 1945 and remained in place until 1989.

[68] An English translation of the Basic Law for the Federal Republic of Germany is available at the website for the German Ministry of Justice at gesetz-iminternet.de.

[69] *See* STRÅTH, *supra* note 2 at 61.

[70] *See* GREBING, *supra* note 27 at 149.

opposed to subordinate to, the trade unions.[71] A new Labour Courts Act was passed in 1953, establishing both trial and appellate labor courts to be in compliance with the demands of Article 95 GG as to the establishment of an independent labor jurisdiction.

The European Coal and Steel Community was founded in 1951 by Germany, France, Italy, and the Benelux countries, regulating these two markets for the purpose of promoting peace in Europe. The 1957 Treaty of Rome, with the same six signatories, created both the European Economic Community and the European Atomic Energy Community. Despite the devastation caused by World War II, within a decade Germany was beginning to be described as an economic miracle. A federal social assistance act was passed in 1961, creating a system of state support in order to help individuals get back on their feet. West Germany suffered its first serious economic recession in the mid-1960s. Unions began to abandon their platform of abolishing capitalism and employers their hostility to trade unions. Both sides began acting more as bargaining partners, working out pragmatic compromises over wages, employment, and social welfare.[72] A Co-Determination Act (*Mitbestimmungsgesetz*) was passed in 1976, legislating significant employee representation—codetermination—by having employee-appointed directors on corporate supervisory boards.[73]

East and West Germany were reunited in 1990, with the Basic Law duly amended so as to be the constitution for the newly formed Federal Republic of Germany. The present Works Constitution Act was adopted in 2001, materially extending the mandate of the works councils, but this time upon a proposal from the unions.[74] The Collective Bargaining Unity Act (*Tarifautonomiestärkungsgesetz*) was adopted in 2015 to strengthen the social partners' autonomy in collective bargaining and introduced minimum wage legislation. An emphasis on social questions, social welfare for workers, and worker representation continues to drive issues now, just as it has done historically for the past two centuries.

---

[71] *See* MÜLLER-JENTSCH, *supra* note 47 at 54.

[72] *See* STRÅTH, *supra* note 2 at 66.

[73] For a history of the transformation from collective agreements to statutory regulation of codetermination in Germany, see Ewan McGaughey, *The Codetermination Bargains: The History of German Corporate and Labour Law* 23(1) COLUMBIA J EUROPEAN LAW 135–42 (2016).

[74] *See* JOHN T. ADDISON, LUTZ BELLMANN, CLAUS SCHNABEL, & JOACHIM WAGNER, *The Long Awaited Reform of the German Works Constitution Act*, IZA DP NO. 422 3 (IZA 2002).

The guild system was historically an ingrained aspect of German society, with the Hansa guilds in many of the city trading centers and the craft guilds in the home towns providing structure and social security at a time when Germany comprised more than one hundred sovereign entities. This explains both the relatively late point at which their existence began to be questioned and the attempts after Napoleon's time to recreate a structure through a reinstatement of the guilds. The social security provided by the guilds was also a motivation for the state creation of social welfare in 1830s Prussia, as an attempt to decrease the guilds' importance. This early social welfare platform led to such a broad acceptance of state intervention that it was recreated by Bismarck on the new national level in the 1870s, this time to counteract radical worker movements. After the Nazi destruction of all worker rights, strong constitutional protections of worker rights and voice, both collective and individual, were put in place in the 1950 Basic Law. They have continued to the present day, as will be seen in Chapter 9.

5. Labor in Sweden: seamless transitions

The development of the guilds and their influence in England occurred parallel to the centralization of royal power and the transition to the nation state, with both paths incremental over the course of centuries. The German craft guilds developed more than five hundred years prior to Germany finally becoming a nation state in 1871, with craft guilds having a strong anchoring in the home towns, and the issue of guild dissolution becoming intertwined with questions of nationalism, social welfare, and the creation of a modern state. Timewise, Sweden sits between these two paradigms, with the craft guilds starting in the fourteenth century but never becoming as strong as in England or Germany, while Sweden became a powerful nation state almost overnight under Gustav Vasa in the 1520s.[1] Despite the many wars in which Sweden was involved during this period, "Swedish history has known no social revolution."[2] The Swedish guild system remained strongly in place until the mid-nineteenth century, when it was almost instantaneously eradicated by statute as part of the implementation of a more liberal economic policy, a component in the dismantling of both aristocratic and burgher power under the 1809 Instrument of Government. Sweden was not industrialized until the late nineteenth century, but by the end of World War II it was one of the world's strongest economies per capita and a model of industrial peace. Within the short span of a century, the guild system was completely dismantled, and the Swedish labor law model based on self-regulation by social partners and the Swedish "folk home" with extensive social welfare benefits were both firmly in place.

[1] *See* JOHAN GABRIEL RICHART, ETT OCH ANNAT, OM CORPORATIONER, PRIVILEGIER, NÄMND I DOMSTOLAR ETC. I ANLEDNING AF CONSISTORII ACADEMICI I UPSALA BETÄNKANDE OM DE ACADEMISKA JURISDIKTION 2 (Stockholm 1822).

[2] *See* FOLKE SCHMIDT, THE LAW OF LABOUR RELATIONS IN SWEDEN 10 (Harvard University Press 1962).

GUSTAV VASA AND THE REFORMATION: 1523–1620

Guilds played a central role in Gustav Vasa's assumption of power and the founding of Sweden: the German Hansa guilds with respect to Swedish secession from the Kalmar Union, and the Swedish guilds as a necessary component in the building of the Swedish nation. The Hansa city of Lübeck supported Gustav Vasa's bid for freedom from Denmark, not only contributing war funds, soldiers, traders, and craftsmen, but also bringing Lutheranism to Sweden. After successfully freeing Sweden from Danish rule, Gustav Vasa began to forge the Swedish state, establishing an extensive and effective national administration including tax and debt execution authorities, founded in part to repay the Lübeck debt but also to finance other wars. Despite his Hansa support, Gustav Vasa began a campaign to build national trade within Sweden, dismantling the privileges the German Hansa had held in Sweden for almost three centuries in the form of monopolies, tolls, and other restrictions. This freedom from Hansa privileges, an emancipation process mirrored in other countries at about the same time, marks the beginning of the decline of Hansa power in the Baltic sea.[3]

Gustav Vasa held two parliamentary meetings in 1527 and 1544, where four estates were represented: the nobility; priests; burghers/merchants; and farmers. Inspired by Henry VIII, the 1544 Västerås parliament proclaimed that the Swedish Lutheran Church was the national church, the Catholic Church was suppressed and its estates confiscated for the Crown and that all religious guilds were to be dissolved.[4] Gustav Vasa also exerted greater royal control over the *skrå* crafts guilds by requiring most craftsmen to move to the cities, allowing for easier taxation, access, and quality control.[5]

The craft guilds became more prominent and more heavily taxed after this point of time—even those craftsmen remaining in the countryside. The master craft guilds were often referred to as *skråämbeten*, with journeymen's associations referred to as *companier*, *gesällskapen*, or

---

[3] *See* ZIMMERN, *supra* chap. 1 note 25 at cxcii. One chapter in Zimmern's book is entitled "The Thirty Year War Kills the League," with the Hansa 1628 Diet given as its last official record: see *id.* at ccliii.

[4] "*Hvarigenom gillen och gilles-gästabud helt och hållet aflystes*": see GUNNAR OLOF HYLTÉN-CAVALLIUS, WÄREND OCH WIRDARNE. ETT FÖRSÖK I SVENSK ETHNOLOGI 163 (Stockholm 1863).

[5] *See* ERIK LINDBERG, BORGERSKAP OCH BURSKAP, OM NÄRINGSPRIVILIGIER OCH BORGERSKAPETS INSTITUTIONER I STOCKHOLM 1820–1846 107 (Acta Universitatis Upsaliensis Uppsala Studies in Economic History 2001).

brödraskapen.[6] Those guilds designated as official suppliers to the Crown were semi-governmental agencies, *handtverksämbetena*. Recognition by the state was necessary in order to become a legal person (*korporation*), with rights and obligations granted within a greater community, often a town or city.

More than 70 crafts were represented in Stockholm by 1580.[7] This centralization of craftsmen in the city facilitated their assertion of cartel privileges, which in turn led to greater control and power by the guilds. Competing craftsmen were often banned from setting up rival businesses within a mile of Stockholm (*bannmil*). The craft guilds were reaching parity with the merchant guilds economically, but still weaker politically even into the seventeenth century—arguably the legacy of the craft guilds' passivity in acquiescing to the merchant Hansa trade guilds.[8]

Journeymen's associations were common by this time, with their own officers, seals, treasury chests, and welcome cups, very much mirrors of the structures of the master guilds. By law, journeymen's associations were not allowed to meet unless two masters were present.[9] Other than that, these associations were very independent, with their own funds for feasts and support for tramping, sickness, burials, and the families of deceased members. The journeymen's associations were also self-policing (*domsrätt*). Journeymen who acted without honor, worked for a master who hired non-journeymen or too many apprentices, or violated a rule would be banned from work. Their names would be written in a black book which would be sent to the journeymen's associations in other towns to prevent them from working anywhere.

Tramping was obligatory for journeymen as early as the sixteenth century, usually for periods of at least two years, often undertaken in Sweden, Denmark, Germany, and Austria.[10] According to the 1621 general Craft Guild Act, a journeyman could not be accepted as a master unless he tramped.[11] Strict rules applied for tramping: a journeyman's letter (*lärobref*) as well as a guild pass (*embetets pass*) had to be

---

[6] *See* HANSSON, *supra* chap. 1 note 73 at 9.

[7] *See* LINDBERG, *supra* chap. 1 note 71 at 46.

[8] *Id.* at 59.

[9] *See* Lars Edgren, *Crafts in Transformation? Masters, Journeymen, and Apprentices in a Swedish Town, 1800–1850*, 1(3) CONTINUITY AND CHANGE 363–83, 376 (1986) and LUNDELL, *supra* chap. 1 note 39 at 73.

[10] *See* HANSSON, *supra* chap. 1 note 73 at 46.

[11] *See* LUNDELL, *supra* chap. 1 note 39 at 67, *citing* General Embetes Skrå 1621, articles 8 and 9.

produced at the new location as proof of status, and a certain "secret" phrase had to be recited.[12]

THE 1621 REFORM OF THE CRAFTS

Criticisms were raised against the unfairly high prices charged by the guilds during the early seventeenth century. Partly in response to this, but also with the aim of creating greater Swedish cities and a stronger nation, Chancellor Axel Oxenstierna set up free markets in Stockholm and Kalmar—"free" as they did not require guild membership in order to trade.[13] The first general Craft Guild Act (*hantverksreform*) was passed in 1621 under King Gustav Adolf. Closed guilds were now illegal, and the master's right to solely determine whether a journeyman was proficient was abolished, with the mayor and council to be present at the presentation of the masterpieces, the master exams.

The first Instrument of Government (*Regeringsformen*)[14] was adopted in 1634, setting out a framework for both central and local administration so that Sweden could be governed in the absence of a warring king.[15] Sweden was at the height of its power after supporting the German Protestants in the Thirty Years' War and after defeating Denmark. One of the first noted worker collective actions occurred in 1665 at the Falun mine in Stora Kopparberget. Eight workers engaged in a work stoppage until their wages in the "new coin" were of the same value as their wages in the old coin.[16]

---

[12] *Id.* at 72.

[13] *Id.* at 103, *citing* a memorial written by Riks-Canzleran Axel Oxenstjerna dated October 8, 1633 from Frankfurt am Main, stating that the insignificance and lack of business in Swedish cities gave rise to the Swedish state's weakness and poverty.

[14] The Instrument of Government (now the 1974 version) is one of the (currently) four constitutional acts in Sweden.

[15] This was a very palpable concern. Sweden was in the middle of the Thirty Years' War (1630–48) at the time. In the period between Gustav Vasa's crowning (1523) and 1634, Sweden was involved in ten wars.

[16] *See* CATRIN ANDERSSON, STEFAN BOHMAN, KERSTIN DAVIDSON, TOMMY GRAHN, LARS LINDER, MARGARETA STÅHL, & JOHAN SÖDERBERG, STREJK! EN BOK OM STREJKER OCH STREJKVISOR FRÅN BAGARIARBETARSTREJKEN 1873 TILL STORTREJKEN 1909 9 (Börås 1974). *See also Placat och förordning om myntet Stockholm den 7 octobris* 1665 which prescribed that only ducats, reichstaler (rijkzdahler), or Swedish silver coins (sölfwermynt) could be used in Sweden.

A general Guild Act of 1669 was enacted in part to address the surplus of journeymen.[17] The tramping requirement was removed, and restrictions as to the numbers of masters were forbidden by the act. Master exams were now to be supervised by a master, the mayor, and the city council. City representatives were also to attend guild meetings.[18] The act prohibited masters from paying journeymen more than the wages set by the mayor and city council. There was a relaxation of the requirement for all craftsmen to live in cities, and under Karl XI (1660–97) each parish was again allowed to have a tailor and a shoemaker in residence, with larger parishes permitted even more of such skilled artisans. The number of journeymen's associations increased in the seventeenth century, some becoming so large that they owned buildings in which the sick could be housed.[19] By the end of the century, a system of milder state regulation of the guilds was in place.

THE EIGHTEENTH CENTURY AND LIBERALISM

The eighteenth century brought significant societal and constitutional changes to Sweden. A new Instrument of Government was adopted in 1718, with the Parliament and Council (*Riksrådet*) abolishing royal absolutism, rendering parliament more powerful than the king. The role of the nobility was also minimized, even more so when the King began to act in coalition with the farmers. The King-farmers' coalition, a Lutheran State Church, and a strong tradition of state administration resulted in strong representation of state and corporate interests, as well as a centralized infrastructural power in combination with strong local democracy.[20]

Queen Ulrika Eleonora passed an ordinance regarding free, unlicensed masters in 1719.[21] Free masters were to have the same rights as guild masters, and their apprentices and journeymen were to be equally respected. The 1720 Guild Act replaced the 1669 act,[22] confirming much of the latter but with certain additions, in effect until 1846. The 1720 act codified the custom that widows had the right to conduct business in their

---

17 Kungl. Mays:tz Allgemene Ordning och Skråå (1669 skråordningen).

18 *See* HANSSON, *supra* chap. 1 note 73 at 19.

19 *Id.* at 38.

20 *See* STRÅTH, *supra* chap. 4 note 2 at 77.

21 Kongl. Maj:ts nådige Förordning Om Fri-Mästare Och Handtwärckarnes fria tilträde här i Riket. Gifwen Stockholm den 26 maj i 1719.

22 Algemene Ordning och Skrå 1720.

deceased husband's trade until remarriage, and recognized a right for women to work generally, such as in the role of apprentice.[23] It also allowed journeymen and masters to agree as to the journeyman's daily and weekly wages. The right to become a master was also strengthened. Article X § 23 of the act regulated prices, prescribing that no one was to take more for their work than it was justly worth, which price was to be attested to by magistrates, aldermen, and guild officers.[24]

Certain individuals received manufacturing privileges (*manufaktur-privilegier*) in trades outside the guild system, creating a dual system of production. Manufacturers and factories were governed by manufacturing ordinances (*hallordningar*) issued in 1722, 1739, and 1770. These often also regulated the relationship between masters and journeymen in nonguild trades.[25] Many craftsmen, and even crafts, did not belong to a guild structure, and only Stockholm guilds could come close to asserting cartel-like privileges.[26] The three main functions of the Swedish guilds were seen as setting prices, cooperating to keep the prices of raw

---

23 This opening for women to work was later limited by the 1734 års lag (1734 general code replacing the 1442 code), however, which in its Marriage Code (*giftermålsbalken*) declared unmarried women generally to be legally incompetent. Women became legally competent in Sweden in 1920.

24 *See* ADLERCREUTZ, *supra* chap. 4 note 35 at 116: "Ingen må taga mer för sitt arbete, än det skäligen är värt, efter magistratens, åldermännens och bisittarnas vitsord, när däröver klagas."

25 *See* JÖRGEN WESTERSTÅHL, SVENSK FACKFÖRENINGSRÖRELSE: ORGANISATIONSPROBLEM, VERKSAMHETSFORMER, FÖRHÅLLANDE TILL STATEN 1 (Tidens förlag 1945). The Swedish manufacturers differed radically from the English of this period with respect to both size and scope: see LUNDELL, *supra* chap. 1 note 39 at 8.

26 *See* TOM SÖDERBERG, HANTVERKARNA I BRYTNINGSTID 1820–1870 47 (Vasatryckeriet 1955). For example, printers were required by a 1752 act, Kongl. Maj:ts Nådige Förordning och Reglemente för Boktryckerierne i Riket. Gifwit Stockholm i Råd-Cammaren den 12 aug 1752, to join printer societies (*boktryckerisociete*) governed by the Cancellie-Collegii—a governmental check on a very influential group, printers, with a very influential media at their disposal, printing presses. The act explicitly excluded journeymen (gesäller) and apprentices (gåssar) from these societies. Prior to this act, journeymen (*konstförvanterna-gesällerna*) had been included in the earlier printers' societies. The journeymen then founded their own societies beginning in 1754 (*Boktryckerie-Konstförvanternas Sjuk-, Begrafningshjelps- och Enke-hjälpsskassa*). A national foundation, Gutenbergska stiftelsen, was founded in 1840 in honor of the 400th anniversary of the printing press. This foundation provided travel funds for journeymen typographers, sickness support, pensions, and provision assistance. Both of the associations also functioned as friendly societies, providing social and professional networking: see BERTIL BJÖRKLUND,

materials down, and setting employment conditions as to wages and hiring. The right to provide goods to the public was to be distributed equally between masters. Complaints as to unreasonably high prices invoked a 1762 ordinance establishing price-setting by impartial individuals, replacing the guilds' right to do so under the 1720 act. Prices were now to be set by a magistrate, trader, broker, and craftsman, who would then submit their votes to the court, and the court would determine the price. The last of the manufacturing ordinances (*hallordningen*) in 1770 forbade the payment of wages to journeymen or other workers that were higher than those set, on penalty of a fine of 20 *riksdalers*.

More and more cities were declared free after 1766, entailing no requirement for a master's exam in order to produce and sell certain goods. The 1720 act was further elaborated upon by a 1773 regulation concerning journeymen, prescribing that no journeyman who had completed training was to be denied master status. Married journeymen were also to have the right to a shorter journey period to allow them to begin working as masters earlier.[27] The freedom from master status had been revoked by 1789, however.

Journeymen's dissatisfaction with the masters' monopoly reached its height in Sweden in the late 1700s. The surplus of unemployed journeymen whom it fell upon the countryside to support was one of the reasons cited for the reforms concerning freedom of trade.[28] Voices were raised against the power of the guilds almost immediately after the passage of the 1669 General Guilds Act. Liberalism began to gain ground after the French revolution. The weakening of the aristocracy's power led to proposals for a comparable weakening of power for the burghers. An anonymous proposal to abolish the guilds was made, with the support of Kommerskollegium,[29] to the Nobility Chamber of the Parliament in 1799; the Merchant/Burgher Chamber naturally rejected it.

The beginning of the nineteenth century was turbulent for Sweden. Finland, a Swedish province since at least the reign of King Magnus

---

SVENSKA TYPOGRAF FÖRBUNDET STF—STUDIER RÖRANDE SVERIGES ÄLDSTA FACKFÖRBUND 16 (Oskarshamn 1965).

[27] 1773 års reskript ang. 1720 års skråordning.

[28] The debates concerned the change in status from guild member, *skråborgare*—a medieval corporative status—to citizen—*medborgare*—an individual status founded in liberalism and individualism.

[29] The National Board of Trade (*Kommerskollegium*), founded in 1651, is still the Swedish governmental agency for trade policy.

Eriksson in 1323,[30] was surrendered to Russia in 1809 after the Napoleonic Wars. Gustav IV Adolf was deposed as a result of the loss, and his uncle became Karl XIII. As Sweden was involved in several wars at the time,[31] a new constitutional order was needed immediately. After two weeks of drafting, the 1809 Instrument of Government (*Regeringsformen*) was quickly adopted. This new Instrument of Government further restricted the power of the monarchy, and a Montesquieu division of state power was introduced as between the King, the council/government, the parliament—still comprising four chambers—and the National Bank. The courts and government agencies received a more independent status, and the Office of the Parliamentary Ombudsman (*Justitieombudsmannen*) was created under the powers of the parliament.[32]

The nobility lost further privileges under the 1809 Instrument of Government and, to compensate for that loss, began to argue that the privileges of the trades should also be reduced. All citizen classes should have the right to participate in trade, not just the burghers. This proposal was also fueled by influences from the French revolution and liberalism. The compromise reached was that any class could participate in trade to the extent that they fulfilled trade requirements. This diffuse compromise gave rise to a more heated debate as to trade freedom, which culminated in the 1846 act described below, commencing the transition from trade regulation to freedom of trade.[33]

The guild structure was very much still intact at this time, as can be seen from an 1813 guild case in Malmö.[34] A journeyman tailor had

---

[30] Certain scholars date the first Swedish expansion into Finland (*Österland*) back to Erik the Holy's crusade in the 1150s: see NORDBERG, *supra* chap. 1 note 72 at 86.

[31] In the short period between 1801 and 1814, Sweden was officially involved in seven different wars: the Barbary Coast War (1801–05); the first Napoleonic war (1805–10); the Finnish war (1808–09); the Danish–Swedish war (1808–09); a war against the United Kingdom (1810–12, only on paper); the second Napoleonic war (1812–14); and a war against Norway (1814), after which Sweden gained Norway, which the Danes had essentially held since the 1397 Kalmar Union. The Swedish policy of neutrality was adopted after this intense period of war; such neutrality has been maintained to date, with the exception of Swedish troops involved in various UN peacekeeping missions and a UN-sanctioned ISAF Afghanistan action.

[32] *See* Riksarkivet, Regeringsformen (2013 updated 2014) available at the website of the Swedish National Archives at riksarkivet.se/regeringsform.

[33] *See* LUNDELL, *supra* chap. 1 note 39 at 203.

[34] *See* EDGREN, *supra* note 9 at 375.

decided to finish work for the day and his master physically prevented him from doing so, arguing that the working day was not yet done. An altercation ensued. A few days later the journeyman brought the case to the guild, which ruled in favor of the master. Despite the negative ruling, this example demonstrates both the independence of the journeyman in terms of deciding his work conditions and his belief in the guild's internal conflict resolution mechanisms to rule fairly.

The journeyman selection process in Malmö demonstrates the same independence. Journeymen as a rule were not to select their master; the masters were to have equal opportunities to hire journeymen. When a journeyman arrived at a town, he was to call at the trade's house-of-call, an inn in a larger city or a master's home in a smaller town. He would then be taken to all the masters (*omskådning*) so they could have equal opportunities to select a journeyman. To avoid a journeyman being claimed by an abusive master, a fellow journeyman would accompany the person on the round, purposefully avoiding any such abusive masters—in essence, boycotting them. A number of these boycott cases were brought to the Malmö guild, but the guild took no action in several of them, as forcing journeymen to work for abusive masters would give the town a bad reputation and no journeymen would then come to the town. Given the effective national and even international communications in place through the tramping system, this was a real concern. Other types of journeymen boycotts included those against masters for poor working conditions, or against other journeymen for either working for an abusive master or with nonapprenticed laborers. All honorable journeymen would refuse to work for such masters or with such journeymen.[35]

FREEDOM OF TRADE AND THE RISE OF LABOR

Despite the fact that the guild system and manufacturing privileges were intact, both were abolished by statute in 1846 as part of the political battle between the nobility and burghers.[36] The craft guilds were replaced by a single craft organization (*hantverksförening*) in each city, to which

[35] *Id.* at 377.

[36] Fabriks och Hantverksordningen av den 22 dec. 1846. At this time, more than 90 percent of the population in Sweden still lived in the countryside, and 80 percent received their income from agriculture: see CHRISTER LUNDH, SPELETS REGLER—INSTITUTIONER OCH LÖNEBILDNING PÅ DEN SVENSKA ARBETSMARKNADEN 1850–2010 45 (2nd ed. SNS Förlag 2010). A new vagrancy law was adopted at the same time: försvarslöshetsstadgan af d. 29 Maj 1846.

all the craftsmen were to belong. Many of the leaders in these new organizations were former guild leaders, with roughly 75 percent of the councilors former guild aldermen, giving the new organizations the "character of an aldermen's collegium from the dying guild period."[37] These new craft organizations had the responsibility of maintaining trade standards through education and qualifications.[38] Though the guilds were abolished, the requirements necessary to practice trades were still in place; a craftsman must have reached a certain age and level of knowledge and skill, assessment of which the city government agencies now handled. Competence for passing the master exams needed to be tried by those knowledgeable in the field and review councils were created to oversee the master exams. The city magistrates now issued all trade licenses, and those licensed had the right to be members of the organization, which consequently still held a monopoly as to who could conduct licensed crafts. The craft organizations were to meet monthly after notifying the city magistrate of the meetings, and the city mayor had the right to be present. Guild foundations continued to administer funds for sick pay and funeral costs. Some of these funds were local; others, such as the typographers, had national foundations for sick insurance and funeral costs.[39] Some of Sweden's oldest trade unions trace their origins to associations founded as a result of the 1846 act.

The journeymen's associations had strived for better working conditions for centuries, but in the mid-nineteenth century they began to act more as a platform for a labor movement in Sweden.[40] The tramping system gave journeymen access to as well as the ability to disseminate information, as well as coherence as groups that easily allowed for new ideas, social and political debates, and at times even radicalism. Organizations similar to friendly societies (*kamratföreningar*) were formed for the purposes of educating journeymen, first in Stockholm and then in other cities in the 1840s; by 1850, 32 cities had such circles.[41] Cooperatives in banking, goods, and eventually housing also began to be founded to support the working class. The first worker organizations began to surface in Stockholm in the 1850s. Strikes after 1846 became more frequent, but were still not seen in anywhere near the numbers in the United Kingdom or United States at that time.

---

[37] *See* ADLERCREUTZ, *supra* chap. 4 note 35 at 161 and AMBROSIANI, *supra* chap. 1 note 87 at 47.

[38] *See* ADLERCREUTZ, *supra* chap. 4 note 35 at 161.

[39] *See* SÖDERBERG, *supra* note 26 at 119.

[40] For a similar discussion, see ADLERCREUTZ, *supra* chap. 4 note 35 at 33.

[41] *See* SÖDERBERG, *supra* note 26 at 130.

The 1860s was marked by an economic depression, voting rights campaigns, and the further removal of medieval corporativistic privileges. The rights (*burskap*) of the burghers and city citizens were removed in 1862.[42] The second step as to abolishing trade privileges was taken with the 1864 Ordinance on Extended Freedom of Trade.[43] The privileges of conducting trade, handicrafts, and manufacturing in cities were abolished. Any citizen could now do so regardless of status.[44] Most of the 1846 statutory craft organizations were dissolved, as licenses were no longer necessary. A new type of craft organization was formed, exemplified by the Stockholm City Craft Association, *Stockholms stads hantverksförening*, which had as its purpose the creation of close ties with craftsmen, promoting work quality, and providing social insurance for the needy or sick.[45] The terminology of master and journeyman was still in use, however, as seen in a song memorializing the 1873 bakers' strike.[46]

For more than five centuries, the Swedish parliament had comprised four chambers (*ståndsriksdag*): the nobility; priests; merchants/burghers; and farmers. Each chamber was elected by a select body of individuals.[47] The majority of the Swedish population was not represented by any of these four chambers, and in 1866, a two-chamber parliament was introduced in response to political pressure. The first chamber was voted

---

[42] The 1862 reform created administrative counties (*landsting*) in Sweden and the right to vote for the governing bodies in these regions, as well as cities outside these regions, was granted to both men and women who were Swedish citizens, had legal capacity (unmarried women over the age of 25), and were assessed for municipal taxes as well as paid them: see 1862 års kommunalförordningar om kommunal styrelse i stad och på landet.

[43] Kongl. Maj:ts Nådige Förordning angående utvidgad näringsfrihet den 18 juni 1864.

[44] *See* LINDBERG, *supra* chap. 1 note 71 at 54.

[45] *See* AMBROSIANI, *supra* chap. 1 note 87 at 48.

[46] "Ja, så gesäll'n gör sig glada dagar och mästaren djupt all strejk beklagar och möten hållas så fort man kan, och 'maggar' gär man så smått hvarann … bättre brödlös än rådlös bli …" see ANDERSSON ET AL., *supra* note 16 at 29.

[47] The origin of the Swedish parliament is debated. Some see it as the 1319 meeting of nobility, farmers, and priests at the Mora stones near Uppsala (Mora ting) that elected Magnus Eriksson King of Sweden: see NORDBERG, *supra* chap. 1 note 72 at 27. Others argue that it was a 1346 meeting held in Uppsala that first comprised the four estates (*stånd*)—nobility, priests, merchants/burghers, and farmers. Still others consider the Arboga meeting in 1435 to be the first Swedish parliament, even though the farmers were not represented. The term for the Swedish Parliament, Riksdag—literally "day of the kingdom" in English—is traced back to a 1544 meeting: "Såsom vi och på then sidst holdne riksdegh til Västerås endrechteligen beslutede."

for indirectly by county and municipal councils. The second chamber was voted for directly by propertied males over the age of 21 years who had paid taxes for ten years—in essence, 20 percent of the Swedish male population in 1866.

This expanded but still rather limited pool of voters began to affect the composition of the political parties and the political issues raised in parliament. The Social Democratic Party was founded in 1889 and the Liberal Party in 1900. These two political parties came to greatly influence the parliamentary debates regarding labor laws. A second significant factor in the development of the structures between the social partners on the labor market at this time is the fact that between 1851 and 1910, almost one million Swedes emigrated to the United States. Of those born in Sweden during the second half of the nineteenth century, 20 percent of men and 15 percent of women left the country, leaving Sweden struggling to retain workers.[48]

One of the first significant employee strikes was the 1869 bricklayers' strike in Stockholm, a collective action by hundreds of workers. The first collective agreement was signed as a result of the strike.[49] A decade later, the 1879 Sundsvall strike was the most extensive strike of the nineteenth century, with five thousand men striking at 18 sawmills.[50] The county governor gave these strikers a choice: return to work or be evicted and jailed in accordance with the vagrancy laws.[51] No negotiations were held with the employer and some strikers were forcibly removed by armed troops. Industrial actions between 1860 and 1885 were at the rate of about ten a year, after which they dramatically increased to about 150 annually.[52]

The first parliamentary motions concerning strikes were brought three years after the Sundsvall strike.[53] These motions proposed expanding the

---

[48] *See* Cecilia Thorborg, *Massutvandring till Amerika slag mot befolkningen*, Nr. 2013:56, available at the Statistics Sweden website, scb.se.

[49] *See* LUNDH, *supra* note 36 at 89.

[50] *See* ANDERSSON ET AL., *supra* note 16 at 30.

[51] The 1846 vagrancy law was repealed in 1885, in part because of the strike, and replaced by the 1885 vagrancy law (lag 1885:27 om lösdrifvares behandling); this meant it was no longer criminal to be unemployed, but a person convicted under the law could be sentenced to forced labor.

[52] Förliknings- och skiljenämndskommitténs betänkande 1901. In the period 1873–89 a total of approximately 190 strikes or lockouts occurred in Sweden: see LUNDH, *supra* note 36 at 128–29.

[53] For a report with respect to the industrial peace legislative proposals from 1887 to 1920 see andra lagutskottets utlåtande no. 22 (1924), and for the period from 1921 to 1933 see andra lagutskottets utlåtande no. 51 (1934).

crime of coercion, or unlawfully forcing another to commit an act, as defined in ch. 15 §§ 22 and 24 of the Penal Act (*strafflag*), to include worker actions. These sections were amended four times during the 1890s to allow prosecutors to indict strikers for coercion used in preventing others from working, as well as to include heavier criminal sanctions for threats and violence used during strikes. These heightened provisions as to strike actions were not repealed until 1938, the same year the Basic Agreement was reached by the social partners.

The issue of labor dispute resolution was taken up as early as the 1880s and initially the viable choices were viewed as either mediation or arbitration by neutral parties, not litigation before the courts. Much in line with the guild system and its internal dispute resolutions mechanisms, many trades already had their own arbitration and mediation councils. A movement toward centralization of the arbitration councils began in the 1890s, with several legislative proposals as to state-sponsored dispute resolution.

The Swedish Social Democrats Labour Party (*Socialdemokratiska arbetareparti*) was founded in 1889 with the support of the trade unions, foundations providing sick and funeral benefits, and various socialist groups, based on a platform of expanded voting rights and an eight-hour working day. The first general Worker's Protection Act was passed in 1899. The number of organized Swedish workers rose from about 9,000 in 1886 to 65,000 in 1900.[54] Cooperatives offering goods, credit, and housing almost at cost were a strong component of the labor movement during this period. The primary objective of the developing Swedish trade unions during the 1880s and 1890s was increasing the power of workers in the labor market, with the actual control of work and work processes deemed to be of lesser importance.[55] National patterns of organization on both employer and employee sides were established, with the blue-collar worker umbrella organization Landsorganisationen ("LO") founded in 1898. The ties between the Social Democratic Labour Party and LO were and still are quite strong. LO required its members to join the Social Democratic Labour Party within three years of joining the union.

Within LO, workers were divided into different central sectoral organizations with local clubs (*avdelningar*) at the different workplaces

---

[54] And one million by 1944: see WESTERSTÅHL, *supra* note 25 at 31.

[55] Bo Stråth, EUI Working Papers in History No. 90/5, *Union Strategies in Historical Perspective: Sweden and Germany* 7 (EUI 1990). *See also* LUNDH, *supra* note 36 at 20.

(*förbundsprincip*).[56] Representative democracy, not local direct democracy, quickly became the model of employee organization.[57] Collective agreements were the approach chosen to pursue union goals. The effect was the emergence of strong trade unions that acted on the basis of a tight labor market due to emigration, giving rise to negotiation strength based not only on industrial action, but also on a potential long-term labor shortage.[58] The system has been described by one scholar as "cartel agreements [since the 1890s] on the conditions for the sale of labor and industrial peace as long as there was standing agreement between the social partners."[59]

The 1890s saw the beginning of constant social democratic/social liberal popular pressure for reformist change.[60] Legislative efforts concerning labor and the relationship between the social partners during this period fell into five main categories: proposals as to criminal sanctions for certain violent strike actions; labor dispute resolution mechanisms; the recognition of collective agreements; freedom of association; and the legal status of trade unions. The legal status of unions was closely tied to the question of freedom of association.[61] Freedom of association (*föreningsfrihet*) had been raised in the Swedish parliament as early as 1899, in terms of both the positive right to join an association and the negative right to refrain from joining one. Sweden's historical treatment of this issue differed greatly from that in the United Kingdom, United States, or Germany. Legal recognition of nonprofit associations was initially pushed for by the free church and teetotaler movements in Sweden, to allow these organizations to own real estate and not to be held accountable for damages as caused by members.[62] Concerns regarding a greater legal status of unions in Sweden were however raised by the English 1901 *Taff Vale* judgment, in which the House of Lords ruled that trade unions could

[56] *See* WESTERSTÅHL, *supra* note 25 at 38.

[57] *Id.* at 85.

[58] *See* KLAS ÅMARK, FACKLIG MAKT OCH FACKLIGT MEDLEMSKAP: DEN SVENSKA FACKFÖRBUDENS MEDLEMSUTVECKLING 1890–1940 11 (Lund 1986).

[59] *See* STRÅTH, *supra* chap. 4 note 2 at 84.

[60] *Id.* at 76.

[61] For a report as to the legislative treatment of this issue up to 1934, see andra lagutskottets utlåtande no. 37 (1935).

[62] *See* WESTERSTÅHL, *supra* note 25 at 281.

be held liable for damages caused by members.[63] There are still no statutory regulations concerning the legal status of trade unions in Sweden.

SOCIAL PARTNER CONSENSUS 1900–1929: THE DECEMBER COMPROMISE

The Social Democrats called for a great strike in 1902 to demand universal suffrage. Voting rights at this time excluded 75 percent of all men and 100 percent of all women at the national level. On April 20, 75,000 individuals demonstrated; a number were injured by police. More than 40,000 demonstrated in Stockholm a week later, and across May 15–18 more than 120,000 took strike action over a three-day period.[64] The strike was successful and voting rights were expanded. By 1908, 60 percent of the male population could vote for representatives in the second chamber, and voting rights reform was adopted in 1909 concerning men over the age of 24 years.[65]

The private sector employer umbrella organization Svenska arbetsgivareföreningen ("SAF") was founded in 1902 in response to the great strike of that year.[66] By 1906, Sweden led Europe with respect to union density.[67] The December Compromise of 1906, a collective agreement between the private sector social partners and the employer and blue-collar employee organizations, SAF and LO, set out the mainframe for the Swedish labor law model. The employers' prerogative (referred to as § 23 SAF) was recognized, in that employers had the right to lead and allocate work, freely hire workers regardless of union membership, and freely fire.[68] In exchange for this prerogative, employers agreed to a

---

63 Taff Vale Rly. Co. v. Amalgamated Society of Rly. Servants, [1901] UKHL 1.

64 *See* ANDERSSON ET AL., note 15 at 74.

65 Women received the right to vote in 1919, with the first eligible election in 1921; the military service restriction for men to vote was lifted in 1924.

66 Now known as *Svenskt näringsliv*, The Confederation of Swedish Enterprise. *See* Anders Kjellberg, *Facklig organisering och partsrelationer i Sverige och Danmark*, in SEPTEMBERFORLIGET OG DET 21. ÅRHUNDREDE. HISTORISKE PERSPEKTIVER OG FREMTIDENS DILEMMAER 57 (Flemming Ibsen & Steen Scheuer eds. Copenhagen 2000).

67 *See* ÅMARK, *supra* note 58 at 11.

68 The origins of the employer's prerogative as adopted in the 1906 December Compromise are found in § 23 of the 1905 SAF Charter, mandating that "[i]n collective agreements drafted between partners or members in the

clause stating that "the right of association was to be kept intact by both parties"[69]—the first legal recognition of the right of association—but only the positive right. The right for both employers and employees to associate was to remain inviolate, and trade unions were now recognized by the employers. The December Compromise set a framework for the self-regulation of the labor market by the social partners that exists to the present day.[70] The employers' prerogative was accepted centrally by LO; however, its acceptance was more controversial at the local level, and this remained the case for several years.[71] A great strike was held in 1909, involving about 300,000 employees, in response to an employer lockout of 80,000 workers demanding wage reductions. The strike concerned several labor market issues, including reduced work time and wages due to the economic crisis and the employer's prerogative clause, § 23 SAF. Despite the strike, the § 23 SAF clause remained. LO membership halved in the following two years.[72]

In the period between 1908 and 1926, 47 million working days were lost due to labor conflicts. Worker conflicts at times resulted in violence. The military was called to Seskarö during a 1917 strike, and more than one hundred shots were fired. This turbulence led Per Albin Hansson, later Swedish Prime Minister, to begin to articulate a vision of the *folkhem* in 1921—a home built on democracy's solid ground, a good home for all Swedes—replacing the class society. This *folkhem* was to be

---

association [SAF] and labour associations or unions, a clause is to be included that the employer has the right to freely hire and fire workers, lead and allocate the work, and use workers from any association or workers who are outside an association." As part of the December Compromise, the employers' prerogative was interpreted into collective agreements unless explicitly derogated, and the Labour Court began to articulate the employer's prerogative as a general rule of law, for example the 29/29 principle stating the employer's right to direct work: see AD 1929 no. 29, 1932 no. 100 and 1934 no. 179. For the history and analysis of the employer's prerogative, *see generally* MIA RÖNNMAR, ARBETSLEDNINGSRÄTT OCH ARBETSSKYLDIGHET: EN KOMPARATIV STUDIE AV KVALITITAV FLEXIBILITET I SVENSK, ENGELSK OCH TYSK CONTEXT (Juristförlaget i Lund 2004).

69 *See* ANDERSSON ET AL., *supra* note 16 at 128.

70 That same year a mediation law was passed, with mediation provided under the auspices of the Kommerskollegium, lag (1906:13) om medling i arbetstvister. For the history of the Swedish mediation institution, *see generally* BIRGITTA NYSTRÖM, MEDLING I ARBETSTVISTER (Norstedts 1990).

71 *See* BERT FREDRIKSSON & ALF GUNNMO, VÅRA FACKLIGA ORGANISATIONER 33 (Uddevalla 1976).

72 For membership statistics from 1900 to 2010, see LUNDH, *supra* note 36 at 95.

characterized by mutual understanding and equality: "The good home knows no privileged or denied, no favorites or outcasts."[73]

The first legislative proposals concerning the recognition of collective agreements were made as early as the 1890s. No legislation was adopted until 1928, and then it was simply an act addressing the recognition of collective agreements and not their content, the Collective Agreements Act.[74] Under the collective agreements entered into at the turn of the twentieth century, arbitration was the resolution mechanism of choice for the social partners, particularly given their skepticism and their desire to keep the state out of all labor market issues. The state supported this by passing the first Labor Mediation Act in 1906 and later by setting up a central labor mediation institution and a central labor arbitration institution in 1920. By then, more than 400,000 Swedish workers were covered by collective agreements, many of which had arbitration clauses. The Labour Court came into existence in 1929 through the Labour Court Act,[75] replacing the arbitration institution set up in 1920. Though this might appear a radical departure from the arbitration and mediation panels that had existed previously, the Labour Court's panels under the act consist of seven members—two judge-trained members, a labor market expert, and four members appointed by the employer and employee sides—in essence still very much an arbitration panel.

The concept behind these two acts, referred to as the "industrial peace legislation," was that by recognizing collective agreements, incentives for industrial peace obligations would be created, which then would be enforced by the newly established Labour Court. This legislation led to strikes by more than 365,000 workers on May 22, 1928, 70,000 of whom marched to the parliament in Stockholm.[76] Despite this protest, LO attended the Industrial Peace Conference in parliament that fall, which was seen as an important step in creating the Swedish industrial consensus (*samförstånd*) approach to the labor market.[77] Once the system

---

[73] "Det goda hemmet känner icke till några privilegierade eller tillbakasatta, inga kelgrisar och inga styvbarn": Per Albin Hansson, Swedish Prime Minister, address to the Swedish Parliament 1928.

[74] Lag (1928:253) om kollektivavtal.

[75] Lag (1928:254) om arbetsdomstol.

[76] *See* KRISTINA BORÉUS, ANN IGHE, MARIA KARLSSON, & RIKARD WARLENIUS, ETT SEKEL AV SYNDICALISM, SVERIGES ARBETARES CENTRALORGANISATION 1910–2010 30 (Stockholm 2012). The Swedish population at this time was 6.1 million according to Statistics Sweden, SCB (scb.se).

[77] The Syndicalist union ("SAC") was formed in 1910 as a counterforce to the consensus policy of the reformist unions in LO: see *id.* at 13.

of conflict regulation was established, the social partners treated the negotiation processes legalistically, with formalized agreements and firm adherence to the letter of the agreements.[78] Consequently, the state could take a fairly neutral stance straight away, as the social partners had at an early stage created the structures needed to handle many types of labor market disputes.[79]

THE BASIC AGREEMENT AND THE *FOLKHEM* 1930–1989

The Great Depression hit Sweden in the 1930s, with a subsequent increase in worker unrest. The military was called in for the 1931 Ådalen strike, where five persons were shot to death. An inquiry was held, union leaders were criminally sentenced, and legislation was passed afterward which allowed no one but the King to call military troops to deal with a civil disturbance—a power which has not been exercised since.

Work began in earnest as to building the *folkhem*, with an even greater focus placed on social protections. The unions had provided sick funds for members, basically continuing the systems set up by the guilds, journeymen's associations, and friendly societies. Legislative reform of sickness insurance was enacted in the 1930s, tidying the system to include only 28 central funds and more than 1,000 local funds, still to be administered and provided by the unions. The unions also administered and provided the unemployment insurance system created in 1935. A minimum state pension was legislated in 1913, the *folkpension*, often supplemented by union insurance. A 1935 Act on Illegal Employment Agency banned employment agencies for profit,[80] with the state employment agency ensuring that unions were to be the only supply of labor. An act on freedom of association and negotiation was finally passed in 1936,[81] again protecting only the positive right of freedom of association. The first holiday legislation was enacted in 1938,[82] with collective

---

[78] For a period of almost 70 years, from 1907 to 1976, the directors of the umbrella employer organization, SAF, were lawyers with little or no industry experience: see GÖRAN THERBORN, BORGARKLASS OCH BYRÅKRATI I SVERIGE 158 (Lund 1989).

[79] *See* STRÅTH, *supra* chap. 4 note 2 at 10.

[80] Lagen (1935:113) med vissa bestämmelser om arbetsförmedling.

[81] Lagen (1936:506) om förenings- och förhandlingsfrihet.

[82] Lagen (1938:287) om semester.

agreements providing additional benefits. Union control over these different funds and benefits is seen as one of the aspects contributing to the historically high union density in Sweden.[83]

Under legislative threat by a Social Democratic government after two years of negotiation,[84] LO and SAF finally entered into the Saltsjöbads Agreement in 1938. This collective agreement, referred to as the Basic Agreement (*Huvudavtal*), is the cornerstone of the Swedish labor model, based on self-regulation of the labor market by the social partners, with the state's neutrality evidenced by the absence of legislative interference. All collective agreements are to have either an express or an implicit industrial peace obligation unless explicitly stated otherwise. Unions are to have the monopoly on the supply of labor.[85] The cartel-like organization of the social partners was now firmly affixed, with both employer and employee organizations acting concertedly and centrally. On the employer side, much of Swedish industry at this time was concentrated in the hands of a few families/spheres.[86] In essence, two powerful constellations of actors controlled the Swedish labor market.

Sweden had been one of the most strike-prone countries in the Western world in the 1920s, and by 1938, it had become the symbol of industrial peace.[87] The leader of the Swedish Social Democratic Party argued already in 1907 that the party was a "folk" party. The Swedish Lutheran State Church was reformed in the 1910s into a modern folk church, *folkkyrka*. Given impetus by Per Albin Hansson's vision of the *folkhem*,

---

[83] *See* STRÅTH, *supra* chap. 4 note 2 at 89. *See also* Anders Kjellberg, *Kollektivavtalens täckningsgrad samt organisationsgraden hos arbetsgivarförbund och fackförbund*, Department of Sociology, Lund University Studies in Social Policy, Industrial Relations, Working Life and Mobility Research Reports 2017:1, 7 (Lund University 2017), who argues that the high union density of 70 percent in Sweden, Finland, and Denmark rests partially on union unemployment insurance.

[84] *See* STEN EDLUND, INGA HELLBERG, TORE MELIN, & BIRGITTA NYSTRÖM, KONFLIKTBEHANDLING PÅ ARBETSMARKNADEN 13 (Arbetslivscentrum 1988) and ARNOLD SÖLVÉN, LANDORGANISATIONENS SKRIFTSERIEN, HUVUDAVTALET 17 (Stockholm 1939).

[85] *See* Ann Numhauser-Henning, *Lagstiftning eller självreglering i arbetsrätten? Svaret är bade ock*, 2001 SVJT 314.

[86] One illustrative example here is Swedish Match (Svenska Tändsticks AB), which controlled 60 percent of the world market with respect to matches. Monopolies and significant ownership constellations—both private and state—were generally accepted in Sweden until its EU membership in 1995, with its incumbent requirements under Union law as to free trade.

[87] *See* STRÅTH, *supra* chap. 4 note 2 at 3.

the political focus in the 1930s, 1940s, and 1950s was on the modernization of Sweden and social welfare. The working class was to be the core of the folk home. Class was an issue in Swedish society, but did not become as volatile as it did in Germany. One reason perhaps is the contrast between the Swedish *folkhem* and the German *Herr-im-Hause*, the former empowering the working class, the latter subjugating it. The Social Democratic Labour Party was and still is the most influential political party in Sweden, with only three minor interruptions in power during the periods 1976–82, 1992–6, and 2006–14.

Industrial peace and general prosperity reigned in Sweden from the 1940s until the 1970s, assisted greatly by an infrastructure left intact after World War II due to Sweden's neutrality. The 1938 Basic Agreement was followed by several different central agreements, for example on company councils (*företagsnämnder*) created for workers to receive information, worker protection (*arbetarskydd*), and company health care (*företagshälsovård*).[88] Central wage negotiations coordinated by the umbrella employer and employee organizations were the rule from the mid-1950s until the 1980s. The situation in the labor market during the period has been described as "a harmony of interests between the social partners and a successful division of roles between the social partners, legislature and courts."[89]

Sweden began the 1970s as one of the wealthiest countries per capita in the world. A new Instrument of Government was adopted in 1974, protecting both freedom of expression and association, as well as the freedom to take industrial action. The bicameral parliament became unicameral. Close ties existed between the social partners and the government, with informal policy meetings referred to as Harpsund's democracy (*Harpsundsdemokrati*) and collective agreements and tax policy synced through unofficial agreements (*Hagauppgörelserna*). Both these unofficial channels between political and labor powers were seen as contributing to the industrial peace Sweden enjoyed at this time. Both, however, were criticized for a lack of transparency and democracy, and it was claimed that the interests of the social partners as organizations overrode those of individuals and their rights.[90]

Changes in technology and in the economic conditions for industry and workers led to a radicalization of the labor movement in the late 1960s and early 1970s, with demands for better work environments, greater

---

88 *See* EDLUND ET AL., *supra* note 84 at 13.

89 *Id.* at 14.

90 *See* FREDRIKSSON & GUNNMO, *supra* note 71 at 14–15.

worker democracy, and more secure employment.[91] A package of legislation favorable to employees was adopted, replacing much of the legislation enacted during the period from 1928 to 1949.[92] A new Work Time Act was passed in 1970.[93] The representation of employees by employee board directors was tested in 1973 and adopted in 1976, the same year as the German Co-Determination Act.[94] A new unemployment insurance act was passed in 1973, replacing the 1934 ordinance, but with the unions still administrating the insurance.[95] In 1974, four relevant acts were passed: the Employment Protection Act,[96] the Trade Union Representative (Status at the Work Place) Act,[97] the Employee's Right to Educational Leave Act,[98] and the Labour Disputes (Judicial Procedure) Act.[99] In 1976 the Employment (Co-Determination in the Workplace) Act,[100] and the Act on the Right to Parental Leave were adopted.[101] In 1977 a new Vacation Act was passed,[102] as was the Work Environment Act. The first Equal Treatment between Women and Men in Employment Act was passed in 1979.[103] A new Employment Protection Act was adopted in 1982.[104] Each of these acts were quasi-mandatory, and were gap-filling to a great extent, in that the social partners were free to agree to derogate through central agreements. The main focus was on the rights

---

[91] *See* EDLUND ET AL., *supra* note 84 at 15.

[92] *See* SVANTE NYCANDER, MAKTEN ÖVER ARBETSMARKNADEN 255 (2nd ed. Stockholm 2008).

[93] Lag (1970:943) om arbetstid m.m. English translations of some of the acts can be found on the website of the Government Offices of Sweden at government.se under the heading "policy," then "labour law and work environment."

[94] Lagen (1976:351) om styrelserepresentation för de anställda i aktiebolag och ekonomiska föreningar.

[95] Lag (1973:370) om arbetslöshetsförsäkring replacing the Förordning (1934:264) om arbetslöshetskassor.

[96] Lagen (1974:12) om anställningsskydd m.m., replaced by lag (1982:80) om anställningsskydd.

[97] Lag (1974:358) om facklig förtroendemans ställning på arbetsplatsen.

[98] Lag (1974:981) om arbetstagares rätt till ledighet för utbildning.

[99] Lag (1974:371) om rättegången i arbetstvister.

[100] Lag (1976:580) om medbestämmande i arbetslivet.

[101] Lagen (1976:280) om rätt till föräldraledighet, replaced already in 1978 by Lag (1978:410) om rätt till ledighet för vård av barn, m.m.

[102] Semesterlag (1977:480).

[103] Lag (1979:503) om jämställdhet mellan kvinnor och män i arbetslivet and then that same year replaced by Lag (1979:1118) om jämställdhet mellan kvinnor och män i arbetslivet.

[104] Lag (1982:80) om anställningsskydd.

of the collective of employees. A telling example of this is that under the Equal Treatment Acts up to 1995, any damages paid for an employer's unlawful discrimination would be based on the harm to one person, and then divided by the group harmed if more than one person had been unlawfully discriminated against.

A new Instrument of Government was adopted in 1974, after almost a decade of different draft proposals, replacing that of 1809, embodying the several constitutional changes that had successively occurred during the interim. The failure of the 1809 Instrument of Government to reflect the political reality, particularly the triumph of parliamentarism and the greatly reduced role of the king leading to the marginalization of this outdated instrument, is seen as having given rise to a sort of anti-constitutionalism. The constitution did not and should not reign in popular sovereignty. A second departure consciously taken from the 1809 Instrument of Government was the decision to change the balance of political power from that of separation of power to a separation of function. Parliament is to be the sole legislator, as seen in the opening paragraph of the 1974 Instrument of Government: "All public power in Sweden proceeds from the people." As a result, a comparatively weak court system was created, with only limited powers. This is also clear from the fact that the third branch of political power, after the legislative and executive branches, is generally not perceived of as the judicial branch in Sweden; rather, the press is considered to be so. The courts were not given a power of judicial review, simply the possibility in the case at hand to declare a law in violation of the constitution.

Given this focus on majoritarianism, only five articles concerning individual rights were included when the Instrument was adopted in 1974. The first addressed freedom of speech, expression, assembly, demonstration, association, religion, and movement. The second concerned the right to information and access to public documents. The third addressed protection from forced disclosures as to associations or religion, and the fourth protection from unlawful searches of person, home, or correspondence. The fifth stated that a "trade union or an employer or employers' association shall be entitled to take industrial action unless otherwise provided in an act of law or under an agreement."[105] These Chapter Two rights, so termed as they were included in the Instrument's second chapter, were expanded as early as 1976 to add protections against race and sex discrimination. The role of the rights as cataloged in

[105] This right is now contained in Article 14 of the 1974 Instrument of Government.

chapter two, however, was still greatly debated in certain circles. Those legal scholars in favor of a weak judicial system argued that Chapter Two rights should be more of a policy declaration, as were certain of the rights in chapter one—in essence, soft law—and not be meant to serve as a legal basis for a remedy. Instead, they should more serve as guidelines for the parliament in its legislative work, giving precedence to the principles of parliamentary rule and popular sovereignty.[106]

The economy had worsened by the end of the decade, and a conservative/liberal coalition government came to power in 1976—for the first time since 1932—and remained in power for six years. Amendments were made to the 1974 Instrument of Government as stated above. Some of the labor legislation was amended, but to the greater extent, the conservative government kept the 1970s legislative package. The Social Democrats came back to power in 1982, and one of the first employment issues raised was the creation of wage earner funds. LO proposed wage earner funds in order to increase workers' influence (through the unions) over the private sector through employee ownership exercised in the funds. A total of five funds were created, financed by taxes assessed at both the corporate profit and dividend levels. These monies were then used to buy up to 7–8 percent of shares on the Swedish stock market, with a limit of 8 percent of voting rights in any one company. The wage earner funds were controversial, seeing protests of 75,000 people in Stockholm in October 1983,[107] and the collection of more than one and a half million signatures in protest. Several companies left Sweden because of the wage earner funds, including Tetra Pak, IKEA, and H&M.[108]

THE 1990S AND FORWARD: EU MEMBERSHIP

The 1990s was another decade of economic distress, with the economy at its worst since the Great Depression in the 1930s. The Social Democrats were out of power from 1991 to 1994. One of the first actions taken by

---

[106] *See* Legislative Bill 1973:90 *med forslag till ny regeringsform och ny riksdagsordning* and Legislative Bill 1975/76:209 *om ändring i Regeringsformen.* The 1974 Instrument of Government was amended effective 2010, removing the former requirement that legislation was "manifestly" in conflict with the constitution, and Chapter 2 was extended to non-Swedish citizens.

[107] *See* NYCANDER, *supra* note 92 at 370.

[108] Another proposal was the Meidner Plan, investing union pension funds in the stock market, giving larger capital ownership to employees, and encouraging long-term investment in the economy. This plan was never adopted.

the conservative government was to liquidate the wage earner funds, distributing the monies across the public pension system and different research foundations. A banking crisis led to the deregulation of the Swedish crown, which eventually proved successful, and the economy grew stronger again.

The greatest change, however, was due to EU membership in 1995. Many Swedish laws were enacted or amended to be in conformity with the requirements of Union law. Particularly affected were the fields of human rights and discrimination protections. Though Sweden had ratified the European Convention in 1952, the Convention was not transformed into Swedish law until 1998, and then as a requirement of EU membership.[109] The Swedish protections against unlawful discrimination were also expanded, as to grounds as well as duty bearers. EU law as based on individual rights challenges the collective perspective upon which the Swedish labor law model is based, with several cases brought to the Court of Justice clearly demonstrating this clash.[110]

A conservative government came to power again in 2006, and changed the financing system for unemployment insurance. Government subsidies to the unions' unemployment insurance were reduced, increasing the unions' costs and entailing that the unions were forced in turn to increase members' fees to cover the actual cost of the insurance (as opposed to the former subsidized cost). The unemployment insurance fees were now also to be assessed based on specific union use as opposed to there being a universal charge, so that costs for unions paying out more unemployment insurance were greater than those for unions with low unemployment rates. For some unions, this resulted in

---

[109] Whether damages could be awarded under the Convention was debated as it contains no remedies provisions. The Swedish Torts Act (skadeståndslag 1972:207) was amended in 2018 to allow damages for violations of the Convention by the State or a municipality.

[110] One of the most telling is the Laval dispute in 2004. A Latvian company, Laval, had been hired to refurbish a school in the municipality of Vaxholm, and used Latvian workers. The Latvian company refused to sign a collective agreement with the Swedish Building Workers' Union, Byggnads. Industrial action was taken, and the issue raised was whether such action was in conflict with the freedom of movement of services. The case was before the Labour Court twice, AD 2004 no. 111 and AD 2005 no. 49. The second time it was sent for a preliminary ruling to the Court of Justice, C-341/05, Laval un Partneri Ltd mot Svenska Byggnadsarbetareförbundet, Svenska Byggnads-arbetareförbundets avd. 1, Byggettan, Svenska Elektrikerförbundet [2007]. The ECJ found the industrial action to be unlawful. The case was again brought to the Labour Court, AD 2009 no. 89, to determine the issue of attorneys' fees and damages.

a quadrupling of the monthly combined fees for unemployment insurance and membership charged to the members.[111] The tax deduction for individual union members was also abolished. As a result, union density decreased from 77 percent in 2006 to 69 percent by 2012,[112] mostly in the blue-collar sector. The subsidy was reinstated by the government in 2014 and the tax deductions for union membership fees in 2018. The employee membership loss over the past decade appears to have plateaued, as seen from the statistics in the years 2013–16, leaving about 2.8 million union members. In all, 70 percent of employees are union members, with almost 90 percent of all employees covered by collective agreements (despite there being no *ergo omnes* mechanism).[113] The number of organized employers in that same period increased by 10 percent to 90 percent in 2012.[114]

The historical timeline from the demise of the guilds to self-regulation of the labor market by the Swedish social partners was a little over 50 years. The guilds were outlawed by 1864, and by 1906 the social partners had entered into a collective agreement that laid the foundations for the present-day Swedish labor law model characterized by strong employer and employee organizations acting as cartels, a model not too dissimilar to the former guild structures. The pragmatic approach of the social partners and the very detailed procedural structures in place with respect to negotiations and industrial actions have resulted in very few working days being lost due to strike—2,570 in 2017.[115] The current challenges

---

[111] For example, the Theater Union monthly fee went from SEK 99 in 2006 (with a 25 percent tax deduction) to SEK 412 in 2013: see Anders Kjellberg, *Växande avgiftsskillnader i a-kassan—och utvecklingen därefter*, 2014(1) STUDIES IN SOCIAL POLICY, INDUSTRIAL RELATIONS, WORKING LIFE AND MOBILITY. RESEARCH REPORTS 16 (Lund University 2014).

[112] *See* Medlingsinstitut (Swedish National Mediation Office), AVTALSRÖRELSEN OCH LÖNEBILDNINGEN 2015—MEDLINGSINSTITUTETS ÅRSRAPPORT 42 (Linköping 2015).

[113] *See* Medlingsinstitut (Swedish National Mediation Office), AVTALSRÖRELSEN OCH LÖNEBILDNINGEN 2016—MEDLINGSINSTITUTETS ÅRSRAPPORT 217 (Linköping 2017).

[114] *See* Medlingsinstitut (Swedish National Mediation Office), SIFFROR OCH DIAGRAM OM MEDLEMSANTAL, ORGANISATIONSGRAD OCH KOLLEKTIVAVTALSTÄCKNING (2014) available at the website of the Medlingsinstitut, mi.se.

[115] *See* Medlingsinstitut (Swedish National Mediation Office), Årsrapport för 2017 (2018) available at the Medlingsinstitut website, mi.se.

facing the Swedish labor law model mostly come from the outside, in the form of international and EU requirements as to individual rights that are to be met by the collective rights approach—a tension discussed further in Chapter 10.

6. Labor in the United States: the Court is king

Thomas Paine claimed that "[I]n America the law is king."[1] The history of labor in the United States demonstrates instead that the Court is king—particularly during the period in which labor was struggling to find an identity, and even more so when unions began asserting rights. Though the timeline was much shorter, European guild structures found their way to the colonies, with guilds or journeymen's associations in many cities. However, the conditions of labor in the colonies were radically different, with constant acute labor shortages and solutions found in slavery, servitude, and immigration.

Industrialism came to the United States piecemeal, starting with the northern states in the mid-eighteenth century. Immigration was actively encouraged during and directly after the Civil War and increased exponentially thereafter. American trade unionism, in the form of the first successful umbrella organization, the American Federation of Labor ("AFL"), was very much an extension of the journeymen's associations, with a focus on craftsmen and skilled labor in specific sectors. Strikes were numerous and involved violence not only from employees and employers, but also on the part of state and federal officials. There were four major strike waves in the 140 years after the Civil War: in 1877, 1919, 1933–43, and 1946. Across the period 1806–2006, more than 130 million workers engaged in at least 275,000 strikes.[2] The pre-New Deal courts consistently found against labor under Lochnerian analyses. It was not until the Great Depression in the 1930s that a government policy protecting workers was successfully defended before the Court, in part due to a presidential threat that resulted in the "switch in time that saved nine." The history set out in this chapter begins with the American colonies, tracing the path of organized labor up to the modern age.

---

1 *See* THOMAS PAINE, FROM THE WRITINGS OF THOMAS PAINE VOL. 1 (1774–1779) (Moncure Daniel Conway ed. G.P. Putnam's Sons, 1894).

2 *See* Aaron Brenner, *Introduction* in THE ENCYCLOPEDIA OF STRIKES IN AMERICAN HISTORY 4 (Aaron Brenner, Benjamin Day, & Immanuel Ness ed. 2015).

LABOR IN THE AMERICAN COLONIES

The efforts of the initial European settlers in the American colonies in the early seventeenth century were naturally focused primarily on survival in their newly adopted home. The strictly applied European demarcations between agriculture and trade, as well as one man–one trade, were not feasible in the face of constant labor shortages. Tradesmen (and women and children) divided their energies between skilled work and whatever opportunities arose offering the best return, from exporting to farming, lodging, and anything else that might be profitable.[3] In certain situations this expansion was not even voluntary, with impressment often used in the colonies for public and even, at times, private works.[4]

The different American colonies fell under the different jurisdictions of their European masters. Jamestown, Virginia was the first successful English colony, established in 1607. After the defeat of France in 1760, all 13 colonies came under the rule of England and its laws. The 1562 Statute of Artificers was applicable in the English American colonies until the founding of the United States.[5] Its enforcement, however, was characterized more by pragmatism than consistency. The labor shortages in the colonies resulted in higher wages for skilled craftsmen than was the case in Europe. Statistics vary as to amounts, but it is estimated that colonial workmen received real wages exceeding those of their English counterparts by anywhere from 30 to 100 percent. One 1694 report stated that labor costs in Sweden and Denmark were just one sixth of the New England prices.[6] These high colonial labor costs did not result in a labor glut, however, as the typical path for many colonialists was to work for wages ("nothing but a high price will induce men to labor at all") and, after a few years, take their savings, purchase land, and become farmers.[7] This pattern remained true even after the American revolution.

Attempts were made to regulate wages, similar to the 1349 English Act after the plague, but such restrictions were difficult to enforce. The Massachusetts General Court abolished one such attempt in 1631,

---

3 *See* SIMON MIDDLETON, FROM PRIVILEGES TO RIGHTS: WORK AND POLITICS IN COLONIAL NEW YORK CITY 2 (University of Pennsylvania Press 2006).

4 *See* RICHARD B. MORRIS, GOVERNMENT AND LABOR IN EARLY AMERICA 7 (Octagon Books 1975).

5 *See generally* SUSAN E. HIRSCH, ROOTS OF AMERICAN WORKING CLASS—THE INDUSTRIALIZATION OF CRAFTS IN NEWARK 1800–1860 (University of Pennsylvania Press 1978).

6 *See* MORRIS, *supra* note 4 at 45–46.

7 *See* APPLEBAUM, *supra* chap. 1 note 8 at 418.

ordering that "the wages of carpenters, joyners, and other artificers and workmen … shall nowe be lefte free and att libertie as men shall reasonably agree."[8] Total freedom was problematic, though, and was quickly replaced by a struggle which lasted decades, attempting to balance wages and the prices of goods. The first organized work stoppage came as early as 1636 in Richmond Island, Maine, and was undertaken by fishermen to protest the withholding of wages.[9]

The labor structures of the different European states were recreated in the colonies to varying degrees. One of the truest examples of the European guild structure in the colonies was in New Amsterdam, now Manhattan, New York. The tradesmen there waged a successful campaign in the 1650s, including strikes, to obtain the "ancient" Dutch freedoms in trade as under Roman Dutch law, which burgher right was granted in 1657.[10] The tradesmen were granted the right to self-police their respective trades, uphold the quality of goods, set prices, train apprentices, accept members, and assist members during periods of sickness and in old age. An apprenticeship system developed as a result, covering training in the trade and often education in literacy and numeracy. In exchange for these rights, the tradesmen agreed to provide certain goods regardless of market conditions, and to contribute to municipal works. This New Amsterdam agreement was based on the systems in Amsterdam, Leiden, and Utrecht. It transformed the city from a fledgling, minimal economy to a thriving community in just over a decade.[11] In the same spirit, a 1659 strike was conducted by master bakers over low prices. Much of this guild/burgher system was retained when the British took over New Amsterdam and it became a part of New York in the 1660s. However, the apprenticeship system gradually changed in the subsequent decades. By the early eighteenth century, it had become an alternative way to manage the poor, "a facade for labor agreements and the putting out of orphans and paupers, in which the provision for the induction into craft skills and mysteries figured

---

[8] *See* MORRIS, *supra* note 4 at 58 *citing* Massachusetts Bay Record I, 84.

[9] *See* BRENNER, *supra* note 2 at xvii.

[10] The Burgher right was denied to persons of color, giving rise to explicit racial distinctions with respect to employment and eventually relegating them, regardless of whether they were free or slave, to the lowest forms of work in New Amsterdam: see MIDDLETON, *supra* note 3 at 144. As to concerted action by white workmen against black artisans, see MORRIS, *supra* note 4 at 182–83: "According to John Adams, the resentment of white labor toward Negro slaves was an important influence in the abolition of slavery in New England."

[11] *See* MIDDLETON, *supra* note 3 at 37–40 and 45.

scarcely at all."[12] New York City cartmen were the first to be sentenced for criminal conspiracy with respect to a strike in 1677.[13]

The very strong identity of the tradesmen in New York, as confirmed first under burgher's rights in the 1650s and later by the racialization of certain work as demeaning during the early 1700s, gave rise to a group identity of craftsmen in the American colonies that was in many ways similar to the English labor aristocracy. During the recession in New York in the 1730s, tradesmen became politically active: "Every cobbler can judge, as well as a stateman … whether he is paid for his work … and whether when a dragoon or parish officer come to him for taxes, if he pay up."[14] The structures set up in terms of burgher's rights in New York paved the way for civic organizations such as lobbying groups and fire brigades, as well as being seen as the forerunners to nineteenth-century trade unions. Combinations of employers for the purposes of trade monopolies, price fixing, and control of the labor market were more common in colonial times than combinations of journeymen, and were basically left untouched by the law.[15] Friendly societies, also known as Box Clubs, included masters as well as journeymen. In return for a monthly fee, each member was entitled to sick benefits.[16]

The same rise in skilled labor occurred in the other colonies, but not to the same geographical extent or with the same set of privileges as in New Amsterdam. In other locations, when guild-like privileges were granted, they were often for specific sectors, for limited periods of time, and in trades seen as being of public interest. Sector examples of licensed trades with granted monopolies include porters, carmen, coopers, butchers, and bakers, such licenses spanning colonial times and continuing after the revolution. These licensed trades acted in concert, petitioning and even striking to enforce their demands for higher wages or product prices.[17] Charters were granted in 1648 for the Boston Shoemakers' Guild and the Coopers of Boston and Charlestown. These included privileges reflecting those of their English counterparts: the rights of self-government and self-policing in the form of electing their own officers, enacting regulations for their trade and affixing penalties for breaches, and levying fines after a trial before the masters and wardens of the guild. The guilds

---

[12] *Id.* at 159.
[13] *See* BRENNER, *supra* note 2 at xvii.
[14] *See* MIDDLETON, *supra* note 3 at 204.
[15] *See* MORRIS, *supra* note 4 at 193.
[16] *Id.* at 198.
[17] *Id.* at 156–66.

were granted a monopoly, having the power to "suppresse" shoemakers or coopers not approved of by the guilds within their respective geographic areas. Three interesting limitations were included in the grant, however: a time limitation of three years, and prohibitions against unlawful combinations to raise prices and against refusing to make goods at a reasonable rate for customers providing the materials. Neither of these charters were renewed after their expiration.[18] A group of journeymen tailors working in New York went on strike in 1768 to protest wage reductions.[19]

LABOR IN THE UNITED STATES

Combinations of mechanics, laborers, masters, journeymen, merchants, and professionals began protesting British rule in the 1760s. The maritime sector organized the Sons of Neptune, who were at the heart of the 1765 New York insurrection in protest against the British Stamp Act. The Sons of Liberty organized that same year under the motto "No taxation without representation," orchestrating the Boston Tea Party. Both these groups included masters and journeymen. The 1770 Boston Massacre was in part caused by a labor dispute due to British quartered soldiers seeking outside work at lower wages, outcompeting the Boston craftsmen.[20]

The different pre-revolution combinations continued after the war. Artisans were commonly referred to as mechanics, encompassing masters, journeymen, and apprentices, and carried significant political weight.[21] The Federal Society of Journeymen Cordwainers was founded in Philadelphia in 1794 and was a union for leather workers and cobblers; it later became involved in the *Pullis* case discussed below.[22] Mutual benefit societies, such as the Newark Ladies' Shoe and Men's Pumpmakers Benevolent Society founded in 1820, provided both employers and employees with insurance, death, and unemployment benefits. Certain collective benefits for workers' actions existed: the shoemakers in

---

18 *Id.* at 139–40.

19 *See* BRENNER, *supra* note 2 at xvii.

20 *Id.* at 190.

21 In Philadelphia in 1772, 1,682 of the 3,350 taxable males were artisans: see Gary B. Nash, *Artisans and Politics in Eighteenth-Century Philadelphia* in THE ORIGINS OF ANGLO-AMERICAN RADICALISM 162 (Margaret Jacob and James Jacob eds. London 1984).

22 *See* LEESON, *supra* chap. 2 note 63 at 96.

Pullis received support during their strike, and in 1809 the New York Society of Printers gave monies to two workers who were fired for refusing to work for less than established prices.[23]

The expectation of apprentices was that with age, experience, and hard work, they would become self-employed masters. Education was seen as an important component in this transition, and societies were founded to support such endeavors, such as the Newark Mechanics Association for Mutual Improvement in the Arts and Sciences. Apprentices who completed their studies, or who simply decided they were ready, moved directly to a position of master due to shortages of labor.[24] Early on, journeymen were rare and viewed with suspicion as they were not working as masters. This changed rapidly, however. For example, in Boston in 1790, there were eight master carpenters for each journeyman; by 1815, the journeymen were the majority. In New England, wage labor was the exception in the urban trades prior to 1800; by 1820 it was the rule. Increasing reliance on technology also changed the conditions of work, with the "American System" of interchangeable machine parts developed by Eli Whitney and others allowing workers to focus on one aspect of production as opposed to the entire craft.[25]

The early American journeymen's associations had close ties to their English counterparts, sharing experiences, tactics, and goals. The "juridical responses they provoked likewise reproduced English practice."[26] Beginning with *Pullis* and the Journeymen Boot and Shoemakers of Philadelphia in 1806, the American courts began to use the English common law doctrine of criminal conspiracy to restrain journeymen associations.[27] These journeymen were convicted of criminal combination and conspiracy to raise their wages.

Journeymen's associations were active in the different parts of the country on different issues, but there was no cross-sector labor movement prior to the 1820s.[28] The "Ten-Hour Day Movement" began in Philadelphia, with an 1827 strike composed of workers in different trades striking

---

23 *See* GEORGE MILTON JANES, THE CONTROL OF STRIKES IN AMERICAN TRADE UNIONS 88 (Johns Hopkins Press 1916).

24 *See* TOMLINS, *supra* chap. 2 note 1 at 111.

25 *See* APPLEBAUM, *supra* chap. 1 note 8 at 417.

26 *See* TOMLINS, *supra* chap. 2 note 1 at 113.

27 Commonwealth v. Pullis (Philadelphia, Pa., Mayor's Court 1806), also known as the Cordwainers' case. The full case can be found in JOHN R. COMMONS & EUGENE A. GILMORE, A DOCUMENTARY HISTORY OF AMERICAN INDUSTRIAL SOCIETY, VOL. 3 59–248 (New York 1910–11).

28 *See* TOMLINS, *supra* chap. 2 note 1 at 152.

for a ten-hour work day. The workers created a city central organization, the Mechanics' Union of Trade Associations, which gave rise to the political labor party called the Working Men's Party. This strike is seen as the "awakening" of the modern American labor movement.[29] Similar independent working men's parties were formed in New York and Massachusetts, gaining support also from artisans and farmers.[30] They all canvassed the same issues: equal, general, and publicly funded education to allow full participation as citizens; simplification of the legal system to allow access to justice; lien laws to protect working classes from victimization by capitalists; the abolition of all chartered monopolies, particularly banks; the abolition of compulsory militia duty; and the abolition of imprisonment for debt and prison labor.[31]

An 1820 strike by canal workers saw the first experience of state intervention. Journeymen's associations were beginning to be viewed as agitators by those in power, while the journeymen perceived themselves—given the active role they had had in the revolution and in the creation of American society—as continuing the role of revolutionary republicanism, "the very axis of society."[32] This tension became marked in the 1830s, with previously unknown levels of vehemence and rancor. The panic and depression of 1837 put an end to joint master/journeymen ventures in Newark.[33] Craftsmen and all Newarkers had divided along class lines by the 1860s, beginning to live according to wealth rather than trade. A split occurred within the crafts, with masters joining the bourgeoisie and journeymen and apprentices falling more into the group of laborers.[34]

THE RISE OF TRADE UNIONISM

United federations of craft unions began to appear on the eastern seaboard during the 1830s. The first, the New York General Trades' Union, was established in 1833 by 12 craft associations, and quickly

---

29 *See* JOHN R. COMMONS, DAVID J. SAPOSS, HELEN L. SUMNER, E.B. MITTELMAN, H.E. HOAGLAND, JOHN B. ANDREWS, & SELIG PERLMAN, HISTORY OF LABOUR IN THE UNITED STATES, VOL. I, 25, 169 (New York 1918).

30 *See* APPLEBAUM, *supra* chap. 1 note 8 at 419.

31 *See* BRUCE LAURIE, ARTISANS INTO WORKERS: LABOUR IN NINETEENTH CENTURY AMERICA 50–51, 63 (New York 1989).

32 *See* TOMLINS, *supra* chap. 2 note 1 at 125.

33 *See* HIRSCH, *supra* note 5 at 88.

34 *Id.* at 98.

began to regulate strikes: "no Trade or Art shall strike for higher wages than they at present receive, with the sanction of the Convention."[35] The Trades' Union of the City and County of Philadelphia was founded that same year, and by 1834 it had 17 affiliates comprising a total of 6,000 organized journeymen. Delegates from these newly formed federations met in 1834 to create the National Trades' Union: "What better means can be devised for promoting a more equal distribution of wealth, than for the producing classes to *claim,* and by virtue of union and concert, *secure* their claims to their respective portions" and thereby establish "the honor and safety of our respective vocations upon a more secure and permanent basis."[36] Asserting rights was best done through combinations and associations among the mechanics and laboring poor, and the right to form any society or association was seen as a constitutional one. Laws against combinations were argued by these employee organizations as being unconstitutional.[37] President Martin Van Buren facilitated the settlement of a strike by shipyard workers, the first government-mediated labor settlement. In 1840, he signed an executive order providing for a ten-hour workday for employees on federal public works projects, stating: "The 10 hour system, originally devised by mechanics and laborers themselves, has by my direction been adopted and uniformly carried out at all public establishments."[38]

American legal scholarship began addressing employment in terms of the employer and the employed in the 1830s, creating a universal paradigm covering all legal relationships in which one party is routinely subjected to the controlling authority of another in a labor exchange.[39] Apprenticeship and agency were treated as specific exceptions to this basic paradigm. The British legal category "master and servant" was subordinated. The legal relationship between employer and employee was entirely contractual, freely entered into by parties of equal bargaining positions, with the contracts then enforced by the courts. Employees were

---

[35] *See* JANES, *supra* note 23 at 11 *citing* J.R. COMMONS & H.L. SUMNER, DOCUMENTARY HISTORY OF AMERICAN INDUSTRIAL SOCIETY, VOL. V 218 (Ohio 1910).

[36] *See* TOMLINS, *supra* chap. 2 note 1 at 158, Ely Moore, New York GTU President, "Address Delivered before the General Trades' Union" at 290–1, emphasis in the original.

[37] *Id.* at 159.

[38] *See* THEODORE WINTER REEDY & JOHN MOFFETT BRUMM, BRIEF HISTORY OF THE AMERICAN LABOR MOVEMENT 7 (U.S. Govt. Print. Off. 1951).

[39] *See* for example TIMOTHY WALKER, AN INTRODUCTION TO AMERICAN LAW 243 (Philadelphia 1837).

bringing cases against employers for workplace injuries as early as the mid-1800s.[40]

Almost 35 years after the judgment in *Pullis* finding criminal conspiracy in a labor combination, Chief Justice Lemuel Shaw held that a union's actions were not a criminal conspiracy in *Commonwealth v. Hunt* (1842).[41] The court found that the objectives of the union, and the action taken of threatening to stop work to prevent Horne's continued employment, were not unlawful under Massachusetts law; consequently, there was no conspiracy regarding a criminal act. The union could exercise "a power which might be exerted for useful and honorable purposes, or for dangerous and pernicious ones." Only if an independently unlawful act could be found, which was clearly laid down in the law, could a combination of people to do the same thing be unlawful. Shaw pointed out that competition among businesses was often treated in the same way, and so the economic loss to the employer or Horne could not count as actionable damage. The workers were "free to work for whom they please, or not to work, if they so prefer … We cannot perceive that it is criminal for men to agree together to exercise their own acknowledged rights, in such a manner as best to subserve their own interests." This judgment rejected the British law of criminal conspiracy that had been in existence, in some form, since the 1304 conspiracy act. The standard now applied as to whether criminal conspiracy existed was if the purpose or means to achieve the purpose were criminal.

Voting reforms beginning in the 1820s entailed that universal white male suffrage was the norm by the 1850s.[42] Trades' Unions, Trades Assemblies, or Trades and Labor Councils became more common. Stable unions were established in the 1850s and 1860s, with the printer's union, the National Typographical Union, becoming the first national union in 1852.[43] New York's trade unions were considered role models by other states. Trade unions were still more state-based at this

---

[40] *See* for example Barnes v. The Boston & Worcester Railroad Corporation, Suffolk County Court of Common Pleas, Oct. term 1837.

[41] *See* Comm. v. Hunt, 35 Mass. (4 Merc.) 111 (1842) distinguishing the Cordwainers' case of 1806 and the English precedent creating criminal conspiracy with respect to workers in England in 1721, in King v. The Journeymen Tailors of Cambridge, 8 Mod. 11 (Nov. 7, 1721) where the court found the actions of the tailors to be a criminal conspiracy.

[42] ROBIN ARCHER, WHY IS THERE NO LABOR PARTY IN THE UNITED STATES? 74 (Princeton University Press 2007).

[43] *See* JANES, *supra* note 23 at 13. The printers were also one of the first trade unions in Sweden, dating from 1846.

time, with effective nationalization beginning only after the Civil War.[44] Conciliation and arbitration were being used to resolve labor disputes by the mid-nineteenth century, with the Benevolent and Protective Spinners' Association of New England stating in its constitution in 1858 that one of its objectives was "to prevent strikes through the medium of arbitration."[45]

THE GILDED AGE 1870–1900

The first federal governmental policy promoting greater immigration was adopted during the Civil War, and remained in place up to World War I.[46] Immigration doubled in the 1870s, with many individuals coming from Southern Europe and working in unskilled and semi-skilled occupations. The new immigrants were perceived as a threat by the established unions, undermining worker rights by accepting work for which they were not qualified ("green hands") at lower wages and under poorer work conditions. In certain sectors, unionized labor was entirely replaced by green hands.[47]

After the Long Depression of 1873–78, which saw an unemployment rate of 20 percent and a drop in wages of 45 percent, the existence of city-based Trades Assemblies became more permanent. Millions of workers took to the road looking for work, referred to as the "tramp problem." During the wave of railway strikes in 1877, referred to as the Great Strike of 1877 or the Great Upheaval, President Rutherford B. Hayes made the decision to send federal troops in to forcibly break the strikes.[48] The strike ultimately involved more than 100,000 individuals and lasted 45 days. More than one hundred people died, hundreds were injured, thousands were jailed, and property worth more than five million dollars was destroyed in this first significant national labor dispute. The year after, Congress forbade the use of federal troops without authorization by either the constitution or Congress.

---

44 *See* COMMONS, *supra* note 29 at 620.

45 *See* JANES, *supra* note 23 at 29.

46 *See* GWENDOLYN MINK, OLD LABOR AND NEW IMMIGRANTS IN AMERICAN POLITICAL DEVELOPMENT: UNION, PARTY, AND STATE, 1875–1920 17 (Cornell University Press 1986).

47 *Id.* at 33. Between 1880 and 1920, 23.5 million immigrants entered the United States.

48 *See* John P. Lloyd, *The Strike Wave of 1877* in THE ENCYCLOPEDIA OF STRIKES IN AMERICAN HISTORY 177 (Aaron Brenner, Benjamin Day, & Immanuel Ness eds. 2015). *See also* APPLEBAUM, *supra* chap. 1 note 8 at 420.

Trade unions grew rapidly after the Great Strike. Craft unions established the Federation of Organized Trades and Labor Unions of the United States and Canada in 1881, the predecessor of the AFL, launched in 1886. Unskilled and semi-skilled workers also began to organize, particularly in mining and railroad industries, but the American union movement was still dominated by a closed model of craft unionism similar to the guild structures.[49] In contrast to the British movement of new unionism in the 1880s, AFL President Samuel Gompers opted for high dues and high benefits, discouraging broad unions and instead preserving trade lines: "[T]he history of the labor movement points to no one thing more clearly than this fact, that it is the manifest duty of the workers to organize in the unions of their trades and pay high dues into their unions."[50] Another aspect of the decision to restrict membership was the desire to keep new immigrants from becoming part of the union ranks. The AFL consistently argued for legislation restricting immigration.[51]

None of these different national systems existed in a vacuum, and Gompers was well versed in the writings of Karl Marx, at one time personally appealing to Friedrich Engels for support.[52] The 1893 AFL political convention voted against establishing a labor party, with Gompers stating that "[w]e shall reward labor's friends and punish its enemies."[53] Lacking any serious contenders, Republicans dominated politics until the Great Depression. Up to the 1890s, the American unions frequently looked to the legislative political process to achieve certain goals.[54] However, in the wake of the 1890s strikes, including the 1894 Pullman national railroad strike,[55] a wave of judicial antipathy began to

---

[49] *See* ARCHER, *supra* note 42 at 37.

[50] *Id.* at 35, *citing* AFL President Samuel Gompers, *Cheap John Unions*, AMERICAN FEDERATIONIST, 223, 226, February 1896. Gompers not only founded the AFL, he was also its president from 1886 to 1924, making him one of the most influential—if not the most influential—individuals in the American labor movement. He also headed the committee that drafted the ILO charter.

[51] *See* MINK, *supra* note 46 at 116.

[52] *See* ARCHER, *supra* note 42 at 221.

[53] *See* WILLIAM B. GOULD IV, A PRIMER ON AMERICAN LABOR LAW 2 (5th ed. Cambridge, 2013).

[54] *See* ARCHER, *supra* note 42 at 93.

[55] The strike involved 18,000 strikers in Chicago protesting a 25–33 percent cut in wages and George Pullman's refusal to lower the rents in his company town. A total of 14,929 police and troops were called in to end the strike, with 13 workers killed. All the union leaders as well as 705 workers were arrested. Nationwide, 150,000 workers participated in the strike, 52,000 state and federal

emerge that would not be reversed until the New Deal in the 1930s. The 1893 Sherman Antitrust Act,[56] intended to curb corporations' monopoly power, was interpreted by the courts to apply to combinations of workers.[57] Injunctions against unions were issued by the courts under the Interstate Commerce Act, despite the fact that Congress had explicitly rejected its application to labor. Labor injunctions on the penalty of imprisonment for contempt of court enabled the courts to directly suppress most employee collective action through broad prohibitions based on the Sherman Antitrust Act, the Interstate Commerce Act, or the need to prevent future damage to an employer's expectations.[58] Parallel to the judicial hostility to employee collective action, state action protecting employers against employees became more commonplace, with the military often called in to end disputes. Disenfranchised with the legislative route, as the courts had the power to interpret, override, or ignore the intended application of legislation, the labor unions' strategy changed. Strengthening the economic position of workers in the marketplace by building the strongest possible organizations was the focus, in order to be able to force concessions directly from employers.

---

troops were called in by President Cleveland, and 25 workers were killed. Property damage exceeded $80 million. See DAVID RAY PAPKE, THE PULLMAN CASE: THE CLASH OF LABOR AND CAPITAL IN INDUSTRIAL AMERICA. LANDMARK LAW CASES & AMERICAN SOCIETY 35–37 (University Press of Kansas 1999). Six days after the Pullman strike ended, legislation was pushed through Congress by President Cleveland to establish a federal holiday, Labor Day. Another effect of the strike was the passage of the Erdman Act in 1898, which facilitated unionization in the railroad industry and was the precursor to the Railway Labor Act: see DOUGLAS E. RAY, CALVIN WILLIAM SHARPE, & ROBERT N. STRASSFELD, UNDERSTANDING LABOR LAW 11 (LexisNexis 1999).

[56] The Sherman Antitrust Act of 1890 (26 Stat. 209) codified at 15 U.S.C. §§ 1-7.

[57] *See* for example, Vegelahn v. Guntner, 167 Mass. 92 (1896), with the court finding that the employees conducting a blockade had committed a tort. Justice Oliver Wendell Holmes dissented, arguing that the use of (non-violent) collective force by employees was comparable to the corporate use of force to compete: "[o]ne of the eternal conflicts out of which life is made up is that between the effort of every man to get the most he can for his services, and that of society, disguised under the name of capital, to get his services for the least possible return. Combination on the one side is patent and powerful. Combination on the other side is the necessary and desirable counterpart, if the battle is to be carried on in a fair and equal way."

[58] *See* for example In re Debs, 158 U.S. 564 (1895) with respect to the 1894 Pullman strike.

Equality of workers, however, was not universal, and the workers' movement still made internal distinctions based on sex and race. In 1894 the American Railway Union rejected a recommendation to open union membership to all and voted to restrict its membership to white persons only, instead creating an auxiliary organization for African-Americans.[59] In the 1890s, the AFL formally denied affiliation to unions that excluded black people. However, if the union charter did not explicitly restrict membership to only whites, the AFL was not critical if in practice only they were allowed as members. Some unions were open in the 1890s, such as the United Mine Workers Unions, but segregation became the rule after the United State Supreme Court's acceptance of apartheid in the 1892 *Plessy v. Ferguson* decision.[60] A minority group falling outside any pretense of protection was that of Chinese Americans. AFL President Gompers published a pamphlet in 1901 entitled "Meat vs. Rice: American Manhood v. Asiatic Coolieism, Which Shall Survive?" to support the extension of the Chinese Exclusion Act of 1882. With its subsequent extension in 1902, the act barred all Chinese people from American citizenship through naturalization.

CONSERVATIVE TRADE UNIONISM 1900–1930

After the 1894 Pullman strike, and given its dissatisfaction with the Democratic Party, the AFL began to work with the Republicans in office. The National Civic Federation ("NCF") was founded in 1900 and remained in place until 1920, comprising chosen representatives of business and organized labor, as well as consumer advocates, for the purpose of resolving labor disputes through peaceful mediation. Though it had no success with the 1902 anthracite strike, President Theodore Roosevelt intervened, not a court, and mediation was the method chosen, not calling in federal troops.[61] The NCF recognized collective agreements as the cornerstone of industrial self-government.[62] These twin pillars of NCF labor policy, mediation and collective agreements,

---

[59] *See* ARCHER, *supra* note 42 at 52.

[60] Plessy v. Ferguson, 163 U.S. 537 (1896) (separate but equal public transportation facilities are not an unconstitutional violation of the fourteenth amendment of the U.S. Constitution).

[61] *See* MINK, *supra* note 46 at 175.

[62] *See* Frank Julian Warne, *The Trade Agreement in the Coal Industry*, 36 AMERICAN ACADEMY OF POLITICAL AND SOCIAL SCIENCES ANNALS 86–95 (September 1910).

allowed the AFL to remain on its course of conservative trade unionism. The AFL opposed social welfare proposals, such as workmen's compensation and unemployment insurance, as well as protective employment legislation regarding wages and hours laws for men.[63] Protective legislation concerning women was acceptable as it minimized competition for male jobs. The AFL argued that the unions should provide social welfare provisions, but at this time most American unions did not and could not provide such benefits themselves. The AFL continued its policy of restrictive immigration.

The American Socialist Party was founded in 1902; one of the most visible among its ranks was Eugene Debs, one of the leaders arrested in the 1894 Pullman strikes. Industrial Workers of the World was founded in 1905 in an attempt to organize all workers, not just the skilled craftsmen who were the focus of the AFL. By 1917, 184 of its members had been convicted of espionage and sedition.[64] Between 1902 and 1904 in the United States, 198 people were killed and almost two thousand injured in labor disputes.[65]

In its seminal decision in the 1905 case of *Lochner v. New York*, the Court struck down a New York law limiting the hours worked for bakers, finding that such protective legislation violated the federal due process clause and freedom of contract. *Lochner* was the first in a series of Court decisions up to 1938 striking down protective labor legislation, in what was referred to as the Lochner Era.[66] In *Danbury*

---

63 *See* MINK, *supra* note 46 at 186.

64 *See* MELVYN DUBOFSKY & FOSTER RHEA DULLES, LABOR IN AMERICA: A HISTORY 201 (8th ed. Wiley-Blackwell 2010). *See also* MELVYN DUBOFSKY, WE SHALL BE ALL—A HISTORY OF THE INDUSTRIAL WORKERS OF THE WORLD (1969).

65 *See* ARCHER, *supra* note 42 at 121.

66 *See* for example Lochner v. New York, 198 U.S. 45 (1905) (New York law limiting the number of hours a baker could work violated the fourteenth amendment's guaranteed "liberty of contract"); Coppage v. Kansas, 236 U.S. 1 (1915) (state law prohibiting yellow dog contracts violated due process guarantee of the fourteenth amendment); Hitchman Coal and Coke Co. v. Mitchell, 245 U.S. 229 (1917) (United Mine Workers was an illegal combination under the Sherman Antitrust Act and that the union violated the company's property rights when it tried to unionize mineworkers); Duplex Printing Press Co. v. Deering, 254 U.S. 443 (1921) (secondary boycott outside the injunction protections of the Clayton Act as they are not lawful/peaceful); American Steel Foundries v. Tri-City Trades Council, 257 U.S. 184 (1921) (picketing not protected under the Clayton Act as it is neither peaceful nor lawful); Truax v. Corrigan, 257 U.S. 312 (1921) (employers protected under the fourteenth amendment against state-level

Hatters,[67] three years later, the Court held that the Sherman Antitrust Act was applicable to labor unions. Secondary boycotts were found to be a violation of the Sherman Antitrust Act, and the Court also determined that individual unionists could be personally liable for damages resulting from the activities of their union. As trebled damages could be awarded under the Sherman Act, the risks involved in findings of individual and personal liability for union members consequently became much higher. A new doctrine of civil conspiracy was then articulated by the courts, with a concomitant new deployment of labor injunctions.[68] One estimate is that more than two thousand such injunctions were issued by the courts in the decade of the 1920s, many of them *ex parte*.[69]

Unionization continued to expand, triggered by both technological demands and outright employer abuses. American employers faced with increased international competition sought to reduce production costs by introducing new production methods, wage incentives, and a systematic management movement referred to as Taylorism. Under Taylorism workers were viewed as cogs in a machinery that could be refined, giving rise to considerable backlash from employees. Flagrant abuses still existed, such as the 1911 Triangle Shirtwaist Factory fire which killed 146 workers, mostly female immigrants, as the building owners had locked the doors to prevent the workers from taking breaks. A strike in 1914 known as the "Ludlow Massacre" became another bloody labor dispute. The Colorado National Guard and company camp guards attempted to stop a strike organized by the United Mine Workers of America involving 1,200 striking coal miners and their families, and two dozen people, including miners and their wives and children, were killed. In retaliation, miners attacked dozens of mines over the next ten days, leading to an entire loss of up to two hundred lives. The owner of the mine, John D. Rockefeller, Jr., was widely criticized for the incident, and in the

---

limitations on labor injunctions, finding for the first time that unions are legal persons and consequently liable for damages); and United Mineworkers v. Coronado Coal Company, 259 U.S. 344 (1922) (unions legal persons under punitive framework of legal liability).

[67] Loewe v. Lawlor, 208 U.S. 274 (1908).

[68] *See* FELIX FRANKFURTER & NATHAN GREENE, THE LABOR INJUNCTION 82 (Macmillan Company 1930).

[69] *See* William E. Forbath, *The Shaping of the American Labor Movement*, 102 HARV. L. REV. 1109, 1249 (1988–89), tracing the progress from 105 injunctions issued in the 1880s, to 410 in the 1890s, 850 in the 1900s, 835 in the 1910s, and 2,130 in the 1920s.

following years he introduced an employee representation plan that came to be referred to as the Rockefeller Plan.[70] Congress responded to the public outrage regarding the strike and deaths, and an investigation by the House Committee on Mines and Mining led to the introduction of child labor laws and an eight-hour working day.

The Clayton Antitrust Act was adopted six months after the Ludlow Massacre, containing safe harbors for union activities.[71] Section 6 of the Act exempts labor unions and agricultural organizations,[72] saying that "[t]he labor of a human being is not a commodity or article of commerce":

> Nothing contained in the antitrust laws shall be construed to forbid the existence and operation of labor … organizations, instituted for the purposes of mutual help, and not having capital stock or conducted for profit, or to forbid or restrain individual members of such organizations from lawfully carrying out the legitimate objects thereof; nor shall such organizations, or the members thereof, be held or construed to be illegal combinations or conspiracies in restraint of trade, under the antitrust laws.

The British immunities system had officially crossed the Atlantic. The Clayton Act also addressed the issue of injunctions in its section 20, stating:

> no restraining order or injunction shall be granted by any court of the United States … in any case between an employer and employees … unless necessary to prevent irreparable injury to property, or to a property right, of the party making the application, for which injury there is no adequate remedy at law.

The wording of the section allowed for extensive judicial interpretation, and the Court found that secondary industrial actions were not protected under the act and that injunctions were still lawful.[73]

Another major strike focusing on the military industry took place in 1917, with one million workers engaged in 4,500 strikes around the country. President Wilson opted to use mediation again, this time through

---

70 *See* GREG PATMORE, WORKER VOICE—EMPLOYEE REPRESENTATION IN THE WORKPLACE IN AUSTRALIA, CANADA, GERMANY, THE UK AND THE US 1914–1939 (Liverpool University Press 2016).

71 The Clayton Antitrust Act of 1914 (Pub.L. 63–212, 38 Stat. 730). The Clayton Act, together with the Sherman Antitrust Act of 1890, regulates practices considered harmful to consumers (monopolies, cartels, and trusts).

72 15 U.S.C. § 17.

73 Duplex Printing Press Co. v. Deering, 254 U.S. 443 (1921).

the newly established Presidential Mediation Commission. The Commission, headed by Felix Frankfurter, concluded in its final report that workers and management needed to develop a "collective relationship" and that workers needed representation in the workplace.[74] Federal policies included eight-hour working days, equal pay for equal work, the right to join a union, an end to employers' unionbusting activities, and a living wage. Collective bargaining rights were promoted, allowing workers under governmental protection to negotiate for better pay and work conditions in legally binding contracts. In the absence of a recognized union, employers had to create shop committees of worker-elected representatives empowered to negotiate on behalf of the employees. By 1920 union membership had doubled from prewar numbers.

Fears of communism and radicalism infected perceptions of the labor movement, as did racism. The media claimed that the Bolsheviks were behind a 1922 strike in which 24 unionists died. Between 1919 and 1922, eight million workers participated in 10,000 strikes. Interpretation of the Clayton Act was still the province of the courts, who continued their Lochnerean, anti-union and anti-protective employment legislation campaign up to the 1930s and the New Deal.[75] The Republicans came to power, and union membership, which had doubled under President Woodrow Wilson, halved again. Unions remained in only a handful of industries by 1929. The Wall Street crash of 1929 commenced the Great Depression, and by 1932 almost 25 percent of the American workforce was unemployed.

THE 1930S AND THE NEW DEAL

The Great Depression of the 1930s forced a new approach to labor, with the Federal Government abandoning the liberal, probusiness approach that had dominated policy choices since the Civil War. Federal legislation, governmental agencies, and work programs were all instituted in order to create work, but also to improve workers' rights. Congress

---

[74] Randi Storch, Working Hard for the American Dream—Workers and Their Unions, World War I to the Present 18 (Wiley Blackwell 2013).

[75] *See*, for example, Hammer v. Dagenhart, 247 U.S. 251 (1918) (federal prohibition on the interstate sale of the products of companies employing children under the age of 14 unconstitutional); Baley v. Drexel, 259 U.S. 20 (1922) (federal tax on the profits of companies employing children unconstitutional); and Adkins v. Children's Hospital, 261 U.S. 525 (1923) (minimum wage legislation for women unconstitutional).

passed the 1932 Norris-LaGuardia Act ("Anti-injunction Bill")[76] barring federal courts from issuing injunctions against nonviolent industrial actions, in part to remedy the harm caused by the courts under the Clayton Act. The federal courts were not to be in the business of formulating rules to govern labor policy—the government was to be neutral, and this neutrality was expected to permit union growth.[77] The act also created protection for employees joining unions and outlawed employer "yellow dog" contracts by which it was required as a condition of employment that employees not join a union.

The National Industrial Recovery Act ("NIRA"),[78] the first New Deal legislation, was passed in 1933, allowing industry certain antitrust exemptions in return for guarantees of minimum wages and maximum hours, as well as a total ban on the use of child labor. Section 7a NIRA supported workers' rights to form unions and bargain collectively free from employer interference. More than 1.5 million workers went on strike in 1934. The Supreme Court ruled the NIRA unconstitutional in 1935.[79] Despite these setbacks, the 1935 National Labor Relations Act ("NLRA")[80] was passed, its declaration of policy stating that:

> Experience has proved that protection by law of the right of employees to organize and bargain collectively safeguards commerce from injury, impairment, or interruption, and promotes the flow of commerce by removing certain recognized sources of industrial strife and unrest, by encouraging practices fundamental to the friendly adjustment of industrial disputes arising out of differences as to wages, hours, or other working conditions, and by restoring equality of bargaining power between employers and employees …
>
> It is hereby declared to be the policy of the United States to eliminate the causes of certain substantial obstructions to the free flow of commerce and to mitigate and eliminate these obstructions when they have occurred by encouraging the practice and procedure of collective bargaining and by protecting the exercise by workers of full freedom of association, self-organization, and designation of representatives of their own choosing, for the purpose of negotiating the terms and conditions of their employment or other mutual aid or protection.

---

[76] Act of March 23, 1932 (Ch. 90, 47 Stat. 70) codified at 29 U.S.C. ch. 6.

[77] *See* Douglas L. Leslie, Labor Law in a Nutshell 4 (West Publishing 2000).

[78] Pub.L. 73–67, 48 Stat. 195.

[79] *See* Schechter Poultry Corp. v. United States, 295 U.S. 495 (1935).

[80] Also referred to as the Wagner Act, after its sponsor, New York Senator Robert Wagner. Pub.L. 74-198, 49 Stat. 449, codified at 29 U.S.C. §§ 151–69.

The NLRA guarantees the basic labor rights of freedom of association, collective bargaining, and representation. The act also set up the National Labor Relations Board ("NLRB"), which has the mandate of enforcement.[81] The Social Security Act was also passed that year, providing retirement and unemployment insurance.[82] The Fair Labor Standards Act ("FLSA")[83] was enacted in 1938, setting out maximum working hours (44 hours a week originally, then 40 by 1941), overtime pay, minimum wages, and significant restrictions as to the use of child labor. Despite this legislative progress, 18 Americans died in 1937 fighting for unionization in the steel industry, ten in the Chicago Memorial Day massacre.

Both management and the AFL were opposed to the NLRA and the Board it created.[84] Dissatisfaction with the AFL's conservative approach led to the 1935 founding within the AFL of the Committee for Industrial Organization. The Committee broke away in 1938, becoming the Congress of Industrial Organizations ("CIO"). The CIO concept was that of a labor organization based on industry and not crafts—in essence, new unionism. Unions in the CIO would represent all workers in industry, from the least to the most skilled, and including women and minorities, in such unions as the United Auto Workers, the United Steelworkers, and the United Rubber Workers. In addition to the pressure exerted by the CIO, the AFL suffered setbacks due to organized crime within the Teamsters.

---

[81] The constitutionality of the NLRA was brought up before the Supreme Court. However, the Court had begun its departure from the Lochner approach already with West Coast Hotel Co. v. Parrish, 300 U.S. 379 (1937), upholding Washington's minimum wage law as being in the state's special interest to protect health and consequently not a constitutional violation of freedom of contract. This case led to the witticism "[t]he Switch in Time that Saved Nine." Continuing down this new path, the Court found the NLRA a constitutional exercise of Congressional power in National Labor Relations Board v. Jones & Laughlin Steel Corp., 301 U.S. 1 (1937).

[82] Social Security Act of 1935 (Pub.L. 74-271, 49 Stat. 620) codified at 42 U.S.C. ch. 7.

[83] Also referred to as the Wages and Hours Bill, codified at 29 U.S.C. ch. 8.

[84] An interesting parallel can be drawn here with the Swedish unions' dissatisfaction with the 1928 acts concerning collective agreements and the labor court.

THE 1940S, WORLD WAR II AND THE PRESENT

The Court held in 1941 that lawful labor union activities are not to be criminally prosecuted under the Sherman Act

> [s]o long as a union acts in its self-interest and does not combine with nonlabor groups, the licit and the illicit under § 20 [under the Clayton Act] are not to be distinguished by any judgment regarding the wisdom or unwisdom, the rightness or wrongness, the selfishness or unselfishness of the end of which the particular union activities are the means.[85]

War led once again to mobilization requirements. President Roosevelt issued Executive Order 8802 Fair Employment Practice in Defense Industries in 1941, prohibiting discrimination by federal defense contractors based on race, creed, color, or national origin. The Court found in 1944 that the

> Railway Labor Act imposes on a labor organization, acting by authority of the statute as the exclusive bargaining representative of a craft or class of railway employees, the duty to represent all the employees in the craft without discrimination because of their race, and the courts have jurisdiction to protect the minority of the craft or class from the violation of such obligation.[86]

This case established the duty of fair representation by unions, in essence the duty to deal fairly on behalf of all of a bargaining unit's employees, both union and nonunion.

One third of all American workers—14.5 million individuals—belonged to unions by 1945.[87] Congress passed the 1947 Taft-Hartley Act,[88] setting out unfair labor practices that can be committed by either employers or unions, including strikes concerning work assignments, unlawful strikes, political strikes, mass picketing, secondary action, closed shops, and political donations by unions. Union officials had to swear that they were not Communists. States were allowed to have even stricter rules regarding union activities in the form of right to work laws, preventing unions from demanding that employers fire workers refusing to join the union. Employers could now deliver antiunion messages.

---

[85] United States v. Hutcheson, 312 U.S. 219 (1941) 232, Justice Frankfurter writing for the Court.

[86] Steele v. Louisville & N. R. Co., 323 U.S. 192 (1944).

[87] *See* STORCH, *supra* note 74 at 104.

[88] Also known as the Labor Management Relations Act, 1947. Pub.L. 80-101, 61 Stat. 136 codified at 29 U.S.C. ch. 7.

Unions also had to give 80 days' notice of the intent to negotiate under the act. The act is seen as being more deferential to management.

The AFL and CIO merged in 1955. Congress passed the Landrum-Griffin Labor Management Reporting and Disclosure Act of 1959 ("LMRDA"),[89] which requires pension and welfare fund administrators to report regarding funds. The ingress of the act begins with the statement:

> from recent investigations in the labor and management fields, that there have been a number of instances of breach of trust, corruption, disregard of the rights of individual employees, and other failures to observe high standards of responsibility and ethical conduct.

The act contains a bill of rights of labor organizations' members, including protections for equal rights, freedom of speech, and assembly, as well as rules concerning dues, initiation fees, and assessments. Rules regarding secret elections and financial reporting are included. Extortionate picketing is made criminal, and unlawful disciplinary measures by unions or deprivations of member rights are sanctioned.

Title VII of the 1964 Civil Rights Act was passed in part as a tribute to the slain American president John F. Kennedy.[90] Title VII prohibits employment discrimination based on race, color, religion, sex, and national origin, and was later extended to include age (1967)[91] and disability (1990).[92] The Equal Employment Opportunity Commission ("EEOC") has the task of enforcing the law. Under Title VII, labor organizations can be found liable for discrimination through an unlawful employment practice:

> (1) to exclude or to expel from its membership, or otherwise to discriminate against, any individual because of his race, color, religion, sex, or national origin;
>
> (2) to limit, segregate, or classify its membership or applicants for membership, or to classify or fail or refuse to refer for employment any individual, in any way which would deprive or tend to deprive any individual of employment opportunities, or would limit such employment opportunities or otherwise adversely affect his status as an employee or as an applicant for

---

[89] Pub.L. 86-257, 73 Stat. 519.

[90] Pub.L. 88-352, codified at 42 U.S.C. 1981.

[91] Age Discrimination in Employment Act of 1967 ("ADEA") (Pub. L. 90-202) codified at 29 U.S.C. §§ 621–4.

[92] The Americans with Disabilities Act of 1990 ("ADA") (Pub.L. 101-336, 104 Stat. 327) codified at 42 U.S.C. ch. 126 § 12101 et seq.

> employment, because of such individual's race, color, religion, sex, or national origin; or
>
> (3) to cause or attempt to cause an employer to discriminate against an individual in violation of this section.

This 1964 inclusion of labor unions as parties to be held liable for unlawful discriminatory behavior was viewed as a necessary component in the legal protection of employees against discrimination, as labor unions are gatekeepers with respect to the labor market.

The labor movement in the United States was faced with radically different challenges from those experienced by the movements in the United Kingdom, Germany, and Sweden. Immigration and race became issues very quickly, even before the founding of the nation. The journeymen structures were quickly embedded in the colonies, and by 1833 the first trade union had been founded. Depressions after the Civil War led to class strife, with the military often called upon and the outcomes in terms of lost lives high. American courts were highly active in industrial action, repressing union activity through injunctions. State action, discrimination, violence, and corruption also significantly mark the history of the union movement, and also led the American legislature to focus on issues other than those considered by its European counterparts. The duty of fair representation was judicially created as a counterpoint to racial discrimination within unions, creating a right to worker voice and union accountability as early as the 1940s.

7. International influences and congruences

Modern international efforts related to labor and particularly collective worker voice can be seen as having two phases: ad hoc national endeavors striving for international cooperation prior to World War I, and the stronger cohesive international and regional approaches espousing greater rights taken by the League of Nations, the International Labour Organization, and the United Nations in the aftermaths of two world wars.[1] The first initiatives with respect to voice and labor were made to end slavery, forced labor, and servitude. Legislation banning the slave trade was proposed in Great Britain as early as 1776,[2] and in passing the 1806 domestic ban Lord Grenville characterized slavery as contrary to the rights of nature, whereby "every human being is entitled to the fruit of his own labour."[3] Great Britain thereafter lobbied strenuously for the international abolition of the slave trade at sea, beginning with the Declaration on the Abolition of the Slave Trade by the 1815 Vienna

[1] For a longer historical overview, *see generally* MICHELINE R. ISHAY, THE HISTORY OF HUMAN RIGHTS FROM ANCIENT TIMES TO THE GLOBALIZATION ERA (2nd ed. University of California Press 2008) and SAMUEL MOYN, HUMAN RIGHTS AND THE USES OF HISTORY: EXPANDED (2nd ed. Verso 2017).

[2] Historically, Great Britain, Portugal, and France accounted for 90 percent of the Atlantic slave trade: see KEITH BRADLEY & PAUL CARTLEDGE, THE CAMBRIDGE WORLD HISTORY OF SLAVERY 583 (Cambridge University Press 2011).

[3] *See* JENNY MARTINEZ, THE SLAVE TRADE AND THE ORIGINS OF INTERNATIONAL HUMAN RIGHTS LAW 17 (Oxford University Press 2012). In Somerset v. Stewart, 98 ER 499 (1772), the English Court of King's Bench held that slavery was not recognized within Britain and consequently the status of "slave" as to any person brought into Britain was not recognized, with Lord Mansfield finding that the law favored freedom. Great Britain banned the slave trade partially with the 1788 (28 Geo. 3) c. 54 Slave Trade Act (Dolben's Act), and then completely with the 1807 (Geo. 3, Sess 1) c. 36 Slave Trade Act 1807. Slavery was outlawed in the UK and all its colonies by 1833. Canada was the first British colony to abolish slavery with An Act to Prevent the Further Introduction of Slaves and to Limit the Term of Contracts for Servitude within this Province in 1793.

Congress of Nations,[4] followed almost immediately by a series of bilateral treaties between Great Britain and other European nations for the purpose of ending the Atlantic slave trade.[5] Despite repeated efforts to eradicate slavery, in 2015 the United Nations estimated that 21 million individuals still live in slavery.[6]

PRIVATELY DRIVEN LABOR INITIATIVES IN THE NINETEENTH CENTURY

The origins of an international labor movement are traced to 1818 meetings of states at Frankfurter and Aix-la-Chapelle. Robert Owen, already active in British labor reform, argued unsuccessfully at both meetings that a prime task for American and European governments was the international setting by law of industrial conditions.[7] Daniel Legrand

---

[4] *See* JEAN ALLAIN, THE LAW AND SLAVERY, PROHIBITING HUMAN EXPLOITATION 4 (Brill 2015) *citing Declaration des 8 Cours, relative à l'Abolition Universelle de la Traite des Nègres*, Annex XV, 8 February 1815, BRITISH AND FOREIGN STATE PAPERS, VOL. 3, 972 (1815–16). The signatories were Austria, Britain, France, Prussia, Russia, Portugal, Spain, and Sweden–Norway.

[5] Great Britain was successful in negotiating bilateral treaties with Portugal (1810), Sweden (1813), Denmark (1814; it had already outlawed slave trade in 1792, effective 1803), France (1814, effective 1826), Spain (1814), The Netherlands (1814), and the United States (1814). Slavery was outlawed in these countries at different times, however: Portugal, 1761 domestically, 1858 in its colonies; Sweden, 1335 domestically, 1847 in all Swedish possessions; Denmark, 1846; France, 1848; Spain, 1811, including its colonies; The Netherlands, 1861; and the United States, 1865. German participation in the Atlantic slave trade is difficult to trace as Germany was not unified as a nation until 1871, but for information on Germany and the slave trade see Andrea Weindl, *The Slave Trade of Northern Germany from the Seventeenth to the Nineteenth Centuries* in EXTENDING THE FRONTIERS, ESSAYS ON THE NEW TRANSATLANTIC SLAVE TRADE DATABASE 250 (David Eltis & David Richardson eds. Yale University Press 2008).

[6] United Nations Secretary-General Ban Ki-moon, *Statement for the International Day for the Abolition of Slavery*, December 2, 2015, available at the UN website un.org: "Slavery has many modern forms, from the children toiling as domestic servants, farmhands and factory workers, to the bonded labourers struggling to pay off ever-mounting debts, to the victims of sex trafficking who endure horrific abuse."

[7] *See* ROBERT OWEN, TWO MEMORIALS ON BEHALF OF THE WORKING CLASSES: THE FIRST PRESENTED TO THE GOVERNMENTS OF EUROPE AND AMERICA, THE SECOND TO THE ALLIED POWERS ASSEMBLED IN CONGRESS AT AIX-LA-CHAPELLE (London 1818). *See also* BOUTELLE ELLSWORTH LOWE,

proposed European cooperation for industrial welfare again 20 years later, with a list of labor-related issues to be addressed internationally, including providing elementary schools, instruction for young workers up to confirmation, Sunday schools, Sunday rest, the encouragement of family life, universal savings banks, and old-age pensions, as well as prohibitions against child labor, excessive labor and night work.

The International Workingmen's Association was founded in London in 1864, with Karl Marx as a member of its General Council. Proposals were made at its first International Labor Congress, two years later in Geneva, regarding restricting child labor, working hour maximums, and the prohibition of night work, particularly for women.[8] The Second International in 1889 demanded a maximum eight-hour working day. The focus of these efforts was combating the worst working conditions and protecting the most exploited groups: children and women.

Cooperation between national trade unions began in the 1860s, with glovemakers in Germany, Austria, France, Denmark, and Sweden sending representatives to each other's congresses.[9] Unions covering several different occupations, such as the Amalgamated Engineers and tobacco, pottery, and glass workers, saw European and even American cooperation. International trade secretariats began to be founded in the late 1880s. The typographers, ever on the frontline, were involved in the creation of the first International Trade Secretariat in 1889, which also included hatters, cigarmakers, tobacco workers, and cordwainers.[10] The early trade union secretariats provided travel aid to journeymen, reciprocity of membership recognition, a clear guild heritage, while discouraging the international movement of strike-breakers. The international secretariats eventually devolved into two groups—trade secretariats with trade unions having manufacturing traditions, and trade secretariats

---

INTERNATIONAL ASPECTS OF THE LABOR PROBLEM 5–10 (Columbia University Press 1918).

[8] *See* GREBING, *supra* chap. 4 note 27 at 47. *See also* Marcello Musto, *Notes on the History of the International*, 28(2) SOCIALISM AND DEMOCRACY 5–38 (2014).

[9] *See* Leon A. Dale, *International Trade Secretariats*, 22(1) RELATIONS INDUSTRIELLES 98–115, 100 (1967).

[10] *See* THE INTERNATIONAL CONFEDERATION OF FREE TRADE UNIONS (Anthony Carew, Michel Dreyfus, Geert Van Goethem, & Rebecca Gumbrell-McCormick eds. Berne 2000). *See also* John P. Windmüller, Stephen K. Pursey, & Jim Baker, *The International Trade Union Movement* in COMPARATIVE LABOUR LAW AND INDUSTRIAL RELATIONS IN INDUSTRIALIZED MARKET ECONOMIES 76 (Roger Blainpain & Jim Baker eds. 10th ed. Wolters Kluwer 2010).

within branches or industries—in essence reflecting the divide between old and new types of unionism.[11]

The International Secretariat of Trade Union Centers, founded at the turn of the twentieth century, renamed itself the International Federation of Trade Unions. By the outbreak of World War I, it had 20 central trade union federations as affiliates, covering 7.7 million workers in Europe and the United States (through the American Federation of Labor), peaking shortly thereafter at more than 20 million workers. Several global international trade union federations still exist today, such as the International Trade Union Confederation ("ITUC"), with 340 national affiliates representing 181 million workers,[12] and Global Unions, with eleven international union federations as affiliates representing more than two hundred million workers.[13] The regional European Trade Union Confederation ("ETUC") was founded in 1973 and now has 89 national trade union confederations and ten European trade union federations, representing 45 million employees.

The turn of the nineteenth century saw various European countries engaging in greater international involvement in the social question of labor. International cooperation was, however, not easy to reconcile with national sovereignty. The first International Labor Conference was convened in 1890 in Berlin at the initiative of German Emperor Wilhelm II, addressing the work of women, children, and young persons; Sunday labor; and mining.[14] The International Association for Labour Legislation was founded in Paris in 1900 and its International Labour Office had the mission of publishing all countries' labor legislation in the French, German, and English languages.[15] The first of the labor proposals to result in concrete action concerning women's night work, the 1905 Berne

---

[11] *See* Petter Rütters, *International Trade Secretariats—Origins, Development, Activities* 9 (Library of the Friedrich-Ebert-Stiftung, library.fes.de, 2003).

[12] ITUC was founded in 2006 after a merger of two bodies, the International Confederation of Free Trade Unions and the World Confederation of Labour. ITUC traces its origins back to the First International Workingmen's Association.

[13] *See* David Huxtable, *A Most Curious Lack of Curiosity: Global Unions as the Missing Link* in Labour Movement Studies in SOCIETY OF SOCIALIST STUDIES 10 (2009).

[14] The countries represented were Germany, France, Austria–Hungary, England, Holland, Spain, Switzerland, Norway, Sweden, Portugal, Denmark, Belgium, Italy, and Luxembourg.

[15] *See* Report of the Committee of Experts, Report International Labor Conference 89th session 3 of the Report III (1B)-2001—Chapter 2, Anatomy of a Prohibition: ILO Standards in Relation to Night Work of Women in Industry 24 (ILO 2001).

Convention, entered into force as an international regulation in 1912.[16] It was hailed as "one of the most glorious pages in the social history of nations."[17] The 1906 Berne International Convention respecting the Prohibition of the Use of White Phosphorus in the Manufacture of Matches was agreed upon the next year.

WORLD WAR I AND THE ILO: A WILD DREAM

A protected right to collective worker voice and action was one of the founding principles of the International Labour Organization ("ILO"). The signatory nations to the Treaty of Versailles created the ILO in 1919 in recognition of the fact that "conditions of labour exist involving such injustice, hardship and privation to large numbers of people as to produce unrest so great that the peace and harmony of the world are imperilled."[18] The ILO Constitution was drafted by a Labour Commission chaired by AFL President Gompers and composed of representatives from Belgium, Cuba, Czechoslovakia, France, Italy, Japan, Poland, the United Kingdom, and the United States. A tripartite organization was created under the ILO Constitution, bringing together representatives of governments, employers and workers in its executive bodies. Inspiration for the constitution was gathered from the work done by the International Association for Labour Legislation.[19] President Franklin Roosevelt, discussing the origins of the ILO, reminisced:

> I well remember that in those days the ILO was still a dream. To many it was a wild dream. Who had ever heard of Governments getting together to raise the standards of labor on an international plan? Wilder still was the idea that the people themselves who were directly affected—the workers and the

[16] The signatories being Austria, Belgium, France, Germany, Great Britain, Italy, Netherlands, Portugal, Spain, Sweden, and Switzerland: see *id.* at 27. The ILO became a specialized agency of the United Nations after World War II in 1946, and currently has 185 members.

[17] *See* Report of the Committee of Experts, Report International Labor Conference 89th Session 27.

[18] *See* ILO, RULES OF THE GAME, A BRIEF INTRODUCTION TO INTERNATIONAL LABOUR STANDARDS 9 (ILO 2014).

[19] For this history, see the ILO website at ilo.org under the section "About the ILO and Origins and History."

employers of the various countries—should have had a hand with Government in determining these labor standards.[20]

Social partners acting in conjunction with states has since been a cornerstone of ILO governance. Six conventions were initially adopted at the first ILO 1919 meeting, creating international labor standards for industrial work hours, unemployment, maternity protections, minimum age requirements, and night work standards for young persons in industry and for women. The ILO Declaration of Philadelphia of 1944 explicitly stated that "labour is not a commodity," reemphasizing its human rights foundation.

The ILO's Governing Body has identified eight conventions as fundamental principles and rights at work, two of which concern collective worker action: the Freedom of Association and Protection of the Right to Organise Convention of 1948 (No. 87)[21] and the Right to Organise and Collective Bargaining Convention of 1949 (No. 98).[22] Many of the principles espoused in these conventions are reinforced by the 1998 ILO Declaration on Fundamental Principles and Rights at Work. The ILO's Governing Body has also designated another four conventions as priority governance instruments, thereby encouraging Member States to ratify them because of their importance to the functioning of an international labor standards system: The Labour Inspection Convention of 1947 (No. 81); the Employment Policy Convention of 1964 (No. 122); the Labour Inspection (Agriculture) Convention of 1969 (No. 129); and the Tripartite Consultation (International Labour Standards) Convention of 1976 (No. 144). The latter once again emphasizes the importance of employee voice in ILO decision-making procedures.

WORLD WAR II AND THE UN

On New Year's Day 1942, US President Franklin Roosevelt, UK Prime Minister Winston Churchill, USSR Ambassador Maxim Litvinov, and

---

[20] *See* GERRY RODGERS, EDDY LEE, LEE SWEPSTON, & JASMIEN VAN DAELE, THE INTERNATIONAL LABOUR ORGANIZATION AND THE QUEST FOR SOCIAL JUSTICE, 1919–2009 1 (ILO 2009).

[21] Convention No. 87 concerning Freedom of Association and Protection of the Right to Organise, adopted in San Francisco on July 9, 1948 and entering into force on July 4, 1950.

[22] Convention No. 98 concerning the Application of the Principles of the Right to Organise and to Bargain Collectively, adopted in Geneva on July 1, 1949 and entering into force on July 18, 1951.

Minister of Foreign Affairs for China Soong Tse-ven signed a short document known as the United Nations Declaration. Representatives of 22 countries still fighting the Rome–Berlin–Tokyo Axis signed the declaration the next day. The United Nations ("UN") was founded as an organization three years later by the signing of the Charter of the United Nations and the Statute of the International Court of Justice. The 1948 United Nations Universal Declaration of Human Rights ("UNDHR") was proclaimed by the United Nations General Assembly[23] as a common standard of achievements for all peoples and all nations, making clear that fundamental human rights are to be universally protected. Among these protected rights are both the positive and negative freedoms of association in Article 20 and the right to work in Article 23, including the specific right to form and join trade unions:

> (1) Everyone has the right to work, to free choice of employment, to just and favourable conditions of work and to protection against unemployment.
>
> ...
>
> (4) Everyone has the right to form and to join trade unions for the protection of his interests.

Twin instruments were adopted in 1966 to buttress and expand the UNDHR rights: the International Covenant on Civil and Political Rights ("ICCPR") and the International Covenant on Economic, Social and Cultural Rights ("ICESCR"). Freedom of association is protected in Article 22 ICCPR, with everyone having the right to freedom of association with others, "including the right to form and join trade unions for the protection of his interests." The right to work is recognized in Article 6 ICESCR, including the right of everyone to the opportunity to gain her living by work which is freely chosen or accepted. Rights to just and favorable working conditions under Article 7 ICESCR include fair wages and equal remuneration, safe and healthy working conditions, equal promotion opportunities, rest, leisure, reasonable working days, and paid holidays. The rights to form trade unions, to freedom of association, and to strike are set out in Article 8 ICESCR. This includes the right of trade unions to establish national federations or confederations and to join international trade union organizations, as well as to function free of restrictions other than those necessary in a democratic society in the interests of national security or public order, or for the protection of the rights and freedoms of others.

---

[23] United Nations General Assembly resolution 217 A.

THE COUNCIL OF EUROPE

The Council of Europe ("COE") was also established in the aftermath of World War II, again with the objective of ensuring lasting peace in Europe, to be achieved through the protection of human rights. The 1949 Treaty of London, signed by ten states—Belgium, Denmark, France, Ireland, Italy, Luxembourg, the Netherlands, Norway, Sweden, and the United Kingdom—is the COE's founding document. West Germany became the fourteenth member state in 1950.[24] The European Convention on Human Rights ("ECHR"), signed in 1950 by Sweden, Germany, and the United Kingdom, among others, protects freedom of assembly and association in its Article 11, interpreted as including the right to form trade unions.[25] Alleged violations of the ECHR are brought to the European Court of Human Rights in Strasbourg.

The European Social Charter of 1961 was drafted by the COE to strengthen the European Convention. Germany and Sweden ratified it in 1962; the United Kingdom in 1965. Part One of the 1961 Charter addresses worker protections, including freedom of association in national or international organizations for the protection of workers' economic and social interests and the right to bargain collectively.

The worker rights in the 1961 Social Charter were reaffirmed in the 1996 (Revised) European Social Charter, with the addition of 23 articles to Part One. A universal right to dignity at work is articulated in Article 26, which can be seen as overarching the entire body of worker rights. Worker voice is taken up in four of the new 1996 Charter articles. Under Article 21, workers have the right to be informed and to be consulted within an undertaking, and through Article 22, they have the right to take part in the determination and improvement of the undertaking's working conditions and working environment. Workers' representatives in undertakings have the right to protection under Article 28 against acts prejudicial to them, and should be afforded appropriate facilities to carry

---

[24] For more on the Convention, the European Council, and the Charters, see the Council's website at coe.int; for the European Court of Human Rights, see the Court's website at echr.coe.int.

[25] An implicit protection for trade unions has been read into Article 11 ECHR by the European Court of Human Rights in several cases, including National Union of Belgian Police v. Belgium, October 27, 1975, Eur. Ct HR Rep., Series A, No. 19 (1975); UNISON v. United Kingdom, judgment of January 10, 2002, [2002] IRLR 497; Enerji Yapi-Yol Sen v. Turkey, Application no. 68959/01 [2009]. *See* CATHERINE BARNARD, EU EMPLOYMENT LAW 718 (4th ed. Oxford 2012).

out their functions. All workers have the right to be informed and consulted in collective redundancy procedures, as articulated by Article 29. Sweden is the only one of the three European countries examined here that has ratified the 1996 (Revised) European Social Charter, which it did in 1998 when taking up EU membership.

Article 5 (Part II) of both the 1961 and 1996 charters addresses the right to organize "[w]ith a view to ensuring or promoting the freedom of workers and employers to form local, national or international organisations for the protection of their economic and social interests and to join those organisations." The Parties agree to undertake that "national law shall not be such as to impair, nor shall it be so applied as to impair, this freedom." Article 6 sets out the right to bargain collectively "[w]ith a view to ensuring the effective exercise of the right to bargain collectively." The Parties undertake:

1 to promote joint consultation between workers and employers;
2 to promote, where necessary and appropriate, machinery for voluntary negotiations between employers or employers' organisations and workers' organisations, with a view to the regulation of terms and conditions of employment by means of collective agreements;
3 to promote the establishment and use of appropriate machinery for conciliation and voluntary arbitration for the settlement of labour disputes;

and recognise:

4 the right of workers and employers to collective action in cases of conflicts of interest, including the right to strike, subject to obligations that might arise out of collective agreements previously entered into.

Both the European Convention and the European Social Charters have unique status in Union law, as will be discussed in the next section.

THE EUROPEAN COMMUNITIES AND UNION

The ultimate modern legal influence on the United Kingdom, Germany, and Sweden is European Union law. Originally formed after World War II to help maintain peaceful relationships between its Member States, the European Union has undergone radical and swift change in recent decades. In 1951 it consisted of six Member States—Germany, France, Italy, and the Benelux countries—while, as of 2018, there are 28 Member States covering more than five hundred million people in Europe. The United Kingdom became a member in 1973, and Sweden in 1995. The

UK held a referendum in 2016 resulting in a vote to leave the EU, which has come to be known as "Brexit," and Article 50 of the Lisbon Treaty regarding a UK withdrawal was triggered by the UK Prime Minister Theresa May in 2017. Despite Brexit, the current laws in the UK are still, and many most likely will remain for some time, consistent with the requirements of Union law.

Addressing social issues of any dimension was not uppermost in the minds of the drafters of the first of the treaties which ultimately established the European Union. The Treaty of the European Coal and Steel Community, signed in 1951,[26] created a common European market in coal and steel, the European Coal and Steel Community (the "ECSC"). Germany, France, and the Benelux countries agreed that "world peace can be safeguarded only by creative efforts commensurate with the dangers that threaten it," and that Europe could "be built only through practical achievements which will first of all create real solidarity, and through the establishment of common bases for economic development."[27] The Treaty establishing the European Economic Community ("EEC"), signed six years later, extended the market sectors from simply coal and steel to all economic sectors in the Member States. The EEC Treaty created a common economic market to be achieved by 1970 through the establishment of the four freedoms of movement of goods, persons, capital, and services.[28] A Social Policy Title was included, with common Community policies agreed upon in certain key areas to insure freedom of movement in the areas of agriculture, transportation, and commerce. A common market operating at maximum efficiency with the removal of all impediments was seen as benefiting everyone—consumers, workers, and employers alike—in turn improving the internal economies of the Member States.

---

[26] The Treaty establishing the European Coal and Steel Community was signed April 18, 1951, entered into force July 24, 1952 and expired July 23, 2003. The ECSC Treaty is not published in the official journals, for the text of this treaty as well as the others cited below, see the official website of the European Union, europa.eu.

[27] *See* the second and fourth paragraphs of the preamble to the ECSC Treaty.

[28] Also referred to as the Treaty of Rome. The EEC treaty is now referred to as the Treaty on the Functioning of the European Union ("TFEU") after the 2007 Treaty of Lisbon, one of the two remaining foundational treaties, the other being the Treaty of the European Union ("TEU"), formerly the 1992 Maastricht Treaty. The Treaty Establishing the European Atomic Energy Community ("Euratom") was also signed in 1957 by the original six members and the Euratom is the only remaining European community after the Treaty of Lisbon.

Despite the focus on economic markets, the principle of equal pay between men and women was included in Article 119 of the EEC Treaty.[29] France argued for the need to counteract social dumping—a reason with a strong economic basis. This market distortion caused by the lawfully unequal wages existing in certain countries was an impediment to the free movement of goods.[30] The Court of Justice gave Article 119 direct effect in *Defrenne II* both vertically and horizontally, laying the groundwork for the EU social platform.[31] In general, however, at this time the EU did not take any broad approach to employment or labor law issues, simply choosing narrow and selective topics to protect worker rights in particular vulnerable situations and in unlawful discrimination, redundancy, bankruptcy, and transfers of undertakings.

The Court of Justice was initially reluctant to address human rights, but by the 1970s it had begun to evaluate legal issues and treaty rights against a background of fundamental rights. The Court held that fundamental rights ranked as general principles of Community law based on two sources: the constitutional traditions of the Member States and the international treaties entered into by the Member States, particularly the ECHR.[32] The European Parliament, the Commission, and the Council signed a Joint Declaration in 1977 in which they undertook to continue to respect fundamental rights arising from these two sources as identified by the Court. The treaties began to mirror the fundamental rights jurisprudence of the Court, incorporating social and political areas. Article 6

---

[29] Now Article 157 TFEU.

[30] France has had legislation on equal pay since World War II, when it had one of the smallest pay gaps between women and men: 7 percent, as compared to up to 40 percent in Italy. France argued that it could not compete with the price of goods from countries in which women were paid less than men: see Catherine Barnard, EC Employment Law 23 (Oxford University Press 2000) *citing* Melitta Budiner, Le Droit de la femme a l'égalité de salaire et la Convention No. 100 de l'organisation internationale du travail (Librairie Générale de Droit et de Jurisprudence, Paris 1975). The drafting of Article 119 was also inspired by the ILO Convention No. 100, Equal Remuneration Convention of 1951: see Barnard, *supra* at 254.

[31] Not retroactively from 1962 but rather from the date of the judgment, 1976: see Case C-43/75, Gabriella Defrenne (No. 2) v. Societe Anonyme Belge de Navigation Aerienne Sabena [1976] 1 ECR-455 at para. 40. This nonretroactive application of Article 119 has been attributed to the Court's consideration of the arguments made by Ireland and the UK that retroactivity from 1962 would expose many employers to claims of unequal pay spanning more than a decade, forcing many employers into bankruptcy.

[32] *See* Case C-44/79, Liselotte Hauer v. Land Rheinland-Pfalz [1979] ECR-3727.

TEU states that the Union "is founded on the principles of liberty, democracy, respect for human rights and fundamental freedoms, and the rule of law, principles which are common to the Member States." The Union is to respect fundamental rights as guaranteed by the ECHR and as they result from the constitutional traditions common to the Member States, as general principles of Community law.[33]

Recognition of the 1961 Social Charter was first made timidly explicit in the Single European Act in 1987. The Community Charter of Fundamental Social Rights of Workers was adopted in 1989 by declaration of all the Member States (and thus was not binding), with the initial exception of the United Kingdom, which acceded to it in 1997. Under the 1989 Charter, the Member States agree to provide for the fundamental social rights of workers, including freedom of association and collective bargaining (Arts 11 to 14) and the right to information and consultation and participation for workers (Arts 17 to 18). Article 151 TFEU states that, having "in mind fundamental social rights such as those set out in the European Social Charter signed at Turin on 18 October 1961 and in the 1989 Community Charter of the Fundamental Social Rights of Workers," the Union and its Member States shall have as their objectives "the promotion of employment, improved living and working conditions, so as to make possible their harmonisation while the improvement is being maintained, proper social protection, dialogue between management and labour, the development of human resources with a view to lasting high employment and the combating of exclusion." Article 152 TFEU states that "[t]he Union recognises and promotes the role of the social partners at its level, taking into account the diversity of national systems. It shall facilitate dialogue between the social partners, respecting their autonomy."

The Charter of Fundamental Rights of the European Union ("EU Charter") also grants protections for worker voice. After a decade of drafting, the EU Charter became legally binding in 2009 through the 2007 Treaty of Lisbon. The Charter is to clarify the rights of EU citizens, not by establishing new rights, but rather by consolidating the rights already existing in other sources, including the EU treaties, the Court of Justice's case law, and the ECHR. The EU Charter's six titles have the objective of protecting dignity, freedoms, equality, solidarity, citizens' rights, and justice. Title IV on Solidarity contains several worker rights and protections. The freedom to choose an occupation and engage in work is provided by Article 15. Article 27 addresses worker rights to

---

[33] *See* Article 6(1) and (2) TEU, formerly Article F.2 EU Treaty.

information and consultation within the undertaking, stating that "[w]orkers or their representatives must, at the appropriate levels, be guaranteed information and consultation in good time in the cases and under the conditions provided for by Union law and national laws and practices." Collective action is protected in Article 28, Right of collective bargaining and action, in that:

> Workers and employers, or their respective organisations, have, in accordance with Union law and national laws and practices, the right to negotiate and conclude collective agreements at the appropriate levels and, in cases of conflicts of interest, to take collective action to defend their interests, including strike action.

Other individual worker rights include protection in the event of unjustified dismissal (Art. 30) and fair and just working conditions (Art. 31).

The growing awareness of the importance of access to justice issues can be seen in the development of Union law, particularly in the area of employment discrimination. While the Member States were initially given great discretion in choosing how to implement Community law requirements under the discrimination directives in the 1970s, under Union law there has been a greater requirement of access to justice for persons who have been discriminated against in the implementation measures taken by Member States. A shifted burden of proof was set out in Council Directive 97/80/EC of 15 December 1997 on the burden of proof in cases of discrimination based on sex, now incorporated in the discrimination directives, entailing that all Member States have to apply this burden of proof in national court cases.[34] There is now also a heightened requirement of real and effective compensation or reparation for loss and damage sustained by persons injured as a result of discrimination, in a way that is dissuasive and proportionate to the damage suffered. Another requirement is for Member States to have enforcement bodies as to these rights, and all of these are seen as necessary components for plaintiffs to successfully bring claims.

The progression from just a sole labor principle of equal pay, as was originally found in the 1957 Rome Treaty, to a broad understanding of

---

[34] The Court first invoked the shifted burden of proof in C-109/88, *Handels- og Kontorfunktionærernes Forbund i Danmark v. Dansk Arbejdsgiverforening, agissant pour Danfoss* [1989] ECR 3199, with the Burden of Proof Directive 97/80/EC following in 1997. For an assessment as to how the burden of proof is used at the EU and national levels, *see* European Commission, REVERSING THE BURDEN OF PROOF: PRACTICAL DILEMMAS AT THE EUROPEAN AND NATIONAL LEVEL (EU 2014), available at the website of the EU Commission, ec.europa.eu.

the importance of worker protections, worker voice, and access to justice as fundamental rights central to a functioning democracy can be easily traced in Union law. The focus of most EU rights is on the individual employee in areas such as unlawful discrimination, work environment health, employee rights in cases of bankruptcy, transfers of undertakings, and collective redundancies, with the articulated objective of increasing labor participation throughout Europe. Employee voice mostly still comes into play from the perspective of the individual employee, in terms of worker involvement in decision-making, information, consultation and participation, and freedom of association. Collective employee action is taken up in the forms of collective bargaining and industrial action, but these rights are necessarily balanced against the free movement of persons, establishment, and services. A good example of the difficulty in this balancing can be seen from several cases decided by the Court of Justice and referred to as the Laval quartet, in which the actions of unions were assessed against free movement.[35] A satisfactory balance between competition and social rights is arguably yet to be achieved within Union law.

THE ORGANIZATION OF AMERICAN STATES

The United States is not bound by the laws of the EU or the COE, but is a member of a regional organization addressing human rights protections, the Organization of American States ("OAS"). Its membership dates back to the founding of the OAS at its First International Conference of American States, held in Washington, DC in 1889/90. The 1948 OAS Charter addresses issues of social justice and the fundamental rights of

[35] *See* C-341/05, Laval un Partneri Ltd v. Svenska Byggnadsarbetareförbundet, Svenska Byggnadsarbetareförbundets avdelning 1, Byggettan and Svenska Elektrikerförbundet [2007] ECR I-11767; C-438/05, International Transport Workers' Federation, Finnish Seamen's Union v. Viking Line ABP, OÜ Viking Line Eesti [2007] ECR I-10779; C-346/06, Dirk Rüffert v. Land Niedersachsen [2008] ECR I-1989; and C-319/06, Commission v. Luxembourg [2008] ECR I-4323. *See also* Jonas Malmberg, Study—Directorate General for Internal Policies—Policy Department A: Economic and Scientific Policy, Employment and Social Affairs: The Impact of the ECT Judgments on Viking, Laval, Rüffert and Luxembourg on the Practice of Collective Bargaining and the Effectiveness of Social Action 13 (2010).

individuals.[36] Article XXII of the 1948 American Declaration of the Rights and Duties of Man protects the right of association with others to promote, exercise, and protect the "legitimate interests of a labour union." The 1948 OAS Charter was amended significantly by a 1967 protocol with a greater emphasis on social justice, setting out in its Article 7 the right to work under just, equitable, and satisfactory conditions and in its Article 8 both the positive and negative rights of association in trade unions.

A Social Charter of the Americas was adopted in 2012, with its Article 1 stating that the "peoples of the Americas legitimately aspire to social justice and their governments have a responsibility to promote it." To achieve social justice, there must be development with equity to strengthen and consolidate democracy, within a framework of solidarity, equity, peace, and freedom. Article 3 mandates that the Member States assume the responsibility "for achieving development with social justice for their peoples, thus contributing to strengthening democratic governance." The importance of cooperation and social dialogue among government representatives, workers, employers, and other stakeholders to promote good governance and a stable economy is stated in Article 8. Observance of the ILO 1998 Declaration of Fundamental Principles and Rights at Work is seen as fostering a quality workforce that drives economic and social progress, providing "a basis for sustained and balanced growth and social justice for the peoples of the hemisphere." Despite the United States' lengthy OAS membership, the organization has not had the same palpable influence on US law that can be clearly seen with the EU and COE and certain of their European members, including Germany, Sweden, and the UK.

Starting as ad hoc efforts by states and individuals to gain legal protections against slavery, indenture, and servitude, and later concerned with the conditions of workers more generally, international and regional efforts gradually evolved into strong cooperations motivated by the devastation caused by two world wars. Certain employee rights are now recognized as human rights on the international level by the UN and the ILO, and also on regional levels by the EU and COE, among others. The

---

[36] The OAS member states are: Antigua and Barbuda, Argentina, Bahamas, Barbados, Belize, Bolivia, Brazil, Canada, Colombia, Costa Rica, Chile, Dominica, Dominican Republic, Ecuador, El Salvador, Grenada, Guatemala, Guyana, Haiti, Honduras, Jamaica, Mexico, Nicaragua, Panama, Paraguay, Peru, Saint Kitts and Nevis, Saint Lucia, Saint Vincent and the Grenadines, Suriname, Trinidad and Tobago, United States of America, Uruguay, and Venezuela. For more information on the OAS see its website, oas.org.

rights recognized have also become more nuanced, having moved from the abolition of slavery and physically unsafe work conditions to now include issues of worker voice, and taking in not only the right to join unions, but also rights of consultation and negotiation. These different international and regional instruments comprise an additional background to the national systems discussed in Part II of this book.

PART II

The Modern National Labor Law Models

8. Employee voice in the United Kingdom

The United Kingdom has served as a forerunner in Western Europe with respect to almost every historical aspect of collective worker action, from the guilds in the early Middle Ages, to journeymen's associations, to the transition to individual laborers, to trade associations, and then to the trade union and cooperative movements in the nineteenth century. Despite this expansive history, UK labor law "has been subject to such multiplicity of changes, initiatives and reforms over recent years that presenting a coherent picture of its current pertinent features is a challenging task."[1] Labor law in the UK today is highly politicized, with certain themes consistently addressed in the legislation, weakening or strengthening the position of trade unions according to the policies of the government in power. These themes include the legal status of trade unions, the legal effects of collective agreements, the financing of the Labour Party by union member political levies, and the parameters of industrial action—all historically contested issues, each of which is taken up in the most recent legislation, the Trade Union Act 2016. The main legislation today comprising the UK labor law model in issues of employee voice is the Trade Union and Labour Relations (Consolidation) Act 1992 ("TULR(C)A"), most recently amended by the Trade Union Act 2016, the Employment Relations Act 2004, and the Employment Rights Act 1996.

THE LEGAL STATUS AND RECOGNITION OF TRADE UNIONS

The UK labor law model is based on a one-channel approach, that the trade union is to be the sole representative of the employees—the model articulated by the Webbs as early as the 1890s. This one-channel

---

[1] *See* Benjamin Jones & Jeremias Prassl, *United Kingdom* in RESOLVING INDIVIDUAL LABOUR DISPUTES 269 (Minawa Ebisui, Sean Cooney, & Colin Fenwick eds. ILO Geneva 2016).

approach contrasts, for example, with the two-channel approach in Germany, where there are both unions and works councils.[2] Section 1 TULR(C)A defines trade unions as organizations (temporary or permanent) broadly consisting mainly of workers, and whose principal purposes include the regulation of relations between workers and employers or employers' associations, or amalgamations of such employee organizations. The majority of trade union rights under the legislation are only given to "independent" trade unions, that is, unions certified by the Certification Officer as free from any type of domination or control by an employer or employer organization.[3]

Trade unions are not bodies corporate under the statute but are seen as having quasi-corporate status,[4] granted the statutory rights of entering into contracts and of suing and being sued in their own name for causes of action based on property, contract, or tort. A union can be liable for offenses committed by that union or on its behalf. Property owned by unions is held in trust, but a judgment can be executed against such property in the same manner as if the trade union were a body corporate. There are fairly detailed rules regarding union assets as well as union tort liability, with caps as to the damages that can be assessed against unions, with certain exceptions for personal injuries, breach of duties, or consumer matters. The system of immunities for trade unions developed during the nineteenth century as to lawful actions in restraint of trade was retained in TULR(C)A.

Despite the lack of legal requirements as to the registration of trade unions as corporate bodies, certain rights under TULR(C)A are tied to

---

[2] Germany's works councils served as a model for the European Works Councils under Directive 2009/38/EC of the European Parliament and of the Council of May 6, 2009 on the establishment of a European Works Council or a procedure in Community-scale undertakings and Community-scale groups of undertakings for the purposes of informing and consulting employees (Recast). The UK implementation of the Recast directive is the Transnational Information and Consultation of Employees (Amendment) Regulations 2010.

[3] A Certificate of Independence is issued under section 6 TULR(C)A by the Certification Officer for Trade Unions and Employers' Associations. Such certificates can only be sought by listed trade unions through an application to the Certification Officer and payment of a fee in the amount of £4,066 (2018). For information on the certification procedure, as well as the listed trade unions, see the Certification Officers website at gov.uk/government/organisations/certification-officer.

[4] *See* Hugh Collins, K.D. Ewing, & Aileen McColgan, Law in Context: Labour Law 495 (Cambridge University Press 2012).

the voluntary list of trade unions kept by the Certification Officer.[5] Trade unions and employer associations enjoy tax-exempt status only if they are listed with the Certification Officer.[6] This tax-exempt status in income is for the purposes of providing provident benefits and not related to trading income or gains.[7] Provident benefits include payments authorized by the association's rules and paid to members during periods of sickness, disability, or unemployment, or through a superannuation based on age, sickness, or disability. Trade unions are taxed on those profits derived from nonmember activities and investment income, but are entitled to deduct from these taxable profits certain costs that they incur when providing benefits to their members. Trade union members can deduct up to 67 percent of their trade union member subscription fees, including the political fund element.[8] However, the fees have to be paid to an approved listed professional organization in order to be eligible for tax relief.

Employer recognition of trade unions was historically voluntary, with no existing statutory recognition procedures until the adoption of the Employment Relations Act 1999. Before that, trade unions could not force employers to recognize them for collective bargaining. The statutory procedures under the Employment Relations Act 2004 allow for both a hybrid form of voluntary recognition and compulsory recognition. An independent trade union wishing to be recognized by an employer in the collective bargaining for a bargaining unit is to request such recognition in writing to an employer having at least 21 employees. This request must include the name of the union, define the bargaining unit, and explicitly state that the request is being made under "Schedule A1 TULR(C)A." The employer has ten days to respond to such a request. If the employer offers to negotiate, such negotiations must occur within 20 days.

---

[5] *See* section 2 TULR(C)A for the provisions concerning the listing of trade unions. Trade unions are to petition to be listed, paying a fee of £150 (2018) to the Certification Officer. The listing is public and available at the website of the Certification Officer at gov.uk/government/organisations/certification-officer.

[6] Employer associations can also be listed publicly with the Certification Officer under section 123 TULR(C)A. An employer organization is defined under the legislation as an organization of employers or individuals owning undertakings, or affiliations of such. Employer associations can be either corporate or quasi-corporate and have immunity for lawful acts that are in restraint of trade. Many of the regulations applicable to trade unions with respect to property and so on are equally applicable to employer associations.

[7] Section 981, Chapter 8, Corporation Tax Act 2010 (c. 4).

[8] Section 457, Chapter 6, Part 8 of the Income Tax Act 2007 (c. 3), *see also* gov.uk/tax-relief-for-employees/professional-fees-and-subscriptions.

In the event that the employer fails to respond to or refuses the request, or where the negotiations fail, the trade union can file an application with the Central Arbitration Committee.[9] This Committee oversees the recognition of trade unions and collective bargaining processes. Under the hybrid employer recognition form, the union files an application with the Central Arbitration Committee for recognition under the act. The employer can then concede to recognition by entering into an agreement for recognition that is binding on them for a period of three years.

The Central Arbitration Committee can only act on applications that are both "valid" and "admissible." The application is deemed valid where the trade union is an independent trade union as demonstrated by having a certificate of independence, the employer has at least 21 employees, and the union has made a written request to the employer seeking recognition explicitly under Schedule A1 TULR(C)A, including a proposed bargaining union. The application is admissible where the union has demonstrated that its application is proper and that the employer has been given proper notice, that the union has not filed any other application in the past three years for this bargaining unit, and that no existing recognition agreement exists for the bargaining unit. In addition, at least 10 percent of the workers in the proposed bargaining unit must be members of the union and the majority of workers in the proposed bargaining unit must most likely favor recognition of the union to conduct collective bargaining. In the event that another union is competing for recognition, the application must also state that the two unions will cooperate with each other if recognized.

If the Central Arbitration Committee finds that the application is valid and admissible, it will assist the parties within 20 days as to reaching an agreement. If no agreement as to a bargaining unit is reached, there is a 20-day period in which the Advisory, Conciliation and Arbitration

---

[9] The Central Arbitration Committee has its origins in the Industrial Court established in 1919. It is currently governed by TULR(C)A as an independent government tribunal under the Department for Business, Innovation and Skills. It works in panels of three: the chair or deputy chair, and one member from each of the social partners. The Committee's mandate includes: the statutory recognition of trade unions; the disclosure of information for collective bargaining; applications and complaints related to information and consultation arrangements; establishing and operating European works councils; complaints about employees' level of involvement in certain decisions covered by regulations related to European companies, cooperative societies, and cross-border mergers; and voluntary arbitration negotiations in collective disputes. More information about the Central Arbitration Committee is available at its website, cac.gov.uk.

Service ("Acas")[10] and the Committee can further assist with negotiations. The employer is to provide certain information about employees in the potential bargaining unit if so requested by the Committee. Failure by the employer to do so can result in the Committee determining the appropriate bargaining unit, taking into consideration the need for the bargaining unit to be compatible with effective management and also:

- the views of the employer and the union;
- existing national and local bargaining arrangements;
- the desirability of avoiding small fragmented bargaining units within the business;
- the characteristics of workers falling within the proposed bargaining unit and other relevant employees; and
- the location of workers.

The inquiry by the Committee is to start with the trade union's proposed bargaining unit, and, if appropriate, the case law states that the Committee need go no further except to the extent of considering the employer's objections.[11] In the event that the parties cannot agree as to recognition after these statutory periods, the Committee will hold a hearing, with both parties given notice and having the opportunity to submit written statements of the case.

After the bargaining union is established, the next issue is to determine whether a majority of the employees in the bargaining unit are members of the union. If the Committee finds this to be the case, it is to issue a declaration that the union is recognized as entitled to conduct collective bargaining on behalf of the workers in the bargaining unit. However, if the majority of employees in the bargaining unit are not members of the union, the Committee ought to arrange for a secret ballot of the relevant

---

[10] Acas traces its history back to 1896, when the government set up a voluntary conciliation and arbitration service. The name was changed to Industrial Relations Service in 1960 and to Conciliation and Advisory Service in 1972. In 1974, the body was renamed the Conciliation and Arbitration Service and separated from government control, with a governing independent council. "Advisory" was added back to the name in 1975 to reflect the fuller range of services. In 1976 Acas was made a statutory body by the Employment Protection Act 1975: *see* Acas website at acas.org.uk.

[11] *See* R v. Central Arbitration Committee and another ex parte Kwik-Fit (GB) Ltd [2002] IRLR 395 CA; and R (on the application of Cable & Wireless Services UK Ltd) v. Central Arbitration Committee and Communication Workers Union (interested party) [2008] IRLR 425 HC.

employees, asking whether they want the trade union to conduct collective bargaining on their behalf. The Committee can also hold a ballot where it finds that it would be appropriate in the interests of good industrial relations, or where there is credible evidence that a significant number of employees within the bargaining unit do not want this union to conduct collective bargaining on their behalf.

The secret ballot is also regulated by statute.[12] The employer must cooperate with the union and the "independent person" holding the ballot, giving the union reasonable access to the workers to inform them of the object of the ballot and to seek their support. The employer is also to give the Committee the names and home addresses of the workers in the bargaining unit and details of any worker who joins or leaves the unit during the conduct of the ballot. The employer is not to make an offer to any of the workers in the bargaining unit to induce them not to attend any relevant union meeting unless it is reasonable in the circumstances, or to take or threaten to take any action against a worker solely or namely because the worker has attended or taken part in any relevant union meeting.

Neither the employer nor the trade union is to use any "unfair practice" during the ballot.[13] Unfair practices include where a party:

- offers to pay money to a worker in return for the worker agreeing to abstain from the ballot;
- makes an outcome-specific offer to a worker;
- coerces or attempts to coerce a worker to disclose whether he or she intends to vote, or how he or she intends to vote or has voted;
- dismisses or threatens to dismiss a worker, takes or threatens to take disciplinary action against a worker, or subjects or threatens to subject a worker to any other detriment; or
- uses or attempts to use undue influence on a worker.

The union wins the ballot if supported by the majority of workers voting and at least 40 percent of the workers constituting the bargaining unit.[14] The cost of the ballot is to be borne by both the employer and trade union. If the employer obstructs the ballot, the Committee may declare

---

[12] Paras. 25–26, Schedule A1, TULR(C)A.

[13] Para. 27A, Schedule A1, TULR(C)A. *See also* the Department of Trade and Industry ("DTI"), Code of Practice, Access and Unfair Practices during Recognition and Derecognition Ballots (2005).

[14] Para. 29, Schedule A1, TULR(C)A.

the union has been recognized to conduct collective bargaining on behalf of the bargaining unit.

A derecognition ballot can also be held by the Committee in certain circumstances. These include where the employer no longer has at least 21 employees, where an employer believes the recognized union no longer has the support of the workers in the bargaining unit, or where fewer than half of the workers in the bargaining union are members of the union. Employees can also petition for derecognition in cases where they believe that the union no longer has the support of the workers in the bargaining unit.[15]

EMPLOYEE CONSULTATION

Employers are always free to invoke employee consultation in forms above the statutory minimum floor. By law, employers of 50 or more employees can be requested by their employees (as employees or through a trade union) to negotiate an agreement in respect of information and employee consultation.[16] Such employee request has to be "valid," entailing that it has to be presented in writing either individually or by a group, representing at least 10 percent of the employees in the undertaking. The request also has to be submitted to both the employer and the Central Arbitration Committee, specifying the names of the employees requesting the agreement.[17] Upon the receipt of a valid request, the employer is to facilitate a procedure for the employees to elect the

---

15 Paras. 101, 106, 128, and 112, Schedule A1, TULR(C)A.

16 These rules are under the Information and Consultation of Employees Regulations 2004 (SI 2004/3426), the UK implementation of Directive 2002/14/EC of the European Parliament and of the Council of 11 March 2002 establishing a general framework for informing and consulting employees in the European Community. No statutory obligation for employers to generally consult with employees existed prior to 2004: see Mark Hall, Sue Hutchinson, John Purcell, Michael Terry, & Jane Parker, *Promoting Effective Consultation? Assessing the Impact of the ICE Regulations*, 51(2) BRITISH JOURNAL OF INDUSTRIAL RELATIONS 355–81 (June 2013).

17 Specific information must also be disclosed to employee representatives by law, such as redundancies under TULR(C)A, transfers of undertakings under the Transfer of Undertakings (Protection of Employment) Regulations 2006, works councils situations under the Transnational Information and Consultation of Employees Regulations 1999, and with respect to pension schemes under the Occupational and Personal Pension Schemes (Consultation by Employers and Miscellaneous Amendment) Regulations 2006 (SI 2006/349).

representatives who are to enter into the negotiations concerning such an agreement. If the employer fails to commence negotiations or where the negotiations are unsuccessful, standard information and consultation provisions are to apply.

These standard provisions include a duty for employers to provide the employee information and consultation representatives with information as to:

- recent and probable developments of the undertaking's activities and economic situation;
- the situation, structure, and probable development of employment within the undertaking and on any anticipatory measures envisaged, in particular, where there is a threat to employment within the undertaking; and
- in general decisions likely to lead to substantial changes in work organization or in contractual relations.

Any consultation committee as set up under the agreement is to constitute a forum for all employees to exchange views and enter into dialogue with the employer as to changes in the working environment that may affect the employees. If a trade union fails to meet the 30 percent threshold for mandatory recognition of the trade union as to collective bargaining, the right of consultation with a 10 percent employee representation requirement provides a fallback position for the trade union to have access to the employer at least with regard to employee information and consultation.[18]

Statutory provisions also regulate the manner, time, and content of the information disseminated by the employer in order to ensure that the employees receive and can process the relevant information in due time. The regulation also imposes upon the parties a duty to work in a spirit of cooperation with due regard for their reciprocal rights and obligations, taking into account the interests of both the undertaking and the employees. Employee representatives have duties of confidentiality, a right to reasonable paid time off to perform the necessary functions, and heightened protection against employment detriments or unfair dismissals. Complaints as to employer failure to provide the required information are to be made to the Central Arbitration Committee, which can then order the employer to comply with the agreement or standard terms. Failure to comply with the order of the Central Arbitration

---

[18] *See* COLLINS ET AL., *supra* note 4 at 654.

Committee can be brought to an Appeal Tribunal, which can order a penalty fine not to exceed £75,000.

COLLECTIVE BARGAINING AND THE LEGAL STATUS OF COLLECTIVE AGREEMENTS

Collective agreements, as a rule, are currently not legally enforceable unless specifically made so in writing. UK trade unions typically do not support binding collective agreements, as these are perceived to create restrictions regarding the right to take industrial action. The legal technique used here instead is that the collective agreement can be given force through its incorporation (of those provisions applicable to individual employees) in the individual employment agreements of the workers covered by the collective agreement. This is seen to have the advantage that the union is able to negotiate new terms in a collective agreement after the date of the individual employment contract, with these new terms automatically becoming part of the latter agreement through incorporation. Because of this mechanism of incorporation, it is the employees who have standing to litigate claims as to violations of the collective agreement. The trade unions and employers are consequently free to engage in industrial action for violations of collective agreements. In other words, there is no duty of industrial peace between the social partners concerning collective agreements, in contrast to the system in effect in both Germany and Sweden.

The procedure for entering into a collective agreement is roughly as follows. After trade union recognition is established, either voluntarily or by ballot, the employer and trade union are to create a joint negotiating body to discuss and negotiate pay, hours, and holidays for the workers comprising the bargaining unit. No other body or group can negotiate these issues unless both the employer and the union agree to such.[19] Recognition status results in certain union benefits in the form of receiving information relevant to the negotiations and union officials receiving the entitlement to paid time off to carry out negotiations. Employers are also obligated to invite union representatives to biannual meetings to discuss employee training. Several different types of union

---

[19] For the procedures as to the actual collective bargaining, see Statutory Instrument 2000 No. 1300, Terms and Conditions of Employment, The Trade Union Recognition (Method of Collective Bargaining) Order 2000, in force as of 6th of June, 2000.

representatives are protected by statutory provisions: union representatives in collective bargaining; union learning representatives; union health and safety representatives; union equality representatives; union environmental representatives; union representatives dealing with individual grievance and disciplinary matters; information and consultation representatives; European works councils representatives; pension representatives; and representatives appointed during a transfer of an undertaking or a collective redundancy.

Collective agreements are defined as agreements or arrangements made by or on behalf of one or more trade unions and one or more employers or employers' associations and relating to one or more of the matters as specified in section 178(2) TULR(C)A. With respect to individual employees, these matters include the terms and conditions of employment; the physical conditions of the work; engagement, termination, or suspension of employment or employment duties as to one or more workers; the allocation of work; the duties of employment between workers or groups of workers; and matters of discipline. On the trade union level, these matters can include a worker's membership or nonmembership in a trade union; facilities for trade union officials; the machinery for negotiation and consultation; and other procedures relating to any of the above matters, including the recognition by employers or employers' associations of a trade union's right to represent workers in such negotiation or consultation or in the carrying out of such procedures.

INDUSTRIAL ACTION AND THE PEACE OBLIGATION

UK law starts from the premise that a strike is an unlawful breach of the employment contract by the striking employees.[20] The system of immunities created in the nineteenth century exempted certain "lawful" industrial actions first from criminal liability and then from civil tort liability. For a strike to be deemed lawful, the union must first notify the employer of the intent to conduct a strike ballot among the employees, no later than a week prior to the ballot. At least 50 percent of the employees entitled to vote must cast paper ballots on the strike question,[21] and then a majority

[20] *See* COLLINS ET AL., *supra* note 4 at 664.

[21] Given the extremely high thresholds of employee voting requirements after the Trade Union Act 2016, an independent review was conducted as to the use of electronic balloting to encourage greater member turnout. The results were set out in Sir Ken Knight's Electronic Balloting Review: The Report of the

of those voting must be in favor of the strike.[22] The employer must be notified of the result of the ballot and two weeks' notice of industrial action is to be given. Strike ballots are to be renewed every four months.

Immunities are granted to trade unions under TULR(C)A for a lawful strike committed in the contemplation or furtherance of a trade dispute and causing a third party to breach a contract. A trade dispute is one between workers and their employer related wholly or mainly to any of the matters listed above with respect to collective bargaining: briefly, the terms and conditions of employment; the engagement, termination, or suspension of employment or employment duties; the allocation of work; discipline; trade union membership; facilities for trade union officials; and negotiation and consultation procedures between the social partners.[23]

In the absence of immunity, the union is liable for any tort damages arising due to the industrial action, for example, by inducing breach of contract, interfering with the performance of a contract, intimidation, and/or conspiracy. Actions excluded from statutory immunity include those taken without proper notice or balloting, unlawful picketing, enforcing trade union membership, retaliation for dismissal for unlawful industrial action, secondary industrial action, and enforcing union recognition by third parties. The requirement of a "trade" dispute has entailed that political disputes are generally unlawful.[24] Unofficial strikes—those not sanctioned by the trade union—are as a rule unlawful. TULR(C)A also contains several criminal offenses resulting from unlawful industrial action, for example relating to breach of contract involving injury to persons or property, intimidation, or annoyance by violence or otherwise. Employees have protection against dismissal for the first 12 weeks of any lawful and official industrial action. Employees dismissed for taking part in an unlawful or unofficial strike or industrial action have no right to bring a claim for unfair dismissal.

Independent Review of Electronic Balloting for Industrial Action (December 2017). The review called for a test of e-balloting on non-statutory ballots as a preliminary step and the need for such to address voting procedures and response rates, cybersecurity issues, and the meeting of other statutory requirements.

[22] These rules have been in effect as of March 1, 2017 under the Trade Union Act 2016. With respect to important public services specified in the regulations—education, fire, health, transport and border security—at least 40 percent of those eligible to vote must approve the industrial action.

[23] Section 244(1) TULR(C)A.

[24] *See* COLLINS ET AL., *supra* note 4 at 672.

TRADE UNION MEMBERSHIP

Approximately one quarter of UK employees today are union members, with union density higher in the public sector (56 percent) than in the private sector (14 percent). About one third of the UK workforce is covered by collective agreements. There is only one trade union confederation, the TUC, comprising trade union members which represent almost six of the approximately seven million union members in the UK. Old and new unionism still exist, but the nature of the majority of unions is now new unionism in that they are industry-wide. More than half of the TUC trade unions (but not the TUC itself) are affiliated with the Labour Party. Affiliation entails that representatives of the trade unions are present and vote at Labour Party conferences and are represented on the Labour Party's executive committee. Trade unions are also the largest source of funding for the Labour Party, comprising more than 60 percent of its funding.[25] Decision-making concerning workplace issues has been kept at the trade union level instead of being delegated to the TUC.

The relationship between trade unions and their members is governed by statutory and case law, as well as internal union documents such as constitutions, charters, and rule books. The TUC's constitution is the governing instrument between this umbrella organization and its affiliate trade unions. According to its constitution, the TUC is to promote the interests of its affiliated organizations, equality for all, and the elimination of all forms of harassment, prejudice, and unfair discrimination, along with generally improving the economic and social conditions of workers in all parts of the world. The TUC is governed by a general council comprising ten sections, with requirements as to representation with respect to large, medium, and small trade unions; women; youths; lesbian, gay, bisexual, and transgender employees; and unionists with disabilities. The general council conducts the daily business of the TUC, monitoring industrial movement and coordinating industrial action where possible, while promoting common action on general questions.

The basic documents between the trade unions and their members are the trade union constitution and the contract of membership, the latter of which is often in the form of a rule book. These documents set out the organizational structure of the trade union and the rights and duties of the trade union and its members, and by law must be made publicly available. Trade unions are generally a form of representative democracy,

---

[25] *See* L. Fulton, Worker representation in Europe (Labour Research Department and ETUI 2013), available at the website worker-participation.eu.

with conferences of members held annually (sometimes less often), where policy decisions are taken and elections held. An elected executive committee or council is typically responsible for decision-making between conferences, with the daily operations carried out by union officers, a general secretary, and a deputy. These are typically the only full-time union officials and take many of the decisions affecting the trade union.[26] Local branches can exist within a trade union, usually with their own constitutions and rule books. For example, Leicester University and College Union, a branch of the University and College Union ("UCU") trade union, sets out the use of funds and governance of the branch in its constitution, including establishing different officers. One such officer is an equal opportunities officer, who is to monitor cases at the workplace involving equal opportunities issues, provide information to members, and negotiate.

MEMBER DUTIES TO TRADE UNIONS

Member duties to trade unions are found in the rule books. Under Section 174 TULR(C)A, union members can be disciplined or expelled from the trade union for violations of the rule book. One universal duty is that of members paying union dues. Otherwise, different lists of duties are found in the different union rule books. For example, under the UCU rule book,[27] in addition to the duty to pay member fees on penalty of suspension, members also have the obligation to abide by the rules, refrain from conduct detrimental to the interests of the union or from breaching the rules, and avoid all forms of harassment, prejudice, and unfair discrimination on the grounds of sex, race, ethnic or national origin, religion, color, class, caring responsibilities, marital status, sexuality, disability, age, or other status or personal characteristic. These obligations can in essence be seen as a duty of loyalty by the members to the trade unions, and also, in a sense, to their fellow union members. In contrast, Unite the Union's rule book includes as member duties the timely payment of contributions, compliance with the rule book, acting consistently with union policy when representing the union or submitting

---

[26] *See* COLLINS ET AL., *supra* note 4 at 502.

[27] *See* Rule 6, University and College Union Rules from 3 June 2016, available at the UCU website, ucu.org.uk.

motions, and not knowingly providing the union with false or misleading information.[28]

UNION DUTIES TO MEMBERS

Union duties to members are set out both by statute and by rule books. There are five broad statutory categories of members' rights which unions must respect: the rights for trade union members to access to information, to proper governance, to not be discriminated against in relationship to membership and the benefits of membership on unlawful grounds, to protection from unjustifiable discipline, and to be able to terminate membership on reasonable notice and compliance with reasonable conditions.

The right of trade union members to access financial information had its origins in the Trade Union Act 1871, but saw a brief hiatus under the Industrial Relations Act 1971. TULR(C)A requires trade unions to keep proper accounting records, including annual reports checked by auditors with statements to members, to be kept by the trade unions for a period of six years and made available for inspection by union members. A trade union member has the right to request access to such accounting, which is to be granted within 28 days. The member is to be allowed to be accompanied by an accountant and to make copies of the records inspected. The union accounting is also to be submitted to the Certification Officer, and the public is to have access to the trade union's annual returns. Any person has a right to request a copy of the union rules for free or at a reasonable cost.

Trade unions are generally to abide by the law as well as by their internal documents and may not act *ultra vires*.[29] Statutory governance requirements include holding secret ballots on certain issues, such as whether to strike. A secret ballot must be held for an industrial action to be deemed lawful. A member's access to the court in questions regarding ballots is not to be restricted by the union. Trade union funds are not to be used for political objectives unless a political resolution has been passed by members for such use of funds. The 2016 Trade Union Act introduced heightened requirements as to political levies, in that union members are to be asked whether they want to opt in to paying

---

[28] Rules 4 and 5 of Unite the Union Rule Book, Effective from Rules Conference 2015 (Approved by Executive Council September 2015), available at the Unite website, unitetheunion.org.

[29] *See* COLLINS ET AL., *supra* note 4; ELIAS & EWING, *supra* chap. 3 note 69 at 97.

contributions to the Labour Party, and then asked again every five years. Senior trade union officers and executive bodies are to be elected at least every five years, with every member having the right to participate in such election ballots. Every trade union member has the right to be a candidate and to receive member information in order to be able to conduct a campaign.

The statutory right not to be discriminated against in relation to membership and the benefits of membership entails that an employer cannot refuse to hire or fire an individual because of the existence or absence of union membership, or their refusal to become or decision to withdraw as a member. Contracts for goods or services cannot require union membership in the form of work being performed by members of trade unions generally or by specific trade union members. Trade unions are not to influence employers to take decisions based on membership. Trade unions can also be liable under Section 57 of the Equality Act 2010 for unlawfully discriminating against members on the basis of a protected ground, these being age, disability, gender reassignment, marriage and civil partnership, pregnancy and maternity, race, religion or belief, sex, and/or sexual orientation.[30]

Under the statutory protections, expulsion of a trade union member is lawful only in three broad categories of situations: member rule violations; lack of eligibility; and unprotected acts. The first concerns the situation in which a member has violated an enforceable membership requirement contained in the rules of the union. The second is where the member is either no longer geographically eligible or no longer works for the employer, where such employment is the basis of the membership. The last category of lawful member expulsion addresses wholly unprotected conduct, such as criminal activity during industrial action.

Union members have the right to not be unjustifiably disciplined by the union, as defined under Section 65 TULR(C)A. Discipline is defined as expulsion, fine, deprivation of services, refusal of membership by another trade union on the first's urging, or any other detriment. Unjustifiable discipline under the statute covers several different types of situations. As regards industrial action, unjustifiable discipline can be based on refusal to participate in or support a strike or other industrial action or failure to violate an employment term or contract during an industrial action. Other situations of unjustifiable discipline include asserting/whistleblowing that a union or union official has violated the rules of the union, a collective agreement, or a law; encouraging or assisting another person to perform

---

30 Part 5 Work, TULR(C)A.

an obligation imposed by a contract of employment; or failing to fulfill a requirement that would infringe the individual's or another's right not to be unjustifiably disciplined. Unjustifiable discipline can also be based on the failure to agree to wage deductions for union fees, resigning from the union or joining another or refusing to join another, or working with nonunion employees or for employers hiring nonunion employees. Finally, disciplinary action taken based on a member requiring the union to do an act which the union by law is required to do upon the requisition of a member is also unjustifiable.

Disciplinary and expulsion procedures must follow due process as set out by law, the trade union's internal documents, and the doctrine of natural justice.[31] Natural justice as articulated by the courts entails two main principles: that the person should have the opportunity to state their case (notice, time, and opportunity)[32] before a negative decision is issued, and that the decision should be made by an unbiased tribunal.[33]

Trade union rule books also typically set out trade union obligations toward members, including rights for members to attend, vote, and stand in elections; to receive copies of the rule book; and to be provided information and advice in professional and educational matters, as well as legal advice in certain cases. A caveat can exist in that legal advice is typically not provided by a trade union regarding actions taken without the union's prior consent.[34]

PURSUING EMPLOYEE GRIEVANCES

With respect to employee grievances against employers, recent legislative amendments attempted to change the thrust of employment dispute resolution from the employment tribunals to conciliation and mediation. Legislation in 2013 imposed a fee system on the previously free employment tribunals, with fees of up to £1,200 for bringing complaints, in order to redirect claimants toward using conciliation services. The impact of the new fee structure was dramatic, with the number of claims filed with the employment tribunals decreasing by 78 percent within one year.[35] Unison brought a case contesting this imposition of fees, and the

---

31 *See* ELIAS & EWING, *supra* chap. 3 note 69 at 212.

32 Annamunthodo v. Oilfield Workers' Trade Union [1961] AC 945.

33 Roebuck v. NUM (Yorkshire Area) No 2 [1978] ICR 676.

34 Rule 4, UCU Rule Book.

35 Ministry of Justice, Review of the Introduction of Fees in the Employment Tribunals—Consultation on Proposals for Reform (January 2017) 22.

UK Supreme Court ruled in 2017 that the tribunal fees impeded the constitutional right of access to justice that is fundamental to the rule of law, and consequently were unlawful.[36] The Court also pointed to the importance not only to individuals but also to society of litigating issues and developing the law. After the fees were removed, the number of employment tribunal cases rose by two thirds already by the third quarter of 2017.[37]

The first stage in an employee grievance procedure usually involves the employer's internal procedures. Acas has issued a statutory Code of Practice on Disciplinary and Grievance Procedures (2015) to provide guidance to employers, employees, and their representatives for handling disciplinary and grievance situations in the workplace. Though not binding on either employers or employees, the employment tribunals are legally required to take the Acas Code of Practice into account where relevant when hearing a case. A tribunal can adjust any award upwards or downwards by up to 25 percent for an unreasonable failure by either the employer or employee to comply with any relevant provisions of the code.

The Code of Practice clearly outlines that fairness and transparency must be present when dealing with employee grievance situations, including developing and applying easily accessible, specific, and clear rules and procedures set out in writing and drafted by both employers and employees. Grievances are to be raised and dealt with promptly and decided consistently, necessary investigations are to be carried out, and employees should be allowed to be accompanied at grievance meetings. If unsuccessful informally, employees are to raise the matter formally and in writing, without unreasonable delay, to a manager who is not the subject of the grievance, setting out the nature of the grievance.

The code sets out a fairly detailed procedure to be followed in formal hearings. Employers are to arrange for a formal meeting to be held without unreasonable delay after receiving the grievance. The employers, the employees, and their companions are to make every effort to attend the meeting, and employees should be allowed to explain their grievance and how they think it should be resolved. Employees have a statutory right to be accompanied by a companion at a grievance meeting dealing with a complaint about a duty owed by the employer to the worker (but not as to renegotiating contract terms). The companion can be a fellow

---

[36] *See* R (Unison) v Lord Chancellor [2017] UKSC 51.

[37] *See* Gavin Jackson, *Employment Tribunal Cases Rise Sharply after Fees are Dropped*, FINANCIAL TIMES, December 14, 2017, available at ft.com.

worker, a trade union representative, or an official employed by a trade union. The trade union representative has to be either employed by the trade union or certified as competent to accompany a worker and has a right to paid time off if with the same employer.[38] After the meeting the employer is to make a decision, which is to be communicated to the employee in writing without unreasonable delay, at the same time informing the employee of the right to appeal. Any appeal is to be dealt with by an impartial manager, and the worker again has the right to be accompanied. The outcome of the appeal is to also be notified to the employee in writing without delay.

Before filing a claim with an employment tribunal, claimants must first notify Acas of their intention to claim so that Acas can offer opportunities for early conciliation, mediation, or arbitration depending on the issue and the parties. About 30 percent of those who used this process in 2015 obtained a formal settlement.[39] If the case is brought to an employment tribunal, a qualified barrister or solicitor acts as the Employment Judge. Two other lay members representing the employer and employee sides can sit on the panel if so directed by the Judge.[40] Tribunals have an overriding statutory objective to deal with cases justly, which includes, so far as is practical, ensuring that the parties are on an equal footing, saving expense, dealing with a case in ways that are proportionate to the complexity or importance of the issues, and ensuring that the case is dealt with expeditiously and fairly.[41] The allocation of trial costs and fees does not follow the typical English rule of the losing party paying the prevailing party's costs and fees; rather, each party bears its own costs and fees, an allocation referred to as the American rule. In certain cases—where a party has acted vexatiously, abusively, disruptively, or otherwise unreasonably during the proceedings; or has made any claim in the proceedings which had no reasonable prospect of

---

[38] The right to paid time off for the trade union representative is in TULR(C)A and covered both in the Acas Code of Practice on time off for trade union duties and activities (2010) and the Acas Code of Practice on Disciplinary and Grievance Procedures (2015) and Acas Discipline and Grievances at Work: The Acas Guide.

[39] *See* Matthew Downer, Carrie Harding, Shadi Ghezelayagh, Emily Fu, & Marina Gkiza, Evaluation of Acas Early Conciliation 2015 65 (Acas 04/15), available at the Acas website, acas.org.uk.

[40] *See* the Employment Rights Act 1996, Employment Tribunals Act 1996, and Employment Rights Dispute Resolution Act 1998.

[41] *See* The Employment Tribunals (Constitution and Rules of Procedure) Regulations 2004 No. 1861, Schedule 1, The Employment Tribunals Rules of Procedure, Regulation 16.

success; or has failed to comply with an order—the tribunal can order the party at fault to pay the legal costs of the other party. Legal aid is available only for employment discrimination (human rights) claims and for those with a monthly income of less than £2,657 before tax and savings of less than £8,000.

The decision of an employment tribunal can be appealed to the Employment Appeal Tribunal ("EAT"). Appeals are limited to questions of law or situations where no evidence supports the facts as found. Cases are heard by an Employment Judge sitting alone, unless the Judge directs otherwise, in which case two lay members sit on the panel. The EAT can order the losing party to pay the prevailing party's fees. After the EAT judgment the issue can be appealed to the Court of Appeal and ultimately to the Supreme Court. Leave to appeal must be granted, and the original decision of the employment tribunal is the object of the appeal.

Union members can request legal assistance from their unions in the pursuit of employment grievances if such provisions exist in the rule book. Where a trade union provides such a type of claims management service, the union is to follow the Code of Practice for the Provision of Regulated Claims Management Services by Trade Unions of 2006.[42] There are six key standards to be followed by trade unions when providing these types of service. First, the union must give honest, impartial advice to members about whether to pursue a claim and, if pursued, the most appropriate method of doing so. Second, the union is to give members relevant information about the funding of their claim and about any relationship between the trade union and any third party (including a solicitor, claims management company, or any other agency) where such a relationship has a direct bearing on the handling of a claim on behalf of a member. Third, the union is to take reasonable steps to ensure that any advice given to members is provided by a competent employee or workplace representative, and that such advisers conduct themselves with honesty and integrity in dealing with a member's claim. Fourth, a complaint procedure should be in place that allows members an effective means to pursue a complaint about the union service in relation to any claim received directly from the trade union. This is to include the ability of the member to complain to the union itself about any fees or charges to members or deductions from a member's damages, and, if the matter cannot be resolved to the satisfaction of both parties, to a third

[42] Ministry of Justice, Claims Management Regulation—Code of Practice for the provision of Regulated Claims Management Services by Trade Unions, November 2006.

party. Fifth, where unjustifiable fees have been charged, these should be repaid by the union. Finally, the union is to give members access to the records it keeps in respect of claims.

An example of a union which follows this Code of Practice is UCU, which has a website page offering legal service FAQs as to when legal services will be provided, with the explicit statement that the union follows the above Code of Practice standards.[43] A UCU Legal Support Review Panel evaluates applications for member legal assistance based on the following articulated criteria to determine whether expenditure on legal casework is proportionate to the objectives sought:

1. The objectives the member seeks to achieve and the suitability of legal processes to achieve them;
2. The complexity and importance of the issues;
3. The legal merits of the case;
4. The costs (including opportunity costs) to the union of providing the legal services;
5. The aims, objectives and policies of the union;
6. The significance of the case both to the individual and other union members;
7. The resource implications for the union;
8. Whether alternative means of resolving the case are available.[44]

The interpretation of the criteria is entirely at the discretion of the National Executive Committee. The Committee is to give particular weight to the Union's objective of promoting equality for all and the opposition of all forms of harassment, prejudice, and unlawful discrimination because of a person's protected characteristics. The member has the right of review of a decision taken under the Legal Scheme by the Committee. If UCU decides to represent a member, UCU pays the tribunal/court fees, but under the UCU scheme the union member pays the opposing party's costs and fees as ordered by the tribunal/court. In contrast to this detailed review procedure for legal assistance as set out by UCU, the Unite union simply states in its rule book that members are to insure that requests for legal assistance are made on the appropriate form and lodged at the appropriate office, in sufficient time, with sufficient information, to enable the request to be considered and appropriate action taken.

---

[43] *See* the UCU website, ucu.org.uk, under the headings "Members," "Getting Support," and "UCU Legal Help."

[44] *See* the UCU Legal Scheme Regulations in force as of November 25, 2016.

In cases of union member complaints against trade unions, several specified types of complaints as to union conduct can be brought to the Certification Officer within 6 or 12 months depending on the complaint. Union members can file complaints where a union has acted or threatened to act in breach of the rule book or statute in relation to disciplinary proceedings; balloting; the appointment, election, or removal of persons from office; or the constitution or proceedings of any decision-making meeting. Complaints can also be brought regarding a union's failure to maintain an accurate member register or comply with a member request for access to accounting records, or for spending monies on political objects outside those permitted, and for any failure to ensure that senior executives and officers have not recently been convicted of certain offenses. A declaration can be made by the Certification Officer as to the breach by the trade union, and in appropriate cases the declaration can be issued with an enforcement order. The parties are to bear their own costs, but certain of the claimant's expenses can be reimbursed by the Certification Officer. The decision of the Certification Officer can be appealed on a question of law to the EAT. Complaints by members as to other types of trade union conduct are to be taken to the courts and not the employment tribunals, as the latter's jurisdiction rests on a contract for work, which the member does not have with a trade union.

The themes addressed in the current UK labor law model as just described—the legal personhood of trade unions, the legal effects of collective agreements, the limits of industrial action, and the granting of immunities—have deep historical roots, as was seen in Chapters 2 and 3. The current treatment of these issues very much reflects the related political debates. Trade unions are quasi-legal persons requiring no legal registration, but certain rights are tied to either registration or at least the listing of the trade union. Trade unions can now apply to be recognized by an employer, but again, the requirements as to the procedure and employee representation are fairly high. Collective agreements do not bind the trade unions; thus they have no industrial peace obligation and can freely take industrial action. However, the immunities from prosecution define the lawfulness of any industrial action very closely. Employees can themselves or through the trade union request consultation, and the thresholds are lower in the first instance: 10 percent of employees, in contrast to the 40 percent required to be a recognized trade union.

Balancing the internal relationship between trade unions and their members has been a legislative concern since the first Trade Union Act in 1871 under which members were given the right to inspect their trade union's financial records. However, the principle of democracy within the trade unions, between members and their organizations, was used politically as a tool to restrict the unions' power, resulting in a backlash against several of the legislative mechanisms created, such as the rejection of the National Industrial Relations Court in the 1970s. Despite this political twisting of issues of democracy, a voluntary trend can be traced within the unions as to greater representation of different worker groups, such as the TUC's representation rules for its council and the different categories of trade union representatives created, including equal opportunities officers, to support the participation of all members.

As to employee voice in the bringing of grievances, the UK system has several avenues available with respect to claims against employers. The employee is to bring such grievances to the employer and the employer is to have procedural safeguards in place, including the right to appeal any decision. The employee has the right to be accompanied, for example by a union representative, as support during the process. Acas offers conciliation, mediation, and arbitration for employee–employer grievances. Most trade unions provide legal assistance in certain types of cases, and as the example of UCU demonstrates, procedural guarantees and even an appeals process are often in place to insure equality of member treatment. The six key standards in the 2006 Code of Practice as to trade unions providing legal services to members emphasize these procedural guarantees. Recently an attempt was made to restrict access to the employment tribunals by imposing fairly high filing and hearing fees, but the Supreme Court struck this fee system down as a violation of the constitutional right to access to justice. Natural justice has also been invoked by the courts to guarantee procedural due process in the forms of the opportunity to present the employee's case and to highlight decisions should be made by unbiased tribunals. The balance achieved in the UK labor law model between statutory regulation and self-regulation by the social partners, resting on constitutional principles such as natural justice and access to justice, provides a unique combination of solutions allowing for employee voice.

9. Employee voice in Germany: dual channels

The dual channel structure of employee voice in place today in Germany was affixed after World War II and features works councils and employee representation on corporate supervisory boards. The aim of the works councils directly after the war was no longer to restrain political radicals, but rather to harness the now more radical unions advocating for the nationalization of industries as well as complete codetermination between employers and employees. A truce of sorts has now been reached between the unions and the works councils with the 2001 Works Constitution Act and the respective roles played by the councils and unions. The main legislation today regarding the German labor law model and employee voice is the 2001 Works Constitution Act, the 1976 Co-Determination Act, and the 1949 Collective Agreement Act, entailing three routes for employee voice: the works councils; employee representation on the supervisory boards; and trade union representation. The divide between works councils and trade unions can roughly be seen as follows: works councils as elected by employees represent their interests in the operations of the employer, while trade unions represent employees' overall interests at the industry level. Works councils cannot enter into collective agreements, only works agreements, but a collective agreement can expressly state that a works agreement can supplement the collective agreement. Industrial action remains the prerogative of the trade unions. The structures and mandates of the works councils are first set out here, followed by those of the trade unions.

THE LEGAL FRAMEWORK OF WORKS COUNCILS

After a turbulent beginning, the present-day existence of works councils is now more or less stable as to both employers and unions. Under the 2001 Works Constitution Act (*Betriebsverfassungsgesetz*),[1] works councils are

[1] Works Constitution Act as promulgated by the Act of September 25, 2001, Federal Law Gazette (Bundesgesetzblatt), Part I, p. 2518, last amended by Art. 3

to be set up in all private sector workplaces having at least five employees.[2] A higher percentage of work councils is found at employers with larger workplaces. In 2014, only 9 percent of all eligible private sector workplaces in western Germany and 10 percent in eastern Germany had a works council; however, these covered 43 percent and 35 percent of all employees respectively. In workplaces with more than 500 employees, 87 percent had works councils in western Germany and 89 percent in eastern Germany.[3]

An overarching principle of equal treatment is imposed on both works councils and employers under section 75 of the Works Constitution Act. In both cases, this is to ensure that all persons working in the establishment are treated in accordance with principles of law and equity. No one is to be subjected to discrimination on the grounds of race, ethnic origin, descent or other origin, nationality, religion or belief, disability, age, political or trade union activities or convictions, or gender or sexual identity. Both works councils and employers are also to safeguard and encourage the personal development of employees, promoting the independence and personal initiatives of employees and working groups.

The employer is to bear the majority of costs for works councils, including compensation for time off for duties as required by employee works council members. Works councils are purely employee bodies, and all employees are covered by the works councils, with the exception of senior management. A separate body may exist to represent senior management (*Sprecherausschuss*). A number of other representative bodies can also be found at workplaces, including trade unions and health and safety committees.

A bifurcation of function within works councils occurs with larger employers. By statute, in companies with more than one hundred permanent employees, an economic committee is to be created. Where employers have more than two hundred employees and, consequently, works councils with nine or more members, a separate works committee is to be elected by the works council to handle the company's daily

---

Law of April 20, 2013 (Bundesgesetzblatt, Part I, p. 868). An English translation of this Act is available from the Language Service of the Federal Ministry of Labour and Social Affairs at gesetze-im-internet.de/englisch_betrvg.

2 There is a system of staff councils (*Personalrat*) in the public sector with similar structures.

3 See L. FULTON, WORKER REPRESENTATION IN EUROPE (Labour Research Department and ETUI 2015) *citing* Peter Ellguth and Susanne Kohaut, Tarifbindung und betriebliche Interessenvertretung: Aktuelle Ergebnisse aus dem IAB-Betriebspanel 2013, WSI-Mitteilungen, 4/20124.

business needs. The works council chair and deputy chair are automatically members of this committee. Works councils can also set up other subcommittees if necessary. Where a company has several workplaces, a central works council is to be established at the company level in addition to those at the plant levels. A works council can also be set up at the corporate group level, but only if works councils covering 50 percent of the total corporate group workforce vote to do so.

Nominations to the works council are made either by a percentage of employees—in most cases, 5 percent of those eligible to vote—or from any trade union with at least one member in the workplace. Elections take place every four years. Specific representation rules exist regarding certain worker categories: blue/white-collar, temporary, sex, age, and disability status. Blue- and white-collar employees are to be represented in proportion to their numbers in the workforce. Temporary agency employees having worked at least three months at the workplace are also entitled to vote, and are to be included in the calculation of the number of employees. The sex that is in a minority in the workforce is to be represented proportionately on all works councils having more than one member.[4] Young workers, as well as workers with disabilities, are to participate in works council discussions concerning topics of importance to these groups.

The size of the works council is set by law, at one member in workplaces with 5–20 employees, three members in workplaces with 21–50 employees, five members in workplaces with 51–100 employees, etc. Works council members are to be given paid leave to carry out their duties and are protected from dismissal during their mandate and for one year after unless extraordinary reasons exist, such as gross misconduct, and only if the works council or the labor court concurs. Protection against involuntary transfers also exists where the consequence of the transfer entails that the employee loses the right to be a works council member, for example by being transferred to a different workplace.

Quarterly works meetings (*Betriebsversammlung*) are to be held by the works councils and a report as to their work provided to all employees.

---

[4] The aim of this 2001 legislative change was to increase the number of women in works councils. This has happened, modestly, with growth from 23.4 percent in 2002 to 27.5 percent in 2014: see FULTON, *supra* note 3 *citing* RALPH GREIFENSTEIN, LEO KIßLER, & HENDRIK LANGE, TRENDREPORT BETRIEBSRATSWAHLEN 2010 (Hans-Böckler-Stiftung 2011) and RALPH GREIFENSTEIN, LEO KIßLER, & HENDRIK LANGE, TRENDREPORT BETRIEBSRATSWAHLEN 2014: ZWISCHENBERICHT (Hans-Böckler-Stiftung 2014), available at the Hans Böckler Foundation's website, boeckler.de.

Departmental or union meetings can be held if necessary or upon the request of the employer or one quarter of the workforce. The employer has the right to attend the works council meetings. The employer has a duty to annually report to the works council as to operational developments affecting employees and their welfare, including issues concerning equal treatment, the economic situation, and environmental protection measures.

THE DUTIES AND RIGHTS OF WORKS COUNCILS

Works councils are to guard against employers unilaterally making key decisions at workplaces without involving representatives of the employees in the decision-making process. In contrast to trade unions, however, works councils are to take a holistic perspective encompassing both employee and employer perspectives, working with the employer "in a spirit of mutual trust having regard to the applicable collective agreements and in co-operation with the trade unions and employers' associations represented in the establishment for the good of the employees and of the establishment."[5] The Act goes on to specifically recognize that trade unions have a separate duty to protect the interests of their members.

The general duties of works councils fall into two basic categories: a duty of protection of all workers, and enhanced duties to certain groups. The general duty of protection entails that the works council is to ensure that the employer follows the law, safety regulations, collective agreements, and works agreements and treats all employees lawfully and equally. Works councils can also make recommendations as to improving the workplace.

The second category contains enhanced duties to certain groups: men and women, youths, the elderly, employees with disabilities, and foreign workers. These groups also coincide with protected nondiscrimination grounds as set out by international, EU, and German law: sex and gender, age (both youths and the elderly), disability, and race. Works councils are to make recommendations as to measures promoting the implementation of equality between women and men, in particular as regards recruitment, employment, training, vocational advancement, and reconciliation of family and work. Works councils are to organize the election of youth and trainee delegations where warranted and to collaborate closely with

---

[5] Section 2 Works Constitution Act.

such in promoting the interests of youth employees up to the age of 25 years, inviting them to submit suggestions and state their views on various matters. Where viable, the works council is to negotiate for their implementation with the employer and inform the employees concerned of the state of those negotiations and their results. Works councils are to promote the employment and rehabilitation of severely disabled employees and others in particular need of assistance, such as the elderly. Works councils are to act in support of the integration of foreign workers in the establishment and better cultural understanding at the workplace, and request measures to combat racism and xenophobia in the establishment.

A further categorization exists with respect to rights the works council has under the act: participation rights and codetermination rights. Participation rights are those rights where the works council is to be informed and consulted about specific issues, and can submit proposals.[6] The right to information includes the employer supplying the works council with the information necessary for the council to carry out its duties, as well as monthly meetings. The right to inspect documents dovetails with the right to information, and includes the works council's right to inspect the payroll.

Codetermination rights are the stronger set of rights, where decisions as a rule are not to be taken without the consent of the works council unless sanctioned by a labor court or arbitration, depending upon the subject matter. The precise rights of the works council vary from area to area, with the strongest rights connected to those issues concerning the actual terms and conditions of employment, and the weakest within areas of business and financial decisions.

Employers must notify the works council of certain decisions before they are effected. For example, in cases of employee dismissals, the works council is first to be consulted and informed of the reasons for the dismissal prior to its execution. A dismissal carried out without this consultation is null and void. The works council has the right to contest the dismissal where the social needs of the employee have not been sufficiently taken into account, where guidelines have not been observed, or where transfer or retraining is possible. The works council is also to be consulted as to any new employments, and has the right to make recommendations regarding manpower and training needs.

---

6 *See* Rebecca Page, *Co-Determination in Germany—A Beginner's Guide*, ARBEITSPAPIER 33, 14 (Hans Böckler Stiftung 2011). *See also* Federal Ministry of Labour and Social Affairs, CO-DETERMINATION 2018 (Federal Ministry of Labour and Social Affairs 2018) available at bmas.de.

The works council has a right to negotiate (codetermination) in many types of decisions affecting employees' work conditions, such as working time, payment of wages, and vacation and safety issues. The employer can make a binding decision on such issues only with the consent of the works council. The employer and works council may also enter into a works agreement, which is then binding on all employees. If the employer has more than one thousand employees, the works council can request from the employer that guidelines on certain employment areas are jointly issued. If no agreement can be reached, the conciliation committee (*Einigunsstelle*) comes into play. This committee is appointed by the works council and employer, with one impartial member appointed jointly or by the other committee members or the Labour Court.

With respect to certain employer actions, such as a breach of the law or collective agreement, failure to observe employer practices, or unlawful dismissals or hirings, the works council has a veto right. Notice has to be given by the works council within one week of being informed of the action, and the employer can then petition a labor court for a favorable decision which would replace the works council's consent. The employer must inform the works councils as to certain decisions, such as closures, mergers, important changes in operations, or the introduction of new work methods. In the event that the employer and works council fail to reach an agreement as to a plan, the parties can resort to mediation by a regional labor court, or conciliation by the conciliation committee.

In the event that an employer grossly violates its duties under the Works Constitution Act, the works council or representative trade union can apply to the Labour Court for an order enjoining the employer for equitable relief under section 23 of the Works Constitution Act. If the employer fails to comply, the Labour Court can, upon request, sanction the employer upon failure to comply. If the employer fails to comply with this second order, the Labour Court can, upon request, order damages of up to €10,000.

INDIVIDUAL EMPLOYEES AND WORKS COUNCILS

Employees are empowered under the Works Constitution Act with regard to both the works councils and employers. Employees have the right to propose that certain issues be discussed by the works council. If the proposal is seconded by at least 5 percent of the employees in the establishment, the works council is to place it on the agenda of a works council meeting within two months.

Employers have a duty to inform employees as to employment, changes in employment, and work environment safety issues, including training. If the changes in employment envisioned require retraining, employees have the right to discuss such with the employer as well as to have a member of the works council present at the discussion. Employees also have a right to a hearing by those competent in the organizational structure on any operational matter concerning their person, and are entitled to state their case and make suggestions. A comparable right exists as to wages, with employees also having the right to have a member of the works council present. Employees are also to have access to their personnel files as well as a right to correction and/or notations in the file, and may also call in a member of the works council in such proceedings.

Each employee is entitled to make a complaint to the competent bodies in the establishment if she feels that she has been discriminated against, treated unfairly, or otherwise put at a disadvantage by the employer or by other employees of the establishment. She may call on a member of the works council for assistance or mediation. The employer is to inform the employee as to how her complaint will be dealt with and, if the employer considers the complaint justified, remedy her grievance. Protections against retaliation are also mandated.

Works councils are given a specific role in dealing with employee grievances under section 85: Employees can bring a grievance against the employer directly to the works council, which is to hear the employee's grievance and, if it appears justified, request that the employer remedy the situation. In the event that the employer and works council disagree as to whether the complaint is well founded, the works council may appeal to a conciliation committee. A decision by the conciliation committee is to be issued, and the employer is to inform both the works council and the employee on how the grievance will be dealt with.

A works council may be dissolved, or a member removed, for grave dereliction of statutory duties upon a petition to the labor court by either one quarter of the employees with voting rights, the employer, or the representative trade union. The works council itself can also petition for the removal of a member. The issue of whether a member of a works council can be held liable in damages for a breach of a duty to an employee is debated within German academic circles:[7] Certain scholars argue that there could be liability in tort; others argue potential liability in

---

[7] *See* DETLEV W. BELLING, LEGAL PROTECTION AGAINST BREACHES OF DUTY ON THE PART OF THE GERMAN WORKS COUNCIL—A FATA MORGANA? 2

the quasi-contractual relationship. Both these legal arguments, however, are treated conservatively and narrowly by the courts. Some maintain that the compulsory representation of employees by works councils with no damage liability has led to individual employees having no true recourse.[8]

CODETERMINATION IN CORPORATE SUPERVISORY BOARDS

An additional avenue for collective employee voice is through employee representation, or codetermination, on the supervisory boards. When the employer is a corporation (*Aktiengesetz*) with at least two thousand employees, there is a requirement under the general Co-Determination Act (*Mitbestimmungsgesetz*) of 1976 that the corporation have two boards: a supervisory board (*Aufsichtsrat*) and a management board (*Vorstand*). The management board is responsible for daily corporate operations. The supervisory board,[9] comprising shareholder-elected directors and employee-representative directors, has two specific functions: to approve the members of the management board, and to monitor its management of corporate operations. The supervisory board can also decide that certain corporate decisions (but not management operations) need its approval, and if the board withholds its approval, the shareholders can override it with a qualified majority of 75 percent.

THE LEGAL STATUS AND RECOGNITION OF TRADE UNIONS

Because of the historical legal treatment of guilds and journeymen's associations, the early trade unions refused to be registered as they could then be required to produce member lists—a concern that materialized

(Springer 2000) *citing* WILFRIED SCHLÜTER, DIE HAFTUNG DER ARBEITNEHMERVERTRETER IM AUFSICHTSRAT EINER AKTIENGESELLSCHAFT BEI NICHTIGKEIT DES JAHRESABSCHLUSSES IN FESTSCHRIFT ZUM 60. GEBURTSTAG FÜR JÖRG BAETGE 983 (Düsseldorf 1997).

[8] *Id.* at 36.

[9] If the employer has 501–2,000 employees, one third of the supervisory board is to comprise employee representatives. If it has more than 2,000 employees, one half of the supervisory board is to be elected by the employees, with the trade union(s) guaranteed a certain number of seats.

during the Nazi persecution of the trade union movement. The trade unions thus organized as nonregistered associations (*nicht rechtsfähhiger Verein*).[10] The majority of trade unions have retained this status to the present day. Trade unions have the capacity to sue and be sued (*Parteifähigkeit*) before the labor courts under § 10 of the Labour Court Act (*Arbeitsgerichtsgesetz*). According to case law, trade unions that are entitled to participate in collective bargaining (*tariffähige Gewerkschaften*) can also sue (*aktive Parteifähigkeit*) in civil proceedings.

As professional associations (*Berufsverbände*), trade unions are tax exempt.[11] Professional associations as a category are exempt from paying corporate taxes unless they pursue commercial activities or use more than 10 percent of their income to directly or indirectly support or promote political parties.[12] Trade union members can take tax deductions from their individual taxes for union fees paid, as contributions to professional associations whose purpose is not directed at an economic activity are tax deductible.[13] In contrast to the works councils, which are highly regulated by statute, the trade unions have very little statutory regulation, particularly under this form of professional association.

Labor organizations are constitutionally protected under Article 9(3) GG.[14] Anyone can form a labor organization and work toward better

---

[10] Eva Kocher and Clemens Sudhof, *Trade Union Representation in Germany* in REPRESENTING EMPLOYEE INTERESTS: TRADE UNION SYSTEMS WITHIN THE EU 157 (Carmen La Macchia ed. Albecete 2013).

[11] *See* section 5(1)Nr 5 of the Corporate Tax Act (Körperschaftsteuergesetz, KStG). *See also* BERND ERLE & THOMAS SAUTER, KÖRPERSCHAFTSTEUERGESETZ: DIE BESTEUERUNG DER KAPITALGESELLSCHAFT UND IHRER ANTEILSEIGNER (3rd ed. 2010) para. 99; R 16(2) KStR 2004 (Körperschaftsteuer-Richtlinien): "Zu den Berufsverbänden ohne öffentlich-rechtlichen Charakter i. S. d. § 5 Abs. 1 Nr. 5 KStG können Berufsverbände der Arbeitgeber und der Arbeitnehmer, z. B. Arbeitgeberverbände und Gewerkschaften [labour unions], und andere Berufsverbände, z. B. Wirtschaftsverbände, Bauernvereine und Hauseigentümervereine, gehören."

[12] *See* section 5(1) Nr 5 KStG.

[13] *See* § 9(1) Nr 3 of the Income Tax Act (*Einkommensteuergesetz*, EStG).

[14] Article 9 [Freedom of association]:

(1) All Germans shall have the right to form corporations and other associations.

(2) Associations whose aims or activities contravene the criminal laws, or that are directed against the constitutional order or the concept of international understanding, shall be prohibited.

(3) The right to form associations to safeguard and improve working and economic conditions shall be guaranteed to every individual and to every

employment conditions. No statutory definitions or requirements exist for either the employee or employer organization. A list of minimum requirements has evolved in the case law of the Federal Labour Court when interpreting the freedom of association rights under Article 9(3) GG and recognition as a labor organization. The organization must:

- have an existence for an unlimited duration;
- have a corporate structure to guarantee continuity even with changing membership;
- follow principles of democratic decision-making, for example, that such organizations are acting on behalf of their members, and that there should be a guarantee that members are able to influence the activities of the organization;
- have only employee or employer members and employee organizations should include members from several workplaces; and
- be independent employee organizations independent of employer, and vice versa, and be independent from the influence of third parties such as the state, political parties, or religious organizations. It is acceptable to have similar goals.[15]

No legal requirements exist as to union registration for employer recognition or concerning membership lists.

Where there is a works council at a workplace, it is to fulfill the statutory duties described above as to representing employee interests. If no works council exists at the workplace, the trade union is then the only collective representative for the employees. This can be the case, for example, where there are fewer than five employees. There is often a high degree of influence and overlap when both a works council and trade union are present at one workplace representing employee interests. Works councils' members are often also trade union members; for example, approximately three quarters of the works council members elected in 2014 were DGB members. Unions can nominate council members and works councils have the right to invite trade unions to attend their meetings where one quarter of the members are in favor of doing so.

---

occupation or profession. Agreements that restrict or seek to impair this right shall be null and void; measures directed to this end shall be unlawful ...

An English translation of the Grundgesetz, or GG, is available from the Minister of Justice at gesetze-im-internet.de.

15 *See* WEISS & SCHMIDT, *supra* chap. 4 note 28 at 170.

EMPLOYEE CONSULTATION

Works councils are by law the main employee representation system at a workplace. There is no separate statutory structure for union workplace representatives, but some unions make provisions for such union workplace representatives, also determining their rights and duties. In some industries these positions are regulated by collective agreements. In an ideal situation, union representatives exist alongside the works council. In practice, there is often no separate specific trade union employee consultation structure and the members of the works council assume such tasks.

COLLECTIVE BARGAINING AND THE LEGAL STATUS OF COLLECTIVE AGREEMENTS

Approximately 58 percent of the workers in western Germany and 47 percent in eastern Germany are covered by collective agreements entered into at the central sector/industry levels. Collective agreements can also be incorporated in the individual employment agreements of nonmembers, unorganized employees, or employees belonging to a different union, extending the coverage of such agreements in western Germany to 77 percent and in eastern Germany to 74 percent.[16] There are no recognition rules for trade unions regarding negotiating for collective agreements. The union simply needs to have enough support among the workers to be deemed representative and able to enforce the agreement. Any objections as to whether this level of representativeness is met are to be raised to the regional labor court and then appealed to the Federal Labour Court.

Collective agreements are regulated by the 1949 Collective Agreement Act (*Tarifvertragsgesetz*). There are generally no form requirements for the validity of a collective agreement. The collective agreement is seen as having two components: the normative part, governing the actual conditions of employment; and a second part setting out the obligations of the parties to the agreement, the employer/employer organization and trade union. These can include, for example, the obligation to execute the agreement or the duty of industrial peace. Only affected trade union member employees have standing to enforce the normative part of the collective agreement determining the conditions of employment; the

---

[16] The figures are for the year 2014: see KAREN ULLMANN & CHRISTIAN LEY, GERMANY: INDUSTRIAL RELATIONS (Xpert database 2016).

social partners do not.[17] Collective agreements may be in force even after their expiration date (*Nachwirkung*) in certain cases. The courts have found that a duty of industrial peace (*Friedensplicht*) exists during the term of the collective agreement.

Wages are the primary subject of collective agreements. Many employers voluntarily follow the sector collective agreements regarding wages. The 2015 Collective Bargaining Unity Act (*Tarifautonomiestärkungsgesetz*) has as its objective promoting collective bargaining and the role of the state in wage setting by strengthening the autonomy of the social partners in collective bargaining. This 2015 act was challenged by several unions as unconstitutional as it infringed on the freedom of smaller unions to enter into coalitions as guaranteed by Article 9(3) GG. The Federal Constitutional Court held in 2017 that though the act was mostly constitutional, it did not include sufficient safeguards to protect the rights of certain occupational groups and the status quo of existing coalitions. The Court ordered that the legislature improve the rules in the act by the end of 2018.[18] The 2015 act also introduced a statutory minimum hourly wage of €8.5 in 2015, and in 2018 the minimum wage was €8.84. A minimum wage joint committee with representatives from the state, employer organizations, and trade unions is to reassess the minimum wage level every two years.

While employers apply collective agreements with a trade union to the union's member employees, in practice the agreement is applied to the other employees in the workforce. Where there are several collective agreements at a workplace (*Tarifpluralität*), the former rule was that the collective agreement covering the most employees was considered to prevail (*Tarifeinheit*). Given the different types of employment now found at most workplaces, the Federal Labour Court has abandoned this rule.[19] This directly affects one of the DGB's four founding principles, one company–one union. The change in rule entails that instead of all workers being represented at the same time, by the same union, with the same strength, employee groups within the workplace negotiate their own terms. This issue was also brought up in the 2017 case discussed above as reducing solidarity across the workplace.

All collective agreements are to be registered with the Federal Ministry of Labour and Social Affairs. The Ministry can declare a collective agreement *ergo omnes* to be generally binding for an entire sector

[17] *See* KOCHER & SUDHOF, *supra* note 10 at 163.

[18] Bundesverfassungsgericht, July 11, 2017-1 BvR 1571/15, 1588/15, 2883/15, 1043/16 and 1477/16.

[19] Bundesarbeitsgericht, June 23, 2010–10 AS 2/10.

(*Allgemeinverbindlicherklärung*) within a German federal state upon the request of the social partners where certain requirements are fulfilled. The collective agreement in question must be of importance with respect to the employment conditions in that sector. The declaration must be of public interest, for example when it is vital for the protection of working conditions in a sector or combatting negative trends such as wage dumping. Sectoral collective minimum wage agreements can also be extended under the Posted Workers Act where the extension is seen as serving the public interest. Objections to a governmental decision declaring a collective agreement generally binding are to be heard by the local labor courts. About 65,000 collective agreements have been registered, and approximately 460 are generally applicable.[20] Collective agreements consequently have a greater reach than union membership; for example, union membership in 2014 was 18 percent, while collective bargaining coverage was 62 percent.[21]

Works councils are not parties to collective agreements. A works agreement can provide better terms for employees than the relevant collective agreement under the "favourability principle" (*Günstigkeitsprincip*). "Opening clauses" (*Öffnungsklauseln*) can be incorporated into collective agreements that allow for deviations, both positive and negative, under certain conditions at the local level, typically with respect to work times and wages. These have been used as a way to retain central collective agreements while at the same time allowing local plant adjustments when necessary.[22]

INDUSTRIAL ACTION AND THE PEACE OBLIGATION

The right to take industrial action in the forms of strikes and lockouts is constitutionally protected under the Basic Law as part of the freedom of association. The Federal Labour Court has held that for a strike to be

---

[20] *See* the website of the Federal Ministry of Labour and Social Affairs, section "Collective Agreements," at bmas.de.

[21] *See* Ralph Greifenstein, Leo Kißler, & Hendrik Lange, Trend-report Betriebsratswahlen 2014: Zwischenbericht: Zwischenergebnisse kurz nach der Wahl (Hans-Böckler-Stiftung, June–August 2014) available at boeckler.de.

[22] *See* Sandra Vogel, *Use of Opening Clauses in Collective Agreements* (Eurofound 2016) available at eurofound.europa.eu.

deemed lawful, it must respect the peace obligation,[23] be fair, be the last resort (*ultima ratio*),[24] and be preceded by a secret ballot of union members.[25] A duty of industrial peace is seen as implicit in collective agreements, so that a strike will be deemed unlawful if it is held when a collective agreement binding the parties and regulating the issue of the dispute is in force. As the purpose of collective agreements is to change the conditions of employment, political strikes are viewed as unlawful.

For a strike to be lawful, negotiations between the social partners must first be held and be unsuccessful. This is to be followed by a secret ballot as to whether to strike. Only a trade union with members who are employees can organize a strike at that employer. Strikes are also governed by a principle of proportionality, entailing that they are not to bring about harm to the common good in a disproportionate manner—an issue often arising with strikes in the public sector concerning vital services. Warning strikes—short strikes held at different locations without any prior ballots or negotiations—are permissible during negotiations under the case law.[26] Secondary actions are lawful only under narrowly defined conditions. Where the strike is lawful, a striking employee is not in violation of the employment agreement. The rights and obligations of the employment relationship are seen as merely suspended.[27]

Employers can temporarily completely shut down their business or invoke a lockout of employees in a strike situation, but only in a proportionate manner. This entails that in a situation where less than one quarter of the workforce is on strike, the employer can lock out only one quarter of the work force from work and pay. If more than one quarter of the employees are on strike, the employer can lock out half the workforce. The lockout is to encompass all workers, not just those who are striking. The employer can contest the lawfulness of the strike by seeking an injunction against the strike from a labor court. There is no statutory system of mediation, conciliation, or arbitration in industrial disputes, but the social partners are free to agree to such as stated under the 1946 Allied Control Council Act on Dispute Resolution Machinery in Labour Conflicts (*Kontrollratsgesetz*).

---

23 Bundesarbeitsgericht, October 31, 1958—1 AZR 632/57, Arbeitsrechtliche Praxis, No. 2 § 1 TVG Friedenspflicht.

24 Bundesarbeitsgericht, April 21, 1971—GS 1/68, Arbeitsrechtliche Praxis.

25 *See* WEISS & SCHMIDT, *supra* chap. 4 note 28 at 203.

26 Bundesarbeitsgericht, December 17, 1976—1 AZR 605/75, *Neue Juristische Wochenschrift,* 1977, 1079.

27 *See* NICOLE ELERT & CHRISTOPHER T. BROOKS, GERMAN EMPLOYMENT LAW 159 (De Gruyter 2014).

TRADE UNION MEMBERSHIP

Both the negative and the positive rights—the right to not join a union and the right to join one—are protected under the German constitution as interpreted by the courts. Consequently, trade unions are not allowed to discriminate as to the terms of collective agreements between members and nonmembers, such as with a closed shop clause. This gives rise to an inherent free-rider problem regarding union membership.[28] Both organization models—old unionism, with organization by craft, and new unionism, with organization based on branch/employer (*Industrieprinzip*)—are in place, but the latter is more prevalent.

Given the status of German trade unions as nonregistered associations, the trade unions are free to determine their internal organization, including the rights of members. The absolute limit to the internal bylaws (*Satzung*) of a trade union is that they may not violate other constitutionally protected rights. Article 9(2) GG states that an association whose "aims or activities contravene the criminal laws, or that are directed against the constitutional order or the concept of international understanding" is to be prohibited.

MEMBER DUTIES TO UNIONS

The obligations and duties of trade unions and their members are set out in the trade union bylaws. Members are to vote on industrial actions, particularly strikes, depending again on the bylaws. The approval rate for strikes is often set at two thirds of the voting union members.[29] A violation of this does not render the strike unlawful as to third parties, however. Another pervasive member duty is to pay member dues. The trade unions that are sector-based can require that their members work in the sector they represent.[30]

Depending upon the bylaws in question, union members can be disciplined for misconduct including persistent objections as to union orders, strikebreaking, membership in other unions, and theft or fraud of union property. The bylaws also set out disciplinary procedures, typically

---

[28] *See* Bernd Fitzenberger, Karsten Kohn, & Qingwei Want, *The Erosion of Union Membership in Germany: Determinants, Densities, Decompositions*, 24(1) JOURNAL OF POPULATION ECONOMICS 141–65, 142 (January 2011).

[29] *See* KOCHER & SUDHOF, *supra* note 10 at 160.

[30] *See* WEISS & SCHMIDT, *supra* chap. 4 note 28 at 171.

initiated by the filing of a complaint, which is followed by an investigation and hearing. Sanctions include union membership exclusion, being banned from functions or voting, or a reprimand. The courts have held that a trade union can exclude a member for misconduct, but only if it is done through a procedure that allows for an adequate defense and where the exclusion is not discriminatory, arbitrary, or abusive. Trade unions with a monopolistic status have a higher threshold with respect to due process in such proceedings, which are often only lawful where the exclusion is based on objective reasons, such as a gross violation of the trade union bylaws.[31] The Federal Constitutional Court has recognized a constitutional right of trade unions to defend their collective unity, so that a trade union member who is at the same time a member of a political party hostile to the union can be excluded.[32]

An interesting feature of the dual channel system in Germany is that minority employee member interests in unions cannot be "totally silenced."[33] A minority expressing an unwanted viewpoint from the union perspective is free to turn to the works councils. Unions then are often more inclined to address the matter in the pragmatic hope of controlling the outcomes. The internal structure of the union is consequently seen as more democratic due to this pressure that can be exerted by minorities, and the participation of individuals also becomes more significant.

UNION DUTIES TO MEMBERS

As previously stated, the basic relationship between unions and their members is set out in the union bylaws. Certain tenants are also imposed by law, such as the right for members to terminate membership on reasonable notice and in compliance with reasonable conditions. Members also have the right to not be discriminated against in relation to members and the benefits of membership. Where there are union political funds, members cannot be forced to contribute. Unions have to follow due process procedures, such as those concerning union ballots.

Paying members are entitled to support from the union in labor disputes, including legal advice. Trade unions are to provide employees

---

[31] *See* Bundesgerichtshof, July 10, 1989—II ZR 30/89.

[32] *See* Bundesverfassungsgericht, February 24, 1999—1 BvR 123/93.

[33] *See* Wolfgang Däubler, *Trends in German Labour Law*, in LABOUR LAW IN THE POST-INDUSTRIAL ERA—STUDIES IN MODERN LAW AND POLICY 109 (Lord Wedderbrun, Max Rood, Gérard Lyon-Caen, Wolfgang Däubler, & Paul van der Heijden eds. Dartmouth University Press 1994).

with legal counsel to assist them in the resolution of legal disputes with an employer. If the conflict cannot be resolved, a trade union may represent a member in court under section 11(2) of the Code of Procedure for the Labor Court (*Arbeitsgerichtsgestz*) even where the trade union counsel is not a registered lawyer. The assistance is usually provided freely to members, with the union paying the trial costs and fees as well as the employer's costs in fees in the case of a loss.

PURSUING EMPLOYEE GRIEVANCES

The system of addressing employee grievances in Germany involves the steps of mediation, arbitration, and litigation. The right for an employee in the private sector to raise a grievance predates the provisions in the Works Constitution Act (*Betriebsverfassungsgesetz*).[34] The right to raise a grievance is based on an implied term in the employment agreement, derived by the courts from the employer's duty of care.[35] This duty requires the employer to consider the employee's moral rights and wellbeing, thus to hear the employee when grievances are raised as to unfair or disadvantaged treatment. Employees consequently have the right, as set out in the Works Constitution Act, to raise a grievance through the works council or individually bring a grievance in the absence of a works council.

The employee can also raise a grievance directly to the relevant workplace body, and ask a member of the works council for assistance or mediation.[36] In the alternative, the employee can raise the grievance with the works council directly or after a failed individual attempt. If the works council finds the complaint justified, it is to act to ensure that the employer remedies the situation. In the event of a disagreement as to whether the grievance is well-founded, the works council, but not the employee, can take the issue to a conciliation committee whose decision is binding. However, the committee does not have mandatory jurisdiction in grievances raising claims of an employee's legal entitlements, and the parties in such cases can only be bound by their consent. Legal entitlements are to be decided by the labor court based on the public

---

[34] *See* Bernd Waas, *Germany* in RESOLVING INDIVIDUAL LABOUR DISPUTES 148 (Minawa Ebisui, Sean Cooney & Colin Fenwick eds. ILO Geneva 2016).

[35] *Id.* at 148 *citing* G. Thüsing, *Section 84 Works Constitution Act* in BERTRIEBSVERFASSUNGSGESETZ (R. Richardi ed. 4th ed. Munich 2014).

[36] *Id.*

policy requirement that legal disputes between employers and employees be heard by the public courts.[37]

GERMAN LABOR COURTS AND DISPUTE RESOLUTION

The labor courts since the passage of the 1926 Act have exclusive jurisdiction over all labor disputes between employees and employers, as well as between trade unions and employers.[38] Two types of dispute can be brought to the trial labor courts: *Beschluss* and *Urteil*. *Beschluss* procedures concern only issues of labor law, disputes arising from codetermination procedures under the Works Constitution Act, the Senior Management Representatives Committee Act, the election of employee representatives to the supervisory board of a company, the capacity to conclude collective agreements, and the collective bargaining jurisdiction of trade unions and employers' organizations. *Urteil* procedures concern disputes that can arise under either employment law or labor law. These can concern an issue arising between employees and employers out of the employment relationship, such as the existence of an employment contract. *Urteil* can also concern labor law disputes, such as those arising from collective agreements; whether such an agreement exists; the rights of the parties, including third parties; the lawfulness of industrial action; freedom of association; and the rights of employer or employee representatives.

There are three tiers of labor courts in place. The local trial labor courts (*Arbeitsgerichte*, 110 in total) and appellate regional/land labor courts (*Landesarbeitsgerichte*, 15 in total) both have panels (chambers) consisting of a judicially trained judge and two lay members representing the social partners, while the highest labor court, the Federal Labour Court (*Bundesarbeitsgericht*), is the court of last resort in labor and employment matters. It has panels (senates) comprising three judicially trained judges and two lay members representing the social partners. A preliminary conciliation hearing is to be held by only a judge prior to the parties bringing the case before the trial court.[39]

---

[37] *Id.* at 149 *citing* Bundestags-Drucksache VI/1786, January 29, 1971, 48.

[38] The current act is the Arbeitsgerichtsgesetz ("AGG"), or Labour Courts Act, enacted 1979 and most recently amended in 2016.

[39] In 2012, 59 percent of all cases (app. 234,920) were settled through conciliation: INGRID SCHMIDT, THE FEDERAL LABOUR COURT 16 (Erfurt 2014).

At the labor trial court level, the parties may represent themselves or be represented by a lawyer or a representative of an employer's association, a trade union, or any other authorized person. Each party is to pay its own fees at the trial court level, which is a deviation from the general rule applied—the English rule that the losing party pay the prevailing party's fees and costs. This reallocation of attorney's fees is deliberate and is aimed at reducing the economic risks to employees, who otherwise could be prevented from seeking judicial redress.[40]

A petition for leave to appeal to the labor appellate courts can be based on an error of law or fact. The petition is to be made to the trial court, which then can grant leave to appeal. Leave to appeal must be granted if the error of law concerns a legal issue that is fundamental and significant for the judgment or if the judgment deviates from the judgments of the Federal Court of Justice, the Joint Senate of the Supreme Federal Courts, or the Federal Labour Court. In the absence of precedent by the Federal Labour Court, leave to appeal is to be granted where there is a split as to the decisions on the appellate level. Leave must also be granted if there are procedural irregularities or if the parties have not had the opportunity to present comments on grounds used for the judgment. In the alternative, leave will be granted if the value of the cause of the appeal exceeds €600, or if the claim relates to the existence, nonexistence, or termination of an employment relationship.

The parties must be represented by either lawyers or union or employer's association representatives at the appellate levels. On appeal, the losing party pays the prevailing party's court costs and attorneys' fees only for the appeal. If an employee cannot pay such costs without endangering his or her livelihood, the employee may apply for legal aid. An award of fees is purposely to be set low, in accordance with the Court Fees Act (*Gerichtskostengesetz*). An employee can request representation by a lawyer if the other party has legal counsel. A petition for leave to appeal an appellate court decision is to be filed with that appellate court. Leave is to be granted only for questions of law. The Federal Labour Court is charged with the administration of justice, with its main tasks being promoting consistency in judicial precedents and developing the law in those areas left unregulated by the legislation.

The German labor law model is built on both strong social partners and strong individual employee rights, particularly with respect to voice. The dual channel system, with employee representation through both works councils and trade unions, provides several avenues for employees to

---

[40] *See* WEISS & SCHMIDT, *supra* chap. 4 note 28 at 156.

raise issues directly with the employer, with support from the works council or the trade union. Having employee directors on the supervisory boards allows another avenue for employee voice. The works councils are given enhanced statutory duties as to certain protected groups based on sex, age, disability status, and race. There are two key points in the procedural rules concerning labor disputes: the necessity for quick and efficient solutions that are transparent and focused on the needs of the public, and the requirement for employees to have access to justice and courts, with a reallocation of trial costs and fees to minimize the economic risks to employees as well as checks to ensure that the costs and fees involved are not excessive.

10. Employee voice in Sweden

The Swedish social partners have in effect been regulating the Swedish labor market uninterruptedly for over a century. Both the employer and employee sides are highly organized, with Swedish employers currently having an organizational density of almost 90 percent and Swedish employees one of approximately 70 percent. Union membership exists even at professional levels, such as for professors, judges, and physicians. The creation and establishment of the Swedish model, based on self-regulation by the social partners and nonintervention by the state, began with the December Compromise of 1906 and was further cemented by the Basic Agreement in 1938, a collective agreement that is still in effect today.[1] An example of this system of self-regulation at work is the absence of minimum wage legislation in Sweden. Wages are set in collective agreements that do not have *ergo omnes* effect; in other words, they are not made generally applicable by statute to parties other than those to the agreement. An indication of the efficacy of the Swedish model is provided in the statistics concerning industrial action, 2,570 work days were lost in 2017 due to industrial conflicts.[2]

One of the most salient features of the Swedish model is the underlying premise that the state should be neutral as to the social partners, the perception being that legislation is an unwanted intervention in the labor market. In private law generally, the majority of Swedish legislation is gap-filling (*dispositiv*), meaning the parties to a transaction have the right to contract out of the law. With respect to labor legislation, on the national level the social partners have historically had the opportunity to contract out of labor law through central agreements, sometimes with the

---

[1] Renegotiations in 2008 targeting the 70th anniversary of the agreement ultimately failed as a result of disagreement with respect to redundancy rehire regulations and labor dispute procedures: see Urban Bäckström, *Om förmågan att lyssna*, Svenskt näringsliv (March 12, 2009) available at the Confederation of Swedish Enterprise's website, svensktnaringsliv.se.

[2] For these statistics, see the Swedish National Mediation Office's website, mi.se.

requirement of a higher level of protection, but not always.[3] A greater number of statutory provisions are now mandatory, particularly those enacted for Sweden to be in compliance with EU law requirements. In such cases, collective agreements can have higher degrees of protection, but still must provide at least the statutory floor of such protections.

Sweden has a single channel system for worker voice, entailing that the trade unions act as the sole representatives of employees as against employers. Given this high degree of self-regulation and the gap-filling function of the legislation, the relationship between the social partners is set out both by statute and in collective agreements. The primary statutes in labor law are the 1976 Employment (Co-Determination in the Workplace) Act (*lag 1976:580 om medbestämmande i arbetslivet*) and the 1982 Employment Protection Act (*lag 1982:80 om anställningsskydd*).[4] Specific work and trade union-related provisions can be found in other legislation, but these two constitute the bones of the labor law model. There are three collective agreements that are key as to the social partners: the 1938 Basic Agreement (*Saltsjöbadsavtalet*), basically defining the Swedish model; the 1982 Agreement on Efficiency and Participation between SAF, LO, and PTK (*Utvecklingsavtalet*),[5] setting out how

---

[3] One example of this gap-filling function can be seen with the 1979 and 1991 acts concerning equal treatment between men and women, lag (SFS 1979:1118) om jämställdhet mellan kvinnor och män i arbetslivet and Jämställdhetslag (SFS 1991:433). Equality Agreements were entered into by the majority of social partners in the private sector to opt out of these acts and out of the Equality Ombudsman's jurisdiction. These Equality Agreements in essence provided no protections against sex discrimination, but simply opted out of the acts and the jurisdiction of the Ombudsman, gutting the possibility of any effective enforcement of the legislation. The 1991 Equal Treatment Act was finally amended in 1994 to be mandatory and no longer gap-filling.

[4] Much of the 1970s legislative package discussed in Chapter 5 is still in place, such as the acts regarding trade union representatives, labor disputes, judicial procedure, annual leave, work environment, working hours, board representation, and parental leave. Newer employment acts have been a result of EU law requirements including posting of workers, discrimination laws, European works councils, and agency work. English translations of the 1976 Employment (Co-Determination in the Workplace) Act and the 1982 Employment Protection Act, as well as many of the above laws, can be found at the website of the Government Offices of Sweden, government.se, under the heading "Swedish Statutes in Translation—Labour Legislation."

[5] PTK is the abbreviation for Privattjänstemannakartellen, the Council for Negotiation and Co-operation, comprising a number of national unions from the umbrella organizations TCO and SACO. Even though national unions can belong

the codetermination act is to be applied by the social partners; and the 2017 Agreement on Industrial Development and Wage Formation (*Industriavtalet*), addressing the procedures concerning wage negotiations.

THE LEGAL STATUS AND RECOGNITION OF TRADE UNIONS

There are no explicit statutory definitions of employee, employer, or employee or employer organization in Swedish law.[6] This lacuna is deliberate in that the legislature reasoned that such definitions would facilitate circumvention, and that the courts could most suitably define the parties in the case at hand. Trade unions are legal persons within the category of nonprofit voluntary unincorporated associations (*ideella föreningar*) for which there is no explicit legislation (aside from certain tax provisions) nor any legal definition. The act governing for-profit unincorporated associations, a form of commercial cooperative, is to some extent applied by analogy.[7] Consequently, trade unions have no statutory requirements as to gaining legal personhood.

Case law has held that organizations falling within the general category of nonprofit voluntary unincorporated associations can acquire legal personhood when they elect a board and adopt bylaws stating the minimum of the association's name, its objective(s), and how decisions are to be taken.[8] If the two requirements of election of a board and adoption of such bylaws are fulfilled, the organization can own assets, be liable for debts and other obligations, and have standing to bring lawsuits and appear before governmental authorities. There is some discussion as to how many persons are required to create this type of organization. The rule of thumb is that three are required, and these can be either individuals and/or legal persons.[9] This rule is based on an analogy to the

---

to different umbrella organizations, they still can enter into negotiating cartels or coalitions on certain issues to strengthen their bargaining position.

6 *See* Legislative Inquiry SOU 1975:1, Demokrati på arbetsplatsen förslag till ny lagstiftning om förhandlingsrätt och kollektivavtal, 722–28, SOU 1993:32 NY ANSTÄLLNINGSSKYDDSLAG 215–54; *see generally* AXEL ADLERCREUTZ, ARBETSTAGARBEGREPPET (Gleerup 1964) and SVANTE BERGSTRÖM, KOLLEKTIVAVTALSLAGEN 38 (2nd ed. Geber 1948).

7 Lag (1987:667) om ekonomiska föreningar.

8 *See* the Swedish Supreme Court's decision in NJA 1973 p. 341 and 1987 p. 394.

9 *See* CARL HEMSTRÖM, UTESLUTNING UR IDEELL FÖRENING 4 (Norstedts 1972).

requirement of three in the act concerning for-profit unincorporated associations.[10] Trade unions are tax exempt as to revenues from member dues, gifts, and contributions.[11] Employees' right to take a tax deduction for union membership fees was removed in 2006 under a conservative government, but reinstated in July 2018 under a social democratic coalition government.

There is no procedure in the Swedish labor law system for trade union recognition by employers. Trade unions that have first entered into a collective agreement with an employer have certain priority rights as "established" or "signatory" unions (*kollektivavtalsbärande fackföreningar*) under the Employment (Co-Determination in the Workplace) Act. This system is argued to encourage employers to enter into collective agreements with only the historically larger, central trade unions.[12]

EMPLOYEE CONSULTATION: CODETERMINATION

With the structure of codetermination as set out in the Employment (Co-Determination in the Workplace) Act, the social partners have been given the power to self-police the enforcement of the collective agreements and legislation, and they generally have the right to institute proceedings on behalf of their members in labor disputes. The employers' prerogative, basically unlimited as set out in the December Compromise in 1906, has been circumscribed in the intervening decades, arguably voluntarily beginning with the Basic Agreement in 1938 limiting the right of employers to freely terminate employment. This erosion of the employers' prerogative can be seen as making way for a parallel expansion of the rights of employees through trade unions to influence the employer's decision-making processes through codetermination. The

---

10 Section 2:1 of the Lag (1987:667) om ekonomiska föreningar.

11 Income Tax Act (*inkomstskattelag* 1999:1229) Ch. 15 § 2 (which applies to all types of member associations). Trade unions are, however, liable for taxes with respect to real estate and operational revenues as well as interest, dividends, and capital gains: see SKATTEVERKET, SKATTEREGLER FÖR IDEELLA FÖRENINGAR 2 (Beskattningsår 2015).

12 *See* for example, The Swedish Engine Drivers' Union v. The State of Sweden, Labor Court Judgment AD 1972 no. 5. As to the negative incentives of entering into collective agreements with smaller and/or newer unions, see BOEL FLODGREN, FACKFÖRENINGEN OCH RÄTTEN 126 (Norstedts 1978).

structure of codetermination and trade union influence comprises the following:[13]

- the primary right to negotiate and the employer's duty to consult with the trade unions;
- the right of interpretation by the union as to certain issues under the collective agreements such as the employee's duty to perform work;
- the trade union's right to information;
- the trade union's right to veto certain employer decisions as to the use of temporary agency labor;
- statutory rights for trade union representatives, including paid time off to conduct union activities;
- the establishment and rights of employee safety delegates at the workplace; and
- mandatory representation of employees on the board of directors for private corporations and public entities.

The primary right to negotiate can be seen as the central component in employee consultation, as the employer has to initiate negotiations with the union before taking decisions that can be viewed as significant in the workplace. Several of the collective agreements set up procedures for the provision of information to employees through trade unions. The 1982 and 2017 Agreements mentioned above set out such information procedures during paid working time, including hiring experts to interpret the information so that employees can be fully informed.

The Act on Board Representation (Private Sector Employees) (*lag 1987:1245 om styrelserepresentation för de privatanställda*) mandates employee representation within boards of directors for corporations, commercial cooperatives, and other types of organizations such as banks and insurance companies. Under this act, two members of the board of directors in such an organization are to act as representatives of the employees if the organization has at least 25 employees, while three members may be appointed in certain organizations having at least one

[13] Terminology, as mentioned several times in this work, is tricky. The term "codetermination" cannot be seen as having a universal meaning, but rather is relative to the system in which it is being used. The components comprising codetermination in the German system differ from those comprising codetermination in the Swedish system. Some Swedish scholars prefer the English term "joint regulation" as more accurate: see, for example, RONNIE EKLUND, TORE SIGEMAN, & LAURA CARLSON, SWEDISH LABOUR AND EMPLOYMENT LAW: CASES AND MATERIALS (Iustus 2007).

thousand employees. However, the number of employee members is never to exceed the number of other board members, so that employee members are always to be at most one half, and more likely in the minority. The local trade unions bound by the applicable collective agreement are to appoint the employee directors. The employee directors are to have the same rights and obligations, including a duty of confidentiality in certain areas, as regular board members.[14]

COLLECTIVE BARGAINING AND THE LEGAL STATUS OF COLLECTIVE AGREEMENTS

There is no statutory requirement that an employer has to have a collective agreement. However, the threat of industrial action, particularly secondary action, acts as a very strong incentive. Collective bargaining in Sweden occurs at the national, sector, and local levels. There has been a movement from the national centralization of agreements that dominated most of the twentieth century to terms of employment, particularly wages, being negotiated more at the local level. Central agreements now typically concern either procedural agreements (such as the 1938 Basic Agreement), agreements on the conditions of employment, or, to a degree, framework wage regulation agreements. Central collective agreements, often referred to as recommended agreements, can be entered into between the umbrella organizations, but such agreements must be adopted at the member level within these organizations to have effect at that level. Such agreements can also be binding on all member organizations if a certain threshold number of organizations ratifies the agreement.

An employer can be bound by several collective agreements regarding its workforce, for example, with respect to salaried employees and blue-collar workers. Employers that are not members of an employer organization can be given the option of signing a simplified form of an already existing collective agreement, an accessory or tie-in agreement (*hängavtal*). This type of agreement usually contains a minimal number of terms and conditions mirroring those found in the sector collective agreement.

The Employment (Co-Determination in the Workplace) Act sets out four categories of negotiations between the social partners: a general

---

[14] A similar right to representation on boards of directors of public entities in the public sector is set out in the Personnel Representation Regulation (*personalföreträdarförordning* 1987:1101).

right in § 10 which can be invoked by any trade union regardless of whether there is a collective agreement; a primary right under § 11 which must be invoked by the employer; and rights under § 12 and § 13 which can be invoked by the established and other trade unions, respectively. The general right to negotiate (*allmän förhandlingsrätt*) was recognized at the turn of the twentieth century in the collective agreements, and first explicitly recognized by statute in the 1936 Act on the Right to Organise and Negotiate. Section 10 of the Employment (Co-Determination in the Workplace) Act now defines the right as belonging to an employee organization "to negotiate with an employer on any matter relating to the relationship between the employer and any member of the organisation who is, or has been, employed by that employer." This right is regardless of whether the union is the established one. If an employee organization approaches an employer with the objective of reaching a collective agreement, the employer must attend the negotiations and discuss the demands presented, a duty sanctioned under the act by damages. Such an obligation to negotiate exists even if the union only has one member at the workplace. This general right to negotiate does not create any obligation on either party to reach an agreement.

The primary right to negotiate (*primär förhandlingsrätt*) is set out under § 11 of the Act. It entails that an employer, before deciding on any important alterations to its activities, must initiate negotiations with the established trade union to which it is bound by collective agreement. The objective of this right is to compel employers to receive input from the employees before taking certain decisions. The rule is also applicable where an employer wishes to make major alterations to the terms of employment or conditions of work in relation to an employee. In certain cases, an employer may make and effect a decision prior to fulfilling its duty to negotiate. However, the Labour Court has interpreted "important alterations" fairly broadly, requiring not only formal but also substantive compliance. The Court has found in several cases that the employer acted too late, as the decision had already been made informally prior to consultation with the trade union. This right to negotiate, however, is limited simply to the fact that, once the negotiations are concluded, the employer is free to make any decision it considers best for the company.

An employer is obliged to negotiate even in matters not involving major alterations, if a trade union party to a collective agreement with the employer, but not the established union, so requests under § 12. In certain cases, a trade union not bound by a collective agreement has a right to negotiate under § 13, namely where a matter specifically concerns the work or employment conditions of an employee belonging to that union. Under § 14 the employer may also be requested to negotiate in these types of matters by a central organization of employees. An employer not bound by any collective agreement must negotiate with all the trade unions involved, that is, all unions having at least one member employee affected by the measure under consideration, before a decision on collective dismissals or transfer of an undertaking can be made.

Upon the request of an employee party under § 32 of the act, the parties are to negotiate as to a collective agreement concerning the employees' right to codetermination. This section encourages the parties to a collective agreement regulating wages and similar matters to enter into agreements about entering into codetermination agreements concerning the conclusion and termination of contracts of employment, the management and distribution of work, and conducting of operations in general.

Collective agreements are legally binding both for the parties to the agreement and for their members.[15] The legislation does not explicitly regulate the legal effects of collective agreements with regard to employees who are members of different unions or not members of unions at all. A collective agreement can be applied in practice (but is not required by statute) to employees of other unions not having an applicable collective agreement at that workplace. This can follow explicitly from the collective agreement, or implicitly under the case law of the Labour Court, which often finds that collective agreements contain implied (in the absence of explicit) commitments by employers to not apply other terms of employment to those employees outside the collective agreement.[16] This broader application insures that the terms of the collective agreement are not circumvented, for example, by employers hiring employees not covered by the agreement at lower costs.

The social partners have fairly extensive freedom regarding the content of collective agreements. According to the Employment (Co-Determination in the Workplace) Act, collective agreements are to be in writing and concern employment terms and conditions or the general relationship between employees and employers. This is the extent of the statutory regulation. The primary issues addressed in collective agreements tend to be wages and employment terms and conditions. This lack of regulation as to the content of collective agreements is seen as one of the strengths of the Swedish model. Collective agreements allow the social partners to adapt the terms and conditions of employment to each

---

15 *See* FOLKE SCHMIDT, FACKLIG ARBETSRÄTT 98 (Reviderad Ronnie Eklund, Håkan Göransson, Ken Källström, Tore Sigeman, Stockholm 1997).

16 *See* for example Labor Court judgment, AD 1990 no. 33.

trade/sector. The parties to the agreement are free to negotiate the terms affecting employees and employers within the specific sector and at a specific workplace. In addition to collective agreements, individual terms in the employment contracts can be entered into between employers and individual employees. An individual employment contract may not, however, be in conflict with the applicable collective agreement.

Because of the duty to keep the industrial peace while a collective agreement is in place, collective agreements are typically renegotiated prior to their expiration. There are more than 670 collective agreements in the Swedish labor market, covering approximately 86 percent of the Swedish workforce. More than 500 collective agreements were scheduled for renegotiation in 2017, covering approximately 2.4 million employees, while in 2018, only 29 collective agreements were renegotiated.[17] Renegotiation procedures are not addressed by statute but are covered by collective agreements. For example, the 2017 Agreement on Industrial Development and Wage Formation (*industriavtal*) concluded between several major parties in private industry contains timetables for bargaining. This is to ensure that bargaining commences in sufficient time so that a new collective agreement can be successfully negotiated before the existing one expires, to allow the duty to keep the industrial peace to remain intact. The parties can also agree to extend an expiring collective agreement until a new one is reached. If the parties are unable to agree one month before the current agreement is to expire, an impartial chair is to be appointed under the agreement to assist the parties in the negotiations. The chair is empowered to order the parties to examine and identify individual bargaining issues, and may make proposals to resolve the issues in hand. Chairs are also entitled to order a cooling-off period for industrial action for which notice has been given, to allow for further negotiations, but not for longer than two weeks. An Industry Committee is established under the agreement, consisting of representatives of the parties, to monitor and encourage the execution of the agreement.

INDUSTRIAL ACTION AND THE PEACE OBLIGATION

Only the social partners can take lawful industrial action; individual employees acting on their own are seen as taking unlawful action. Two main categories of industrial conflict are set out in Swedish labor law: rights disputes and interest disputes. Rights disputes concern issues

[17] For these statistics, see the website of the Swedish National Mediation Office at mi.se, under the heading "avtalsrörelse."

covered by collective agreements and must ultimately be taken to the Labour Court for resolution. Where there is a collective agreement at a workplace, the parties bound to the collective agreement are deemed to have waived their right to take industrial action and are under a duty of peace (*fredsplikt*). As soon as a collective agreement is reached, the right of the parties to take industrial action in principle ceases according to Sections 41–42 of the Employment (Co-Determination in the Workplace) Act. Neither may industrial action be taken in order to amend a collective agreement. This is also seen as a rights dispute and must be first negotiated and then, failing a resolution by the parties, ultimately taken to the Labour Court. This gives rise to the function of collective agreements as peace instruments and acts as an incentive for employers to sign collective agreements. A party to a collective agreement, however, is generally entitled to take secondary action (*sympatiåtgärder*) without restriction in order to assist another party in an ongoing lawful labor conflict.

If no collective agreement is in place between the social partners, and the employer and employee parties cannot come to an agreement, the social partners are normally free to take industrial action (*stridsåtgärder*), a right constitutionally protected by ch. 2 § 14 of the Instrument of Government. Such conflicts are interest disputes for which industrial action is deemed the appropriate resolution mechanism. Industrial action can take the form of a strike, lockout, or boycott or any similar measure against the other party, failing any provision to the contrary by law or agreement. Industrial action is not defined by statute, but rather purposely not defined to allow for greater flexibility and protection of rights. The 1938 Basic Agreement sets out self-regulation procedures concerning blue-collar industrial actions, with respect to negotiations as well as to handling conflicts threatening essential public services. The National Mediation Office is currently authorized to provide assistance in resolving industrial disputes through mediation. Parliament is empowered under the Instrument of Government to intervene only in certain, very limited cases of industrial action.

TRADE UNION STRUCTURE AND MEMBERSHIP

The social partners are represented by strong centralized organizations, each having a hierarchy comprising umbrella organizations, national sector organizations belonging to the umbrella organizations, then local/regional and club organizations belonging to the national sector organizations. The major umbrella organizations on the employee side are known as LO, TCO, and SACO. *Landsorganisationen* ("LO") is the largest, covering mainly blue-collar workers, with 14 unions and nearly 1.5 million members.[18] Historically, it has had close ties with the political Social Democratic Workers Party, giving the political party SEK 6 million annually and presenting plans to spend SEK 30 million to support it in the 2018 election.[19] The Swedish Confederation for Professional Employees ("TCO") is the largest organization in the salaried employee sector, with 14 affiliated national unions and 1.3 million members.[20] The Swedish Confederation of Professional Associations ("SACO") organizes primarily university-educated employees, with 23 unions and slightly more than 670,000 members.[21] There are only a few smaller central organizations aside from these three. Further away from these organizations is the Swedish Workers Central Organisation—Syndicalists (*Sveriges arbetares centralorganisation—Syndikalisterna*), which perceives its role as being the counterpoint to the more traditional and, in its view, stagnant workers' movement.[22]

As to employer organizations, within the public sector there is the Swedish Agency for Government Employers ("SAGE") for the state, covering 250 employer members with a total of 250,000 employees.[23] The Swedish Association of Local Authorities and Regions ("SALAR") represents the municipalities and county councils as employers, covering employer members with nearly 1.2 million employees, approximately one quarter of the Swedish workforce.[24] On the private employer side, the main umbrella organization is the Confederation of Swedish Enterprise, with 50 sectoral and employer associations encompassing over 60,000 member companies covering almost 1.5 million employees.[25] There are also several smaller private employer organizations. The percentage of employers belonging to employer organizations, almost 90 percent, is today higher than the union density among employees, approximately 70 percent.

---

18 For more information on LO see its website, lo.se.

19 *See* Birgitta Forsberg, *LO statser 30 miljoner på S till valet—trots vikande stöd*, SVENSKADAGBLADET, December 23, 2017.

20 For more information on TCO see its website, tco.se.

21 For more information on SACO see its website, saco.se.

22 For more information on SAC see its website, sac.se.

23 For more information on SAGE see its website, arbetsgivarverket.se.

24 For more information on SALAR see its website, skl.se.

25 For more information on the Confederation of Swedish Enterprise, see its website, svensktnaringsliv.se.

Under the umbrella organizations, the national organizations are organized mostly by industry or employer, with only a few still organized by craft or trade. An objective expressed by LO since 1909 has been to move from craft unions over to industrial unions.[26] Examples of remaining craft unions include the Electricians' Union (*Elektrikerförbundet*) and Painters' Union (*Målareförbundet*). Under the national organizations, there may also be local clubs for particular workplaces. As there are no direct statutory regulations governing the formation of any of these organizations, the bylaws (*stadgar*) as adopted by their members alone govern the organizations. There are also no statutory regulations regarding elections or ballots, recognition, governance, or the taking of decisions concerning industrial action.

On the national umbrella level, as well as the national sector levels, the organizations' governance structures are similar. Congresses (*kongresser*) are to be held at regular intervals; in the majority of cases, these intervals are longer than one year, sometimes up to every fourth year.[27] Councils (*representantskap/förbundfullmäktige*) and boards (*förbundstyrelse*) make decisions in the periods between congresses if authorized to do so in the bylaws. The national sector unions are members of the umbrella organizations, sending representatives to these, and the local unions are members of the national sector organizations, sending representatives to these. Individuals are members of the local unions.

The LO bylaws require member unions to enact certain provisions, for example that the national sector's board is to make any decisions as to accepting, rejecting, or terminating a collective agreement, as well as concerning taking industrial action. In general, LO members are to obtain opinions from the LO Board before taking any significant decision. Members of LO must allow all workers in their area of operation to be members.[28] Individual trade union members must transfer their union membership if new employment requires this. The national unions are not to strike (primary or secondary) without the consent of the LO Board

---

[26] *See* FOLKE SCHMIDT, LAW AND INDUSTRIAL RELATIONS IN SWEDEN 18 (Stockholm 1977).

[27] *See* for example the bylaws of *Industrifacket Metall*, adopted at the 2017 Congress, which state in § 14(1) that the ordinary congress is to be held every third year. *Byggnads* holds its congresses every four years: see its *Stadgar för Svenska Byggnadsarbetareförbundet* (2014–18).

[28] This clause in the LO bylaws allows the rejected individual union members to appeal to the LO regarding a local union's decision against allowing membership: see FOLKE SCHMIDT, KOLLEKTIV ARBETSRÄTT 106 (4th ed. Stockholm 1962) 106.

where the strike or potential employee action concerns more than 3 percent of the national union's members. Where the national union has followed LO's procedures and been granted permission to take industrial action, the national union has the right to strike compensation from LO. In the same vein, every national union member has the duty to contribute to LO's strike fund.[29]

The bylaws of the labor market organizations also define the mutual rights and duties between the members and the organizations. There is no Swedish legislation explicitly regulating the internal affairs of labor market organizations. However, the 2008 Discrimination Act expressly prohibits unlawful discrimination by employee and employer organizations on the basis of sex, transgender identity or expression, ethnicity, religion or other belief, disability, sexual orientation, or age with respect to employment, labor market policy, professional recognition, and membership in organizations.

MEMBER DUTIES TO UNIONS

There is no statutory regulation of members' duties to trade unions, only that which is included in each organization's bylaws. There is no universal model for union bylaws and no statutory requirement as to dissemination to members or public access to either bylaws or collective agreements generally.[30] By way of example of duties under union bylaws, according to the Swedish Association of Health Professionals (*Vårdförbundet*) bylaws effective as of 2014, members agree to work for the solidarity and development of the union. Members also agree to follow the union's fundamental values and strive toward democratically made decisions. In cases of changed employment circumstances, members are to provide updated details as to employment as well as personal contact information. Members are to pay fees, and if membership is to be terminated this must be in writing.[31] In cases where members fail to pay

---

[29] LO and several of its union members have significant assets. From the most recent publicly available annual accounts, for example, it can be seen that the LO group had stated assets in 2015 of 2.8 billion Swedish crowns. That same year a national union, *Industrifacket Metall*, had 8.4 billion Swedish crowns in assets.

[30] There is a requirement for the social partners to submit copies of collective agreements to the Swedish National Mediation Office, mi.se.

[31] Until the 1970s, membership in a union was basically considered to be for life unless the member switched to a position of management. The other

their fees, or obviously violate the union's bylaws or in another manner work against the interests of the union, members can be expelled.[32] Another example of duties under bylaws can be seen in those of the finance sector union (*Finansförbundet*). These bylaws state the members' duties as being loyal to the union's purpose and objectives and, during situations of industrial conflict, following the union's directions and showing solidarity with the goals that the conflict seeks to achieve; providing the union with necessary personal information; paying membership fees; and informing the union if the member wishes it to intervene in a question as to employment conditions.

The 2017 bylaws of *Industrifacket Metall* include explicit sections concerning member rights and benefits, and one concerning member duties. Under the rights and benefits, members have the right to make motions to the local clubs, local sections, and national organization, and to the congresses. They have the right to compensation for harassment due to union membership and also for taking lawful industrial action. The national council can approve legal assistance for individual members. Under the member duties, members have the explicit obligation to follow the bylaws and any decision taken in accordance with them. Members are to strive for the cohesion and development of the union and be loyal to it. Member fees are to be paid, and the union updated as to personal information. Members have the right to terminate their union membership after two months' notice. The union can expel a member for failure to pay fees, for receiving compensation based on false information, for acting as a strike or blockade breaker, for supporting organizations that are not compatible with the union's objectives, or more generally for intentionally violating the bylaws or in another manner acting disloyally to the union.

UNION DUTIES TO MEMBERS

There are no specific statutory duties that trade unions must fulfill as regards their members that can give rise to a member claim. The most common remedy for a union member is to leave the union. Under the statutory framework of the labor law model, trade unions represent

---

alternative was to stop paying dues and be expelled: see SCHMIDT, *supra* note 26 at 54. Now due written notice of membership termination is sufficient to act as a resignation: see AD 1966 no. 11, AD 1971 no. 17.

[32] *See Vårdförbundets stadgar*, available at the Swedish Association of Health Professionals' website at vardforbundet.se.

member employees on both the collective and the individual levels. Unions can conclude collective agreements that bind their members. Unions are also to negotiate with an employer on behalf of employee members. Local signatory unions have the right to nominate a safety delegate at a workplace as well as employee representatives on the company's board of directors.[33] The union can also decide to pursue an employee member grievance, first through negotiations with the employer and then, if unsuccessful, by bringing a case to the Labour Court.[34] The decision to pursue a case is at the sole discretion of the trade union as there is no general duty of fair representation by trade unions as to their members.

Looking again at the bylaws of the Swedish Association of Health Professionals, it can be seen that members have the right to free assistance in matters concerning employment, but decisions as to litigation assistance that can be seen as costly are to be taken by the Board of the Union, with no appeal procedure in place. Members have the right to participate in meetings and activities within the union, nominate and participate in elections, propose motions, and stand as candidates, and have the right to strike pay.[35]

The bylaws of the finance sector union state that the members have the right to be active, to be elected to union positions, to introduce motions, to receive information as to the union's operations, to strike pay after three months' membership and after six months, to apply for certain membership funds, to transfer membership time from another union, and to be released from paying dues due to unemployment or long-term sick leave. Members have the right, after three months' membership, to apply for assistance with advice, negotiations, or legal aid with respect to an employment issue. The union council decides the form and extent of the assistance to be provided. Members have the right to request that the council hears a matter in which the member feels a decision has been wrongly taken by the union. A member can appeal a decision of the

---

[33] *See* KENT KÄLLSTRÖM, LOKALA KOLLEKTIVAVTAL—OM LOKALA PARTERS RÄTTSLIGA STÄLLNING INOM FACKLIGA ORGANISATIONER 104 (Liber 1979).

[34] LO and TCO have a joint law firm, LO-TCO rättsskydd AB, that provides help to union members in the areas of occupational injuries and employment disputes. A member of an LO or TCO union first needs to apply to the union for legal aid, after which the union assesses the merits of the case with regard to whether there is a reasonable chance of success. If approved by the union, the member then can use the services of the law firm. For more information see fackjuridik.com.

[35] Section 3.3 of *Vårdförbundets stadgar* as adopted by the 2014 congress.

board in writing within 30 days after notice of the decision has been given, and the appeal is then heard by the ordinary congress, which is held every third year.[36]

General legal principles as found in the areas of contracts or agency can also regulate the relationship between the union and its members. Those legal areas not covered by the labor legislation or collective agreements are, according to the labor law model, to be regulated by general private law. An example of this can be seen in a case brought by an employee against a trade union that had negotiated away certain vested rights of the employee in relation to the employer. The Labour Court found that the trade union had not explicitly been given authority by the employee to negotiate issues concerning vested rights and that trade unions generally only had the mandate to negotiate as to future employment issues. Thus, the union had acted outside the scope of its authority under general rules of agency. It can also be mentioned here that there is no overriding principle of fiduciary duties in Swedish law generally; any such duty must be based on explicit legislation (or bylaws/agreement). Trade unions are to follow general principles of procedural fairness, for example with decisions as to expelling members,[37] or decisions by a union board concerning member benefits.[38] A general principle of equal treatment of members is argued in the legal scholarship.[39]

PURSUING EMPLOYEE GRIEVANCES

The social partners are under a statutory obligation to negotiate most issues, almost always at the local and often also at the central levels, after

---

[36] Sections 4.1.4 and 4.1.8 of *Finansförbundets Stadgar* (bylaws), valid from July 1, 2012 and amended as of November 2016. It should be pointed out that the statute of limitations in employment issues is generally very short, measured in terms of weeks and months. The requirement that the member wait until the ordinary annual congress for a decision concerning support in litigation—which could take as much as three years—means the claim would long have been barred by the time the congress addressed the decision.

[37] *See* NJA 1945 p. 299, union expulsion decision invalid as member had not refused to comply with instructions from the union's national board as required by the bylaws; NJA 1946 p. 83, member expulsion due to belonging to a national socialist party invalid.

[38] *See* NJA 1987 p. 394 as to the invalidity of a union board's decision regarding union members' collective home insurance.

[39] *See* HEMSTRÖM, *supra* note 9 at 15.

which they can bring a case to the Labour Court.[40] Unions must have the employee's consent before they can bring an action to the Labour Court on behalf of the employee. However, as can be seen in the union bylaws cited above, in the majority of cases of employee grievance the individual employee has no mechanism to force a union to litigate a claim and the unions have no duty to provide legal assistance.

The system with respect to labor and employment law claims is very much based on a collective and not individual approach. Cases involving the social partners, including where a union represents an employee, are brought directly to the Labour Court as it has exclusive jurisdiction in such issues.[41] The composition of the Labour Court, as well as the relevant procedure, is regulated in the Labour Disputes (Judicial Procedure) Act and to the extent a specific issue is not regulated there, the procedural rules as found in the Code of Judicial Procedure are applicable. A judging panel for the Labour Court consists of at most seven members in total. Typically, three are nonpartisan members: a chair and a vice-chair trained in law, and an expert in the labor market. Another four members are partisan, with two appointed by the employer organizations and two by the employee organizations.

The Labour Court is limited in the relief it can grant. It can grant a motion for a declaratory judgment (*fastställesletalan*), such as whether an employment relationship exists; order performance based on a legal obligation (*fullgörelsetalan*); or declare invalid certain acts by the social partners, as well as collective agreements or clauses therein contained (*ogiltigförklaring*). The other primary remedy that the Labour Court can award is damages to either the individual employer or employee, the organization, or both. The damages are modest on a comparative scale.

---

40 *See* Jenny Julen Votinius, *Sweden* in RESOLVING INDIVIDUAL LABOUR DISPUTES 239 (Minawa Ebisui, Sean Cooney, & Colin Fenwick eds. ILO Geneva 2016), stating that 90–98 percent of all claims are settled before coming to the Labour Court, but citing no references and giving no further definition of "resolved" in terms of, for example, settlements and withdrawals.

41 The Labour Court's primary task was to resolve labor law issues, disputes regarding the interpretation and application of collective agreements, and the non-strike regulations of the Collective Agreements Act. The present expanded jurisdiction of the Labour Court over most issues of labor and employment law has several causes: Collective agreements now exist in most of the labor market, having been extended in the 1970s to include salaried private employees and the public sector; much labor law was codified in the 1970s package; and there was an expansion in certain areas due to EU membership so that the Labour Court's jurisdiction was broadened to include even employment law issues brought by unions on behalf of members, such as discrimination claims.

For example, in discrimination cases, the average of damages for the 2010s has been SEK 63,000 (as against the average trial costs and fees per party of SEK 192,000).[42] The Labour Court has no equitable remedies, such as the authority to order an employer to hire an individual. In addition, the Labour Court is the final instance, and its judgments cannot be appealed to any higher Swedish court.

With respect to the costs of pursuing an employee grievance after unsuccessful negotiations, if the union chooses to litigate the case, it bears all the costs and fees, and the case is brought directly to the Labour Court. If the individual employee brings the employment grievance, it must be to the general courts, which judgment can be then appealed to the Labour Court. Sweden generally follows the English rule with respect to trial costs and fees, which means that the non-prevailing party pays the trial costs and fees for both parties. According to § 5(2) of the 1974 Labour Disputes (Judicial Procedure) Act, the Labour Court may also order that each party bear its own costs if the losing party had reasonable cause to have the dispute tried, but this reallocation is seldom invoked by the Court, and then it is evenhanded between losing employers and losing employees.

If a union pursues an employee grievance, they risk only the trial costs and fees of one instance, that before the Labour Court. The unions have greater economic resources than individuals, so that the financial risks associated with litigating claims are not as decisive. However, there are limits even to these resources and there is no requirement that the unions pursue such claims. There is no duty of representation under Swedish labor law, so unions are basically free to decline to represent a claim, with the union member/employee having only the form of redress against the union of leaving it. Added to this is the complication of the very short statute of limitations in employment claims. For example, if the claim concerns unlawful dismissal, notice has to be given to the employer of the alleged unlawfulness within two weeks of the notice of dismissal, and if negotiations are not held, the case has to be filed within a second period of two weeks, or, where negotiations are held, two weeks after the end of negotiations. An individual with an unlawful dismissal claim consequently must receive a response from the union within two weeks or be barred from bringing the claim.

---

[42] For these statistics see Laura Carlson, *Discrimination Damages—Promoting or Preventing Access to Justice?* in FESTSKRIFT TILL ANN NUMHAUSER-HENNING 129 (Mia Rönnmar ed. Juristförlaget i Lund 2017).

If the individual employee pursues litigation of the grievance, they risk liability for the trial costs and fees of both parties and two instances, both before the general court and before the Labour Court.[43] There is a limited right to receive legal aid (for example, an individual cannot have assets and yearly income of more than SEK 260,000), with a ceiling of one hundred hours of legal advice. If the individual is a member of a trade union, the trade union is to be contacted before legal aid can be provided. If an individual has legal assistance coverage as part of their home insurance, the insurance coverage is to be used instead. With respect to home insurance covering legal assistance, the range of coverage varies per policy, often from SEK 75,000 to SEK 200,000, regularly with a deductible of 20 percent. Some policies also cover liability for the other party's fees up to 80 percent. A caveat here, though, is that most, if not all, insurance policies exempt employee employment disputes, referring instead to the trade unions as the avenue for pursuing such claims (regardless of whether the insured is a union member). Given the financial risks for plaintiffs, many claimants have opted to take employment claims to the small claims court, which has a ceiling of approximately SEK 22,000 in damages (with a filing fee of SEK 900) but a limited risk of being found liable to pay the other party's trial costs and fees. Given this limit in damages, it is questionable whether this can be seen as a suitable or deterring alternative from an access to justice perspective.

The Swedish labor law model is unabashedly concerned with the social partners and collective solutions to labor market issues. Union members have no statutory rights with respect to the unions, and no voice with

[43] *See*, for example, AD 2006 no. 54, in which a former employee argued that his employment termination was unlawful as it was based on sexual harassment of another employee. The employee prevailed in the trial court (applying the case law of the Labour Court) and was awarded SEK 85,000 in damages for the unlawful termination and SEK 15,525 for the employer's failure to give notice. The employer appealed the case to the Labour Court, which departed from its earlier case law and found that termination based on sexual harassment was lawful but that the former employee was correct in that he did not receive proper notice, for which the Labour Court awarded him SEK 5,000 in damages. Determining that the former employee had not prevailed as to the majority of the issues in the case, the Labour Court ordered him to pay the employer's trial costs and fees before the Labour Court in the amount of SEK 50,184, as well as the employer's costs and fees for the proceedings in which the employee prevailed in before the trial court, in the amount of SEK 185,968—making a total of SEK 236,152 plus interest to be paid by the former employee.

regard to employers except through the unions or through pursuing litigation themselves. Elaborate procedures have been put in place concerning the negotiations between the social partners, with extensive rights as to industrial action and secondary or sympathetic actions lawful. The claim could be made that the Swedish trade unions are some of the strongest in the world, with little or no legal accountability. The low damages awarded and the relatively higher attorneys' costs and fees create a significant deterrent for individuals considering the pursuit of employment grievances. Litigation is arguably not an affordable option for most individual plaintiffs. This is particularly true in light of the fact that such cases often involve employment grievances in terms of hiring or firing, and consequently individuals who are unemployed.

11. Employee voice in the United States

Union density in the United States generally was 10.7 percent in 2017, with rates of 6.5 percent in the private sector and 34.4 percent in the public sector, the latter which historically has strong union roots. Union density varies greatly by sector, with two sectors—education and protective service occupations—having the highest density rates, at approximately 34 percent. Union density also varies significantly by state, with New York having the highest at 23.6 percent (a New Amsterdam legacy, perhaps) and South Carolina the lowest at 1.6 percent. Despite downward trends and the lowest union density of the four countries examined here, these statistics also demonstrate union success. In those sectors where unions have historically been most active, union density is significantly higher, such as in local government, at 40.3 percent. The median weekly earnings of nonunion workers were 80 percent of the earnings of union members.[1]

The federal legislation governing labor relations today came out of the Great Depression and the New Deal in the 1930s, with the National Labor Relations Act of 1935 (the Wagner Act or the NLRA) still the centerpiece. Three other federal acts also address labor market relations: the Labor Management Relations Act of 1947 (the Taft–Hartley Act); the Labor Management Reporting and Disclosure Act of 1959 (the Landrum–Griffin Act); and the Labor Management Reporting and Disclosure Act of 1959.[2] Labor organizations are not allowed to unlawfully discriminate, as set out explicitly in the Civil Rights Act of 1964. The Social Security Act of 1935 and the Fair Labor Standards Act of 1938 set out social benefits and workplace standards, including a minimum wage.

The US approach to employee collective voice has been that of a single channel, the trade unions, representing employees against employers. Employees can bring also certain issues to governmental agencies for

---

1 *See* U.S. Bureau of Labor Statistics, *Economic News Release, Union Members Summary 2017*, January 19, 2018, available at the website of the U.S. Bureau of Labor Statistics, bls.gov.

2 States are allowed to legislate certain issues within this field, but an exhaustive account of the different states' legal systems is beyond the scope of this work.

resolution, such as claims of unfair labor practices by either employer or labor unions. The statutory framework created by the federal legislation has several policy objectives, including promoting industrial peace through collective bargaining and employee organizations, and ensuring that unions follow democratic principles.

THE LEGAL STATUS AND RECOGNITION OF TRADE UNIONS

There are no requirements for labor organizations to file articles of incorporation with either state or federal governments to gain legal personhood. However, de facto requirements can be found in both tax and reporting regulations, as well as in the Clayton Act. Labor organizations have been federally tax exempt since 1909.[3] Labor organizations have the right to collect member dues to pay for operational costs, with such collection generally not seen as revenue for business purposes and not taxable to the organization. Section 501(c)(5) of the US Internal Revenue Code sets out the definition and parameters for the tax-exempt status of labor organizations.[4] The term "labor" within the tax code is commonly accepted as meaning the performance of service as an employee.[5] For tax-exempt purposes, a labor organization is normally defined as:

---

[3] This was under the Corporation Excise Tax Act of 1909 (36 Stat. 113) ch. 6 § 38. The legislative bill explicitly included labor organizations, but the Senate Finance Committee struck it as it considered the definition "fraternal beneficiary societies … operating under a lodge system and providing for the payment of life, sick, accident, and other benefits" sufficiently inclusive. "Labour organizations" as a term was put back into the bill with the first income tax act, the Tariff Act of 1913, which then explicitly excluded "labor, agricultural, or horticultural organizations" from income tax liability: see the Tariff Act of 1913 (38 Stat. 172) ch. 16, § 11(G). All subsequent tax bills and revisions have retained this language: see John Francis Reilly, Carter C. Hull, & Barbara A. Braig Allen, IRC 501(c)(5) Organizations, Exempt Organizations Technical Instruction Program for FY 2003 (2003) j-3, available at the IRS website, irs.gov, *citing* 44 Cong. Rec. at 4148–49.

[4] 26 U.S.C. § 501(c).

[5] *See* Rev. Rul. 78-288, 1978-2 C.B. 179, *citing* Rev. Rul. 76-420, 1976-2 C.B. 153.

- An association of workers
- who have combined to protect or promote the interests of the members
- by bargaining collectively with their employers
- to secure better working conditions, wages, and similar benefits.[6]

The term "labor organization" includes labor unions, councils, and committees. IRC 501(c)(5) labor organizations do not need to be recognized labor unions.

To be tax exempt, a labor organization must meet two requirements: the net earnings of the organization may not inure to the benefit of any member, and the objective of the organization must be the betterment of conditions of those engaged in the pursuits of labor. Lobbying for legislation germane to a labor organization's program, even as a primary activity, is a permissible means of attaining its exempt purposes. However, a section 501(c)(5) labor organization engaging in lobbying may be required to either provide notice to its members regarding the percentage of dues paid applicable to lobbying activities, or pay a proxy tax.

The tax-exempt purposes of a labor organization do not include direct or indirect participation or intervention in the political campaigns of candidates for public office. A section 501(c)(5) labor organization may engage in political activities to the extent that it is not its primary activity. Expenditures regarding political activities may be subject to taxes. Labor organizations carrying on business activities, such as employing union members, collecting taxes, or creating a savings plan, are not tax exempt with respect to those activities. Union members prior to income tax year 2018 could take tax deductions for union dues and expenses paid (with the exception of lobbying) as unreimbursed job-related expenses to the extent that they exceeded 2 percent of the employee's adjusted gross income. Tax deductions for unreimbursed job-related expenses were removed starting in 2018 under the Tax Cuts & Jobs Act in an effort to simplify the federal tax code.[7]

Every labor organization also must comply with federal reporting requirements. Under Section 201 of the Labor Management Relations Act of 1947, every labor organization is to adopt a constitution and bylaws and submit copies of such with the Secretary of Labor. A report signed by the president of the labor organization and its secretary, or

---

6 *See* REILLY ET AL., *supra* note 3 at j-4.

7 *See* IRS Publication 529 (2015) for the income tax years prior to 2018 available at irs.gov. The Tax Cut and Jobs Act of 2017 applies as of 2018, see Pub.L. 115-97 codified at 131 Stat. 2054.

corresponding principal officers, is also to be filed, containing the particulars of the labor organization, including the name, mailing address, and address of its principal office; the name and title of each of its officers: the initiation fee or fees required from a new or transferred member; fees for work permits required by the reporting labor organization; and any regular dues or fees or other periodic payments required to remain a member of the reporting labor organization. In addition to this information, the labor organization is to submit a report including the following information:

- qualifications for or restrictions on membership;
- levying of assessments;
- participation in insurance or other benefit plans;
- authorization for disbursement of funds of the labor organization;
- audit of financial transactions of the labor organization;
- the calling of regular and special meetings;
- the selection of officers and stewards and of any representatives to other bodies composed of labor organizations' representatives, with a specific statement of the manner in which each officer was elected, appointed, or otherwise selected;
- discipline or removal of officers or agents for breaches of their trust;
- imposition of fines, suspensions, and expulsions of members, including the grounds for such action and any provision made for notice, hearing, judgment on the evidence, and appeal procedures;
- authorization for bargaining demands;
- ratification of contract terms;
- authorization for strikes; and
- issuance of work permits.

Consequently, while there may not be any requirements as to the incorporation of labor organizations, there are significant requirements as to their continued existence.

There are also requirements regarding the status of the lawfulness of labor organizations in order to be granted immunities under Section 6 of the 1914 Clayton Antitrust Act.[8] These are found under the heading of "Antitrust laws not applicable to labor organizations":

> The labor of a human being is not a commodity or article of commerce. Nothing contained in the antitrust laws shall be construed to forbid the

---

[8] 15 U.S.C. § 17.

> existence and operation of labor, agricultural, or horticultural organizations, instituted for the purposes of mutual help, and not having capital stock or conducted for profit, or to forbid or restrain individual members of such organizations from lawfully carrying out the legitimate objects thereof; nor shall such organizations, or the members thereof, be held or construed to be illegal combinations or conspiracies in restraint of trade, under the antitrust laws.

Consequently, labor organizations are given immunity from liability for antitrust violations if they are created to provide mutual help and are nonprofit, noncorporate organizations.

The procedures regarding labor union recognition are set out in the NLRA, which grants private employees the right to bargain collectively through representatives of their own choosing or, in the alternative, to refrain from making such a choice. A private employer may voluntarily agree to recognize a union as the bargaining representative for the employees at that workplace. In the absence of a voluntary employer agreement, the National Labor Relations Board ("NLRB") can be requested to conduct a secret ballot to determine whether a union will represent, or continue to represent, a unit of employees.[9] There are two types of certification cases: first, where the union files a petition to be certified; second, where an employer files a petition for an election of one or more individuals or unions seeking recognition as the bargaining representative. Of the 1,854 representation petitions filed with the NLRB in fiscal year 2017, elections were held in 1,366 and the unions won 940.[10] The union formation process commences when employees file an election petition with the NLRB showing that at least 30 percent of the employees at a given business wish to organize as a labor union and elect representatives for collective bargaining. Employee support is often demonstrated with signed and dated cards, which are not revealed to the employer and are authenticated by the NLRB. After a successful counting of cards showing at least 30 percent support as monitored by the NLRB, the labor union is formed.[11]

---

[9] The NLRB is an independent federal agency that has been empowered since 1935 to enforce the NLRA. It consists of a Board and a General Counsel, with 32 regional offices. The NLRB states its mission as being to protect "the rights of private sector employees to join together, with or without a union, to improve their wages and working conditions": see its website at nlrb.gov.

[10] NLRB, Representation Petitions, RC statistics, available at nlrb.gov.

[11] Criticism has been raised concerning the recognition process with the NLRB: *see*, for example, Cynthia Estlund, *The Ossification of American Labor Law*, 102 COLUMBIA LAW REVIEW 1527–1612, 1527 (2002); Benjamin Sachs,

After the procedural requirements are fulfilled by the parties concerned—that is, union and employer—including notice of the elections, secret ballots are held. Each party is permitted to have an observer present at the election. The side gaining the majority of votes cast wins. If the union receives the majority, it is then certified as the employees' bargaining representative and is entitled to be recognized by the employer as the exclusive bargaining agent for the employees in the unit. An employer's failure to bargain with the union at this point counts as an unfair labor practice. Objections to an election can be made by either of the parties concerned for failures to follow procedure or unfair labor practices.

Two types of decertification processes can be requested of the NLRB. The first is where 30 percent of the employees file a petition to remove the currently recognized union as the bargaining representative. This has to occur within very limited and defined timeframes, and not before the expiration of the first year after certification. Under the contract bar rule, during the first three years of a collective bargaining agreement, employees have the power to decertify the union with a majority vote within a 30 day window generally beginning 90 days and ending 60 days prior to the expiry of the agreement. In the second process, an employer files a petition based on a good faith reasonable uncertainty as to a union's continuing majority status.[12]

The dynamism of this process has been seen recently in the case of Yale University graduate students/adjunct teachers. Universities can use lower-paid adjuncts and doctoral students rather than full-time professors

---

Revitalizing Labor Law, 31(2) BERKELEY JOURNAL OF EMPLOYMENT AND LABOR LAW 333–47 (2010); and Benjamin Sachs, *Despite Preemption: Making Labor Law in Cities and States*, 1224 HARVARD L. REV. 1153–1224, 1162–63 (2011). The Employee Free Choice Act, H.R. 1409, S. 560, 111th Congress (2009–10) was introduced into both chambers of the US Congress in 2009 to address some of the criticism. The bill's purpose was to amend the National Labor Relations Act in three aspects. First, this was to be accomplished by streamlining union certification and allowing a union to be certified based on a majority of the employees' signatures without a NLRB ballot. Second, a requirement would be introduced that the employer and union enter into a collective agreement within 90 days after the union is recognized, or notify the Federal Mediation and Conciliation Service of the dispute. If mediation is unsuccessful after 30 days, the parties were to refer the dispute to an arbitration board, which would issue a decision that would be binding for two years. Third, the proposed act strengthened enforcement by allowing injunctions and liquidated damages in certain cases. This legislative proposal was not adopted.

[12] *See* Levitz Furniture Co. of the Pacific, 333 NLRB 105 (2001).

to teach, a model widely criticized as exploitative. In March 2015, Yale University graduate students chartered a union, Local 33 Unite Here, anticipating the 2015 NLRB decision that found graduate students were employees.[13] One week after the NLRB decision was taken, in September 2016, Local 33 filed for union elections and was certified for its first vote, which took place on February 23, 2017. The newly formed union requested negotiations with Yale University in April 2017, and the university responded by appealing the NLRB decision to allow the vote to take place, as well as the Columbia decision. The union withdrew its petition with the NLRB in 2018 and has decided to pursue voluntary negotiations with Yale.[14]

EMPLOYEE CONSULTATION

Within the duty of the employer to bargain in good faith is also the requirement that the employer furnish information to a recognized labor union in the bargaining process to assist the union in its negotiations under sections 8(a)(1) and (5) NLRA. The failure to provide such information in certain cases has been seen as an unfair labor practice.[15] This duty to provide information is even extended to information necessary for policing the administration of an existing collective agreement, as well as assessing grievances.[16] The employer has no duty to inform unless the recognized labor union has made a timely and

---

[13] The National Labor Relations Board decision of August 23, 2016 in the petition filed by the Graduate Workers of Columbia-GWC and the United Autoworkers in Union Case Number: 02-RC-143012 to represent graduate student assistants at Columbia University. According to the 2016 NLRB press release, "[f]ederal courts have made clear that the authority to define the term 'employee' rests primarily with the Board absent an exception enumerated within the National Labor Relations Act. The Act contains no clear language prohibiting student assistants from its coverage. The majority found no compelling reason to exclude student assistants from the protections of the Act": see NLRB, Board: Student Assistants Covered by the NLRA (August 23, 2016) available at nlrb.gov.

[14] *See* the website of the Union of Graduate Employees at Yale University, Local 33 Unite Here, at local33.org.

[15] *See* NLRB v. Truitt Mfg. Co., 351 U.S. 149 (1956) (employer's claim—that the financial situation of the company did not allow a wage increase—needed to be honest and subject to review, that is, verified through documentation).

[16] *See* NLRB v. Acme Industrial Co., 385 U.S. 432 (1967); Schrock Cabinet Co., 339 NLRB 182 (2003); King Scoopers, Inc., 332 NLRB 4 (2000).

somewhat clear request for information, and the duty to provide information in no way triggers a right to employee consultation.

There is no statutory requirement that an employer consult with employees with respect to its state of affairs. In fact, the historical development has been the opposite, with the issue of employee consultation intimately intertwined with employer-initiated company unions. At the time of the passage of the NLRA, company unions accounted for 60 percent of union membership. Company-controlled unions were viewed as easily dominated by employers, skewing the collective bargaining process in favor of employers. Section 8(a)(2) NLRA outlaws company unions, making it an unfair labor practice for an employer to engage in such conduct, as company unions lack the "unfettered power of the independent organization to determine its own actions." Company unions consequently lack the "independence of action and free choice" required by section 7 NLRA.[17]

Voluntary systems of employee consultation can be found, as created within collective agreements. The University of California, which has negotiated collective agreements with 15 unions representing 77,000 employees, has in its collective agreements the duty to consult with the employees and appropriate labor union in cases of:

- extensions or releases of employees during a probationary period;
- disciplinary actions (letters of warning, suspensions, terminations) for career employees;
- investigatory leave (prior to or immediately after placing employee on leave);
- layoffs or reductions in time;
- medical separation (of employees who are unable to return to work due to a medical condition); and
- early release of limited appointment employees (before the normal end of their expected appointment end date).[18]

---

[17] For the argument that company unions should be allowed in workplaces which have no significant labor union presence, to allow workers to take up grievances and suggestions, see PATMORE, *supra* ch. 6, note 70 at 41–42. *See also* Laura J. Cooper, *Letting the Puppets Speak: Employee Voice in the Legislative History of the Wagner Act*, 94 MARQUETTE LAW REV. 837–868 (2011).

[18] *See* for example the Collective Bargaining Agreement entered into between the University of California and the Teamsters Local 2010, effective December 31, 2011–November 20, 2016, available at the website of the University of California at ucnet.universityofcalifornia.edu/labor/bargaining-units/cx/contract.html.

Another example of a voluntary agreement as to employee consultation can be seen in the Collective Bargaining Agreement dated February 11, 2016 between the Boeing Company and the Society of Professional Engineering Employees in Aerospace, The International Federation of Professional and Technical Engineers ("IFPTE") Local 2001, in effect until 2022. The employer has to notify the union of several different types of decisions in advance, and under the agreement's section 10.1, "Joint Meetings," it is stated:

> 10.1(a) Should either party desire to discuss with the other any matter affecting generally the relationship of the parties, a meeting of Union and management representatives shall be arranged upon request of either party. Such meeting shall take place at a time mutually convenient to both parties. Any use of Company time for attendance at such meetings shall be arranged in advance by mutual agreement.
>
> 10.1(b) This Article is intended to provide a free avenue of communication between the Union and the Company, and suggestions, complaints, or other matters may be presented by either party, provided that neither party shall be required to discuss any item brought up by the other party nor be bound to act upon any item presented. However, both parties agree to discuss informal grievances and complaints.[19]

The basic underlying premise of the NLRA is that the parties are to have arm's length negotiations without undue influence by either side, leading to skepticism regarding any employer efforts in this area.

CONCERTED ACTIVITY

Employees who are not represented by a union also have rights under the NLRA. Section 7 NLRA protects employees' right to engage in concerted activity without retaliation by the employer. Concerted activity is when two or more employees take action for their mutual aid or protection regarding the terms and conditions of employment. A single employee may also engage in protected concerted activity if he or she is acting on the authority of other employees, bringing group complaints to the employer's attention, trying to induce group action, or seeking to prepare for group action. A fairly broad range of cases can be found here with respect to concerted activities. Employees who refuse to work

[19] The Collective Bargaining Agreement dated February 11, 2016 between the Boeing Company and the Society of Professional Engineering Employees in Aerospace, IFPTE Local 2001 available at speea.org.

overtime or who leave their employer's premises in protest over wages, hours, or other working conditions are engaged in protected activities under the NLRA.[20] Although a truck driver's continued protests about fuel surcharges were presented individually, the driver was found by the NLRB and the Seventh Circuit Court of Appeals to be engaged in concerted activity protected by the NLRA. The individual employee, who had asked that the surcharges be shown on his paycheck stub as the driver, had been engaged in an ongoing debate with the company concerning exactly how much was being taken from his paycheck, and was reiterating a shared employee complaint.[21]

COLLECTIVE BARGAINING AND THE LEGAL STATUS OF COLLECTIVE AGREEMENTS

Once a labor union is recognized, either through the NLRB election process or voluntarily by an employer, it is irrebuttably presumed to represent a bargaining unit at a workplace during the certification year or the period of the collective agreement. Once the certification year or agreement expires, the union enjoys a rebuttable presumption as to continued representation until it is decertified or suffers a loss of majority status.[22] Before the expiry of a collective agreement, the parties have the obligation to bargain in good faith for a successor contract, or for the termination of the agreement, while the terms of the expiring contract continue. A party wishing to end the contract must notify the other party in writing 60 days before the expiration date, or 60 days before the proposed termination. The party must offer to meet and confer with the other party and notify the Federal Mediation and Conciliation Service of the existence of a dispute if no agreement has been reached by that time.[23]

---

20 *See* NLRB v. Mike Yurosek & Son, Inc, 53 F.3d 261 (9th Cir. 1995).

21 *See* Alton H. Piester, LLC v. NLRB, 591 F.3d 332 (7th Cir. 2010).

22 An employer acquiring another employer is not required to take over a collective agreement as entered into by the previous employer. However, if the new employer is found to be a successor to the previous employer, they may have a duty to recognize and bargain with the union recognized by the predecessor.

23 The Federal Mediation and Conciliation Service was established in 1947 and is an independent agency whose mission is to preserve and promote labor management peace and cooperation. Headquartered in Washington, D.C., with ten regional offices and more than 60 field offices, the agency provides mediation

The recognized labor union has the exclusive authority to negotiate on behalf of the employees regarding wages, hours, and other terms and conditions of employment.[24] The employer's refusal to bargain collectively with representatives of the employees is an unfair labor practice under section 8(a)(5) NLRA.[25] The parties have a mutual obligation to negotiate in good faith, as stated in section 8(d), but there is no obligation for either party to agree or compromise. "Good faith" is not defined by statute, with the case law addressing this issue on a case-by-case basis. The NLRB distills the duty to bargain in good faith into "an obligation to participate actively in the deliberations so as to indicate a present intention to find a basis for agreement. This implies both an open mind and a sincere desire to reach an agreement as well as a sincere effort to reach a common ground."[26] Good faith rules out surface bargaining, meeting and merely going through the motions of negotiations with no intent of reaching an agreement, and unilateral, take-it-or-leave-it proposals. The failure to negotiate in good faith is also an unfair labor practice. Objective criteria at which the NLRB looks when determining a lack of good faith include: whether the party is willing to meet at reasonable times and intervals; whether the party is represented by someone who has the authority to make decisions at the table; and conduct away from the bargaining table. One example of bad faith given by the NLRB is where an employer makes a unilateral change in the terms and conditions of an employee's employment without bargaining. After sufficient good faith efforts where no agreement is reached, the employer may declare an impasse and implement the last offer presented to the union. This can be contested by the union, which may declare that no true impasse had been reached and that the employer bargained in bad faith. The NLRB then determines whether a true impasse had been reached. If the NLRB finds that no impasse was reached, the employer will be ordered to return to the bargaining table.

The duty to bargain in good faith under section 8(d) NLRA includes an obligation to commit the agreement to writing. The Court has stated that "an employer, who, by his refusal to honor, with his signature, the

---

and conflict resolution services to industry, government agencies, and communities: for more information see its website at fmcs.gov.

[24] *See* sections 9 and 8(d) NLRA.

[25] *See also* Virginian Railway v. System Federation No. 40, 300 U.S. 515 (1937) and NLRB v. Jones & Laughlin Steel Corp., 301 U.S. 1 (1937), holding that compulsory collective bargaining is constitutional.

[26] *See* NLRB, Employer/Union Rights and Obligations: How Is "Good Faith" Bargaining Determined? at the NLRB website, NLRB.gov.

agreement which he has made with a labor organization, discredits the organization, impairs the bargaining process and tends to frustrate the aim of the statute to secure industrial peace through collective bargaining."[27] The parties are also prohibited from reneging on any agreement reached. During the term of the agreement, the duty to bargain includes a duty to negotiate any questions arising under the collective agreement, as well as a continuous duty to provide information as well as refrain from making unilateral changes. The NLRB can order the parties to sign a written contract evidencing the agreement, and also order that the agreement be honored. The NLRB can also void employers' unilateral acts taken without bargaining and order restoration of the status quo, including back pay, resumption of operations, and reinstatement. However, the ineffectiveness of the NLRB's remedial authority in cases of violation of the duty to bargain has been raised by the Court,[28] by the NLRB itself,[29] and by scholars.[30]

Exclusivity with respect to the recognized union and bargaining entails that no person or group other than the recognized labor union can represent the same employees within the bargaining unit. This rule of exclusivity was put into place as the economics of pluralism were seen to favor employers. In order to promote effective representation, exclusivity bars employers from using divide and conquer tactics, encouraging interunion rivalries, and negating strike threats.[31] The Court has interpreted the NLRA and the Railway Labor Act as prohibiting individual employees from negotiating their own terms and conditions of employment where an exclusive bargaining representative has been recognized.[32] This requirement of direct dealing between employers and recognized labor unions as a facet of industrial self-determination has had three themes in the case law: an employer refusing to recognize the union's monopoly over the labor market, an employer depriving the collective of the right to redistribute individual assets to the benefit of the collective,

---

[27] *See* H.J. Heinz Co. v. NLRB, 311 U.S. 514, 526 (1941).

[28] *See* H.K. Porter Co. v. NLRB, 397 U.S. 99 (1970).

[29] *See* Ex-Cell-O Corporation, 185 NLRB 107 (1970).

[30] *See* for example, *Notes: NLRB Remedies*, 351 DUKE LAW JOURNAL 354 (1975). The Labor Law Reform Act of 1978 was presented to Congress with the aim of amending the National Labor Relations Act to strengthen the remedies and expedite the procedures under the NLRA. The 1978 proposal passed the House but not the Senate.

[31] *See* RAY ET AL., *supra* chap. 6 note 55 at 190.

[32] *See* J.I. Case Co. v. NLRB, 321 U.S. 332 (1944). *See also* Order of Railroad Telegraphers v. Railway Express Agency, Inc., 321 U.S. 342 (1944) and Medo Photo Supply Corp. v. NLRB, 321 U.S. 678 (1944).

and an employer not giving the union the chance to act upon its bargaining mandate.[33] Exclusivity applies, however, only to the mandatory subjects of bargaining: wages, hours, and terms and conditions of employment. Employers can negotiate directly with employees as concerning nonmandatory subjects. In addition, a collective agreement can set a floor regarding certain employment terms, such as wages, and the individual employees can then negotiate wages higher than the floor. Employees and groups of employees that are not the recognized labor union can, despite exclusivity, bring grievances directly to the employer.

INDUSTRIAL ACTION AND THE PEACE OBLIGATION

Industrial action and the peace obligation are regulated both by legislation and by collective agreement. The framework established by the NLRA is mandatory, but still gives great leeway for the collective agreements entered into by the social partners.

Industrial Action and the NLRA

Industrial action is considered a necessary element of the collective bargaining process under the NLRA. The act guarantees the right of employees to lawfully strike, while at the same time placing limitations and qualifications on the exercise of the right.[34] Strikes can be unlawful if their purpose is unlawful, if they are taken in violation of a no-strike cause, if there is a failure to follow procedure, or due to the misconduct of the strikers. Two categories of lawful strikers are created under the act: economic strikers and unfair labor practice strikers.

There is in essence a peace obligation with respect to economic terms during the validity of a collective agreement. Economic industrial actions are those with the objective of economic goals, of terminating or modifying a collective agreement. In cases of economic industrial action where a collective agreement is in place, the party taking the industrial action—the labor union in the case of a strike, or the employer in the

---

[33] *See* RAY ET AL., *supra* chap. 6 note 55 at 194.

[34] In 2017 there were 7 work stoppages involving more than 25,000 or more workers and 440,000 idle days affected in the United States: see BLS News Release, *MAJOR WORK STOPPAGES 1947–2017* (USDL-18-0206), February 9, 2018 available at the website of the Bureau of Labor Statistics, U.S. Department of Labor, bls.gov. These statistics have been compiled by the BLS since 1947, with the highest number of idle days in one year reaching almost 61 million in 1959.

case of a lockout—has to first give notice under section 8(d) NLRA. The acting party has to give 60 days' notice of termination or modification to the other party, and notify the Federal Mediation and Conciliation Service within 30 days of the notice as to the dispute. Strikes and lockouts are barred for either the 60 notice days or until the agreement expires, whichever date occurs later.[35] Economic strikers retain their status as employees and cannot be discharged. Under the *Mackay* doctrine, an employer may hire replacements for economic strikers and need not discharge the replacements after the strike is over.[36] If the economic striker applies unconditionally to go back to work, the economic striker is not entitled to reinstatement at that time. Economic strikers are then entitled to be recalled during limited time periods to jobs for which they are qualified when openings in such jobs occur.

The Court has held that the requirements of notice under the NLRA as applicable to economic strikes are not applicable to strikes caused by unfair labor practices or dangerous work conditions.[37] Unfair labor practice strikers have greater protection than economic strikers as they can neither be discharged or permanently replaced.

If an employer responds improperly to a strike, it commits an unfair labor practice. If an employer unlawfully discharges a striker or fails to recall a striker when there is a duty to do so, the employer can be ordered to reinstate the employee and pay back pay. Employees engaging in unlawful strikes can be lawfully dismissed by employers. Secondary boycotts are prohibited under sections 8(b)(4)(b) and 8(e) NLRA, entailing that all union picketing activity is barred against employers with whom the labor union does not have a primary labor dispute. If either the recognized labor union or the employer breach the industrial actions provisions of the NLRA, they commit an unfair labor practice.

The provisions of the NLRA generally preempt state legislation in the areas of labor representation and strikes. However, the NLRA exempts federal, state, and local governments from its definition of "employer." States then have legislative jurisdiction as governing public employers,

---

[35] Strikes are totally barred in cases of emergencies affecting the nation's safety and health, see Section 206 NLRA and United Steelworkers v. United States, 361 U.S. 39 (1959), and certain limitations are placed on health care institutions.

[36] *See* NLRB v Mackay Radio & Telegraph Co., 304 U.S. 333 (1938) and NLRB, *The Right to Strike*, available at nlrb.gov/strikes.

[37] *See* Mastro Plastics Corp. and French-American Reeds Mfg. Co., Inc. v. NLRB, 350 U.S. 270 (1956).

and also if a "compelling state interest"[38] such as preventing violence can be argued, giving rise within a limited context to an additional layer of regulatory norms.

Industrial Action and Collective Agreements

Certain labor organizations, often national labor unions, also internally regulate issues of industrial action, often in charters or constitutions. By way of example, the 2015 IFPTE Constitution states in its Article 16 that the Federation is opposed to strikes and lockouts for adjusting differences between employers and employees, preferring arbitration.[39] No local union member is to call or engage in a strike until it is cleared by the IFPTE, which is to determine within one week whether a strike would be legal and proper. The IFPTE's Executive Council is authorized to grant strike, lockout, or victimization benefits to members and local unions from the Federation's funds.

Procedures for calling a strike are set out both in the Teamsters Constitution and local union bylaws. After a statement that employment disputes are to be resolved through good faith collective bargaining, the strike voting rules are found in Article XII(b) of the International Brotherhood of Teamsters Constitution.[40] During negotiations, the executive board of a local Teamster union can order a secret strike ballot to be taken. Where the employer has made a final offer of settlement, the offer is to be submitted to the membership involved for a secret ballot. If at least one half of the members eligible to vote cast valid ballots, any majority of those voting in favor of the final offer is to result in the acceptance of the submitted offer. In the event that the majority votes against accepting the final offer, a strike is authorized without the need for any additional vote. If less than one half of the eligible members cast valid ballots, then a qualified majority of two thirds of the vote is necessary to reject the final offer and to authorize a strike.

Section 29(D) of the Teamsters Local 2010 Union Bylaws picks up where the Teamsters Constitution leaves off,[41] providing that if a

---

[38] San Diego Building Trades v. Garmon, 359 U.S. 236 (1959).

[39] The 2015 Constitution is available at the IFPTE website, at ifpte.org.

[40] Adopted by the 28th International Convention June 27–July 1, 2011. The International Brotherhood of Teamsters has member unions representing 1.4 million employees.

[41] The Local Union Bylaws for the Teamsters Local 2010 (2017), available at the website of the Teamsters Local Union 2010 at teamsters2010.org.

settlement with the employer is not reached after the union negotiators have used reasonable means to achieve settlement through collective bargaining, "the matter shall be subject to the strike procedure, conditions and qualifications set forth in the Constitution. The Local Union Executive Board may, in its discretion, provide that the strike vote be limited to the members employed in a particular division, craft, chapter or place of employment." In addition, a strike vote is not required where the existing collective bargaining agreement authorizes strikes for the purpose of enforcing the terms of the agreement. Strike votes are also not required for strikes in support of demands that an employer agree to the terms and conditions of an agreement already negotiated and approved on a state, multistate, multiarea, multiemployer or national, companywide, or area basis of which unit such employer is a member. In either case, the Local Union Executive Board, subject to the approval of the General President, may call the strike in support of its position, and may also, with the approval of the General President, terminate such strike without vote. Striking members are eligible for out-of-work benefits as provided by the Teamsters Constitution. Strikes not terminated by the conclusion of a collective agreement or by arbitration may otherwise be terminated in such manner as the Local Union Executive Board deems appropriate.

The University of California collective agreement entered into with the Teamsters Local 2010 contains a no-strike clause in its Article 20. That clause states that both the employer and the employee organization, the Coalition of University Employees ("CUE") Teamsters, agree not to take industrial action, whether lockouts, strikes, stoppages or interruptions of work, or other concerted activities that interfere directly or indirectly with university operations during the life of the collective agreement or any written extension thereof. The CUE Teamsters further agrees, on behalf of its officers and agents, that it shall not in any way authorize, assist, sanction, condone, or participate in any activities, including sympathy strikes, in violation of the agreement. Employees violating this clause are to be subject to discipline up to and including termination of employment. The CUE Teamsters also assumes the obligation to "immediately take whatever appropriate action is necessary to prevent and bring about an end to any concerted activity in violation of this Article," including notice to employees engaged in such conduct. This collective agreement expired on November 30, 2016 and after almost a year of unsuccessful negotiations the CUE Teamsters called their members to a strike in January 2017 over fair wages, and won concessions as to a pay increase of 19.4 percent over five years. More than 97 percent of members voted for the employer's offer in April 2017.[42]

UNFAIR LABOR PRACTICES

Both employers and labor unions can be liable for unfair labor practices under the NLRA[43]—employers since the passage of the NLRA in 1935 under its section 8(a); labor unions since 1947 with the passage of the Taft–Hartley Act under section 8(b) NLRA.[44]

Employers are barred under section 8(a) NLRA from interfering with, restraining, or coercing employees in the exercise of the rights:

- to self-organization;
- to form, join, or assist labor organizations;
- to bargain collectively through representatives of their own choosing; or
- to engage in concerted activities for the purpose of collective bargaining or other mutual aid or protection.

Employers are also barred from dominating or interfering with the formation or administration of any labor organization, or contributing financial or other support to it (with the exception of allowing employees time off with pay to confer with the employer). Employers are also not to discriminate against any individual worker because of union activity, such as in terms of hiring or employment conditions. Employers and the representative union can however enter into an agreement under the act as to requiring union membership as a condition of employment. The prohibition as to discrimination extends to employees with regard to filing charges with the NLRB or taking part in any NLRB proceedings. As stated above, the employer also has a duty to bargain collectively in good faith.

---

[42] *See* the Teamsters 2010 website for more information on this bargaining process, at teamsters2010.org.

[43] An unfair labor practice is not the same thing as a violation of a fair labor standard as defined in the Fair Labor Standards Act ("FLSA"). A complaint as to a violation of a fair labor standard, such as failing to pay minimum wages as defined by that act, is filed with the U.S. Department of Labor, which has the mandate to enforce the FLSA.

[44] Codified at 29 U.S.C. § 158—Unfair Labor Practices.

Section 8(b) NLRA lists unfair labor practices as committed by labor organizations and their agents. Labor unions or their agents are not to restrain or coerce individual employees in the exercise of the employees' rights to self-organization, bargain collectively through representatives of their own choosing, or engage in concerted activities for the purpose of collective bargaining or other mutual aid or protection. A breach of the labor union's duty of fair representation of all members is also an unfair labor practice.

With respect to the labor union's relationship with the employer, the labor union also has a duty to bargain in good faith. Labor unions are not to restrain employers in the selection of their representatives for collective bargaining or handling grievances, nor cause employers to discriminate against an employee based on union membership or lack thereof. Unions are not to require employers to pay for unnecessary workers, nor force employers to join an organization, recognize an employee organization, or distribute work based on union membership. With respect to industrial action, unfair labor practices by labor unions include engaging in certain types of secondary boycotts, picketing for recognition for more than 30 days without petitioning for an election, or refusing to handle goods from an anti-union employer.

A charge citing an unfair labor practice can be filed with the NLRB within six months of the event by basically any party, including employees, labor organizations, employers, civil society, relatives or friends. Charges can be filed electronically with the NLRB and there are no filing fees. Each charge is investigated by Board agents who gather evidence and may take affidavits from parties and witnesses. Their findings are evaluated by the Regional Director and, in certain novel or significant cases, reviewed by NLRB attorneys at the Division of Advice in Washington, DC. Typically, a decision is made about the merits of a charge within 7–12 weeks, although in certain cases this can take much longer. During this period, the majority of charges are settled by the parties, withdrawn by the charging party, or dismissed by the Regional Director. Between 20,000 and 30,000 charges are received annually by the NLRB.[45] Of the 18,874 charges as to unfair labor practices brought in 2017, 7,344 (39 percent) settled, 6,575 (35 percent) were withdrawn, 4,512 (24 percent) were dismissed and Board Orders were issued in 443 (2 percent) charges. Decisions to dismiss a charge may be appealed to the Office of Appeals in Washington, DC within two weeks of the dismissal. Each appeal is assigned an attorney and supervisor for a review of all the

---

[45] *See* NLRB, What We Do, Investigate Charges, available at nlrb.gov.

documents in the case, including new information submitted by the charging party. The Office of Appeals handles about 2,000 appeals annually.

A structural weakness exists with respect to the NLRB's unfair labor practices under section 8(a)(5), in that employers can delay the enforcement of remedies literally for years by invoking the appeal process. An employer can contest the finding of an unfair labor practice (or even a union election, as seen in the case of Yale University). A hearing must then be held and a NLRB decision issued, and in the event that the employer refuses to comply with the decision, enforcement must be sought by the NLRB from a federal circuit court of appeal. This process can take years, during which period the employer has no duty to bargain with the union. Even if the Board is successful at the circuit court, the remedy is a bargaining order commencing as of the date of the court of appeal's judgment. There is naturally a time-cost aspect to any delay—the employer may have saved money by not having to bargain with the union during this period. In addition, the union may have been weakened in the eyes of its members by such delays as are caused by the employer.[46]

THE STRUCTURE AND MEMBERSHIP OF LABOR UNIONS

Positive freedom of association—the right of workers to join unions—is explicitly protected by the NLRA. Negative freedom of association, the right to not join a labor organization, is not as highly protected on the federal level. According to section 8(a)(3) NLRA, union shop agreements,[47] collective agreements binding the employer to employ only members of a single labor union, are valid after the 30th day of employment.[48] States began to adopt right-to-work laws prohibiting

---

46 *See* LESLIE, *supra* chap. 6 note 77 at 220.

47 In a closed shop, employees must be members of the union as a condition of employment and if the employee ceases to be a member, they are to be discharged. A union shop allows for the hiring of non-union employees, provided that they then join the union within a certain time period. An agency shop is where employees must pay the equivalent of union dues, regardless of union status, but need not formally join the union. An open shop is where employees need neither be members nor pay dues.

48 *See* E.H. Schopler, *Closed Shops and Closed Unions*, 160 A.L.R. 918 (1946 with cumulative supplements).

these traditional union security devices of the closed shop and/or agency shop at an early stage. Before 1947, the question existed whether state right-to-work legislation was invalid due to conflicting with the NLRA. The 1947 Labor Management Relations Act added § 14(b) to the NLRA, specifically granting states the right to prohibit union and agency shops. The Court also held at an early stage that state right-to-work statutes were constitutional.[49] Today, 28 states and the Guam Territory have either constitutional provisions or legislation concerning right-to-work provisions.[50]

A three-tiered system exists with respect to employee labor organizations, with umbrella labor union federations, such as the AFL-CIO (representing a total of 12 million workers)[51] and the Change to Win Federation (representing a total of 5.5 million workers),[52] having national

---

[49] *See* Lincoln Federal Labor Union No. 19129, A.F. of L. v. Northwestern Iron & Metal Co., 335 U.S. 525 (1949) and American Federation of Labor v. American Sash & Door Co., 335 U.S. 538 (1949) (right-to-work laws of three states—Arizona, Nebraska, and North Carolina—did not violate the due process and equal protection clauses of the Fourteenth Amendment).

[50] As with any legal issue in the United States, the variances between the different states' legal treatments are considerable and any systematization is beyond the scope of this work. The following 28 states have right-to-work legislative or constitutional provisions: Alabama (1943), Arizona (State Constitution 1948), Arkansas (Constitution 1944), Florida (Constitution 1944), Georgia (1947), Idaho (1985), Indiana (2012), Iowa (1947), Kansas (Constitution 1958), Kentucky (2017), Louisiana (1976), Michigan (2012), Mississippi (Constitution and statute 1954), Missouri (2017, citizen vote to be held in 2018), Nebraska (Constitution and statute 1946), Nevada (1952), North Carolina (1947), North Dakota (1947), Oklahoma (Constitution 2001), South Carolina (1954), South Dakota (1946), Tennessee (1947), Texas (1993), Utah (1955), Virginia (1947), West Virginia (2016), Wisconsin (2015), Wyoming (1963), and Guam (2000). For the specific state laws, see the website of the National Right to Work Legal Defense Foundation at nrtw.org. In 2016 the Sixth Circuit Court of Appeals upheld the right of local governments to enact local right-to-work laws in Kentucky and Ohio: *see* United Automobile, Aerospace and Agricultural Implement Workers of America Local 3047, et al. v. Hardin County, Kentucky, et al., 842 F.3d 407 (6th Cir. 2016).

[51] For these statistics see the AFL-CIO website, aflcio.org, under the heading "AFL-CIO Unions."

[52] For these statistics see the Change to Win website at changetowin.org.

labor unions as their members.[53] The umbrella organizations are governed by constitutions approved by the national member labor unions at conventions,[54] with issues between conventions addressed by leadership councils.

The two models existing today at the national labor union level are old unionism, based on the trades/crafts, and new unionism, or industrial/employer-specific unions—reflecting the divide between the AFL-CIO and Change to Win. The AFL-CIO has retained its historic trade union model focus. The Change to Win unions broke free of the AFL-CIO in 2005 (mirroring the previous breakout of the CIO), emphasizing an industry focus. Change to Win currently spends three quarters of its membership revenues on strengthening union density and organization.[55] The trade union model, almost directly taken from the guilds and journeymen's organizations, as discussed in previous chapters, facilitates access to jobs for specialized workers and, in the guild tradition, often provides benefits not provided by employers. The industrial unions, which are employer-specific, often comprise nonmanagerial employees seeking to bargain with one specific employer. Consequently, to be a member of an industrial union, the individual must already be employed by the targeted employer. Employment, not skill, is then the determinative qualification. Both these national types typically have constitutions approved by members, conventions convened regularly, and executive councils and officers. Under the national labor unions are local unions, as seen in the example of the Teamsters at the University of California cited previously. Employees belong to the local unions, and their rights are set out in the local union bylaws.

Every labor organization is to adopt a constitution and bylaws, submitting them and certain other reports to the Secretary of Labor under the requirements of section 201 of the 1947 Labor Management Relations Act. The process for labor organization elections is also set out in sections 401–403 of the act, with each national or international labor

---

[53] The structure of the labor unions varies across the different umbrella organizations. A third umbrella organization, Industrial Workers of the World, was founded in 1905; it presently has about four thousand individuals as members, who are organized within the industry of their employment: see the IWW website at iww.org.

[54] The AFL-CIO conventions are held every fourth year.

[55] *See* Rachel Aleks, *Estimating the Effect of "Change to Win" on Union Organizing* [Electronic version], 68(3) INDUSTRIAL & LABOR RELATIONS REVIEW 584–605 (2015).

organization, with the exception of a federation of national or international labor organizations, to elect its officers at least every five years either by secret ballot among the members in good standing or at a convention of delegates chosen by secret ballot. Each local labor organization is to elect its officers at least every three years by secret ballot among the members in good standing, while committees and councils are to have elections at least every four years.

To ensure fair elections, labor organizations are to comply with all reasonable requests by any candidate to distribute campaign literature by mail or otherwise, at the candidate's expense, to all members in good standing, and to refrain from favoring any candidate with respect to the use of member lists. Each bona fide candidate has the right to inspect the member list once before elections, and the member list is to be maintained and kept at the principal office of the labor organization by a designated official. A reasonable opportunity for candidate nomination is to be provided, and every member in good standing is to be eligible to be a candidate and to hold office and have the right to vote for or otherwise support the candidate or candidates of her or his choice, without being subject to penalty, discipline, or improper interference or reprisal of any kind by such organization or any member thereof. No monies received by any labor organization by way of dues, assessment, or similar levy, and no monies of an employer, are to be used to promote the candidacy of any one person.

Additional adequate safeguards to insure a fair election are to be provided, including the right to have an observer at the polls and at the counting of the ballots. Notice of the election is to be mailed to each member not less than 15 days prior to the election. Each member in good standing is entitled to one vote. No dues-paying member is to be declared ineligible to vote or be a candidate by reason of alleged delay or default in the payment of dues. The votes cast by members of each local labor organization are to be counted, the results published separately, and the ballots preserved for one year. Elections are to be conducted in accordance with the constitution and bylaws of such organization and the law. The same holds where officers are chosen by a convention of delegates elected by secret ballot.

The constitution and bylaws of local labor organizations must also contain adequate procedures for the removal of an elected officer guilty of serious misconduct. Such officers may be removed, for cause shown and after notice and hearing, by members in good standing voting in a secret ballot conducted by the officers of such labor organization in accordance with its constitution and bylaws.

LABOR UNION DUTIES TO MEMBERS

The Bill of Rights of Members of Labor Organizations set out in the Labor-Management Reporting and Disclosure Act ("LMRDA") is a balancing act by Congress to insure democratic forms of self-government without excessively interfering with intraunion government.[56] The act strives for a minimum floor of due process as to the internal workings of the labor organization, but each labor organization is to have its own constitution and bylaws as voted on by their members. As a guarantee of member rights, the act mandates that all labor organizations have the statutory duty to inform their members of their rights under the act, and, upon request from the employee, to provide copies of the relevant collective agreements. Under the LMRDA, every member of a labor organization is to have equal rights and privileges within the organization:

- to nominate candidates;
- to vote in elections or referendums;
- to attend membership meetings; and
- to participate in deliberations and voting upon the business of such meetings.

Each of these rights and privileges is subject to reasonable rules and regulations as found in such labor organization's constitution and bylaws. Every member is to have the right to meet and assemble freely with other members and to express any views, arguments, or opinions. Each member also has the right to express at the meetings of the labor organization her views as to candidates in an election of the labor organization or upon any business properly before the meeting, subject to the organization's established and reasonable rules pertaining to the conduct of meetings. Union dues are to be decided by secret ballot of the members of the labor organization. A member's right to sue is protected from restrictions by labor organizations, with two exceptions: the member can be required to exhaust reasonable hearing procedures not to exceed a four-month lapse of time; and no interested employer or employer association is to directly or indirectly finance, encourage, or participate in, except as a party, any such action, proceeding, appearance, or petition.

---

[56] The Labor-Management Recording and Disclosure Act of 1959, also known as the Landrum-Griffin Act: *see* 29 U.S.C. § 411. *See also* Marcia Greenblatt, *Union Officials and the Labor Bill of Rights*, 57 FORDHAM L. REV. 601 (1989).

Labor organizations are prevented from fining, suspending, expelling, or otherwise disciplining a member unless the member has been served with written specific charges, given a reasonable time to prepare a defense, and afforded a full and fair hearing. The exception to this due process guarantee is where the union action is due to a member's failure to pay the labor union's dues.

Other union duties can be set out in the labor organization's constitution or bylaws. An example here is the Teamsters Human Rights Diversity Commission. Established under the Teamsters Constitution, it has a mandate to assist local unions in promoting diversity; work to eliminate all forms of discrimination in the workplace; and develop educational materials on related topics, such as sexual harassment, family leave, and disabilities. In addition, the Teamsters has an international women's caucus and national Black, Hispanic, and LGBT caucuses promoting their interests on local, state, and national levels.

MEMBER DUTIES TO LABOR UNIONS

The selection of a union as a representative by the majority of employees "extinguishes the individual employer's power to order his own relations with his employer and creates a power vested in the chosen representative to act in the interests of all employees."[57] Unions are entitled to expect the support of their members, and can discipline members for certain breaches of union rules where the rule has been properly adopted, reflects a legitimate union interest, impairs no policy Congress has imbedded in the labor laws, and is reasonably enforced against union members who are free to leave the union and escape the rule.[58] The policy of the NLRA is to "insulate an employee's job from their organizational rights … as a union member, so long as he chooses to remain one, he is subject to union discipline."[59] Union bylaws set out many of the member duties, including actual participation in organizing efforts, forbidding members to work with nonmembers or union members who are not in good standing.

---

[57] *See* NLRB v. Allis-Chalmers Manufacturing Company et al., 388 U.S. 175, 179 (1967).

[58] *See* Scofield v. NLRB, 394 U.S. 423 (1969). *See also* International Union of Operating Engineers Local 513, AFL-CIO v. NLRB, 635 F.3d 1233 (D.C. Cir. 2011) (not an unfair labor practice for a union to fine a member for reporting another member's safety violation to management).

[59] *See* Radio Officers' Union v. NLRB, 347 U.S. 17, 40 (1954).

The definition of "member" or "member in good standing" in the LMRDA includes any person who has fulfilled the requirements for membership in the organization, and who has neither voluntarily withdrawn from membership nor been expelled or suspended from membership after appropriate proceedings consistent with lawful provisions of the organization's constitution and bylaws. The Teamsters Local 2010 bylaws include provisions as to due payments, and an oath of obligation to be taken by the union member as set out in its section 31 Obligation:

> Fellow worker, you will now take an obligation that will bind you to the International Brotherhood of Teamsters and this Local Union, and that will in no way conflict with your religious belief or your duties as a citizen:
>
> I, ______(give name)_____, pledge my honor to faithfully observe the Constitution and the laws of the International Brotherhood of Teamsters and the Bylaws and laws of this Local Union.

The member then continues to pledge compliance with all the rules and regulations for the government of the international union and the local union, to faithfully perform all the duties assigned to the best of ability and skill, to conduct themselves at all times in a manner so as not to bring reproach upon the union, to take an affirmative part in the business and activities of the union and accept and discharge any responsibilities during any authorized strike or lockout, to not divulge to nonmembers the private business of the union unless authorized to reveal the same, to never knowingly harm a fellow member, and to never discriminate against a fellow worker on account of race, color, religion, sex, age, physical disability, national origin, or sexual orientation. The oath concludes with the new member swearing:

> I will refrain from any conduct that would interfere with the Union's performance of its legal or contractual obligations.
>
> I will at all times bear true and faithful allegiance to the International Brotherhood of Teamsters and this Local Union.

These words reflect a very personal bond between the union and its members reminiscent of many aspects of the guilds and journeymen associations.

PURSUING EMPLOYEE GRIEVANCES

The structures set up in the American context are on both federal and state levels, involving mediation, agency action, arbitration and litigation. Many collective agreements include arbitration clauses, entailing that disputes arising under the collective agreement are first to be brought to arbitration—usually decided by a single arbitrator appointed jointly by the employer and union. Most collective agreements have a "just cause" requirement for the termination of a member's employment by the employer, in contrast to the prevailing rule of employment-at-will. Claims of unlawful termination under the collective agreement are then brought to arbitration by the union as the employee is not a party to the contract.[60]

In the collective context, labor union members are owed a duty of fair representation by labor unions.[61] This duty is seen as a counterbalance to the exclusivity rule in order to prevent the potential "tyranny of the Majority" by labor unions.[62] The unions, as the exclusive representative of the employees within the bargaining union, have a duty to accord equal protection to all employee interests within the unit. The Court has addressed this balance on several occasions: "For the representative

---

[60] *See* Aaron Halegua, *United States* in RESOLVING INDIVIDUAL LABOUR DISPUTES 315 (Minawa Ebisui, Sean Cooney, & Colin Fenwick eds. ILO Geneva 2016).

[61] Canada enacted a very similar structure regarding a duty of fair representation by unions, as first framed by Canadian courts as early as 1969: see Fisher v. Pemberton (1969) 8 D.L.R. (3d) 521 (B.C.S.C.). The Supreme Court of Canada found a national common obligation on unions to represent their members fairly in 1984: see Gagnon v. Canadian Merchant Service Guild et al. [1984] 9 DLR (4th) 641, 654. Several provinces have legislated a duty of fair representation, such as Ontario in its Labour Relations Act of 1995. Section 74 of the Act, "Duty of fair representation by trade union, etc.," states:

> A trade union or council of trade unions, so long as it continues to be entitled to represent employees in a bargaining unit, shall not act in a manner that is arbitrary, discriminatory or in bad faith in the representation of any of the employees in the unit, whether or not members of the trade union or of any constituent union of the council of trade unions, as the case may be.

Federal employees and all the provinces, with the exceptions of Prince Edward Island, Nova Scotia, and New Brunswick, have such statutory protection: *see generally* BRIAN BELL RICHARD, THE EVOLVING DUTIES OF TRADE UNIONS TOWARD THEIR MEMBERS: DEFINING THE DUTIES AND DETERMINING THE STANDARDS (Proquest 1998).

[62] *See* Emporium Capwell Co. v. Western Addition, 420 U.S. 50, 64 (1975).

[union] is clothed with power, not unlike that of a legislature, which is subject to constitutional limitations on its power to deny, restrict, destroy or discriminate against the rights of those for whom it legislates, and which is also under an affirmative constitutional duty equally to protect those rights."[63]

The duty of fair representation was developed in the 1940s in a series of cases involving alleged racial discrimination by unions certified as exclusive bargaining representatives under the Railway Labor Act.[64] The collective bargaining system, as encouraged by Congress and administered under both the Railway Labor Act and the NLRA, of necessity subordinates the interests of an individual employee to the collective interests of all employees in a bargaining unit.[65] The US Supreme Court recognized in *Steele* that "the Congressional grant of power to a union to act as exclusive collective bargaining representative, with its corresponding reduction in the individual rights of the employees so represented, would raise grave constitutional problems if unions were free to exercise this power to further racial discrimination."[66] Since *Steele*, the duty of fair representation has "stood as a bulwark to prevent arbitrary union conduct against individuals stripped of traditional forms of redress by the provisions of federal labor law."[67] The Court found in *Vaca* that the federal courts had jurisdiction in claims of a breach of the duty of fair representation by unions, as "[t]he existence of even a small group of cases in which the [NLRB] would be unwilling or unable to remedy a union's breach of duty would frustrate the basic purposes underlying the duty of fair representation doctrine."[68]

Although section 8(b) NLRA was enacted in 1947, the NLRB did not interpret a breach of a union's duty of fair representation as an unfair labor practice until 1962, in the case *Miranda Fuel*.[69] There the Board's majority held that section 7 NLRA gives employees "the right to be free from unfair or irrelevant or invidious treatment by their exclusive bargaining agent in matters affecting their employment." Section

---

63 *See* Steele v. Louisville & N. R. Co., 323 U.S. 192, 199 (1944) (duty under the Railway Labor Act).

64 *See* Steele and Tunstall v. Brotherhood of Locomotive Firemen, 323 U.S. 210 (1944).

65 *See* J. I. Case Co. v. NLRB, 321 U.S. 332 (1944).

66 *See* Steele 198–99.

67 *See* Vaca v. Sipes, 386 U.S. 171 (1967) at 182.

68 *Id.* at 183.

69 *See* Miranda Fuel Company, Inc. and Michael Lopuch and Local 533, International Brotherhood of Teamsters, 140 NLRB 7 (1962).

8(b)(1)(A) NLRA accordingly prohibits labor organizations, "when acting in a statutory representative capacity, from taking action against any employee upon considerations or classifications which are irrelevant, invidious, or unfair." The Board also held that an employer who "participates" in such arbitrary union conduct also violates section 8(a)(1), and that the employer and the union may violate sections 8(a)(3) and 8(b)(2), respectively, "when, for arbitrary or irrelevant reasons or upon the basis of an unfair classification, the union attempts to cause or does cause an employer to derogate the employment status of an employee."[70]

Under the doctrine of a duty of a fair representation, the exclusive agent's statutory authority to represent all members of a designated unit includes the obligation to serve the interests of all members without hostility or discrimination toward any, to exercise its discretion with complete good faith and honesty, and to avoid arbitrary conduct. As the exclusive bargaining representative, the recognized union has a duty to fairly represent all employees, both in its collective bargaining and in its enforcement of the resulting collective bargaining agreement.

In one case, nonunion medical center employees brought action against the union claiming that the union imposed a policy allowing the union to charge nonunion members, within its bargaining unit fees, for individual representation in grievances, hearings, and arbitrations, in violation of Nevada's right-to-work laws. The court found that that the exclusive bargaining relationship establishes:

> [a] "mutuality of obligation": a union has the obligation to represent all employees in the bargaining unit without regard to union membership, and the employee has a corresponding obligation, if permissible under the CBA and required by the union policy, to share in defraying the costs of collective bargaining services from which he or she directly benefits … Our recognition of this mutuality of obligation will, in part, serve to discourage "free riders"—employees who receive the benefits of union representation but are unwilling to contribute to its financial support.

The court held that the policy did not discriminate against the nonunion employees, as paying the service fee for grievance representation was not

---

70 *Id.* at 186.

a condition of employment; individuals could opt to forgo the fees and hire their own private attorney without fear of losing their job.[71]

Apart from the labor union's duty of fair representation, employees also have the right to directly file charges as to unfair labor practices with the NLRB as discussed above. There is, however, no private right of action for such violations, which means the NLRB is the only path available. Violations of fair labor standards are monitored by the US Department of Labor ("DOL"), and a complaint concerning a violation of pay or hours can be filed with DOL's Wage and Hour Division ("WHD"), which has over 200 offices throughout the country. The Division will commence an investigation as to compliance by an employer without disclosing whether an employee has complained or whether the investigation is for other reasons. In fiscal years 2013–2017 the WHD recovered over $1.2 billion in back wages for more than 1.3 million workers.[72]

Claims of unlawful discrimination by either employers or labor unions based on race, color, religion, national origin, sex, pregnancy, age, and/or disability can be brought to the Equal Employment Opportunity Commission ("EEOC"), the agency charged with enforcing the federal anti-discrimination legislation. All of the laws enforced by EEOC, except for the Equal Pay Act, require that the individual file a Charge of Discrimination with the EEOC prior to commencing litigation against the employment. In addition, an individual, organization, or agency may file a charge on behalf of another person in order to protect the aggrieved person's identity. Mediation is typically the first step for each charge, and if not successful, the charge is given to an investigator. If the investigation finds no violation of the law, the individual is given a Notice of Right to Sue, which allows litigation to be commenced. If a violation is found, the EEOC will attempt to reach a voluntary settlement with the employer. If no settlement can be reached, the case is referred to the EEOC legal staff, or in certain cases the Department of Justice, which then decides whether the agency should file a lawsuit. If the decision is made not to file a lawsuit, the individual is given a Notice of Right to Sue. In some cases—if a charge appears to have little chance of success, or if it is something that the EEOC does not have the authority to investigate—the charge will simply be dismissed without an investigation or mediation. In the year 2017, 540,000 calls were made to the EEOC

---

71 Cone v. Nevada Service Employees Union, 998 P.2d 1178 (Nev. 2000) 1183 *citing* Schaffer v. Board of Education, 869 S.W.2d 163, 166–68 (Mo.Ct.App. 1993); Opinion of the Justices, 401 A.2d 135, 147 (Me. 1979); and NLRB v. General Motors Corp., 373 U.S. 734, 743 (1963).

72 For this information, see the WHD website at dol.gov/whd.

toll-free number, 155,000 contacts made in field offices, 84,254 charges filed, $355.6 million in monetary relief obtained through mediation and conciliation settlements, with the EEOC filing 184 lawsuits and recovering $42.4 million for plaintiffs.[73]

Many states and local jurisdictions have their own employment and anti-discrimination laws and comparable state agencies responsible for enforcing those laws (a Fair Employment Practices Agency or "FEPA"). If a discrimination charge is filed with a FEPA, it will automatically be "dual-filed" with EEOC if federal laws apply and the individual does not need to file with both agencies. The status of a charge can be checked by the individual online on the EEOC website.

COURTS AND DISPUTE RESOLUTION

Employees can also raise certain employment claims in court, particularly of unlawful discrimination, unlawful retaliation, or unlawful termination of employment. Recent research has shown that in discrimination cases, plaintiffs have a 35.4 percent success rate in federal court, with average damages of $150,500; a 59 percent success rate in state (California) court, with average damages of $296,991; and a 21.4 percent success rate in private arbitration, with average damages of $36,500.[74]

Another aspect to keep in mind is the fee-shifting that occurs in cases claiming violations of civil or human rights, such as unlawful discrimination or pay cases. Individuals can file claims with the courts at any level *pro se*, without the assistance of legal counsel. On plaintiff's motion, a court can where appropriate waive any filing fees. As to trial fees and costs, the main rule in American procedural law is that each party bears its own trial costs and fees. However, in claims concerning civil and human rights, the court will order that the defendant pay a prevailing plaintiff's reasonable trial costs and fees. This fee-shifting is based on the legislature's intent to increase access to justice by individuals. Although technically a one-channel system of employee representation, federal and state laws create several avenues of employee voice in addition to labor organizations. Individual employees can bring claims to state and federal agencies alleging unfair labor practices or unlawful discrimination, and these agencies will investigate the claims. Employees can also act

---

[73] For this information, see the EEOC website at eeoc.gov.

[74] *See* Alexander J.S. Colvin, *American Workplace Dispute Resolution in the Individual Rights Era*, in 23(3) INTERNATIONAL JOURNAL OF HUMAN RESOURCE MANAGEMENT 459–75 (2012).

together concertedly outside the scope of a labor organization and still be afforded legal protection. There are extensive statutory requirements as to labor organizations and procedural due process demands, particularly concerning member participation, elections, and disciplinary measures. The labor unions also have a duty of fair representation, entailing that they must, as the exclusive representative of employees, represent all employees equally. This duty is regardless of an individual's union membership status, sex, race, religion, disability status, or age, a right enforcement by both members and nonmembers. This emphasis on employee voice and access to justice in American law is very much a legacy of past discrimination.

12. Voice, democracy, and collectivism in the different systems

Democracy and worker voice have been vital elements more or less present at each stage of worker collectivism, whether guilds, journeymen's associations, or labor unions. The system dynamics approach to comparative law has been used in this work to lay the groundwork for a comparison based on its four principal sources: legal texts, institutions, decision-making communities, and patterns of thought. The presentations of the history, development, and modern legal approaches to worker collectivism in the different national systems have lent themselves well to this approach. The texts explored and compared have included the legislative treatment of employee collectivism and voice, codes of practice and other agency guidelines, and collective agreements as reached by the social partners. The institutions have also been easily identifiable: collective worker organizations, first as guilds; then as journeymen's associations and trade societies and associations; then as trade and labor unions, employee organizations, and employer organizations. The state has also played a varying role in each of the national models, either through legislation or through services provided by government agencies. Both texts and institutions have been placed in their broader national communities to the extent that this is possible in such a short work, and the patterns of thought at each stage have been traced. This chapter presents a system comparison, first by identifying certain common threads, as well as events, that transcend the national borders. After this, the modern national labor law models are assessed against two of the components of procedural democracy: the responsiveness of the system and the interests protected.

"WHY WOULD YOU DESTROY COMMUNITY?"

This plaint posed by the journeymen woolcombers of Norwich to their masters in 1752 captures both the strengths of the early guild system and the causes of its unraveling. The first common thread for all the national systems is the guild system, the prototype for worker collectivism. Based on mutual aid and democracy, the guilds in Europe became very sophisticated structures of self-governance and self-policing, often with their own court system. The early guilds in each of the European systems examined here—England, Germany, and Sweden—were all based on direct democracy. Each of the members had equal rights of voting and participation, and, in most of these early guilds, equal responsibility and strict liability for the acts of other guild members: "If all misdo, let all bear it; let all share the same lot."[1] This equality also entailed mutual aid, with the guilds often providing benefits in the form of funds during times of sickness, funeral costs, and financial support for families of deceased members. Apprentices and journeymen became a part of both the master's family and the guild. Some of the early guilds allowed journeymen and, at times, apprentices voting rights, but all took into consideration the future of the craft, ensuring a balance between skilled artisans and apprentices and journeymen in terms of wages, prices, and production. All were bound by the guild's charter, and could assert rights and claims that were heard by the guild in either arbitration-like proceedings or actual courts. The law intervened only sparingly, with kings often exercising power to generate revenues and control loyalties, as seen in Charlemagne's demand that no oaths of loyalty be taken except to him. These demands of loyalty are easily understood against the background of the Hansa guild's trading empire, which at times could be a king-maker, as in the case of Gustav Vasa.

A distinction must be drawn, however, between the governance of the early guilds and that of their later forms. The growing degree of legalization and institutionalization was the result of the use of the law by the Crown, and later the state, to harness the guilds. Legislation as early as the 700s in England and Germany required certain standards of behavior and loyalty to the Crown instead of the guild. Much of the relevant legislation in England from the thirteenth century up to the Reformation concerned the legalization and incorporation of guilds in order for the Crown to gain greater control and revenues. The structure of the guilds was transformed by the sixteenth century, characterized by a greater degree of institutionalization, assumption of public authority, legalization, and greater distance between masters and their apprentices and journeymen. This institutionalization is most visible in England, where the exercise of royal power with respect to affirming guild charters and granting monopolies was perhaps most pervasive and regular, and the Twelve Livery Companies the most powerful. The Reformation also had a significant impact on the guilds in England, Germany, and Sweden,

---

1 *See* BRENTANO, *supra* Introduction note 1 at 5.

stripping them of their religious (Catholic) affiliations and related assets, ensuring that trade and craft were now the main focus. The Reformation's acceptance of profits also exacerbated the growing distance between masters and their apprentices and journeymen. Profits in trade were no longer seen as being against God's will. The delicate balance maintained by the early guilds between skilled artisans, prices, and production began to be abandoned.

Journeymen in all three European countries had been organized for several centuries by the time the journeymen woolcombers asked their question in 1752; however, the early guild structures based on democracy and mutual aid had radically changed. Becoming a journeyman was no longer a step toward being a master, but rather a status in itself, with masters in a more antagonistic relationship with both apprentices and journeymen, now focused more on profits than on the future of the craft. Since the creation of their own organizations, journeymen had self-policed as to working conditions and protested against unfair masters. At this point, however, the struggle was for a broader spectrum of rights, as well as cutting across sectors. The tramping system, created to gain greater knowledge and skill in the craft, was used in all these countries as a set of networks to be invoked as support for protests, as seen with the 1720 London tailors' strike involving 30,000 tailors.

The English state had attempted to legislate away labor conflicts at an early stage, with the 1351 Statute of Labourers placing a wage ceiling on workmen that would stay in place until the 1562 Statute of Artificers, which then allowed for wages to be set by the state. Journeymen and apprentices appealed to the Crown and legislative powers in England, Germany, and Sweden for protection against low wages; the use of unskilled workers; excess apprentices and journeymen; and the prohibitive barriers of entry to the trade as masters. The English 1562 Statute of Artificers and the Swedish 1620 Guild Act can be seen as responses to these criticisms. The early American colonies are outliers here, as early attempts during colonial times to legislate the conditions of work, particularly wages, were unsuccessful and eventually abandoned by the courts.

"UNITED TO PROTECT, NOT COMBINED TO INJURE"

This slogan, as adopted by the United Society of Brushmakers in 1840, reflects the legal treatment of worker collectivism at that point of time. The focus of the journeymen's associations was on protecting rights and even on larger social issues, with journeyman now a status in itself and not just a career step. The focus of the law also changed at this point, taking less care over balancing rights between masters and journeymen and instead perceiving the organization of journeymen as a societal threat, particularly in England, the United States, and Germany. England began to outlaw combinations of workers and any collective agreements reached by them, first through judicial interpretation of criminal conspiracy under the 1304 act, and then explicitly through legislation, beginning in 1718 and moving through several different acts up until the Trade Union Act 1871. The journeymen in Germany were equally active and equally banned, with the 1731 Imperial law prohibiting journeymen's associations due to their "senseless rebellion and refusal to work." Swedish legislation took a different path, with the 1720 Guild Act expanding the rights of free masters and journeymen's access to the trades, with journeymen and masters agreeing as to wages. Stockholm and Malmö had already been declared free in 1633, and the same was happening in the case of more and more Swedish cities at this time, greatly weakening the power base of guilds and masters generally.

Given the hostility to combinations of workers exhibited by the legislation and the courts, these groups tried to circumvent the reach of the law by using different designations, such as friendly societies, trade societies, and trades associations. This redesignation did not place these groups beyond the reach of the law, as the English Tolpuddle Martyrs discovered. The United Kingdom and United States had "trade unions" early on, with central organizations already in place by the 1830s—in the United Kingdom, for example, Robert Owen's 1834 Grand National Consolidated Trades Union, and in the United States, for example, the 1833 New York General Trades' Union. The Typographers' Unions in both Germany and Sweden were among the first unions in these countries, with the former having already drafted a program by 1858 and entering into the first German collective agreement in 1872. In Sweden this union traces its origins to 1846; it claims to be Sweden's oldest union.

The national central labor organizations in each of the countries considered in this book were founded within 40 years of each other. In the UK, the TUC was founded in 1860, the American AFL in 1886, the German General Commission of Trade Unions in 1890, and the Swedish LO in 1898. New unionism—organization not simply by trade but rather by employer, and covering a broader range of workers, including unskilled workers—had begun in the UK by the 1860s, in Germany by the 1890s, and in Sweden by the early 1900s, but was flatly rejected by the AFL in the 1890s. The CIO's break from the AFL in 1935 was over the question of new unionism and representation of skilled as well as unskilled workers;

this is also the current platform of Change to Win, which split off from the AFL in 2005 over this same issue.

THE INSTITUTIONALIZATION OF LABOR

Trade unions and collective agreements were recognized by legislation in these four countries within a time span of 60 years. Germany recognized trade unions and collective agreements under the 1869 GO, but also originally severely curtailed union activities. The UK Trade Union Act 1871 legalized trade unions, granting them immunity from conspiracy and restraint of trade for lawful activities. Trade unions in Sweden were first recognized by the social partners through the central collective agreement, the 1906 December Compromise, and later by the 1928 Collective Agreements Act. An American court held in 1842 that a labor combination was not unlawful simply by reason of its existence, but safe harbors would not be created for union activities until the 1914 Clayton Antitrust Act. Legislation as to trade union recognition has been complicated, as legal status is intimately intertwined with the issue of recognition. The rejection of legal personhood by the trade unions in all four countries is a direct result of the historical treatment of combinations of workers and the use of legislation by the state to legalize and then control such groups. As to political labor parties, the United States had several workers' labor parties by the 1830s: these were the Working Men's parties, which quickly disappeared. The German Social Democratic Workers' Party emerged in 1875. The Swedish Social Democratic Labour Party was founded in 1889 and the UK Labour Party in 1906. A Socialist Party of America was formed in 1901, but never gained anything close to the political clout of the German, Swedish, and UK labor parties.

Social security benefits, as part of the social question, were also established in these different countries—in Prussia they were in place as early as the 1830s, and they were an aspect of Bismarck's program to counteract the socialists in the 1880s. The UK began to offer worker compensation benefits in 1897, and over the next decade continued to pass acts providing old-age pensions, regulation of work hours, labor exchanges, a minimum wage, and national sickness and employment insurance. Sweden passed its first general worker protection act in 1899, but most of the social security benefits were administered by the unions, particularly sickness and unemployment benefits. Federal social security protections were finally legislated in the United States during the 1930s as part of the New Deal package to combat the Great Depression.

Certain labor questions arose in all four countries at the turn of the twentieth century. The resolution of industrial disputes was one, with arbitration and mediation the favored mechanism of dispute resolution by the 1890s. Another common issue was that of worker voice, with worker committees used during World War I in the United Kingdom, United States, and Germany. Given Sweden's neutrality in World War I, the same degree of nationalization of industry did not occur, and the need for worker voice was perhaps not as palpable. Tripartite structures can be found in all four countries at this time, and were even taken up in the governance structure created for the ILO by a drafting committee chaired by AFL President Gompers.

Despite the similarities of the issues raised first by the journeymen's organizations and later by trade and labor unions, the solutions achieved in the national models differ as to key points. Here discourses in the different systems under the system dynamics approach to comparative law can be examined as possible explanations as to these divergences. The starting points and challenges faced by labor greatly differed between the four national systems. In the United Kingdom, the law had been used as a means for state control over labor for a period of, arguably, more than six hundred years, starting with the 1349 Statute of Labourers. Several acts—at least six—addressed unlawful worker actions and conspiracies in the 1700s, up until the passing of the Trade Union Act 1871. Labor law underwent as many, if not more, legislative changes in the latter half of the twenty-first century depending on the political party in power, concerning many of the same issues, as well as state registration requirements as to trade unions, the status of collective agreements, and the extent of immunities and limitations on industrial action.

German labor law had an entirely different historical background. Social security protections were introduced as early as the 1830s in Prussia, and used by conservatives as a means to counteract socialists in the 1890s. The social unrest and devastation caused by World War I eventually led to the central collective agreement still in effect today between the social partners, as well as protections under the 1919 Weimar Constitution as to certain labor law issues. Germany, consequently, was the first of these four countries to specifically include labor protections in a written constitution. The total decimation of labor unions, leaders, and rights during the Third Reich gave impetus to equally strong, if not stronger, constitutional protections after the end of the war, with a focus on both collective and individual rights and voice. Several avenues of employee voice were put in place, such as trade unions, works councils, and employee representation on corporate supervisory boards.

In less than a century, Sweden went from having a guild system to having one of the highest union and employer organizational densities in Europe and it had become a prime example of industrial peace by 1938. The architecture of the folk home put in place in the early 1900s was a response to social unrest and poverty in Sweden, as well as depopulation caused by emigration mostly to America. There needed to be a reason for workers to stay in Sweden. The Swedish labor model has never faced extensive or recurring legislative changes, with minimal labor legislation adopted until the comprehensive 1970s package, which was favorable to employees, and most of which is still in place. The most significant challenge to this model has historically been the economy; today, perhaps the most important is the reconciliation of this very corporativistic structure with individual rights as protected under EU and international law.

Labor law in the United States had to address yet another different set of parameters in the form of labor shortages, slavery, racism, and an intense judicial hostility to worker collectives that took the form of labor injunctions prohibiting most union activity. The violence and deaths involved in industrial actions eventually led to the 1914 Clayton Antitrust Act. The Great Depression brought about a new set of problems, leading to the passage of the NLRA and the creation of the NLRB. Extensive racism led to the courts imposing a duty of fair representation on the unions. Corruption within certain unions led to the 1959 LMRDA creating stronger individual member protections and greater transparency as to internal union operations.

RESPONSIVENESS AND INTERESTS IN THE DIFFERENT MODELS

Against this system dynamics approach comparison of the different national legal models, aspects of a procedural democracy model are now assessed. Procedural democracy combines a procedural account of democratic legitimacy with deliberative politics. Two aspects of Habermas' analysis are focused on here: the responsiveness of the system to the needs of its constituency, and the interests actually represented. These require that laws and decisions involve all citizens, particularly those affected by the act, in a discursive process in order to be viewed as legitimate. There must be a basic right to equal opportunities, to participate in processes of opinion and will formation, in which citizens exercise their political autonomy and through which they generate legitimate law. In addition, citizens must be able to claim rights and bring them to bear as against one another. The general right to equal liberties, along with the correlative membership rights and guaranteed legal remedies, establish the legal code as such. In other words, "there is no legitimate law without these rights."[2]

Procedural Democracy within the Guild Structures

A model of direct democracy permeated the early guilds, the journeymen's associations, and the early trade unions, based on the ethos of mutual aid and equal participation. The entirety of Habermas' procedural concept of democracy can be seen at work with the early guilds, which is not so surprising considering the size and scope of these institutions. This was a period in which personal ties very much defined individuals' roles in society, before, as Maine summarized it, contract replaced status.

From the perspective of internal democracy and voice, the later guilds can be seen as going over to a system of indirect democracy at best. The growing divide between masters and their journeymen and apprentices entailed that the latter had less participation in the internal procedures. In the case of the London Livery, the distance had become so great that those who had the power to vote no longer even needed to have ever practiced the trade. The journeymen's associations instead became the forum for the exercise of voice, often vociferously, as seen by the 1720 London strike involving 30,000 journeymen tailors. Though the later guilds cannot be seen as still falling within the Habermasian procedural concept of democracy, particularly in light of their appeals to external parties, such as the King and parliament, to resolve conflicts, the journeymen's associations took up the torch. Tramping contributed not only to greater skills in the trades but also to the dissemination of knowledge across large areas. For England, tramping on the continent was common; for Sweden, tramping took place in other Nordic countries and Germany; and for Germany, across the entirety of the Holy Roman Empire. Tramping became an unemployment system for journeymen, who informed each other of possible work and provided funds for tramping. Tramping also facilitated early industrial action, allowing for a control mechanism as to masters and even unskilled workers. Journeymen could protest against masters using unskilled labor or paying low wages by tramping en masse and relaying information about such masters to others. Direct democracy was the rule in the journeymen's associations, with mutual aid and solidarity still very strong components.

---

2 *See* HABERMAS, *supra* Introduction note 39 at 125.

The activities of the journeymen's associations in each of the four countries studied here were eventually assumed by the trade union movement.

Trade Union Member Grievances in the United Kingdom

The themes addressed in the current UK labor law model—for example, the statutory regulation of the legal status of trade unions, collective agreements, and industrial action—have deep historical roots. The UK model has kept decision-making with respect to workplace issues at the plant level, allowing those closest to the decision to vote on the outcome. The objective of trade union democracy has been used as a political tool to restrict trade union power. The political concern for member voice that is articulated would ring truer if not for the fact that in the past decade high fees were imposed for bringing cases to the industrial tribunals. Unison contested this 2013 imposition of fees, and the UK Supreme Court ruled that the fees impeded the constitutional right of access to justice that was fundamental to the rule of law.

The UK system has several avenues available as to employee grievances. The first involves employees bringing grievances directly to the employer. The lawmaker has required employers to have certain procedural guarantees in place, including an appeal process. The government agency Acas provides conciliation, mediation, and arbitration if the employee still wishes to pursue the grievance, and after this, she may take it to the employment tribunals at no cost. The employment tribunals have an overriding statutory duty to deal with cases justly, ensuring that the parties are on an equal footing. Trade unions provide legal assistance in certain cases, and must observe procedural requirements as to transparency and candor in any decisions made concerning the provision of legal assistance. UCU's rule book, by way of example, places particular weight in such cases on the Union's objective of promoting equality for all and the opposition of all discrimination. Union members can also bring complaints to the Certification Officer regarding union procedural violations, and again this is at no cost. Complaints falling outside the jurisdiction of the Certification Officer are to be brought to the courts. One of the principles espoused by the courts in such situations is that the union's actions must adhere to a standard of natural justice.

That there has been such a focus in UK law on procedural safeguards, natural justice, and access to justice is not surprising given the early societal acceptance that litigation by private parties is a necessary aspect of law enforcement. This is much in line with Habermas' requirement of the actionability of rights and the ability of citizens to claim rights and bring them to bear against each other—the communicative power of the citizenry. The balance achieved in the UK labor law model between statutory regulation and self-regulation by the social partners, resting on constitutional principles such as natural justice and access to justice, allows several channels for individual employee voice.

Trade Union Member Grievances in Germany

The German labor law model is built on both strong social partners and strong individual employee rights, particularly concerning employee voice. The dual emphasis on both collective and individual employee rights arguably stems at least in part from the devastation wreaked by the Nazis on employment rights and trade unions. Germany is the archetype dual channel voice system, with its works council used as a model in the European Union's directive. Not all workforces have works councils, and where this is the case the labor unions assume many of the functions of works councils. The works council legislation creates strong rights for employees, with the councils having representation rules as to certain worker categories and enhanced duties as to certain equality issues based on sex, age, and national origin. The option of turning to works councils is also seen as offering leverage with respect to trade unions, as members have a choice of whether to turn to the works council or the trade union.

Where an employee wishes to pursue a grievance, she can bring the grievance to the competent bodies at the workforce herself and be accompanied by either a works council member or a labor union representative. The employee has the right to bring a claim under the Works Constitution Act even in the absence of a works council at the workplace, based on the employers' duty of care; this is a judicial doctrine predating the works council legislation, which holds employers to an implied term in the employment contract to consider the employee's moral rights and wellbeing. In the alternative, the employee can bring the grievance directly to the works council, which, if it finds the grievance justified, can request that the employer remedies the situation. The works council and employer can also appeal to a conciliation committee for a resolution of the case. The employee can also turn to the labor union for assistance. In all of these alternatives, the employee incurs no costs by pursuing the grievance.

The employee can also take a grievance to court. At the trial court level, the employee only risks her own trial cost and fees—a conscious deviation from the English rule as typically applied in Germany, in order to minimize the employee's economic risks. At this level the employee can represent herself or be represented by a lawyer or trade union representative. If the case is appealed, the English rule concerning costs and fees is then applied, and the losing party has to pay the prevailing parties' costs and fees. However, even here, awards of fees are consciously set at low levels, and if the employee risks economic harm in having to pay them, legal aid is available.

The dual channel system, with employee representation through both works councils and labor unions, provides several avenues for employees to raise issues, either directly with the employer, to the works council, or to the trade union. The works councils are given enhanced statutory duties concerning certain protected groups based on sex, age, disability, and race. Two important issues can be seen in the procedural rules concerning labor disputes: first, quick and efficient solutions that are transparent and focused on the needs of the public; second, that employees are to have access to justice through the courts, with a reallocation of trial costs and fees to minimize the economic risks to employees, as well as checks that the costs and fees are not excessive.

Through this awareness of the economic risks employees take when contesting employer decisions, as well as the need to have different groups of employees represented at workplaces, the German model also takes into account many of the facets of procedural democracy within its labor law model. Employees have the right to submit matters to be addressed by the works council, and even to force the issue if 5 percent of the employees in the establishment second the proposal—the lowest threshold for legally exercising employee representative rights among the four different systems examined here. Although it is an entirely different solution than the other three, the dual channel system in Germany incorporates many of the features of procedural democracy: discursive processes, equal opportunities, and participation in opinion formation, as well as the bringing of claims as to rights.

Trade Union Member Grievances in Sweden

Of the four systems examined here, the Swedish labor law system can be seen as the one that is most true to a single-channel voice system, focusing on the collective of employees as represented solely by the labor unions. The Swedish labor law model is about the social partners and collective solutions to labor market issues. Union members have no statutory rights regarding their unions, and no voice with respect to employers except through the unions or litigation. Elaborate procedures have been put in place concerning the negotiations between the social partners, with extensive rights as to industrial action. The Swedish system is the only one included here in which secondary industrial actions are lawful as long as the primary action is lawful. This extensive right of the unions can be contrasted with the rights of employees under Swedish law. Mediation/agency procedures outside of the unions do not exist for individual employee complaints, such as with Acas and the Certification Officer in the United Kingdom, the works councils in Germany, and the NLRB, DOL Wage and Hour Division, or EEOC in the United States. The unions are the central means for their members as to negotiations with employers.

Another lacuna in the Swedish legislation, case law, and internal union documents is the approach to ensuring that issues of equality are addressed. As seen in the United Kingdom in the TUC's constitution, the objective is to achieve broad representation through mandatory quotas of different groups. The German works councils also have representation rules and enhanced duties with respect to equality issues for certain groups and the United States has a duty of fair representation placed upon the unions, not only between members, but also encompassing nonmembers. No such equivalent can be found in the law or collective agreements in Sweden. The unions have been very strong in protecting the collective, in a system very much based on majoritarianism.

The Swedish system is also the only one that has not addressed any reallocation of costs and fees as to employee claims in an effort to make litigation generally more affordable and consequently accessible. The English rule is applied in Sweden, in that the losing party pays the prevailing party's costs and fees. Where the unions take up the claims, they then pay the costs and fees. There are no formal internal procedures in place regarding decisions by unions as to whether to litigate, with one collective agreement stating that board decisions, such for example whether to provide such legal assistance, are to be appealed to the general congress held every third year. Certain employees have opted to take claims against employers to small claims courts to avoid the economic risks of costs and fees, but then the damages are set at a ceiling of SEK 22,000, a negligible sum for most employers. If the employee member wishes to raise a claim against their labor union, they have litigated the issue before the general courts, risking the costs and fees that may be incurred. Or the member can simply leave the union. Neither choice is very satisfactory with respect to the resolution of an employee grievance.

The trend of low damages awards and relatively higher attorneys' costs and fees creates a significant deterrent for individuals considering the pursuit of employment grievances. Litigation is arguably not an affordable option for most individual plaintiffs, particularly in cases of employment grievances as to hiring or firing—that is, in cases where individuals are likely to be unemployed. Little focus has been placed on individual member rights either under the law or by the unions. This is very much a reflection of the Swedish legal system as a whole, in which many individual rights, such as those granted under the European Convention, were not given the force of law until Sweden took up EU membership in 1995.

Trade Union Member Grievances in the United States

Although technically a one-channel system of employee representation, American federal and state law creates several avenues of employee voice in addition to labor organizations. Individual employees can bring claims to state and federal agencies alleging unfair labor practices, violations of fair labor standards, or unlawful discrimination, and these agencies will investigate such claims. Employees can also act together concertedly outside the scope of a labor organization and still be afforded legal protection. Extensive statutory requirements exist with respect to labor organizations and procedural due process demands.

Several routes are available for employees when it comes to pursuing grievances. Both employers and labor organizations can commit unfair labor practices, and three protected routes for raising grievances exist under the NLRA: raising claims through the unions; concerted activity; or charges filed by parties (whether directly affected or not) with the NLRB. The individual charges can be filed with the NLRB electronically and at no cost, with the right to appeal to an Office of Appeals. Similar complaint procedures also exist regarding violations of fair labor standards with the WHD, and for unlawful discrimination with the EEOC. An employer's failure to provide information to unions relating to employee grievances is in itself an unfair labor practice. A duty of candor under the legislation can also be seen as being imposed on labor organizations. They must make their internal governance instruments, constitutions, and bylaws publicly available, as well as certain information concerning membership, benefit plans, accounting records, and the disciplining of members. In addition, they must inform their members of their rights under the law.

With respect to employee grievances against employers, the labor unions have a duty of fair representation to all their members. This was initially a judicial doctrine adopted in 1944 to counterbalance any potential "tyranny of the majority" within labor unions. The legitimate concern at this time was discrimination on the basis of race within unions at a time when apartheid, as allowed under the separate but equal doctrine, was reaching its height in many states. The duty of fair representation entails that the labor union must, as the exclusive representative of employees, represent all employees equally. This duty is regardless of an individual's union membership status, sex, race, religion, disability, or age. A union's failure to fulfill the duty of fair representation is deemed an unfair labor practice. This emphasis on employee voice and access to justice in American law is very much a legacy of past racial discrimination.

Unions representing members in litigation against employers bear the costs and fees. Union members can directly sue employers and/or unions, for employment decisions taken either alone or together. Individuals filing with a court *pro se*, without the assistance of legal counsel, can have their filing fees waived. If the employee/member pursues litigation, a fee-shifting rule comes into place. The American rule entails that each party bears its own trial costs and fees. However, with respect to claims concerning civil rights, such as issues of discrimination or fair labor standards, the court will order that the defendant pay the prevailing plaintiff's reasonable trial costs and fees, and, if the plaintiff loses, that each party bear their own costs and fees. This rule is in place to facilitate access to the courts for individual plaintiffs as a necessary component in access to justice. The American labor law model rests on statutory and self-regulation, with employees given the ability to turn to government agencies at no cost in disputes with employers or with labor unions. Even where litigation is chosen, the allocation of costs and fees and the amount of damages ensure that the economic risks to employees are minimized.

THE ROLE OF THE LAW AND WORKER COLLECTIVISM

The focus of this work has been the relationship between the law, workers, and the collective, with the question raised as to whether requirements of procedural democracy, specifically the responsiveness of the systems, are addressed in these different models. A specific marker invoked was facilitating employee voice in the collective, particularly concerning employee grievances, as well as rights of access to justice as to voicing grievances. The law has historically been used both to oppress and to encourage worker collectivism. Oppression by law, when invoked, has been devastating, as seen in the too numerous examples such as the Roman forced guild membership over generations, Charlemagne's nose-slitting, the use of conspiracy and then later combination to suppress all worker collectivism, and Nazi Germany's total annihilation of any worker movement.

There are common legal threads among the four systems considered here. All four have constitutional protections with respect to freedom of association and freedom of expression. All are bound by the UN Declaration of Human Rights. The three European countries are all required to follow the European Convention on Human Rights and Union law, which has entailed a harmonization of certain labor and employment law issues such as individual rights against unlawful discrimination and freedom of movement with respect to persons and services.

As to differences, the UK labor law system, as the oldest of these four national systems, has naturally had the most complicated relationship with the law, given its age span. There is today a strong emphasis on procedural safeguards, natural justice and access to justice, and the reallocation of trial costs and fees, which forms the foundation for the balance of statutory, agency, and self-regulation in the field of labor law. The German system also has strong explicit constitutional protections, both for the collective and the individual, in the labor context, again with a focus on procedural safeguards and the reallocation of trial costs and fees. Individual employee voice has been facilitated through the works councils and labor unions under a concept of the employer's overriding duty of care, actively taking into consideration both the responsiveness of the system and the interests to be protected. The United States does not have explicit constitutional protections per se, but has strong civil rights protections that have entailed a focus on access to justice and the reallocation of trial costs and fees. Access to justice has included the duty of fair representation and that allegations as to unfair labor practices, violations of wage or hour laws, or unlawful discrimination can all be reported at no cost to government agencies, usually at both the state and federal levels, and will be investigated. This is also a two-channel system of sorts, but instead of works councils, it involves governmental agencies and labor unions.The Swedish system is that which most closely mirrors Kahn-Freund's collective laissez-faire. Sweden's explicit constitutional protections are to the benefit of the trade unions and the trade unions are the gatekeepers as to employee voice. The employer and employee organizational sides are treated as equally strong—a presumption in the law that mirrors a reality in existence since the 1930s. The focus on the social partners and self-regulation has entailed that individual members are not empowered to the same extent as in the other three systems. It is an accepted proposition that the Swedish system is built on a system of collective justice—a communitarian approach to the law and its role in society. This has also meant that procedural guarantees are not in place to the same extent and that there is no natural justice reasoning by the courts, no duty of fair representation by which to hold unions accountable, no overriding duty of care, as in Germany. This is not saying that the Swedish legal system is necessarily fundamentally unfair, but simply that the individual perspective has not been a focus in this very communitarian system that works more for the collective than the individual.

This book began with the premise that procedural guarantees for union members with regard to labor union decisions, particularly responsiveness and the interests protected in line with Habermas' procedural concept of democracy, create legitimacy within existing labor law structures. What the history of worker collectivism reveals is that procedural due process has always been a component, but perhaps not always an expressly articulated one, in worker collectivism, since the time of the early guilds. Solidarity, equality, and mutual aid have been ever present, to various degrees and in different forms. A way forward is to consciously build on and strengthen procedural democracy for union members, through legal protections as to transparency and procedural due process for union members. Given the greater focus today on human rights in the labor law context, the mechanisms necessary to invoke these rights need to be in place to give them effect.

Bibliography

BOOKS

AXEL ADLERCREUTZ, ARBETSTAGARBEGREPPET (Gleerup 1964)

AXEL ADLERCREUTZ, KOLLEKTIV AVTALET—STUDIER ÖVER DESS TILLKOMSTHISTORIA (Gleerup 1954)

JEAN ALLAIN, THE LAW AND SLAVERY: PROHIBITING HUMAN EXPLOITATION (Brill 2015)

SUNE AMBROSIANI, FRÅN DE SVENSKA SKRÅÄMBETENAS DAGAR (Svenska teknologföreningens förlag 1920)

CATRIN ANDERSSON, STEFAN BOHMAN, KERSTIN DAVIDSON, TOMMY GRAHN, LARS LINDER, MARGARETA STÅHL & JOHAN SÖDERBERG, STREJK! EN BOK OM STREJKOR OCH STREJKVISOR FRÅN BAGARIARBETARSTREJKEN 1873 TILL STORTREJKEN 1909 (Börås 1974)

ANONYMOUS, A LOVER OF HIS COUNTRY, A SHORT ESSAY UPON TRADE IN GENERAL (London 1741)

HERBERT APPLEBAUM, THE CONCEPT OF WORK: ANCIENT, MEDIEVAL AND MODERN (SUNY 1992)

ROBIN ARCHER, WHY IS THERE NO LABOR PARTY IN THE UNITED STATES? (Princeton University Press 2007)

W.J. ASHLEY, SURVEYS HISTORIC AND ECONOMIC (London 1900)

CATHERINE BARNARD, EC EMPLOYMENT LAW (Oxford University Press 2000)

CATHERINE BARNARD, EU EMPLOYMENT LAW (4th ed. Oxford University Press 2012)

DETLEV W. BELLING, LEGAL PROTECTION AGAINST BREACHES OF DUTY ON THE PART OF THE GERMAN WORKS COUNCIL—A FATA MORGANA? (Springer 2000)

SVANTE BERGSTRÖM, KOLLEKTIVAVTALSLAGEN (2nd ed. Geber 1948)

BERTIL BJÖRKLUND, SVENSKA TYPOGRAF FÖRBUNDET STF—STUDIER RÖRANDE SVERIGES ÄLDSTA FACKFÖRBUND (Oskarshamn 1965)

ANTONY BLACK, GUILD & STATE—EUROPEAN POLITICAL THOUGHT FROM THE TWELFTH CENTURY TO THE PRESENT (Transaction Publishers 2003)

MARC BLOCH, FEUDAL SOCIETY (Routledge & Kegan Paul Ltd. 1961)

ALAN BOGG, THE DEMOCRATIC ASPECTS OF TRADE UNION RECOGNITION (Oxford University Press 2009)

KRISTINA BORÉUS, ANN IGHE, MARIA KARLSSON, & RIKARD WARLENIUS, ETT SEKEL AV SYNDICALISM, SVERIGES ARBETARES CENTRALORGANISATION 1910–2010 (Federativ förlag 2012)

KEITH BRADLEY & PAUL CARTLEDGE, THE CAMBRIDGE WORLD HISTORY OF SLAVERY (Cambridge University Press 2011)

LUJO BRENTANO, DIE ARBEITERGILDEN DER GEGENWART (Duncker & Humblot 1871)

LUJO BRENTANO, ON THE HISTORY AND DEVELOPMENT OF THE GILDS AND THE ORIGIN OF TRADE-UNIONS (London 1870)

J. BREUILLY, LIBERALISM AND LABOUR IN NINETEENTH-CENTURY EUROPE (Manchester University Press 1992)

EDMUND BURKE, THOUGHTS ON THE CAUSE OF THE PRESENT DISCONTENT (Printed for J. Dodsley in the Pall-Mall, London 1770)

MICHAEL BURLEIGH, THE THIRD REICH: A NEW HISTORY (Hill & Wang 2001)

JAMES BURN, AN HISTORICAL SKETCH OF THE INDEPENDENT ORDER OF ODDFELLOWS (Manchester 1845)

RICHARD BURN, SIR GEORGE CHETWYND, JUSTICE OF THE PEACE AND PARISH OFFICER VOLUME 4 (Straham 1820)

IAIN CAMERON, AN INTRODUCTION TO THE EUROPEAN CONVENTION ON HUMAN RIGHTS (7th ed. Iustus 2014)

ANTHONY CAREW, MICHEL DREYFUS, GEERT VAN GOETHEM, & REBECCA GUMBRELL-MCCORMICK (EDS.), THE INTERNATIONAL CONFEDERATION OF FREE TRADE UNIONS (Peter Lang 2000)

EDWARD P. CHEYNEY, AN INTRODUCTION TO THE INDUSTRIAL AND SOCIAL HISTORY OF ENGLAND (New York 1916)

G.D.H. COLE, GUILD SOCIALISM (The Fabian Society 1920)

HUGH COLLINS, K.D. EWING, & AILEEN MCCOLGAN, LAW IN CONTEXT: LABOUR LAW (Cambridge University Press 2012)

JOHN R. COMMONS, ULRICH PHILLIPS, EUGENE GILMORE, HELEN SUMNER, & JOHN ANDREWS (EDS), A DOCUMENTARY HISTORY OF AMERICAN INDUSTRIAL SOCIETY VOLUMES 1–10 (Cleveland 1910)

JOHN R. COMMONS, DAVID J. SAPOSS, HELEN L. SUMNER, E.B. MITTELMAN, H.E. HOAGLAND, JOHN B. ANDREWS, & SELIG PERLMAN, HISTORY OF LABOUR IN THE UNITED STATES, VOL. I (New York 1918)

K.P. COMPANJE, R.H.M. HENDRIKS, K.F.E. VERAGHTERT & B.E.M. WIDDERSHOVEN, TWO CENTURIES OF SOLIDARITY—GERMAN, BELGIAN AND DUTCH SOCIAL HEALTH CARE INSURANCE 1770–2008 (Aksant 2009)

Margaret Gay Davies, The Enforcement of English Apprenticeship: A Study in Applied Mercantilism 1563–1642 (Harvard University Press 1956)

Simon Deakin & Gillian S. Morris, Labour Law (6th ed. Oxford University Press 2012)

C.R. Dobson, Masters and Journeymen: A Prehistory of Industrial Relations 1717–1800 (Croom Helm 1980)

Ian Doolittle, The City of London and its Livery Companies—A History of Survival (Guildhall Library Publications 2010)

Anton Drexler, My Political Awakening (Preuss 1920)

Melvyn Dubofsky, We Shall Be All—A History of the Industrial Workers of the World (Quadrangle Books 1969)

Melvyn Dubofsky & Foster Rhea Dulles, Labor in America: A History (8th ed. Wiley-Blackwell 2010)

John Dunn, Democracy—A History (Penguin 2005)

Sten Edlund, Inga Hellberg, Tore Melin, & Birgitta Nyström, Konfliktbehandling på arbetsmarknaden (Arbetslivscentrum 1988)

Nicole Elert & Christopher T. Brooks, German Employment Law (De Gruyter 2014)

Patrick Elias & Keith Ewing, Trade Union Democracy—Members' Rights and the Law (Mansell 1987)

Steven A. Epstein, An Economic and Social History of Later Medieval Europe (Cambridge University Press 2009)

Bernd Erle & Thomas Sauter, Körperschaftsteuergesetz: Die Besteuerung der Kapitalgesellschaft und ihrer Anteilseigner (3rd ed. C.F. Müller Verlag Heidelberg 2010)

Joseph V. Femia, Marxism and Democracy (Oxford University Press 1993)

James S. Fishkin, When the People Speak—Deliberative Democracy and Public Consultation (Oxford University Press 2009)

Boel Flodgren, Fackföreningen och rätten (Norstedts 1978)

Felix Frankfurter & Nathan Greene, The Labor Injunction (Macmillan Company 1930)

Bert Fredriksson & Alf Gunnmo, Våra fackliga organisationer (Rabén & Sjögren 1976)

Carola M. Frege, Employment Research and State Traditions: A Comparative History of Britain, Germany and the United States (Oxford University Press 2007)

L. Fulton, Worker representation in Europe (Labour Research Department & ETUI 2015)

Otto von Gierke, Community in Historical Perspective (Antony Black ed. reprint Cambridge 2002)

OTTO VON GIERKE, DAS DEUTSCHE GENOSSENCHAFTSRECHT (Weidmann 1868)

WILLIAM B. GOULD IV, A PRIMER ON AMERICAN LABOR LAW (5th ed. Cambridge University Press 2013)

HELGA GREBING, HISTORY OF THE GERMAN LABOUR MOVEMENT—A SURVEY (Berg Publishing 1969)

ANDREAS GRIESSINGER, DAS SYMBOLISCHE KAPITAL DER EHRE: STREIKBEWEGUNGEN UND KOLLEKTIVES BEWUSSTSEIN DEUTSCHER HANDWERKSGESELLEN IM 18. JAHRHUNDERT (Ullsteing 1981)

RICHARD GRUNBERGER, A SOCIAL HISTORY OF THE THIRD REICH (Phoenix 1971)

JÜRGEN HABERMAS, BETWEEN FACTS AND NORMS (Polity Press 1997)

G.D.G. HALL (ED.), THE TREATISE OF THE LAWS AND CUSTOMS OF THE REALM OF ENGLAND COMMONLY CALLED GLANVILLE (Reprint Seldon Society 1965)

MARK HALL & JOHN PURCELL, CONSULTATION AT WORK: REGULATION AND PRACTICE (Oxford University Press 2012)

THEODORE S. HAMEROW, RESTORATION, REVOLUTION, REACTION—ECONOMICS AND POLITICS IN GERMANY, 1815–1871 (Princeton University Press 1970)

ALEXANDER HAMILTON, JAMES MADISON, & JOHN JAY, THE FEDERALIST PAPERS (1787)

SIGFRID HANSSON, BLAND MÄSTARE, GESÄLLER OCH LÄRPOJKAR (Norstedt & söners förlag 1931)

GUNNAR HAZELIUS, OM HANDTVERKSAMBETENA UNDER MEDELTIDEN (Nordiska museet 1906)

L.C. HECTOR & BARBARY HARVEY, THE WESTMINSTER CHRONICLE 1381–1394 (Oxford University Press 1982)

CARL HEMSTRÖM, UTESLUTNING UR IDEELL FÖRENING (Norstedts 1972)

BOB HEPPLE (ED.), THE MAKING OF LABOUR LAW IN EUROPE—A COMPARATIVE STUDY OF NINE COUNTRIES UP TO 1945 (Mansell Publishing 1986)

WILLIAM HERBERT (LIBRARIAN TO THE CORPORATION OF LONDON), THE HISTORY OF THE TWELVE GREAT LIVERY COMPANIES OF LONDON; PRINCIPALLY COMPILED FROM THEIR GRANTS AND RECORDS WITH AN HISTORICAL ESSAY AND ACCOUNTS OF EACH COMPANY, ITS ORIGIN, CONSTITUTION, GOVERNMENT, DRESS, CUSTOMS, HALLS, AND TRUST ESTATES AND CHARITIES, INCLUDING NOTICES AND ILLUSTRATION OF METROPOLITAN TRADE AND COMMERCE AS ORIGINALLY CONCENTRATED IN THOSE SOCIETIES, WITH ATTESTED COPIES AND TRANSLATIONS OF THE COMPANIES' CHARTERS, VOL. 1 (London 1837)

SUSAN E. HIRSCH, ROOTS OF THE AMERICAN WORKING CLASS—THE INDUSTRIALIZATION OF CRAFTS IN NEWARK 1800–1860 (University of Pennsylvania Press 1978)

THOMAS HOBBES, DE CIVE PHILOSOPHICAL RUDIMENTS CONCERNING GOVERNING AND SOCIETY (London 1651)

THOMAS HOBBES, EIGHT BOOKES OF THE PELOPONNESIAN WARRE (London 1648)

THOMAS HOBBES, LEVIATHAN (Printed for Andrew Crooke, at the Green Dragon in St. Paul's Churchyard, 1651)

RICHARD HOFSTADTER & WALTER METZGER, ACADEMIC FREEDOM IN THE AGE OF THE COLLEGE (Columbia University Press 1961)

HORNE'S MIRROR OF JUSTICES, 7 Selden Society 1, vol. VII (W.J. Whittaker & F.W. Maitland trans. 1893)

GEORGE HOWELL, TRADE UNIONISM NEW AND OLD (London 1900)

GUNNAR OLOF HYLTÉN-CAVALLIUS, WÄREND OCH WIRDARNE. ETT FÖRSÖK I SVENSK ETHNOLOGI (P.A. Norstedt & Söner 1863)

MICHELINE R. ISHAY, THE HISTORY OF HUMAN RIGHTS FROM ANCIENT TIMES TO THE GLOBALIZATION ERA (2nd ed. University of California Press 2008)

GEORGE MILTON JANES, THE CONTROL OF STRIKES IN AMERICAN TRADE UNIONS (Johns Hopkins Press 1916)

JUSTINIAN, DIGEST OF JUSTINIAN (Alan Watson trans. PennPress 2009)

OTTO KAHN-FREUND, DAS SOZIALE IDEAL DES REICHSARBEITSGERICHTS: EINE KRITISCHE UNTERSUCHUNG ZUR RECHTSPRECHUNG DES REICHSARBEITSGERICHTS IN ABHANDLUNGEN ZUM ARBEITSRECHT VOL. 7 (BENSHEIMER 1931)

G.E. KLEMMING, SAMLINGAR UTGIFNA AV SVENSKA FORNSKRIFTSÄLLSKAPET—SKRÅ ORDNINGAR (Stockholm 1856)

STELLA KRAMER, THE ENGLISH CRAFT GILDS AND THE GOVERNMENT—AN EXAMINATION OF THE ACCEPTED THEORY REGARDING THE DECAY OF THE ENGLISH CRAFT GUILDS (Columbia University Press 1905)

JOHN KROON, GULDSMEDERNAS SKRÅ AV ÅR 1501 FAKSIMILTRYCK (AM Malmö Ljustrycksanstalt 1959)

KENT KÄLLSTRÖM, LOKALA KOLLEKTIVAVTAL—OM LOKALA PARTERS RÄTTSLIGA STÄLLNING INOM FACKLIGA ORGANISATIONER (Liber 1979)

J. MALET LAMBERT, TWO THOUSAND YEARS OF GILD LIFE—OR AN OUTLINE OF THE HISTORY AND DEVELOPMENT OF THE GILD SYSTEM FROM EARLY TIMES, WITH SPECIAL REFERENCE TO ITS APPLICATION TO TRADE AND INDUSTRY (London 1891)

PAUL LANGFORD & WILLIAM B. TODD (EDS.), THE WRITINGS AND SPEECHES OF EDMUND BURKE, VOL. 2: PARTY, PARLIAMENT, AND THE AMERICAN WAR: 1766–1774 (Oxford University Press 1981)

RICHARD M. LANGWORTH & WINSTON CHURCHILL, CHURCHILL BY HIMSELF: THE LIFE, TIMES AND OPINIONS OF WINSTON CHURCHILL IN HIS OWN WORDS (Ebury Press 2008)
BRUCE LAURIE, ARTISANS INTO WORKERS: LABOUR IN NINETEENTH CENTURY AMERICA (Hill & Wang 1989)
ROBERT A. LEESON, UNITED WE STAND—AN ILLUSTRATED ACCOUNT OF TRADE UNION EMBLEMS (Dart 1971)
ROBERT A. LEESON, TRAVELLING BROTHERS (Granada 1979)
DOUGLAS L. LESLIE, LABOR LAW IN A NUTSHELL (West Publishing 2000)
ERIK LINDBERG, BORGERSKAP OCH BURSKAP, OM NÄRINGSPRIVILIGIER OCH BORGERSKAPETS INSTITUTIONER I STOCKHOLM 1820–1846 (Acta Universitatis Upsaliensis Uppsala Studies in Economic History 2001)
FOLKE LINDBERG, HANTVERK OCH SKRÅVÄSEN UNDER MEDELTID OCH ÄLDRE VASATID (Prisma 1989)
CARL LIVIJN, OM MODERNA SOCIALPOLITISKA LAGAR OCH LAGFÖRSLAG ANGÅENDE ARBETSKLASSENS BETRYGGANDE MOT DE EKONOMISKA FÖLJDERNA AF S.K. OLYCKSFALL I ARBETET (Beckman 1893)
JOHN LOCKE, TWO TREATISES OF GOVERNMENT (Thomas Hollis ed. A. Millar 1689)
PHILIPP LOTMAR, DER ARBEITSVERTRAG NACH DEM PRIVATRECHT DES DEUTSCHEN REICHES (Duncker & Humblot 1902)
BOUTELLE ELLSWORTH LOWE, INTERNATIONAL ASPECTS OF THE LABOR PROBLEM (Columbia University Press 1918)
JACOB LUNDELL, OM HANDTVERKSSKRÅN, NÄRINGSFRIHET OCH ARBETS ORGANISATION (Lund 1846)
CHRISTER LUNDH, SPELETS REGLER—INSTITUTIONER OCH LÖNEBILDNING PÅ DEN SVENSKA ARBETSMARKNADEN 1850–2010 (2nd ed. SNS Förlag 2010)
FRANK MCVEY, MODERN INDUSTRIALISM (D. Appleton & Company 1904)
SIR HENRY SUMNER MAINE, ANCIENT LAW (London 1861, reprint Legal Classics Library 1982)
JENNY MARTINEZ, THE SLAVE TRADE AND THE ORIGINS OF INTERNATIONAL HUMAN RIGHTS LAW (Oxford University Press 2012)
SIMON MIDDLETON, FROM PRIVILEGES TO RIGHTS: WORK AND POLITICS IN COLONIAL NEW YORK CITY (University of Pennsylvania Press 2006)
GWENDOLYN MINK, OLD LABOR AND NEW IMMIGRANTS IN AMERICAN POLITICAL DEVELOPMENT: UNION, PARTY, AND STATE, 1875–1920 (Cornell University Press 1986)
RICHARD B. MORRIS, GOVERNMENT AND LABOR IN EARLY AMERICA (Octagon Books 1975)

SAMUEL MOYN, HUMAN RIGHTS AND THE USES OF HISTORY: EXPANDED (2nd ed. Verso 2017)

THE NATIONAL GUILDS LEAGUE, THE POLICY OF GUILD SOCIALISM (London 1921)

MICHAEL J. NEUFELD, THE SKILLED METALWORKERS OF NUREMBERG—CRAFT AND CLASS IN THE INDUSTRIAL REVOLUTION (Rutgers University Press 1989)

MICHAEL NORDBERG, I KUNG MAGNUS TID, NORDEN UNDER MAGNUS ERIKSSON 1317–1374 (Norstedts 1995)

SVANTE NYCANDER, MAKTEN ÖVER ARBETSMARKNADEN (2nd ed. Stockholm 2008)

BIRGITTA NYSTRÖM, MEDLING I ARBETSTVISTER (Norstedts 1990)

JOHN V. ORTH, COMBINATION AND CONSPIRACY—A LEGAL HISTORY OF TRADE UNIONISM 1721–1906 (Clarendon Press 1991)

ROBERT OWEN, TWO MEMORIALS ON BEHALF OF THE WORKING CLASSES: THE FIRST PRESENTED TO THE GOVERNMENTS OF EUROPE AND AMERICA, THE SECOND TO THE ALLIED POWERS ASSEMBLED IN CONGRESS AT AIX-LA-CHAPELLE (London 1818)

OXFORD ENGLISH DICTIONARY (1st ed. 1884–1928)

THOMAS PAINE, FROM THE WRITINGS OF THOMAS PAINE VOL. 1 (1774–1779) (Moncure Daniel Conway ed. New York: G.P. Putnam's Sons, 1894)

DAVID RAY PAPKE, THE PULLMAN CASE: THE CLASH OF LABOR AND CAPITAL IN INDUSTRIAL AMERICA. LANDMARK LAW CASES & AMERICAN SOCIETY (University Press of Kansas 1999)

GREG PATMORE, WORKER VOICE—EMPLOYEE REPRESENTATION IN THE WORKPLACE IN AUSTRALIA, CANADA, GERMANY, THE UK AND THE US 1914–1939 (Liverpool University Press 2016)

ALEXANDER PENNECUIK, BURGESS AND GUILD-BROTHER OF EDINBURGH, AN HISTORICAL ACCOUNT OF THE BLUE BLANKET, OR CRAFTS-MEN'S BANNER, CONTAINING THE FUNDAMENTAL PRINCIPLES OF THE GOOD-TOWN, WITH THE POWERS AND PREROGATIVES OF THE CRAFTS OF EDINBURGH & C. (Edinburgh 1722)

PLATO, THE REPUBLIC (Benjamin Jowett trans. Project Gutenberg 2008)

PLUTARCH, THE RISE OF ROME: TWELVE LIVES BY PLUTARCH: ROMULUS, NUMA, PUBLICOLA, CORIOLANUS, CAMILLUS, FABIUS MAXIMUS, MARCELLUS, ARATUS, PHILOPOEMEN, TITUS FLAMININUS, ELDER CATO, AEMILIUS PAULLUS, NUMA (Christopher Pelling, Ian Scott-Kilvert, & Jeffrey Tatum trans. Penguin 2013)

JAMES POOL, WHO FINANCED HITLER: THE SECRET FUNDING OF HITLER'S RISE TO POWER, 1919–1933 (Gallery 1979)

R.W. POSTGATE, THE BUILDERS' HISTORY (Labour Publishing Company 1923)

DOUGLAS E. RAY, CALVIN WILLIAM SHARPE, & ROBERT N. STRASSFELD, UNDERSTANDING LABOR LAW (LexisNexis 1999)

THEODORE WINTER REEDY & JOHN MOFFETT BRUMM, BRIEF HISTORY OF THE AMERICAN LABOR MOVEMENT (US Government Printing Office 1951)

BRIAN BELL RICHARD, THE EVOLVING DUTIES OF TRADE UNIONS TOWARD THEIR MEMBERS: DEFINING THE DUTIES AND DETERMINING THE STANDARDS (Proquest 1998)

JOHAN GABRIEL RICHART, ETT OCH ANNAT, OM CORPORATIONER, PRIVILEGIER, NÄMND I DOMSTOLAR ETC. I ANLEDNING AF CONSISTORII ACADEMICI I UPSALA BETÄNKANDE OM DE ACADEMISKA JURISDIKTION (Stockholm 1822)

JOHN ROBERTS (ED.), OXFORD DICTIONARY OF THE CLASSICAL WORLD (Oxford University Press 2007)

GERRY RODGERS, EDDY LEE, LEE SWEPSTON & JASMIEN VAN DAELE, THE INTERNATIONAL LABOUR ORGANIZATION AND THE QUEST FOR SOCIAL JUSTICE, 1919–2009 (ILO 2009)

JOEL ROGERS & WOLFGANG STREECK (EDS.), WORKS COUNCILS: CONSULTATION, REPRESENTATION AND COOPERATION IN INDUSTRIAL RELATIONS (University of Chicago Press 1995)

MIA RÖNNMAR, ARBETSLEDNINGSRÄTT OCH ARBETSSKYLDIGHET: EN KOMPARATIV STUDIE AV KVALITITAV FLEXIBILITET I SVENSK, ENGELSK OCH TYSK CONTEXT (Juristförlaget i Lund 2004)

ALICE SALOMON, LABOUR LAWS FOR WOMEN IN GERMANY (Women's Industrial Council London 1907 Leopold Reprint 2010)

WILLIAM SCHIRER, THE RISE AND FALL OF THE THIRD REICH (Mandarin 1999)

WILFRIED SCHLÜTER, DIE HAFTUNG DER ARBEITNEHMERVERTRETER IM AUFSICHTSRAT EINER AKTIENGESELLSCHAFT BEI NICHTIGKEIT DES JAHRESABSCHLUSSES IN FESTSCHRIFT ZUM 60. GEBURTSTAG FÜR JÖRG BAETGE (Düsseldorf 1997)

FOLKE SCHMIDT, FACKLIG ARBETSRÄTT (Reviderad Ronnie Eklund, Håkan Göransson, Ken Källström, Tore Sigeman Stockholm 1997)

FOLKE SCHMIDT, LAW AND INDUSTRIAL RELATIONS IN SWEDEN (Stockholm 1977)

FOLKE SCHMIDT, THE LAW OF LABOUR RELATIONS IN SWEDEN (Uppsala 1962)

J.H. SCHRÖDER, STATUTA CONVIVII A S. GEORGIO DICTI AD MAGNUM CUPRIMONTEM DALEKARLIAE (Uppsala 1833)

JOSEPH A. SCHUMPETER, CAPITALISM, SOCIALISM AND DEMOCRACY (2nd ed. 1947, Martino Publishing, reprint 2011)

KIRSTEN A. SEAVER, THE LAST VIKINGS: THE EPIC STORY OF THE GREAT NORSE VOYAGERS (Tauris 2014)

Hugo Sinzheimer, Der korporative Arbeitsnormenvertrag: Eine Privatrechtliche Undersuchung (Duncker & Humblot 1907)

Adam Smith, An Inquiry into the Nature and Causes of the Wealth of Nations (London 1776)

Toulmin Smith, English Gilds—The Original Ordinances of more than one hundred Early English Gilds (Oxford University Press 1870)

K.D.M. Snell, Annals of the Labouring Poor—Social Change and Agrarian England, 1660–1900 (Cambridge 1985)

Michael Stolleis, A History of Social Law in Germany (Springer 2013)

Michael Stolleis, Origins of the German Welfare State: Social Policy in Germany to 1945 (German Social Policy) (Springer 2014)

Randi Storch, Working Hard for the American Dream—Workers and Their Unions, World War I to the present (Wiley Blackwell 2013)

Bo Stråth, The Organisation of Labour Markets—Modernity, culture and governance in Germany, Sweden, Britain and Japan (Routledge 1996)

Arnold Sölvén, Landorganisationens skriftserien, Huvudavtalet (Stockholm 1939)

Thucydides, Eight bookes of the Peloponnesian warre written by Thucydides the Sonne of Olorus Date: 1648 (Thomas Hobbes trans. 1648)

Thucydides, Thucydides in Four Volumes: Vol. 1, the History of the Peloponnesian War Books I and II 320–21 (Charles Forster Smith trans. Harvard University Press 1956)

Suetonius Tranquillus, Divus Iulius (Harold Edgeworth Butler & Max Cary eds. Clarendon 1970)

Suetonius: The Lives of the Twelve Caesars; An English Translation, Augmented with the Biographies of Contemporary Statesmen, Orators, Poets, and Other Associates (J. Eugene Reed & Alexander Thomson eds. 1889)

Tom Söderberg, Hantverkarna i brytningstid 1820–1870 (Vasatryckeriet 1955)

Göran Therborn, Borgarklass och byråkrati i Sverige (Arkiv förlaget Lund 1989)

Michael Thomsett, The German Opposition to Hitler, The Resistance, the Underground and Assassination Plots 1938–1945 (Crux 2016)

Christopher L. Tomlins, Law, Labor, and Ideology in the Early American Republic (Cambridge University Press 1993)

ROLF TORSTENDAHL, BUREAUCRATIZATION IN NORTHWESTERN EUROPE 1880–1895 (Routledge 1991)
HENRY ASHBY TURNER, GERMAN BIG BUSINESS AND THE RISE OF HITLER (Oxford University Press 1987)
ÖSTEN UNDÉN, KOLLEKTIVAVTALET ENLIGT GÄLLANDE SVENSK RÄTT (Berlingska boktryckeriet 1921)
MARTIN UPCHURCH, GRAHAM TAYLOR, & ANDREW MATHERS, THE CRISIS OF SOCIAL DEMOCRATIC TRADE UNIONISM IN WESTERN EUROPE: THE SEARCH FOR ALTERNATIVES (Ashgate 2009)
GEORGE URWIN, INDUSTRIAL ORGANIZATION IN THE SIXTEENTH AND SEVENTEENTH CENTURIES (London 1957)
MACK WALKER, GERMAN HOME TOWNS, COMMUNITY, STATE, AND GENERAL ESTATE 1648–1871 (Cornell 1971)
TIMOTHY WALKER, AN INTRODUCTION TO AMERICAN LAW (P.H. Nicklin & T. Johnson 1837)
SIDNEY WEBB & BEATRICE POTTER WEBB, INDUSTRIAL DEMOCRACY (Longman, Green & Co. 1897)
SIDNEY WEBB & BEATRICE POTTER WEBB, THE HISTORY OF TRADE UNIONISM (Longman, Green & Co. 1894)
SIDNEY WEBB & BEATRICE POTTER WEBB, THE HISTORY OF TRADE UNIONISM 1666–1920, VOL. 1, 2 (1920 Palgrave reprint 2003)
DAVID B. WEISBERG, GUILD STRUCTURE AND POLITICAL ALLEGIANCE IN EARLY ACHAEMENID MESOPOTAMIA (Yale University Press 1967)
MANFRED WEISS & MARLENE SCHMIDT, LABOUR LAW AND INDUSTRIAL RELATIONS IN GERMANY (4th ed. Kluwer 2008)
JÖRGEN WESTERSTÅHL, SVENSK FACKFÖRENINGSRÖRELSE: ORGANISATIONSPROBLEM, VERKSAMHETSFORMER, FÖRHÅLLANDE TILL STATEN (Tidens förlag 1945)
CHRIS WICKHAM, THE INHERITANCE OF ROME: ILLUMINATING THE DARK AGES 400–1000 (Penguin 2010)
HELEN ZIMMERN, THE HANSA TOWNS AND THE HANSEATIC LEAGUE (Florence 1889)
KLAS ÅMARK, FACKLIG MAKT OCH FACKLIGT MEDLEMSKAP: DEN SVENSKA FACKFÖRBUDENS MEDLEMSUTVECKLING 1890–1940 (Arkiv förlag Lund 1986)

ARTICLES AND CHAPTERS

John Adams, *7th "Novanglus" letter*, BOSTON GAZETTE (1774)
John T. Addison, Lutz Bellmann, Claus Schnabel, Joachim Wagner, *The Long Awaited Reform of the German Works Constitution Act*, IZA DP No. 422 (IZA 2002)

Rachel Aleks, *Estimating the Effect of "Change to Win" on Union Organizing* [Electronic version], 68(3) INDUSTRIAL & LABOR RELATIONS REVIEW 584–605 (2015)

Alan Apperley, *Hobbes on Democracy*, 19(3) POLITICS 65–171 (1999)

Joyce Appleby, *The Radical Double-Entendre in the Right to Self-Government* in THE ORIGINS OF ANGLO-AMERICAN RADICALISM (Margaret Jacob & James Jacob eds. George Allen & Unwin London 1984)

Michael Berlin, *Guilds in Decline? London Livery Companies and the Rise of a Liberal Economy, 1600–1800* in GUILDS, INNOVATION AND THE EUROPEAN ECONOMY, 1400–1800 (S.R. Epstein & Maarten Prak eds. Cambridge University Press 2008)

Lujo Brentano, *Introduction* in Toulmin Smith, ENGLISH GILDS—THE ORIGINAL ORDINANCES OF MORE THAN ONE HUNDRED EARLY ENGLISH GILDS (Oxford University Press 1870)

Laura Carlson, *Discrimination Damages—Promoting or Preventing Access to Justice?* in FESTSKRIFT TILL ANN NUMHAUSER-HENNING (Mia Rönnmar ed. Juristförlaget i Lund 2017)

G.D.H. Cole, *A study in British Trade Union History. Attempts at a 'General Union' 1829–1834*, 4 INTERNATIONAL REVIEW OF SOCIAL HISTORY 359–462 (January 1938)

Taylor Cole, *The Role of the Labor Courts in West Germany*, 18(3) THE JOURNAL OF POLITICS 479–98 (Aug. 1956)

Alexander J.S. Colvin, *American Workplace Dispute Resolution in the Individual Rights Era*, 23(3) INTERNATIONAL JOURNAL OF HUMAN RESOURCE MANAGEMENT 459–75 (2012)

Laura J. Cooper, *Letting the Puppets Speak: Employee Voice in the Legislative History of the Wagner Act*, 94 MARQUETTE LAW REV. 837–868 (2011)

Leon A. Dale, *International Trade Secretariats*, 22(1) RELATIONS INDUSTRIELLES 98–115 (1967)

Patrick Diamond, *From Fatalism to Fraternity: Governing Purpose and the Good Society* in AFTER THE THIRD WAY—THE FUTURE OF SOCIAL DEMOCRACY IN EUROPE 3 (Olaf Camme & Patrick Diamond eds. London 2012)

Ruth Dukes, *Hugo Sinzheimer and the Constitutional Function of Labour Law* in THE IDEA OF LABOUR LAW 57 (Guy Davidov & Brian Langille eds. Oxford 2011)

David Dunér, *Helvetet i Falun*, 3 POPULÄR HISTORIA 48–53 (2009)

Wolfgang Däubler, *Trends in German Labour Law* in LABOUR LAW IN THE POST-INDUSTRIAL ERA—STUDIES IN MODERN LAW AND POLICY (Lord Wedderburn, Max Rood, Gérard Lyon-Caen, Wolfgang Däubler, & Paul van der Heijden eds. Dartmouth 1994)

Lars Edgren, *Crafts in Transformation? Masters, Journeymen, and Apprentices in a Swedish Town, 1800–1850*, 1(3) CONTINUITY AND CHANGE 363–83 (1986)

Peter Ellguth & Susanne Kohaut, *Tarifbindung und betriebliche Interessenvertretung: Aktuelle Ergebnisse aus dem IAB-Betriebspanel 2013*, WSI-Mitteilungen, 4/20124

Cynthia Estlund, *The Ossification of American Labor Law*, 102 COLUMBIA LAW REVIEW 1527–1612 (2002)

James S. Fishkin & Robert C. Luskin, *Experimenting with a Democratic Ideal: Deliberative Polling and Public Opinion*, 40 ACTA POLITICA 284 (2005)

Bernd Fitzenberger, Karsten Kohn, & Qingwei Want, *The Erosion of Union Membership in Germany: Determinants, Densities, Decompositions*, 24(1) JOURNAL OF POPULATION ECONOMICS 141–65 (January 2011)

Jeffrey Flynn, *Communicative Power in Habermas's Theory of Democracy*, 3(4) EUROPEAN JOURNAL OF POLITICAL THEORY 433 (2004)

William E. Forbath, *The Shaping of the American Labor Movement*, 102 HARV. L. REV. 1109 (1988–89)

Birgitta Forsberg, *LO statser 30 miljoner på S till valet—trots vikande stöd*, SVENSKADAGBLADET, December 23, 2017

Ian Anders Gadd & Patrick Wallis, *Reaching beyond the City Wall: London Guilds and National Regulation 1500–1700* in GUILDS, INNOVATION AND THE EUROPEAN ECONOMY, 1400–1800 (S.R. Epstein & Maarten Prak eds. Cambridge University Press 2008)

Dick Geary, *Socialism and the German Labour Movement before 1914* in LABOUR AND SOCIALIST MOVEMENTS IN EUROPE BEFORE 1914 (Dick Geary ed. Berg 1992)

David J. Gerber, *System Dynamics: Toward a Language of Comparative Law?*, 46 AM. J. COMP. L. 719 (1998)

Marcia Greenblatt, *Union Officials and the Labor Bill of Rights*, 57 FORDHAM L. REV. 601 (1989)

Gavin Jackson, *Employment Tribunal Cases Rise Sharply after Fees Are Dropped*, THE FINANCIAL TIMES, December 14, 2017

Aaron Halegua, *United States* in RESOLVING INDIVIDUAL LABOUR DISPUTES (Minawa Ebisui, Sean Cooney, & Colin Fenwick eds. ILO Geneva 2016)

Mark Hall, Sue Hutchinson, John Purcell, Michael Terry, & Jane Parker, *Promoting Effective Consultation? Assessing the Impact of the ICE Regulations*, 51(2) BRITISH JOURNAL OF INDUSTRIAL RELATIONS 355–81 (June 2013)

David Huxtable, *A Most Curious Lack of Curiosity: Global Unions as the Missing Link* in LABOUR MOVEMENT STUDIES IN SOCIETY OF SOCIALIST STUDIES (2009)

Benjamin Jones & Jeremias Prassl, *United Kingdom* in RESOLVING INDIVIDUAL LABOUR DISPUTES (Minawa Ebisui, Sean Cooney, & Colin Fenwick eds. ILO Geneva 2016)

Otto Kahn-Freund, *Labour Law* in LAW AND PUBLIC OPINION IN BRITAIN IN THE TWENTIETH CENTURY (Morris Ginsberg ed. London 1959)

Otto Kahn-Freund, *On Uses and Misuses of Comparative Law*, 37 MOD. L. REV. 1, 27 (1974)

Otto Kahn-Freund, *The Legal Framework* in THE SYSTEM OF INDUSTRIAL RELATIONS IN GREAT BRITAIN: ITS HISTORY, LAW, AND INSTITUTIONS (Alan Flanders & Hugh Clegg eds. Oxford University Press 1954)

Ernst Kallenberg, *Akademisk jurisdiktion. Studenternas rättsliga undantagsställning*, 2 STATSVETENSKAPLIG TIDSKRIFT 97–121 (1906)

Anders Kjellberg, *Facklig organisering och partsrelationer i Sverige och Danmark* in SEPTEMBERFORLIGET OG DET 21. ÅRHUNDREDE. HISTORISKE PERSPEKTIVER OG FREMTIDENS DILEMMAER (Flemming Ibsen & Steen Scheuer eds. Copenhagen 2000)

Anders Kjellberg, *Kollektivavtalens täckningsgrad samt organisationsgraden hos arbetsgivarförbund och fackförbund,* 2013(1) STUDIES IN SOCIAL POLICY, INDUSTRIAL RELATIONS, WORKING LIFE AND MOBILITY, RESEARCH REPORTS (Lund University 2013)

Anders Kjellberg, *Växande avgiftsskillnader i a-kassan – och utvecklingen därefter*, 2014(1) STUDIES IN SOCIAL POLICY, INDUSTRIAL RELATIONS, WORKING LIFE AND MOBILITY, RESEARCH REPORTS (Lund University 2014)

Eva Kocher and Clemens Sudhof, *Trade Union Representation in Germany* in REPRESENTING EMPLOYEE INTERESTS: TRADE UNION SYSTEMS WITHIN THE EU (Carmen La Macchia ed. Albecete 2013)

John P. Lloyd, *The Strike Wave of 1877* in THE ENCYCLOPEDIA OF STRIKES IN AMERICAN HISTORY (Aaron Brenner, Benjamin Day, & Immanuel Ness eds. 2015)

Graeme Lockwood, *An Epitaph to CROTUM and CPAUIA*, 31(5) INDUSTRIAL RELATIONS JOURNAL 471–81 (2000)

Alf Lüdtke, *The "Honor of Labor": Industrial Workers and the Power of Symbols under National Socialism* in REWRITING HISTORIES: NAZISM AND GERMAN SOCIETY, 1933–1945 (David Crew ed. Routledge 2013)

James Madison, NOTES ON THE DEBATES IN THE FEDERAL CONVENTION, Tuesday September 17, 1787, available at the website of The Avalon Project, Documents in Law, History and Diplomacy, Yale Law School: avalon.law.yale.edu

Robert W. Malcolmson, *Workers' Combinations in Eighteenth-Century England* in THE ORIGINS OF ANGLO-AMERICAN RADICALISM (Margaret Jacob & James Jacob eds. London 1984)
Ewan McGaughey, *The Codetermination Bargains: The History of German Corporate and Labour Law*, 23(1) COLUMBIA JOURNAL OF EUROPEAN LAW 135–42 (2016)
Wolfgang Merkel, *Social Democracy in Power: Explaining the Capacity to Reform*, 1(1) ZEITSCHRIFT FÜR VERGLEICHENDE POLITIKWISSENSCHAFT 125–45, 134–5 (2007)
Marcello Musto, *Notes on the History of the International*, 28(2) SOCIALISM AND DEMOCRACY 5–38 (2014)
Walther Müller-Jentsch, *Germany: From Collective Voice to Co-Management* in WORKS COUNCILS: CONSULTATION, REPRESENTATION AND COOPERATION IN INDUSTRIAL RELATIONS (Joel Rogers & Wolfgang Streeck eds. Chicago 1995)
Gary B. Nash, *Artisans and Politics in Eighteenth-Century Philadelphia* in THE ORIGINS OF ANGLO-AMERICAN RADICALISM (Margaret Jacob & James Jacob eds. London 1984)
Notes: NLRB Remedies, 351 DUKE LAW JOURNAL 354 (1975)
Carole M. Nottingham, *The London Middle English Guild Certificates of 1388–9* in *Historical Introduction*, 39 MEDIEVAL STUDIES 108 (1995)
Ann Numhauser-Henning, *Lagstiftning eller självreglering i arbetsrätten? Svaret är bade ock*, 2001 SVJT 314
Rebecca Page, *Co-determination in Germany—A Beginner's Guide*, ARBEITSPAPIER 33 (Hans Böckler Stiftung 2011)
Cinzia Peraro, *Right to Collective Action in Cross-Border Employment Contexts: A Fundamental Social Right Not Yet Covered by EU Private International Law*, 2(2) UNIO—EU LAW JOURNAL 20–38 (2016)
Ewa Persson, *Högsta organisationsgraden på sju år för tjänstemannen*, ARBETSVÄRLDEN February 18, 2015
Maarten Prak, *Preface: S.R. Epstein (1960–2007) and the Guilds* in THE RETURN OF THE GUILDS (Jan Lucassen, Tine De Moor, & Jan Luiten van Zanden eds., Intl. Review of Social History supp. 16 2008)
Petter Rütters, *International Trade Secretariats—Origins, Development, Activities* (Library of the Friedrich-Ebert-Stiftung, library.fes.de, 2003)
Benjamin Sachs, *Revitalizing Labor Law*, 31(2) BERKELEY JOURNAL OF EMPLOYMENT AND LABOR LAW 333–47 (2010)
Benjamin Sachs, *Despite Preemption: Making Labor Law in Cities and States*, 1224 HARVARD LAW REVIEW 1153–1224 (2011)
E.H. Schopler, *Closed Shops and Closed Unions*, 160 A.L.R. 918 (1946 with cumulative supplements)
Jo Shaw, *Gender Mainstreaming and the EU Constitution*, 15(3) EUSA REVIEW 3–4 (2002)

Eric Stein, *Uses, Misuses—and Nonuses of Comparative Law*, 72 NW. U. L. REV. 198 (1977)

Bo Stråth, *EUI Working Papers in History No. 90/5, Union Strategies in Historical Perspective: Sweden and Germany* 7 (EUI 1990)

Jelle Visser, *Union Membership Statistics in 24 Countries*, 38 MONTHLY LABOUR REVIEW 39–49 (January 2006)

Jenny Julen Votinius, *Sweden* in RESOLVING INDIVIDUAL LABOUR DISPUTES (Minawa Ebisui, Sean Cooney, & Colin Fenwick eds. ILO Geneva 2016)

Bernd Waas, *Germany* in RESOLVING INDIVIDUAL LABOUR DISPUTES (Minawa Ebisui, Sean Cooney, & Colin Fenwick eds. ILO Geneva 2016)

Frank Julian Warne, *The Trade Agreement in the Coal Industry*, 36 AMERICAN ACADEMY OF POLITICAL AND SOCIAL SCIENCES ANNALS 86–95 (September 1910)

Alan Watson, *Legal Transplants and Law Reform*, 92 L. QUART. REV. 79 (1976)

Andrea Weindl, *The Slave Trade of Northern Germany from the Seventeenth to the Nineteenth Centuries* in EXTENDING THE FRONTIERS, ESSAYS ON THE NEW TRANSATLANTIC SLAVE TRADE DATABASE 250 (David Eltis & David Richardson eds. Yale 2008)

George S. Werner, *Traveling Journeymen in Metternichian South Germany*, 125 PROCEEDINGS IN THE AMERICAN PHILOSOPHICAL SOCIETY NO. 3 190–219 (1981)

John P. Windmüller, Stephen K. Pursey, & Jim Baker, *The International Trade Union Movement* in COMPARATIVE LABOUR LAW AND INDUSTRIAL RELATIONS IN INDUSTRIALIZED MARKET ECONOMIES (Roger Blainpain & Jim Baker eds. 10th ed. Wolters Kluwer 2010)

Patrick Wintour, *Trade Unions—Biggest Crackdown on Trade Unions for 30 Years Launched by Conservatives*, THE GUARDIAN, July 15, 2015

Donald Woodward, *The Background to the Statute of Artificers: The Genesis of Labour Policy, 1558–63*, 33(1) THE ECONOMIC HISTORY REVIEW, NEW SERIES 32–44 (Feb. 1980)

REPORTS

Rev. J.T. Becher, OBSERVATIONS UPON THE REPORT FROM THE SELECT COMMITTEE OF THE HOUSE OF COMMONS ON THE LAWS RESPECTING FRIENDLY SOCIETIES (1826)

BLS News Release, MAJOR WORK STOPPAGES 1947–2017 (USDL-18-0206), February 9, 2018

Committee on Trades' Societies, Trades' Societies and Strikes, REPORT OF THE COMMITTEE ON TRADES' SOCIETIES APPOINTED BY THE NATIONAL ASSOCIATION FOR THE PROMOTION OF SOCIAL SCIENCE, PRESENTED AT THE FOURTH ANNUAL MEETING OF THE ASSOCIATION AT GLASGOW, SEPTEMBER 1860 (London 1860)

European Commission, REVERSING THE BURDEN OF PROOF: PRACTICAL DILEMMAS AT THE EUROPEAN AND NATIONAL LEVEL (EU 2014)

Matthew Downer, Carrie Harding, Shadi Ghezelayagh, Emily Fu, & Marina Gkiza, EVALUATION OF ACAS EARLY CONCILIATION 2015 (Acas 04/15)

Federal Ministry of Labour and Social Affairs, CO-DETERMINATION 2018 (Federal Ministry of Labour and Social Affairs 2018)

ILO, RULES OF THE GAME, A BRIEF INTRODUCTION TO INTERNATIONAL LABOUR STANDARDS (2014)

Ralph Greifenstein, Leo Kißler, & Hendrik Lange, TRENDREPORT BETRIEBSRATSWAHLEN 2010 (Hans-Böckler-Stiftung 2011)

Ralph Greifenstein, Leo Kißler, & Hendrik Lange, TRENDREPORT BETRIEBSRATSWAHLEN 2014: ZWISCHENBERICHT: ZWISCHENERGEBNISSE KURZ NACH DER WAHL (Hans-Böckler-Stiftung, June–August 2014)

IRS PUBLICATION 529 (2015)

Anders Kjellberg, KOLLEKTIVAVTALENS TÄCKNINGSGRAD SAMT ORGANISATIONSGRADEN HOS ARBETSGIVARFÖRBUND OCH FACKFÖRBUND, Department of Sociology, Lund University Studies in Social Policy, Industrial Relations, Working Life and Mobility Research Reports 2017(1) (Lund University 2017)

Sir Ken Knight, ELECTRONIC BALLOTING REVIEW: THE REPORT OF THE INDEPENDENT REVIEW OF ELECTRONIC BALLOTING FOR INDUSTRIAL ACTION (December 2017)

Richard Koch (ed.), NATIONAL MONETARY COMMISSION, GERMAN IMPERIAL BANKING LAWS, 61ST CONGRESS 2D SESSION DOCUMENT NO. 574 (Washington DC 1910)

LAWS FOR THE CONSTITUTION AND GOVERNMENT OF THE LONDON JOURNEYMEN'S TRADES HALL ENROLLED ACCORDING TO ACT OF PARLIAMENT (London 1839)

Jonas Malmberg, STUDY—DIRECTORATE GENERAL FOR INTERNAL POLICIES—POLICY DEPARTMENT A: ECONOMIC AND SCIENTIFIC POLICY, EMPLOYMENT AND SOCIAL AFFAIRS: THE IMPACT OF THE ECT JUDGMENTS ON VIKING, LAVAL, RÜFFERT AND LUXEMBOURG ON THE PRACTICE OF COLLECTIVE BARGAINING AND THE EFFECTIVENESS OF SOCIAL ACTION (2010)

Medlingsinstitut (Swedish National Mediation Office), SIFFROR OCH DIAGRAM OM MEDLEMSANTAL, ORGANISATIONSGRAD OCH KOLLEKTIVAVTALSTÄCKNING (2014)

Medlingsinstitut (Swedish National Mediation Office), AVTALSRÖRELSEN OCH LÖNEBILDNINGEN 2015—MEDLINGSINSTITUTETS ÅRSRAPPORT (Linköping 2015)

Medlingsinstitut (Swedish National Mediation Office), ÅRSRAPPORT FÖR 2017 (2018)

Mick Marchington, JOINT CONSULTATION REVISITED (Centre for Research in Industrial Democracy and Participation 1985)

OBSERVATIONS ON THE RISE AND PROGRESS OF FRIENDLY SOCIETIES (1824)

John Francis Reilly, Carter C. Hull & Barbara A. Braig Allen, IRC 501(C)(5) ORGANIZATIONS, EXEMPT ORGANIZATIONS TECHNICAL INSTRUCTION PROGRAM FÖR FY 2003 (2003) J-3

Report of the Committee of Experts, REPORT INTERNATIONAL LABOR CONFERENCE 89TH SESSION 3 OF THE REPORT III (1B)-2001—*Chapter 2 Anatomy of a Prohibition: ILO Standards in Relation to Night Work of Women in Industry* (ILO 2001)

Report of the Royal Commission on Trade Unions and Employers' Associations (the "Donovan report"), 23(4) RELATIONS INDUSTRIELLES (1968)

Ingrid Schmidt, THE FEDERAL LABOUR COURT (Erfurt 2014)

John Simkin, TRADE UNIONS IN NAZI GERMANY (Spartucus-educational.com 1997)

US Bureau of Labor Statistics, ECONOMIC NEWS RELEASE, UNION MEMBERS SUMMARY, January 28, 2016

UNPUBLISHED WORKS

Esmée Myfanwy Thomas, Guilds of Craftsmen and Small Traders in the Ancient World (exclusive of Egypt) from the Earliest Greek Times to the End of the 5th Century A.D. (Unpublished thesis, Oxford University, St. Anne's Society 1934)

INTERNET MATERIALS

Urban Bäckström, *Om förmågan att lyssna, Svenskt näringsliv* (March 12, 2009) available at the Confederation of Swedish Enterprise website, svensktnaringsliv.se

Deutscher Gewerkschaftsbund, *DBG—Functions and Principles* (2016) available at the DGB website, dgb.de

M.H. Hansen, *Democracy/Athenian* in OXFORD CLASSICAL DICTIONARY (2015) available at classics.oxfordre.com

ILO, *About the ILO and Origins and History*, available at the ILO website, ilo.org

NLRB, *Employer/Union Rights and Obligations: How Is "Good Faith" Bargaining Determined?* available at nlrb.gov

NLRB, *Representation Petitions, RC Statistics* available at nlrb.gov

NRLB, *The Right to Strike* available at nlrb.gov/strikes

NRLB, *See What We Do, Investigate Charges* available at nlrb.gov

Project Samnordisk Runtextdatabas Svensk—*Rundata entry for Ög 64 and Ög MÖLM1960:230*, available at nordiska.uu.se/forskn/samnord.htm

Riksarkivet, *Regeringsformen* (2013 updated 2014) available at the Swedish National Archives website, riksarkivet.se/regeringsform

Cecilia Thorborg, *Massutvandring till Amerika slag mot befolkningen*, Nr. 2013:56, available at the Statistics Sweden website, scb.se

Chris Trueman, *Trade Unions and Nazi Germany* (2013) available at the History Learning Site website, historylearningsite.co.uk

Karen Ullmann & Christian Ley, *Germany: Industrial Relations* (Xpert internet database 2016)

United Nations Secretary-General Ban Ki-moon, *Statement for the International Day for the Abolition of Slavery*, 2 December 2015, available at the UN website, un.org

Sandra Vogel, *Use of Opening Clauses in Collective Agreements* (Eurofound 2016) available at eurofound.europa.eu.

LEGAL SOURCES

International Laws

United Nations

The 1948 United Nations Declaration of Human Rights

The 1966 International Covenant on Civil and Political Rights

The 1966 International Covenant on Economic, Social and Cultural Rights

United Nations General Assembly 1948 Resolution 217 A, Universal Declaration of Human Rights, A/res/3/217A

UN International Labour Organisation

ILO Declaration on Fundamental Principles and Rights at Work (1998)

ILO Convention No. 81 The Labour Inspection Convention of 1947

ILO Convention No. 87 concerning Freedom of Association and Protection of the Right to Organise of 1948
ILO Convention No. 98 concerning the Application of the Principles of the Right to Organise and to Bargain Collectively of 1949
ILO Convention No. 100 Equal Remuneration Convention of 1951
ILO Convention No. 122 The Employment Policy Convention of 1964
ILO Convention No. 129 The Labour Inspection (Agriculture) Convention of 1969
ILO Convention No. 144 The Tripartite Consultation (International Labour Standards) Convention of 1976

Regional Cooperations

Council of Europe

Instruments

The 1950 Convention for the Protection of Human Rights and Fundamental Freedoms
The 1961 European Social Charter
The 1996 (Revised) European Social Charter

Case law

National Union of Belgian Police v. Belgium, October 27, 1975, Eur. Ct HR Rep., Series A, No. 19 (1975)
UNISON v. United Kingdom, judgment of January 10, 2002, [2002] IRLR 497
Enerji Yapi-Yol Sen v. Turkey, Application no. 68959/01 [2009]

European Union law

Treaties

The 1951 Treaty establishing the European Coal and Steel Community ("ECSC Treaty")
The 1957 European Economic Community ("EEC")
The 1957 Treaty establishing the European Atomic Energy Community ("Euratom")
The 2007 Treaty of Lisbon amending the Treaty on European Union and the Treaty establishing the European Community, signed at Lisbon, 13 December 2007
The 2007 Treaty on the European Union ("TEU")
The 2007 Treaty on the Functioning of the European Union ("TFEU")

Directives

Council Directive 97/80/EC of 15 December 1997 on the burden of proof in cases of discrimination based on sex

Directive 2002/14/EC of the European Parliament and of the Council of 11 March 2002 establishing a general framework for informing and consulting employees in the European Community

Directive 2009/38/EC of the European Parliament and of the Council of 6 May 2009 on the establishment of a European Works Council or a procedure in Community-Scale undertakings and Community-scale groups of undertakings for the purposes of informing and consulting employees (Recast)

Council resolutions

Council Resolution of 21 January 1974 concerning a social action programme, OJ 1974 C 13/1

Court of Justice case law

Case C-43/75, *Gabriella Defrenne (No. 2) v. Societe Anonyme Belge de Navigation Aerienne Sabena* [1976] 1 ECR-455

Case C-44/79, *Liselotte Hauer v. Land Rheinland-Pfalz* [1979] ECR-3727

C-109/88, *Handels- og Kontorfunktionærernes Forbund i Danmark v. Dansk Arbejdsgiverforening, agissant pour Danfoss* [1989] ECR 3199

C-341/05, *Laval un Partneri Ltd v. Svenska Byggnadsarbetareförbundet, Svenska Byggnadsarbetareförbundets avdelning 1, Byggettan and Svenska Elektrikerförbundet* [2007] ECR I-11767

C-438/05, *International Transport Workers' Federation, Finnish Seamen's Union v. Viking Line ABP, OÜ Viking Line Eesti* [2007] ECR I-10779

C-319/06, *Commission v. Luxembourg* [2008] ECR I-4323

C-346/06, *Dirk Rüffert v. Land Niedersachsen* [2008] ECR I-1989

Organization of American States

1948 American Declaration of the Rights and Duties of Man

1948 Charter of the Organization of American States

1967 Protocol of Buenos Aires amending the 1948 Charter of the Organization of American States

2012 Social Charter of the Americas

National Law

Canadian law

Statutes
Ontario Labour Relations Act of 1995

Case law
Fisher v. Pemberton [1969] 8 D.L.R. (3d) 521 (B.C.S.C.)
Gagnon v. Canadian Merchant Service Guild et al. [1984] 9 D.L.R. (4th) 641

German law

Laws
Arbeitsgerichtsgesetz (1979 Labour Court Act)
Bertriebsverfassungsgesetz (2001 Works Constitution Act)
Einkommensteuergesetz (2009 Income Tax Act)
Gerichtskostengesetz (2004 Court Fees Act)
Gesetz gegen die gemeingefährlichen Bestrebungen der Sozialdemokratie (1878 Law Against the Publicly Dangerous Endeavors of Social Democracy)
Gesetz über den vaterländischen Hilfsdienst (1916 Act on Patriotic Service)
Grundgesetz (1949 Basic Law)
Kontrollratsgesetz (1946 Allied Control Council Act on Dispute Resolution Machinery in Labour Conflicts)
Körperschaftsteuergesetz (2002 Corporate Tax Act)
Mitbestimmungsgesetz (1976 Co-Determination Act)
Tarifautonomiestärkungsgesetz (2015 Collective Bargaining Unity Act)
Tarifvertragsgesetz (1949 Collective Agreement Act)

Case law
Bundesarbeitsgericht, October 31, 1958—1 AZR 632/57
Bundesarbeitsgericht, April 21, 1971—GS 1/68
Bundesarbeitsgericht, December 17, 1976—1 AZR 605/75
Bundesarbeitsgericht, June 23, 2010—10 AS 2/10
Bundesgerichtshof, July 10, 1989—II ZR 30/89
Bundesverfassungsgericht, February 24, 1999—1 BvR 123/93
Bundesverfassungsgericht, July 11, 2017-1 BvR 1571/15, 1588/15, 2883/15, 1043/16 and 1477/16

Swedish law

Laws (chronological order)

Magnus Erikssons landslag (1350)
Kristofers landslag (1442)
Placat och förordning om myntet Stockholm den 7 octobris 1665
Kungl. Mays:tz Allgemene Ordning och Skråå (1669 skråordningen)
Kongl. Maj:ts nådige Förordning Om Fri-Mästare Och Handtwärckarnes fria tillträde här i Riket. Gifwen Stockholm den 26 maj i 1719
Algemene Ordning och Skrå 1720
1734 års lag
Kongl. Maj:ts Nådige Förordning och Reglemente för Boktryckerierne i Riket. Gifwit Stockholm i Råd-Cammaren den 12 aug. 1752
1773 års reskript ang. 1720 års skråordning
Fabriks och Hantverksordningen av den 22 dec. 1846
Försvarslöshetsstadgan af d. 29 maj 1846
1862 års kommunalförordningar om kommunal styrelse i stad och på landet
Kongl. Maj:ts Nådige Förordning angående utvidgad näringsfrihet den 18 juni 1864
Lag (1885:27) om lösdrifvares behandling
Lag (1906:13) om medling i arbetstvister
Lag (1928:253) om kollektivavtal
Lag (1928:254) om arbetsdomstol
Förordning (1934:264) om arbetslöshetskassor
Lagen (1935:113) med vissa bestämmelser om arbetsförmedling
Lagen (1936:506) om förenings- och förhandlingsfrihet
Lagen (1938:287) om semester
Lag (1970:943) om arbetstid m.m.
Lag (1973:370) om arbetslöshetsförsäkring
Lagen (1974:12) om anställningsskydd m.m.
Lag (1974:358) om facklig förtroendemans ställning på arbetsplatsen
Lag (1974:371) om rättegången i arbetstvister
Lag (1974:981) om arbetstagares rätt till ledighet för utbildning
Lag (1976:580) om medbestämmande i arbetslivet
Lagen (1976:280) om rätt till föräldraledighet
Lagen (1976:351) om styrelserepresentation för de anställda i aktiebolag och ekonomiska föreningar
Semesterlag (1977:480)
Lag (1978:410) om rätt till ledighet för vård av barn, m.m.
Lag (1979:503) om jämställdhet mellan kvinnor och män i arbetslivet
Lag (1979:1118) om jämställdhet mellan kvinnor och män i arbetslivet
Lag (1982:80) om anställningsskydd
Lag (1987:667) om ekonomiska föreningar

Inkomstskattelag (1999:1229)
Diskrimineringslagen (2008:567)
Lag (2011:427) om europeiska företagsråd

Agency regulations
RSV, *Skatteregler för ideella föreningar* (Beskattningsår 2015)

Legislative preparatory works
Förliknings- och skiljenämndskommitténs betänkande 1901
Andra lagutskottets utlåtande no. 22 (1924)
Andra lagutskottets utlåtande no. 51 (1934)
Andra lagutskottets utlåtande no. 37 (1935)
Legislative Bill 1949:214 Kungl. Maj:ts proposition till riksdagen angående godkännande av Sveriges anslutning till Europarådet
Legislative Inquiry SOU 1975:1 Demokrati på arbetsplatsen förslag till ny lagstiftning om förhandlingsrätt och kollektivavtal
SOU 1993:32 Ny anställningsskyddslag

Case law
Swedish Supreme Court case law
NJA 1973 p. 341
NJA 1973 p. 423
Swedish Supreme Administrative Court case law
RÅ 1974 p. 121
Labour Court case law
AD 1929 no. 29
AD 1932 no. 100
AD 1934 no. 179
AD 1972 no. 5
AD 1983 no. 107
AD 1990 no. 33
AD 2004 no. 111
AD 2005 no. 49
AD 2009 no. 89
AD 2011 no. 37

United Kingdom law

UK statutory law (chronological order)
1304 (33 Edw. 1) st. 2, Who be Conspirators and who be Champertors
1305 (33 Edw. 1) st. 3, The punishment of such as commit Champerty
1330 (4 Edw. 3.) st. 1, Confirmation of all statutes not repealed

1349 (23 Edw. 3) stat. 1, c. 1-8, Statute of Labourers (Cap. 1 What persons shall be compelled to labour, cap. 2 Departing before the time agreed upon shall be imprisoned, cap. 3, 4, and 5 Regulation of labourers wages, cap. 6 Of victuallers, cap. 7 Of beggars, cap. 8 Of artificers)
1350 (25 Edw. 3) stat. 2, c. 1-7, Labourers, artificers, etc.
1353 (27 Edw. 3) Letter-Book G. fol. x. (Latin)
1360 (34 Edw. 3) c. 9-11, Concerning labourers
1362 (36 Edw. 3) stat. 1, c. 5-6, 8-14, Purveyance
1376 (50 Edw. 3) cc. 1-8, Confirmation of liberties and charters, pardon, arrest of clergy, fraudulent conveyances, cloth
1388 (12 Ric. 2) c. 1, Confirmation of liberties, etc.
1388 (12 Ric. 2) c. 3-9, Labourers, beggars
1405 (7 Hen. 4) c. 17, Concerning putting out apprentices
1425 (3 Hen. 6) c. 1, Labourers
1436 (15 Hen. 6) c. 6-7, Marshalsea, exportation of corn, safe-conducts, sub-poenas, attaints, etc.
1530 (22 Hen. 8) c. 4, Concerning exactions levied on apprentices
1545 (37 Hen. 8) c. 4, Dissolution of Colleges Act 1545
1547 (1 Edw. 6) c. 14, Dissolution of the Colleges Act 1547
1548 (2 & 3 Edw. 6) c. 15, Victuallers
1562 (5 Eliz. 1) c. 4, Statute of Artificers
1721 (7 Geo. 1) st. 1, c. 13, Journeymen Tailors, London Act 1720
1725 (12 Geo. 1) c. 34 and 35, cap. 34 To prevent unlawful combinations of workmen employed in woolen manufactures, and for better payment of their wages, Woollen Manufactures Act 1725, and cap. 35 To prevent abuses in the making of bricks and tiles, to ascertain the dimensions thereof, and to prevent all unlawful combinations amongst any brickmakers or tilemakers within fifteen miles of the city of London. . .
1748 (22 Geo. 2) c. 27, Frauds by Workmen Act 1748
1788 (28 Geo. 3) c. 54 Slave Trade Act (Dolben's Act)
1793 (33 Geo. 3) c. 54, Friendly Societies Act 1793
1795 (35 Geo. 3) c. 111, Friendly Societies Act 1795
1795 (36 Geo. 3) c. 7, Treason Act 1795
1795 (36 Geo. 3) c. 8, Seditious Meetings Act 1795
1796 (36 Geo. 3) c. 111, Combinations of Workmen Act 1796
1799 (39 Geo. 3) c. 81, Unlawful Combinations of Workmen Act 1799
1800 (39 & 40 Geo. 3) c. 90, Disputes Between Masters and Workmen Act
1800 (39 & 40 Geo. 3) c. 106, Unlawful Combinations of Workmen Act 1800
1807 (Geo. 3, Sess 1) c. 36 The Slave Trade Act 1807

1819 (59 Geo. 3) c. 66, Cotton Mills and Factories Act 1819
1824 (5 Geo. 4) c. 95, Combinations of Workmen Act 1824
1825 (6 Geo. 4) c. 129, Combinations of Workmen Act 1825
1832 (2 & 3 Wm. 4) c. 45, Representation of the People Act 1832
1833 (3 & 4 Wm. 4) c. 63, Apprentices Act 1833
1835 (5 & 6 Wm. 4) c. 76, Municipal Corporations (England) Act 1835
1855 (18 & 19 Vict.) c. 63, Friendly Societies Act 1855
1859 (22 Vict.) c. 34, Combination of Workmen Act 1859
1867 (30 & 31 Vict.) c. 102, Representation of the People Act 1867
1871 (34 & 35 Vict.) c. 31, Trade Union Act 1871
1875 (38 & 39 Vict.) c. 86, Conspiracy and Protection of Property Act 1875
1884 (48 & 49 Vict.) c. 3, Representation of the People Act 1884
1897 (60 & 61 Vict.) c. 37, Workmen's Compensation Act 1897
1906 (6 Edw. 7) c. 47, Trade Disputes Act 1906
1906 (6 Edw. 7) c. 58, Workmen's Compensation Act
1908 (8 Edw. 7) c. 40, Old Age Pensions Act 1908
1908 (8 Edw. 7) c. 57, The Coal Mines Regulation Act
1909 (9 Edw. 7) c. 7, Labour Exchanges Act 1909
1909 (9 Edw. 7) c. 22, Trade Boards Act 1909
1911 (1 & 2 Geo. 5) c. 55, National Insurance Act
1913 (3 & 4 Geo. 5) c. 30, Trade Union Act 1913
1920 (10 & 11 Geo. 5) c. 15, Representation of the People Act 1920
1920 (10 & 11 Geo. 5) c. 35, Representation of the People (No. 2) Act 1920
1922 (12 & 13 Geo. 5) c. 12, Representation of the People Act 1922
1922 (12 & 13 Geo. 5) c. 41, Representation of the People (No. 2) Act 1922
1927 (17 & 18 Geo. 5) c. 22, Trade Disputes and Trade Unions Act 1927
1928 (18 & 19 Geo. 5) c. 12, Representation of the People (Equal Franchise) Act 1928
1928 (18 & 19 Geo. 5) c. 25, Representation of the People (Reading University) Act 1928
1948 (11 & 12 Geo. 6) c. 65, Representation of the People Act 1948
1964 c. 24, Trade Union (Amalgamations, etc.) Act 1964
1968 c. 55, Friendly and Industrial and Provident Societies Act 1968
1969 c. 15, The Representation of the People Act 1969
1971 c. 66, Friendly Societies Act 1971
1974 c. 46, Friendly Societies Act 1974
1974 c. 52, Trade Union and Labour Relations Act 1974
1975 c. 65, Sex Discrimination Act 1975
1975 c. 71, Employment Protection Act 1975
1976 c. 7, Trade Union and Labour Relations (Amendment) Act 1976

1976 c. 71, The Race Relations Act 1976
1978 c. 44, Employment Protection (Consolidation) Act 1978
1982 c. 46, Employment Act 1982
1984 c. 49, Trade Union Act 1984
1984 c. 62, Friendly Societies Act 1984
1988 c. 19, Employment Act 1988
1989 c. 38, Employment Act 1989
1990 c. 38, Employment Act 1990
1992 c. 52, Trade Union and Labour Relations (Consolidation) Act 1992 (TULR(C)A 1992)
1993 c. 19, Trade Union Reform and Employment Rights Act 1993
1995 c. 50, Disability Discrimination Act 1995
1996 c. 18, Employment Rights Act 1996
1998 c. 8, Employment Rights (Dispute Resolution) Act 1988
1998 c. 42, Human Rights Act 1998
1999 c. 26, Employment Relations Act 1999
2004 c. 24, Employment Relations Act 2004
2007 c. 3, Income Tax Act 2007
2008 c. 24, Employment Act 2008
2010 c. 4, Corporation Tax Act 2010
2010 c. 15, Equality Act 2010
2014 c. 4, Transparency of Lobbying, Non-Party Campaigning and Trade Union Administration Act 2014
2016 c. 15 Trade Act 2016

Statutory instruments

Statutory Instrument 2000 No. 1300, Terms and Conditions of Employment, The Trade Union Recognition (Method of Collective Bargaining) Order 2000

Regulations

Transnational Information and Consultation of Employees (Amendment) Regulations 2010

Codes of Practice

Acas Code of Practice on Time Off for Trade Union Duties and Activities (2010)
Acas Code of Practice on Disciplinary and Grievance Procedures (2015)
Acas Discipline and Grievances at Work: The Acas Guide (2017)
Department of Trade and Industry ("DTI") Code of Practice, Access and Unfair Practices during Recognition and Derecognition Ballots (2005)

Ministry of Justice, Claims Management Regulation—Code of Practice for the Provision of Regulated Claims Management Services by Trade Unions, November 2006

Proclamations

1718 Proclamation Against Combinations of Woollen Weavers comp 4 Hughson's London 337, reprinted in Notes and Queries, September 21, 1867

Case law (alphabetical order by case name)

Annamunthodo v. Oilfield Workers' Trade Union [1961] AC 945
Hornby v. Close, 10 Cox CC 393 (QB 1867)
King v. The Journeymen Tailors of Cambridge, 8 Mod. 11 (Nov. 7, 1721)
Lumley v. Gye (1853) 2 E. & B. 216
R (on the application of Cable & Wireless Services UK Ltd) v. Central Arbitration Committee and Communication Workers Union (interested party) [2008] IRLR 425 HC
R v. Central Arbitration Committee and another ex parte Kwik-Fit (GB) Ltd [2002] IRLR 395 CA
R v. Lovelass and Others (1834) 172 ER 1380
R (Unison) v. Lord Chancellor [2017] YJSC 51
Rex v. Marks et al., 3 East 157 (1802)
Roebuck v. NUM (Yorkshire Area) No 2 [1978] ICR 676
Rookes v. Barnard [1964] UKHL 1
Somerset v. Stewart, 98 ER 499 (1772)
Taff Vale Rly. Co. v. Amalgamated Society of Rly. Servants, [1901] UKHL 1

United States law

Federal

LEGISLATION (CHRONOLOGICAL ORDER)

The Sherman Antitrust Act of 1890 (26 Stat. 209) codified at 15 U.S.C. §§ 1-7
The Corporation Excise Tax Act of 1909 (36 Stat. 113) ch. 6 § 38
The Tariff Act of 1913 (38 Stat. 172) ch. 16 § 11(G)
The Clayton Antitrust Act of 1914 (Pub.L. 63–212, 38 Stat. 730) codified at 15 U.S.C. § 17
Norris–LaGuardia Act of March 23, 1932 (Ch. 90, 47 Stat. 70) codified at 29 U.S.C. ch. 6
National Industrial Recovery Act of 1933 (Pub.L. 73-67, 48 Stat. 195)

National Labor Relations Act of 1935, The Wagner Act (Pub.L. 74-198, 49 Stat. 449) codified at 29 U.S.C. §§ 151–69
Social Security Act of 1935 (Pub.L. 74-271, 49 Stat. 620) codified at 42 U.S.C. ch. 7.
The Fair Labor Standards Act of 1938, The Wages and Hours Bill (Pub.L. 75-718, 52 Stat. 1060) codified at 29 U.S.C. ch. 8
The Labor Management Relations Act of 1947 (Pub.L. 80-101, 61 Stat. 136) codified at 29 U.S.C. ch. 7
The Labor-Management Recording and Disclosure Act of 1959, Landrum-Griffin Act (Pub.L. 86-257, 73 Stat. 519) codified at 29 U.S.C. § 411
Civil Rights Act of 1964 (Pub.L. 88-352, 78 Stat. 241) codified at 42 U.S.C. 1981
Age Discrimination in Employment Act of 1967 ("ADEA") (Pub. L. 90-202, 81 Stat. 602) codified at 29 U.S.C. §§ 621–4
The Americans with Disabilities Act of 1990 ("ADA") (Pub.L. 101-336, 104 Stat. 327) codified at 42 U.S.C. ch. 126 § 12101 et seq.

EXECUTIVE ORDERS

Executive Order 8802 Fair Employment Practices in Defense Industries (1941)

UNITED STATES SUPREME COURT CASE LAW (CHRONOLOGICAL ORDER)

In re Debs, 158 U.S. 564 (1895)
Lochner v. New York, 198 U.S. 45 (1905)
Loewe v. Lawlor, 208 U.S. 274 (1908)
Coppage v. Kansas, 236 U.S. 1 (1915)
Hitchman Coal and Coke Co. v. Mitchell, 245 U.S. 229 (1917)
Hammer v. Dagenhart, 247 U.S. 251 (1918)
Duplex Printing Press Co. v. Deering, 254 U.S. 443 (1921)
American Steel Foundries v. Tri-City Trades Council, 257 U.S. 184 (1921)
Truax v. Corrigan, 257 U.S. 312 (1921)
Baley v. Drexel, 259 U.S. 20 (1922)
United Mineworkers v. Coronado Coal Company, 259 U.S. 344 (1922)
Adkins v. Children's Hospital, 261 U.S. 525 (1923)
Schechter Poultry Corp. v. United States, 295 U.S. 495 (1935)
West Coast Hotel Co. v. Parrish, 300 U.S. 379 (1937)
Virginian Railway v. System Federation No. 40, 300 U.S. 515 (1937)
NLRB v. Jones & Laughlin Steel Corp., 301 U.S. 1 (1937)
H.J. Heinz Co. v. NLRB, 311 U.S. 514 (1941)
United States v. Hutcheson, 312 U.S. 219 (1941)
J.I. Case Co. v. NLRB, 321 U.S. 332 (1944)

Order of Railroad Telegraphers v. Railway Express Agency, Inc., 321 U.S. 342 (1944)
Medo Photo Supply Corp. v. NLRB, 321 U.S. 678 (1944)
Steele v. Louisville & N. R. Co., 323 U.S. 192 (1944)
Tunstall v. Brotherhood of Locomotive Firemen, 323 U.S. 210 (1944)
Lincoln Federal Labor Union No. 19129, A.F. of L. v. Northwestern Iron & Metal Co., 335 U.S. 525 (1949)
American Federation of Labor v. American Sash & Door Co., 335 U.S. 538 (1949)
Radio Officers' Union v. NLRB, 347 U.S. 17 (1954)
Mastro Plastics Corp. and French-American Reeds Mfg. Co., Inc. v. NLRB, 350 U.S. 270 (1956)
NLRB v. Truitt Mfg. Co., 351 U.S. 149 (1956)
San Diego Building Trades v. Garmon, 359 U.S. 236 (1959)
United Steelworkers v. United States, 361 U.S. 39 (1959)
NLRB v. General Motors Corp., 373 U.S. 734, 743 (1963)
NLRB v. Acme Industrial Co., 385 U.S. 432 (1967)
NLRB v. Allis-Chalmers Manufacturing Company et al., 388 U.S. 175 (1967)
Scofield v. NLRB, 394 U.S. 423 (1969)
H.K. Porter Co. v. NLRB, 397 U.S. 99 (1970)
Emporium Capwell Co. v. Western Addition, 420 U.S. 50 (1975)
Teamsters v. United States, 431 U.S. 324 (1977)

FEDERAL CASE LAW (CHRONOLOGICAL ORDER)
NLRB v. Mike Yurosek & Son, Inc., 53 F.3d 261 (9th Cir. 1995)
Alton H. Piester, LLC v. NLRB, 591 F.3d 332 (7th Cir. 2010)
International Union of Operating Engineers Local 513, AFL-CIO v. NLRB, 635 F.3d 1233 (D.C. Cir. 2011)
United Automobile, Aerospace and Agricultural Implement Workers of America Local 3047, et al. v. Hardin County, Kentucky, et al., 842 F.3d 407 (6th Cir. 2016)

NLRB CASES (CHRONOLOGICAL ORDER)
Miranda Fuel Company, Inc. and Michael Lopuch and Local 533, International Brotherhood of Teamsters, 140 NLRB 7 (1962)
Ex-Cell-O Corporation, 185 NLRB 107 (1970)
King Scoopers, Inc., 332 NLRB 4 (2000)
Schrock Cabinet Co., 339 NLRB 182 (2003)

STATE CASE LAW (CHRONOLOGICAL ORDER)
Commonwealth v. Pullis (Philadelphia, Pa., Mayor's Court 1806)

Barnes v. The Boston & Worcester Railroad Corporation, Suffolk County Court of Common Pleas, Oct. term 1837 (Massachusetts)
Comm. v. Hunt, 35 Mass. (4 Merc.) 111 (1842)
Vegelahn v. Guntner, 167 Mass. 92 (1896)
Opinion of the Justices, 401 A.2d 135, 147 (Me. 1979)
Schaffer v. Board of Education, 869 S.W.2d 163, 166-68 (Mo.Ct.App. 1993)
Cone v. Nevada Service Employees Union, 998 P.2d 1178 (Nev. 2000)

Index